Thriving!

A Manual for Students in the Helping Professions

Thriving!
A Manual for Students in the Helping Professions

LENNIS G. ECHTERLING
ERIC COWAN
WILLIAM F. EVANS
A. RENEE STATON
GRACE VIERE
J. EDSON McKEE
JACK PRESBURY
ANNE L. STEWART

James Madison University

LAHASKA PRESS
HOUGHTON MIFFLIN COMPANY
BOSTON   NEW YORK

Editor-in-Chief: Kathi Prancan
Publisher, Lahaska Press: Barry Fetterolf
Editorial Assistant: Nirmal Trivedi
Associate Project Editor: Martha Rogers
Editorial Assistant: Reba Frederics
Senior Production/Design Coordinator: Jodi O'Rourke
Senior Manufacturing Manager: Jane Spelman
Senior Marketing Manager: Katherine Greig

Lahaska Press, a unique collaboration between the Houghton Mifflin College Division and Lawrence Erlbaum Associates, is dedicated to publishing books and offering services for the academic and professional counseling communities. Houghton Mifflin and Lawrence Erlbaum will focus on becoming the major conduit for educational and academic materials in the psychological and educational counseling fields. The partnership of Lahaska Press was formed in late 1999. The name "Lahaska" is a Native American Lenape word meaning "source of much writing." It is also a small town in eastern Pennsylvania, named by the Lenape.

Printed in the U.S.A.

Library of Congress Catalog Card Number: 2001131489

ISBN: 0-618-13118-3

23456789-QF-06 05 04 03 02

Contents

Foreword   xv

Preface   xviii

CHAPTER 1   The Thriving Principles   1

     ▲ How Shall We Begin? *Jean's Story*   2

   Use It—Don't Lose It!   4

   Thriving   5

     Pack Wisely   5

     Make the Journey Your Destination   7

       ▲ The Journey: *A Parable*   9

     Have Traveling Companions   10

       ▲ Worst Parents of the Year Award: *Jen's Story*   13

     Keep Your Bearings   15

       ▲ You'll Go Far in Life: *Andrea's Story*   16

       ■ Exercise 1.1. Whatcha Gonna Be?
         A Magic Mirror Exercise   18

     Let the Trip Take You   19

     Always Take the High Road   20

   Summary   22

   Resources   22

   References   23

CHAPTER 2 Making Your Training Journey 25

▲ Why Not Enjoy the Ride? *Cathy's Story* 26

Being an Applicant 28

Gain Experience 28

Complete the Academic Prerequisites 29

Explore Your Training Options 29

Take the Required Standardized Tests 29

Arrange for References 30

Write a Personal Statement 31

Participate in a Selection Interview 31

Consider Your Options Carefully 32

Being a Novice 32

Opening Rituals 33

■ Exercise 2.1. Traditions:
    A Reminiscing and Planning Exercise 34

Communication 36

Handling Personal Problems 38

Keeping a Portfolio 38

Dualistic Thinking 39

▲ The One: *Juanita's Story* 40

Perfectionism 40

Being an Apprentice 41

Multiplistic Thinking 42

▲ A Deer Caught in the Headlights: *Bill's Story* 42

The "Sophomore Slump" 43

Comprehensive Examination 44

An Emerging Professional 46

Relativistic Thinking 46

Research Project 48

Graduation and Commencement 50

Summary 50

Resources 50

References 52

CHAPTER 3   Meeting Your Basic Needs   55

Your Personal Hierarchy of Needs   56

▲ A Constant Challenge: *Ellen's Story*   58

Basic Needs and Self-Actualization   59

■ Exercise 3.1. Take That Job And . . . :
A Guided Fantasy Exercise   61

Conducting a Needs Inventory   62

▲ Touch the Sun: *Renee's Story*   62

■ Exercise 3.2. The Sea Star: *A Balancing Exercise*   64

Crafting a Balanced Life   65

▲ We Have Nothing to Fear But . . . : *Beth's Story*   66

■ Exercise 3.3. Your Needs in Context:
A Systemic Exercise   67

Pathways to Balance   67

Housing   68

▲ Adventures in Subsidized Housing Land:
Chris' Story   69

■ Exercise 3.4. It Takes a Community:
An Exercise in Imagination   71

Financial Assistance   72

Wellness   76

▲ Kicking and Sleeping: *Martin's Story*   77

Finding and Creating Perspective   78

▲ The Road from Orange Crackers to Rice: *Anne's Story*   78

■ Exercise 3.5. I'll Have the Combo:
Meeting Multiple Needs   79

Summary   81

Resources   81

References   82

CHAPTER 4   Enhancing Your Academic Skills   84

▲ More Than I Had Bargained For: *Bonnie's Story*   85

Hearts and Minds   86

Developing Critical Reflection Skills   88

Learning by Heart   90

   Riding the Perturbation Wave   91

    ■ Exercise 4.1. The Bird Cage:
        Encountering Oppression   92

   Finding "The Zone"   93

   Using the Zeigarnik Effect   94

The Core Academic Skills   95

   Reading   95

    ■ Exercise 4.2. What? So What? Now What?   98

    ▲ I Learned How to Read All Over Again:
        Brian's Story   99

   Researching   99

    ■ Exercise 4.3. Doing a Little Detective Work   102

    ■ Exercise 4.4. Critiquing   104

   Writing   105

   ▲ Learning the Hard Way: *Susan's Story*   105

    ■ Exercise 4.5. Writing Twice-Told Stories   107

    ■ Exercise 4.6. Reading: *A Writing Exercise*   108

    ■ Exercise 4.7. Structuring: *A Writing Exercise*   109

   Presenting   110

    ■ Exercise 4.8. Preparing and Practicing   113

    ■ Exercise 4.9. Imagining Success   116

    ■ Exercise 4.10. Breathing   116

Summary   117

Resources   117

References   118

CHAPTER 5   Embracing Your Stress   120

    ▲ Stressed Out: *Bill's Story*   122

Stress   123

   The Stress of Helping   124

   Distress   125

   Stressful Events   125

    ▲ When It "Hurts Good": *Rachel's Story*   126

Responding to Stress   127
■ Exercise 5.1. Your Success with Stress   128
■ Exercise 5.2. Ways of Saying "No" and "Yes!"   132
Beyond Stress   134
Resilience Under Stress   135
Making Meaning of Stress   136
Telling Your Story   136
■ Exercise 5.3. The Embracing Attitudes:
    A Quick Check Exercise   137
Thriving Under Stress   138
Envisioning Your Goals   138
■ Exercise 5.4. Mission: Possible:
    An Exercise in Envisioning   138
Using Your Strengths   139
■ Exercise 5.5. Panning for Gold:
    Uncovering Strengths and Resources   139
Connecting with Others   140
Exercise 5.6. The Sea Star II: *A Revisiting Exercise*   140
Stress and Character   142
Stress into Strength   144
Summary   145
Resources   146
References   147

CHAPTER 6 Exploring Yourself   149
Make Personal Growth Your Goal   149
▲ Thanksgiving Leftovers: *Edna's Story*   150
■ Exercise 6.1. "I Am . . . " versus "A Counselor Is . . . "   152
Ontological Security   153
"I" and "Me"   154
The Need for Personal Growth   155
Being a "Do-Gooder"   155
■ Exercise 6.2. Things I Hope My Clients Never Say:
    An Aversion Exercise   157

Consider Counseling for Yourself   160

▲ It Feels Weird for a Counselor to Be a Client:
  Robert's Story   161

Allow Yourself to Mess Up   162

Explore Your Assets   163

Avoid the "Groucho Paradox"   164

Be a Beginner, Not an Expert   165

Assimilation and Accommodation   166

Accommodating Information About Yourself   167

Hold to Your Center   168

The Demands of Others   169

▲ Learning from the Inside Out: *Teresa's Story*   170

Honor, But Modify, Your Style   170

■ Exercise 6.3. Toward, Against, or Away?
  A Moving Exercise   171

Countertransference   173

Getting Clear   175

Finding Your Roots   176

▲ I Need to Pay Attention to Who I Am:
  Michelle's Story   176

Find the "I AM" Experience   178

Summary   178

Resources   179

References   180

CHAPTER 7 Being with Others   183

▲ Being "Processed":
  Rebecca's Story   184

What's in Your Backpack?   186

Self and Relationship   186

Exploring Your Relational Worldview   187

■ Exercise 7.1. Visitor from Another Planet:
  A Guided Fantasy   189

Growing in Relation   191

Mirrors 192

▲ The Childlike Feeling of Possibility:
Antoinette's Story 193

The Counseling Qualities 194

"Truth" with a Capital "T" 196

■ Exercise 7.2. Your Hard-Belly Response: A Quiz 197

Giving and Receiving Feedback 198

Giving Helpful Feedback 199

The Johari Window 201

■ Exercise 7.3. Giving and Receiving Feedback 201

Authenticity 202

Social Masks 203

Being and Seeming 203

Important People in Your Training 205

Mentors 205

Support Staff 208

Significant Others 208

Summary 211

Resources 211

References 212

CHAPTER 8 Thriving in Your Practicum and Internship 213

You Are Ready, Although You May Have Doubts 214

▲ How Old Are You? Grace's Story 215

Your Practicum 216

Accommodating to Your Practicum 217

▲ Pipe Dreams: Lennie's Story 217

Taking Pictures Along the Way 218

▲ Sometimes the Therapist Learns More Than the Client:
Jane's Story 219

Internship 220

Choosing a Site 221

■ Exercise 8.1. Refreshing Your Memory and Plotting
Your Course: A Decision-Making Exercise 221

Writing an Internship Agreement 222

Professional Liability Insurance 222

Adhering to Ethics Codes 223

Putting It All Together 225

Taking the High Road 227

▲ *Eric's Story* 229

Making Rest Stops Along the Way 232

▲ *Nathaniel's Story* 233

■ Exercise 8.2. First Thoughts: *An Exploratory Exercise* 234

Stages in the Journey 237

Juggling 239

Making the Most of Your Internship 239

Summary 240

Resources 240

References 241

CHAPTER 9 Launching Your Career 243

▲ Around the Next Corner: *Bill's Story* 244

■ Exercise 9.1. Life-Span Time Line 245

From Student to Professional 246

Exploring Your Values 246

■ Exercise 9.2. Building a House: *A Values Exercise* 246

Exploring Your Roots 248

▲ The Legacy of My Parents: *Gabe's Story* 248

■ Exercise 9.3. Career Genogram 249

Using the Campus Career Center 250

Seeking Career Counseling 251

Career Possibilities by Degree 251

Careers with a Master's or Ed.S. 251

Careers with a Doctorate 253

Planning Your Career 254

Being Intentional 254

Where to Look for Jobs 254

■ Exercise 9.4. Interviewing Two Masters:
  A Journal Exercise 255

Becoming Professionally Involved 256

Conducting Your Search 257

Designing an Effective Resume 257

Writing Persuasive Correspondence 258

Successful Job Interviewing 259

Your Career and Your Life 260

Lifelong Learning 260

Fitting In and Standing Out 260

Think You're Not Creative? 262

Clock-Watchers and Workaholics 264

Leaving the Nest and Making Mistakes 264

■ Exercise 9.5. Putting It All Together:
  A Balancing Exercise 266

Summary 268

One Final Point 268

Resources 268

References 270

APPENDICES

Appendix A: Our Favorite Counseling and
  Therapy Books 272

Appendix B: American Counseling Association's *Code of
  Ethics and Standards of Practice* 279

Appendix C: American Psychological Association's
  *Ethical Principles of Psychologists and
  Code of Conduct* 312

Index 343

Foreword

Breaking new ground in any field represents a significant accomplishment, and *Thriving!* does just that. It provides important inroads into largely uncharted graduate school territory and develops an effective map that leads towards greater growth and satisfaction as a graduate student. Step-by-step, the book guides the student through otherwise unfamiliar territory with effective signs that mark the fast track to success. Importantly, the directions it provides are much more than cautionary signals that point out various hazards in the road towards the completion of the degree. To be sure, the book does identify points at which students can expect "falling rocks ahead," or "ice on the bridge," and it points as well to the periodic "winding road" or "sharp turn ahead" that customarily punctuate the passage through graduate training. But equally important is the book's proactive posture in informing students about the opportunities and joys of graduate training, and how to get the most out of those opportunities. In short, the authors are dedicated to maximizing a student's traction, rather than merely to minimizing their friction, on the road to graduate school success. And they succeed admirably en route to this goal.

Reading *Thriving!* reminded me of my own introduction to graduate training, which was surely a product of a time and place that have long since vanished from the landscape of graduate education. In our opening orientation meeting, our graduate coordinator began by asking us to "look at the person on your left, then look at the person on your right; only *one* of those people is likely to make it through this graduate training program!" Needless to say, this inauspicious introduction to graduate training triggered the release of all of our native apprehensions and insecurities in a stampede of unbridled anxiety. *Thriving!* represents a systematic, dynamic, and fully human compendium of strategies for reigning in this anxiety and directing its collective energy towards the constructive pursuit of personal and professional development. Indeed, by blurring the boundary between the personal and the professional, the book succeeds in underscoring the key relationship between them: professional development in counseling and mental health is, in fact, deeply personal, and personal development is equally crucial to professional vitality. In this way and scores of other ways, the book conveys the kind of wisdom that every graduate student would love to have and that every faculty member would love to have the time and ability to convey. In the process, it provides a treasure trove of novel, detailed, and effective strategies for helping the student get the most out of his or her graduate school experience.

One of the most compelling features of the book is the voice it is written in. Its clear, engaging, and turbo-charged prose combines the effective voice of an "executive coach" with the exhilarating impact of a personal trainer. Together they combine to promote the kind of self-actualization that is designed to maximize graduate success, not only for the student but for his or her faculty, as well. In fact, one of the most striking features of the volume is how effectively it recognizes the contexts that shape, frame, and scaffold otherwise diverse graduate school experiences. Rather than promoting the image of the student as a "salmon swimming upstream," the book projects a more positive, productive image by furnishing knowledge of the cross-currents, eddies, shallows, and depths that graduate training can sometimes provide. With *Thriving!* as their guide, graduate students can take a rollicking ride through the coursing currents of graduate training, and experience the satisfaction of a job well done when the trip comes to a conclusion.

In *Thriving!*, Echterling, McKee, Presbury, Staton, Evans, Stewart, Cowan, and Viere do more than provide a manual for graduate school; they invite a reconceptualization of it. In this reconceptualization, the content and structure of the graduate program are joined by equally vital forces that the student brings to bear on the experience. Personal engagement with, critical reflection on, and a thoroughgoing participation in the graduate program cultivate the skills that ultimately lead to more than just successful graduation; they lead to the creation of a life-long learner who reflects the very goals and values that the field seeks to promote. Whether you are an aspiring applicant, a current graduate student, or a seasoned graduate faculty member, it is a pleasure to introduce you to this book and to invite you to begin *Thriving!*

Greg J. Neimeyer, Ph.D.
Professor of Psychology and
Graduate Coordinator
University of Florida

Preface

It has been said that what you get from graduate training depends on what you put into it. We agree that, with hard work, deep commitment to your desired profession, and cooperative interactions with your peers and professors, you will profit greatly from graduate school. If, on the other hand, you adopt the attitude that while you are in school you will be preparing for "real life," you will miss the point. Graduate school *is* real life. So what you must put into it is your openness to fully being there—in each moment, with each experience, and with each person you encounter.

Back when you were an undergraduate student, you probably skated through some of the experiences that were offered to you, holding your breath and waiting for them to be over. We certainly did! You also may have held on to many of the ideas you were taught only long enough to mark the correct answer on the final examination. Now the ideas that inform you will be those that carry you into a successful professional career.

Graduate school will be amazingly short, and, as in a well-crafted short story, nothing in your schooling will be beside the point. Everything will be useful and, indeed, essential to your becoming a skilled counselor. You will find that if you are willing to live each day in the here and now, dropping some of your defenses and opening yourself to new growth, you will get much more out of your graduate training than you put into it.

This guidebook offers practical and positive strategies that you can use to make the most of your training experience. These strategies are based on six principles for thriving in your graduate training—come well prepared, live your training, learn from others, explore yourself, be open to opportunities, and always act with character. In each chapter, we explore one facet of succeeding in training. The format includes inspirational quotes, personal accounts of students' experiences, practical hints and suggestions, structured activities, recommended resources, and references. The tone of the book is conversational, and we invite you to be actively involved as you read it.

We hope this book will be helpful to you as you make your training journey. As you encounter obstacles along the way, you will find that, by coming back and rereading these chapters, they will make more and more sense to you. Pay particular attention to the stories that were written by students who have traveled the same road that you face. Their experiences will reassure you that you are still on the right path—even though at times it will seem that you have lost your way.

We wish to thank the many students and colleagues who have generously offered their personal stories so that you can discover that the doubts and struggles you are experiencing are normal. In fact, going through these painful experiences is essential to becoming an enlightened helping professional.

Producing this book has truly been a team effort. We greatly appreciate the insightful comments of those who reviewed earlier drafts of this book, including Alan Caviola, Moumoth University; Ronald S. Kiyuna, Ed.D., California State University, Fresno; Don C. Locke, North Carolina State University; Oliver Morgan, University of Scranton; Greg J. Neimeyer, Ph.D., University of Florida; and Mike Robinson, University of Central Florida. The final version is much better as a result of their feedback. We are particularly grateful to Greg Neimeyer for his enthusiastic endorsement and for his many creative contributions to the project. Of course, we also want to acknowledge our debt to Barry Fetterolf for his energetic support and ongoing commitment to our vision of a guide for helping students thrive in their training to become counselors and therapists.

Finally, we offer special thanks to Robert Anderson, April Bennett, Christine Carmouze, Constance Cromartie, Jane Halonen, Karen Hannam, Christy Hartford, Rachel Heberle, Teresa Hiney, Andrea Hollister, Melissa Lewis, Ellen Neill-Dore, Kimberley Payne, Jennifer Phillips, Antoinette Roberts, and A. Renee Wilson.

Thriving!
A Manual for Students in the Helping Professions

CHAPTER 1

▲▲▲
▼▼▼

The Thriving Principles

> The question is not how to survive, but how to
> thrive, with passion, compassion, humor, and style.
>
> —Maya Angelou

Whether you have watched it or not, you've certainly heard of the immensely popular reality TV series *Survivor*. The show involved dropping a group of castaways on a primitive island somewhere in the South Pacific or in a desolate spot in the Australian outback. Week after week, the contestants had to suffer through ordeals—such as eating rats—that were hatched up by the program's producers. The castaways held tribal councils, schemed to form temporary alliances, voted contestants off the program, and competed with one another until only one lone survivor was left standing at the conclusion of the series.

No matter what kind of helping professional you aspire to become—counselor, psychologist, clinical social worker, or counselor educator—you first must complete an intensive and rigorous training program. We can guarantee you that, whatever program you enter, you'll sometimes feel as if you're a contestant on *Survivor*. Of course, instead of tribal councils, you'll have committee meetings. Instead of foraging for berries, you'll be subsisting on macaroni and cheese. And instead of enduring physical challenges, you'll have comprehensive examinations. In spite of these superficial differences, you'll face ordeals and obstacles in your training that can be just as intimidating and challenging as anything on a reality TV show.

At times, you may feel so overwhelmed by the demands and so plagued with self-doubts that you wonder whether you'll ever make it through the program. Quoting Winston Churchill, one former graduate student described those times as "full of blood, sweat, and tears." Whereas other trainees may seem to have the knack for picking up the skills almost effortlessly, you may feel that you have to struggle to master even the basics. As you face your first research methods test or your first client, you may wonder if you're even going to survive.

We also guarantee that, as you progress through your training, you will regularly hear a certain phrase. Someone will say to you, with a heavy dose of irony, "Just think of this as a 'learning experience' for you." By themselves, these words typically suggest an opportunity for enrichment. However, the person's tone of voice, deep sigh, and shaking head strongly suggest that a frustrating, disappointing, and demanding time is in store for you. After a few of these difficult experiences, you may begin to suspect that there's a "no pain, no gain" philosophy of training in the helping professions. We believe, however, that the most productive "learning experiences" you encounter can actually be tremendously satisfying, fulfilling, and joyful.

In this chapter, we describe the principles that can help you do much more than just *survive* your training experiences. Following these principles can help you *thrive*—to succeed, flourish, and even enjoy your training with, as Maya Angelou said, "passion, compassion, humor, and style."

▲▲▲

How Shall We Begin?
Jean's Story

I CAN REMEMBER vividly the first time I opened that door and stepped into the Psychology Building as one of its newest and freshest trainees. I was so excited! Finally, after years of effort, I had fulfilled my long-standing dream of being accepted into a graduate program with a fine reputation. It was exactly what I wanted, and I couldn't have been happier. Of course, before applying, I had obsessively read all the information I could find about the program. It was credentialed, well known for its innovative methods, and respected for its commitment to professionalism. I had traveled to the campus, met with one of the professors, and even talked to several students. After all this research and preparation, I thought I had a pretty good idea of what I was getting into. Boy, was I wrong.

I had my rude awakening at my first class. Days before the semester began, I had bought all my textbooks and had even read several chapters ahead in each of them, diligently highlighting nearly every sentence I read. Back then, I had the delusion that learning took place only by a strange form of osmosis. Somehow, the knowledge contained in the sentence had to travel through the highlighter, up my arm, and finally into my brain. Of course, with this method, I was only turning my black-and-white textbooks into black-yellow-and-white textbooks. Somehow, though, the process seemed comforting to me in its familiarity. That's the way I had studied all through college, so I assumed that I would continue learning in the same tried and true way—by hunting for the absolute truth in a book and pouncing on it with my highlighter.

I came to that first class feeling eager, as well as a bit smug that I had already captured some truth in yellow. I was ready with my sharpened pencils, brand new spiral-bound notebooks, and an academic year calendar in pristine condition. I found a desk in front, struck a pose of thoughtful attentiveness, and waited for the professor to enter the room and begin revealing the hidden truth that would make everything meaningful. My plan was to neatly write those messages down in my notebook and later highlight them all in that yellow shade of truth—just to be sure.

That's when it happened, when all my expectations were destroyed. My professor came in, asked us to form our desks into a circle, and sat down with us. That's the thing—she just sat there, smiling and looking at each of us with kind, but penetrating, eyes. What was her problem? Why didn't she begin lecturing?

Finally, one of the other students timidly raised her hand and asked, "Are you the professor?"

"Yes," she replied.

After a pause, the student reluctantly continued, "Well, isn't it time for us to start?"

"Yes, you're right," she answered. "How shall we begin?"

I was sitting there wondering, "What the hell is going on here? Is this woman playing some sadistic joke on us?"

Another student suggested, "Maybe we could introduce ourselves?"

"Sounds good!" the professor said. "Who would like to begin?" It suddenly dawned on me that I was in new, uncharted territory here. I felt like Dorothy landing in Oz and telling Toto the obvious, "I don't think we're in Kansas any more." I was disoriented but curious, anxious but intrigued, and a little dazed but ready to begin.

▼▼▼

USE IT—DON'T LOSE IT!

The essential of everything you do . . . must be choice, love, passion.

—Nadia Boulanger

If you are already a trainee, your first experience may not have been as memorable for you as it was for the student who wrote this account, but you probably had some similar feelings. You are likely to find that training to become a counselor or therapist is dramatically different from your undergraduate education.

As you begin your training, you may sometimes think that you're embarking on a long and arduous journey with seemingly no end in sight. Although you will enjoy many aspects of your training, at times you may feel overwhelmed and lost. That is why we have conceived this book as a survival guide for you. Because you can feel lonely when you're lost and confused, this book is also like having a support group at hand. As you read it, you can share the reactions of other students. At times, you may want to set aside this book to take some time to explore your own experiences. When you read the stories of other students, you may learn from their mistakes and feel encouraged by their successes. Finally, you can take advantage of the advice and tips from these students as you forge your own training journey.

The earlier in your career training you read this book, the better. And be sure to keep it handy even after you have read it. You will want to refer to it regularly throughout your training. When a training problem—or opportunity!—catches you off guard, you can refresh your memory and review strategies. In other words, "use it—don't lose it."

The book provides you with practical information on programs, policies, and procedures and also helpful hints on gaining the most from the experiences your training program has to offer.

THRIVING

Life is either a daring adventure or nothing. To keep our faces toward change and behave like free spirits in the presence of fate is strength undefeatable.

—Helen Keller

As you enter your training program, you may have just completed your undergraduate education or you may be embarking on your second career path. You may be coming from an urban neighborhood in Los Angeles, a suburban community near Chicago, or a rural area in the Appalachian Mountains. Perhaps you're African American, white, Latino, Asian American, or Native American. However, no matter what your background or circumstances may be, you are joining with others who have one dream in common—to become a helping professional. As you make this training journey, which we describe in Chapter 2, you can thrive if you use the following simple principles.

Pack Wisely

What do you pack when you pursue a dream?
And what do you leave behind?

—Sandra Sharp

The first principle of thriving involves meeting your basic needs and bringing along the resources you'll require in your training. On any long journey, you'll want to stock provisions, pack the right gear, prepare for emergencies, and travel light.

Caring for your basic needs enables you to focus your energies on the personal and professional growth you can achieve in your training. In Chapter 3, we present useful information and guidelines for obtaining educational loans, applying for assistantships and scholarships, finding safe and affordable housing, taking care of your nutritional needs, and maintaining an active and healthy lifestyle.

Because you will be preparing to practice the craft of counseling and therapy, you will need to bring along some tools of the trade. Of course, a personal computer, notebooks, pens and pencils, a dictionary, the *Publication Manual of the American Psychological Association*, and other reference books are some of the essentials. While you're deciding what to take, keep in mind that how you use this gear is far more important than the equipment itself. For example, like many people in the helping professions, you may have a touch of technophobia, treating your computer as if another HAL from *2001: A Space Odyssey* may be lurking in it. As a result, you may not be taking full advantage of the computer in writing reports, doing presentations, conducting research, exploring resources, and communicating with others. On the other hand, you may be more of a technophile. You may find yourself salivating over any new gadget with all the latest "bells and whistles." In that case, keep in mind that these tools are only as good as your skill in using them.

Of course, a computer and reference books are examples of the obvious tools that you will be using. However, there are other resources you will want to bring to your training endeavors. These include your academic, time management, and stress management skills. Basic academic skills, such as reading and writing, do much more than just help you earn good grades. In fact, they are an indispensable part of being an effective professional helper. Reading allows you to broaden and enrich your own experiences by tapping into the minds of healers and thinkers throughout time and from around the world. Writing is a process in which you can give voice to your experiences, make your thoughts visible, and clarify your vague hunches by putting them into words. Keeping your curiosity alive, thinking critically about assumptions, and thoughtfully examining issues help you maintain your professional vitality throughout your career. In Chapter 4, we offer tips on improving your reading, writing, researching, and presentation skills.

Another resource you bring to your training is time. Unlike money, you cannot bank or buy time. You must learn to choose wisely how to spend the time you have available. One of the challenges you will face throughout your journey will be to balance the opportunities of your training program with other aspects of your life.

It's impossible to eliminate all the stressors you face in your training program. These stressors are a lot like Arnold Schwarzenegger's character in *The Terminator*—even when you successfully cope with one, you can almost hear it warning, "I'll . . . be . . . back." In fact, you will continue to deal with stressors throughout your professional career. Therefore, it is vital that you include stress management skills among the resources you pack for this journey. In Chapter 5, you will explore specific tips for managing your time and successfully handling the stressors that you will inevitably confront in your graduate and professional life. Finally, do your best to travel light. If you are bringing a lot of emotional baggage to your training, then it is hard to stay focused on the needs of your clients. One of the best ways to deal with your emotional issues is to participate in your own counseling or therapy. Many training programs strongly recommend that their trainees seek counseling, and they have developed resources to provide this service at little or no cost. It makes perfect sense for you to take advantage of this opportunity, even if it's not required. Being a client yourself certainly is a powerful way to appreciate the risks, vulnerabilities, and pain that clients face. More important, however, this level of involvement helps you to truly trust the process of counseling and therapy. Once you have been in counseling, you have no longer only read about or observed its benefits; you've encountered them personally. Besides, you will be encouraging others to engage in counseling and therapy; shouldn't you practice what you preach?

Make the Journey Your Destination

To travel hopefully is a better thing than to arrive.

—Robert Louis Stevenson

With many trips, getting there is half the fun; but when it comes to your personal and professional journey, the trip is *all* there is. You began this journey to become a counselor or therapist long before you entered a training program, and you will continue your journey long after you leave. The second principle of thriving involves the important point that, just as life is not a rehearsal, neither is your training. From day one, your training is the real thing, not merely a rite of passage you have to endure to do counseling or therapy after graduation. You actually have chances to practice therapeutic principles in every facet of your training. Consider your helping skills to be like muscles that are strengthened by regular use.

In the nineteenth century, Horace Greeley extolled a "manifest destiny" in the United States by urging, "Go West, young man." Joseph Campbell (1986), on the other hand, recommended, "Follow your bliss." In other words, your destiny is not found in a particular geographic territory. Instead, it lies in the joy you experience as you fulfill your potential, express your talents, and pursue your dreams *now*.

One of the biggest mistakes you can make on this journey is to view yourself as a customer and your program as merely a service station along the roadside. When you are truly learning, you are never only a passive recipient of training services or only a consumer of educational goods. Instead, you are a dynamic, full, and equal participant in the learning endeavor (Corey & Corey, 1998).

Your teachers and supervisors will be expecting you to actively collaborate with them by always "bringing something to the table." In virtually every class and training experience, you will have an opportunity to practice the craft of counseling—the processes of encountering others, of observing, of gathering information, of conceptualizing, and of taking action. You may participate in a structured exercise, respond to a videotape segment, act out a role-play, or engage in some group task that demonstrates a principle that you are studying. Actively participating in your readings means more than merely underlining or highlighting words. It means involving yourself by jotting down ideas and reactions in the margins, organizing the material into important concepts, critically evaluating the arguments, and talking about the readings before coming to class. It is only when you invest your whole self in these endeavors that you make the most of these learning opportunities. Many of your classes will be small and will have the format of a seminar, which literally means "seedplot." Do your part to tend these gardens so that the seeds will grow and be fruitful.

The depth and breadth of your program's curriculum reflect the high standards that trainers have set for you. Certainly, they expect that you will fulfill all the course requirements, but they also want you to extend yourself, to challenge yourself by pursuing knowledge and skills beyond the minimal course requirements. Coming to each class ready and willing to engage fully in the active, exciting process of learning is a great strategy for success, not only in school but also in your career.

Of course, you'll also want to take full advantage of all the many enriching experiences that take place outside the classroom. During virtually any week of the academic year, you are likely to find an exciting array of talented artists, authors, scholars, and performers coming to your campus. Art exhibits, theater performances, poetry readings, invited lectures, musical performances, and films are just a few of the cultural opportunities you will have available—many of which are free to students.

Truly successful counselors and therapists do not limit their development to their academic careers. Whether you are a trainee or a professional, you need to recognize that you have two simple options: either you can continue to grow personally and professionally by challenging yourself, or you can stagnate. Completing your training program with a curiosity about what makes people tick and a zest for discovery will guarantee that your learning will not end when you earn a diploma. Instead, you will see graduation as another step in the lifelong pursuit of professional mastery. One of the reasons that the counseling and therapy professions are so exciting is that the field is still in its infancy and is wide open for new breakthroughs. You can look forward to a long career of refining your skills, revising your thinking, and stretching the envelope.

Of course, you're familiar with Einstein's formula, $E = MC^2$. However, his friends recalled at his death that Einstein also had developed a formula, as simple and profound as its famous counterpart, for personal success in life: Personal Success = Work + Play + Not Bragging About Your Success. Einstein's formula sounds like good advice for almost anyone, especially if you're in training to help *others* achieve their personal success. Just remember—your tires should always be inflated, but your ego should not.

▲▲▲

The Journey
A Parable

KIONE WAS DISAPPOINTED. The people were having a grand feast to honor the Great Chief, and entire clans were planning to attend. But Kione's village was located on the opposite end of the island. There was room in the village's lone outrigger canoe only for several local officials, four paddlers, and gifts. He begged his parents to allow him to go—after all, wasn't he named after the Great Chief himself? His father told him that there was not enough room.

"Besides," Kione's mother smiled when she asked him, "What present could you give the Great Chief?"

Kione awoke just before dawn and, while the others were still sleeping, began the long trek to the Chief's village. He carried only some dried mullet and fruit wrapped tightly in a large cassava leaf, his bamboo knife, and a pouch containing his favorite seashell.

When the sun god was directly over his head, the boy stopped to eat beside a cool stream. As he was eating, an old man sat down beside him. Politely, Kione offered to share his meager fare with the stranger, who carefully consumed his portion. Thanking the boy, the old man said, "I want to offer you something in return, but all I have is my wisdom. People can be like a pack of monkeys—chattering, mimicking one another, and fighting for a better place in their pack. Or they can be like a pride of lions—sharing food, caring for one another, and protecting both the old and the young. You have been a lion with me. Can you be a lion surrounded by monkeys?" Kione did not know what the old man meant, but he politely thanked him for the advice and continued on his way.

In the early evening, Kione reached the village, full of music and revelers. He quietly joined the line of people waiting before the *bai* (council house) to offer their gifts. When his turn came, Kione bowed and solemnly handed his only treasure to the Chief, who showed it to everyone within sight and exclaimed rather loudly that this boy had brought a seashell to honor him! The crowd laughed uproariously, and Kione felt his face grow hot with shame. The laughter quickly subsided, however, as three distinguished-looking older women, moving quietly, gracefully, and majestically, gathered beside the Chief. They spoke quietly but intently to him while the festivities halted. Even the children and animals became quiet, for these women were very powerful—they decided who was to be chief and when it was time for a chief to be replaced. The women beckoned Kione to them and began asking him gentle questions about his village and his trip. After a few minutes, the trio went back to the Chief, spoke briefly, and moved back into the small group of elder women at the bai.

The Great Chief beckoned Kione to come and sit beside him. Then he announced in a humble voice, "This boy is a hero. He was willing to give us his only possession, but his long, hard journey here made his present the most magnificent gift of all."

The story has been told and retold throughout the years, and the message is always the same at the end. The gift *is* the journey.

▼▼▼

Have Traveling Companions

When we can share—that is the poetry in the prose of life.

—Sigmund Freud

Every culture has its folk tales and myths that portray a heroic figure on a quest. No matter how talented and strong this protagonist may be, the person neither travels nor triumphs alone. Before the journey, the heroic figure may recruit traveling companions or, along the way, may encounter strangers who become comrades. Jason had his Argonauts. Dorothy had her Cowardly Lion, Tin Man, and Scarecrow. Luke Skywalker had his Obi-Wan Kenobi, Princess Leia, and Han Solo. As the journey progresses, these companions serve vital roles by giving guidance to the traveler, using special powers to help overcome obstacles, or offering useful gifts to provide physical and emotional sustenance.

Like the protagonists in those archetypal stories, you also will encounter others—peers, mentors, instructors, supervisors, and clients—who will have a profound impact on your training journey. The third principle of thriving in your program is being open to the resources that others offer you. This openness is essential because you cannot be trained as successfully, as completely, or even as joyfully on your own. Of course, you need to engage in the solitary work of reading, writing, reflecting, and studying if you expect to be successful in any training program. But to become an effective counselor or therapist, you also need to come together with others to engage in the collaborative work of observing, discussing, practicing, giving feedback, challenging, and encouraging one another.

Our society is one that emphasizes individual achievement and competition. In fact, most of your previous educational experiences probably reinforced a "do it yourself" approach to learning. Homework involved assignments that you completed on your own. Group activities, from elementary school spelling bees to high school debates, emphasized competition. Even your class ranking system translated into scholarship offers for those at the top and rejection letters for those at the bottom. In the education game, when there are winners, there have to be losers.

Because you were probably a successful student, it may be a challenge for you to participate in a program designed to train *helping* professionals—counselors and therapists who work effectively with others. Now your learning experiences will emphasize relating, listening, communicating, and collaborating. It may be hard for you to admit it, but it's absolutely true that you are not an island unto yourself in this kind of training—you cannot learn it all on your own.

As a matter of fact, such a collaborative approach to learning is closer to the roots of a true college experience. The word *college* comes from the same Latin word as *colleague*—*collega*, which means "one chosen to work with another." In other words, you need trainers, supervisors, fellow learners, and clients to inform, inspire, prod, and even provoke you to refine your thinking, develop your skills, and make discoveries about yourself and others. For example, you will be receiving feedback from others on a regular basis. In every instance, you have the chance to be open to their observations, reactions, and suggestions. Just remind yourself that your mind is like a parachute—it works best when it's open.

Based on this principle of having traveling companions on your training journey, you have two daunting, but crucial, tasks. First, with each of your instructors, supervisors, fellow trainees, and clients, you need to develop a working relationship that is based on honesty, understanding, and acceptance. It is essential that you get to know, trust, and respect others if you are going to work well with them. Your second, but equally important, task is to do your part to contribute to developing your program into a learning community. Instead of competing with one another for individual accolades, members of a learning community make a commitment to share information and ideas. They respect—and even value—different points of view. And they support one another in the formidable enterprise of becoming helping professionals. This way, *everybody* wins.

Because you learn by example, the heart of a training program is not the curriculum, but its people. Actions do speak louder than words, so it is vital that you seek out trainers and supervisors who exemplify the knowledge and skills you want to learn. You want to be with those whom you respect and admire, because the most important lessons in this line of work are not taught but caught. Like chicken pox at a day care center, openness to feedback, commitment to helping, and curiosity about the human heart can be highly contagious. So take a close look at the people in a training program. What do you want to catch from them? Is it obvious that they are enthusiastic about training new professionals? Are they dedicated to the art of doing counseling and therapy? Do they have a sense of awe about the mysteries of the mind? Instead of looking for trainers who merely spoon-feed simplistic answers, seek out those who truly educate by demonstrating their professionalism and who challenge you to do likewise. The counseling profession, like a fidgety kid, is never still—it is a living, breathing, kicking, and constantly evolving entity. Look for mentors and trainers who personify the kind of professional you want to become.

Of course, you can also serve as an example to others. You can demonstrate the fundamental helping attitudes of genuineness, caring, and openness. You can practice the skills that you are developing. In class discussions, you can share your own discoveries and observations. Whatever the situation, you bring a wealth of experience and ideas to this training, and your colleagues will appreciate your generosity in sharing it. Keep in mind that your training program has changed in one important way since you applied to it—you are now a member of it! A vibrant, thriving training program, like the entire profession, is continually changing and growing as members like you contribute to its vitality. The African Mbuti have a ritualized song that is a wonderful example of what every learning community should aspire to achieve. In the song, individual singers are responsible for specific notes, but no one carries the entire melody. As a result, only the community can sing the song (Turnbull, 1990). You can follow the spirit of this song by adding your voice to your learning community. Practice making a difference by volunteering for committees, offering suggestions, and making your program a better one by the time you leave it.

When you join a community, one of the things you need to do is communicate with other members. Of course, effective communication is important to any organization, but it is particularly essential to one that is dedicated to training counselors. Virtually every day, you will have opportunities to engage in all sorts of stimulating, intriguing, encouraging, and challenging interactions with your teachers, supervisors, and colleagues. In Chapter 7, we offer suggestions for ways you can connect with others in your program, broaden your experiences with diverse populations, and network with your professional colleagues. We also explore how the personal changes you make will have an impact on your relationships with significant others, friends, and relatives.

▲▲▲

Worst Parents of the Year Award
Jen's Story

YOU WOULD have thought by the look on their faces that I had just handed them the award for "Worst Parents of the Year." They sat confused, hurt, and angry. On my left, my father was perched on his chair, waiting for me to give him a better explanation for all of this. To my right was my mother, fighting back tears as she struggled to understand what I had just told them. I was in the middle, feeling like this conversation I was having in my living room was just about the worst mistake I had ever made.

My intentions had been so noble, so heartfelt. I wanted to share with my parents my desire for a closer relationship with them. I wanted our conversations to reach beyond everyday chitchat and into depths of who we were. I wanted to know my parents as people and I wanted the same from them in return. And why not? After the first three months in my counseling program, I was having conversations like this on a daily basis. My whole world was about sharing, listening, reflecting, and accepting the ideas of others. As classmates, we laughed together, we cried together, and we always had someone to pour our souls out to. I thought for sure I could take home all the treasures I had learned and initiate the same experiences with my parents.

Unfortunately, as they say about baseball pitchers, my windup was great, but my delivery stunk. In my naïvete, I had assumed that, because I had been living in a counselor's world, everyone else had been doing the same. I had forgotten that most people aren't having intimate discussions about the meaning of life on a daily basis. Therefore, when I brought my request to my parents, I chose words that had worked so well with my peers and professors. As you might think, their reactions were not what I had expected. They couldn't understand how, after all the love and support they had given me, I could ask for something more. How could I suggest that we were not close enough, or that we didn't talk enough about the right things? The more I tried to explain, the more unhappy they got. By the end of the conversation, I truly felt like I was speaking a different language. Needless to say, what started out as the perfect plan ended up as a complete failure. Or was it?

After I returned to school, strange things started happening. I began to get calls from my mom for no particular reason. My dad stopped asking me if I had gotten my oil changed and started inquiring what I wanted to do after graduation. E-mails began to appear from them, filling me in on how they were feeling about different things. I even went home out of the blue to spend the weekend with them.

What started out as a disaster turned into something amazing. I learned that we are all on a journey to find closeness with our loved ones but that not all of us go about it at the same pace. Those who are in training on a regular basis must resist the urge to carry those who prefer to walk. In this way, we will all feel comfortable when we reach the finish line.

▼▼▼

Keep Your Bearings

Our life's journey of self-discovery is not a straight line.

—Stuart Wilde

The fourth principle of thriving is based on the fact that, although you need company on your training journey, you also need time alone to check your bearings, process your experiences, and reflect on the discoveries you are making. As Paul Tournier (1957) explained, "The real meaning of travel . . . is the discovery of oneself" (p. 57). No matter what classes you take, the subject you're likely to learn most about is yourself. As a result, your training experiences will be like your fingerprints—uniquely your own.

You probably have access to information about your program's policies and procedures in your school catalog and student handbook. However, because embarking on any important journey is neither a certain nor an easy venture, you need to rely on more than this information to gain your bearings. As with any trip, you need to remember where you've been, determine where you are now, and envision where you're heading. In other words, you need to explore yourself in order to find the internal compass that can offer you a sense of direction, to develop a training time line and map, and to assess your progress regularly.

Keeping a journal is one excellent way to recollect important events, explore ideas, sort out reactions, and work through personal issues. Your journal then becomes a reservoir of discoveries, the place in which you face and answer your own questions and carry on an ongoing written conversation with yourself. You can use your journal to reflect on and tie together all of your learning experiences: readings you encounter, relationships you establish, observations you make, and skills you practice.

At the very least, it is vital that you set aside personal time for yourself—to meditate, ponder, speculate, pray, relax, or simply *be*. Throughout your training, from your admissions interview to the graduation ceremony, you will have countless opportunities for personal growth and greater self-awareness. It is up to you to take full advantage of these opportunities and to make meaning of these experiences. You will find that the most important discoveries you make in your training—the greatest learning experiences you have—take place when you are truly open to looking at yourself.

Training programs repeatedly invite you to explore yourself, because in no other profession is the adage, "Know thyself," more important or more central. The many videotapes you will watch, the extensive feedback you will hear, and the countless occasions for introspection you will have can help you tremendously in knowing your most important tool as a counselor—yourself. However, the process is neither easy nor pain free. For example, you may begin a course on multiculturalism feeling pretty self-satisfied, confident that you do not have a racist or sexist bone in your entire body, only to discover quickly that you need to confront your own ethnocentrism and racism (Kiselica, 1999).

It's sometimes tempting to stay right where you are, remaining in familiar territory, avoiding the troubling questions, and never breaking out of your routine. But just remember—if you have both feet firmly planted on solid ground, then you're not moving. You only advance when you lean forward enough to become momentarily imbalanced and then take a step. Simply put, progress is knocking yourself off balance and regaining it in a new position. Nobody can become a counselor or therapist without a spirit of adventure, without the willingness to try something different, to take a few risks, and to make lots of mistakes along the way. You might as well abandon any perfectionistic tendencies you may have, because they will do you no good in this field. There's an Inuit saying that expresses this spirit of adventure: "Only the air-spirits know what lies beyond the hills, yet I urge my team farther on."

As you engage in this process, remember to focus on your strengths, too. It's easy to ruminate on your mistakes, limitations, and blunders. If that is your inclination, then you are bound to keep yourself restless, troubled, and awake on many a night. Of course, many trainees occasionally feel demoralized (Watkins, 1996). At these times, it may be helpful to remind yourself that you were selected for training because of your strengths, talents, and potential—and that you also chose to accept this challenge. So give yourself credit for having the chutzpah to think that perhaps you have what it takes to enter what Janet Malcolm (1982) called "the impossible profession."

▲▲▲

You'll Go Far in Life
Andrea's Story

LIKE MOST graduate students, I've had my share of moments of self-doubt. There were times when I've wondered how I ever got to graduate school in the first place. I sometimes believed that my acceptance to graduate school was a fluke and that I got in by the skin of my teeth. It was during one of these low points that I had what I consider a moment of clarity.

I was in one of my first graduate courses, and the professor was explaining to my class that his course was not part of the admissions process. I remember thinking, "Admissions process? What the heck is he talking about? What would this course have to do with the admissions process anyway?" Sensing our confusion, he went on to explain himself. He told us that his class was not designed to "weed out" any of us. He said that getting accepted into graduate school was a difficult task, but it was a task that we had already accomplished. He told us that he firmly believed that each and every one of us deserved to be there. He explained that he would expect a lot out of us, because he believed that we were all quite capable. He concluded by telling us that as long as we were willing to work hard, he would do whatever he could to help us in our graduate careers. I left class that day feeling as though my professor had a personal investment in each and every one of us. I also knew that not living up to his expectations would result in my feeling as though I had personally let him down.

Reflecting on that particular class experience helped me to understand graduate school overall. I began to realize that it isn't about proving myself over and over again. I finally understood that everyone assumed that I deserved to be here. Furthermore, I realized that my professors were all willing to do whatever they could to help me succeed. And as I began to look around, I became aware of the feeling that they all had a personal investment in me.

On the last day of that particular class, my professor told me how much he had enjoyed having me in his class. I thanked him and told him that I had thoroughly enjoyed it. He went on to say that he knew that I would go far in life. Not being one to accept a compliment easily, I kind of brushed his comment aside with a little bit of humor. Days later, though, I could not get his words out of my head. What did I ever do to deserve such a compliment?

This man, one of the most brilliant people I have ever met, believes that I am going to go far in life? Those words still echo in my mind at times, and I know that I will spend the rest of my life trying to do just that.

▼▼▼

Of course, you're going to encounter roadblocks along the way in your training journey, but how you view them can turn these stumbling blocks into stepping stones. It was during a particularly tough time that one student, Christine, found it helpful to give herself this motivational nudge: "If I look at challenges as only obstacles, then I'll have trouble handling them, but if I look at them as opportunities, I'll be enriched."

Another way to cope with this turmoil is to appreciate the humor in your situation, particularly if the joke is *yourself*—your own hang-ups, idiosyncrasies, limitations, and foibles. For example, during one class, when students were discussing their consultation projects, one participant, John, instead of presenting a successful experience, decided to talk about a session in which he "blew it." During a meeting with his consultees, John found himself making one mistake after another. His description of his frantic but futile attempts to salvage his image made the discussion a memorable learning experience. It was not only a hilarious story, but John's willingness to share his predicament was liberating for everyone in the class. They realized that they did not have to be perfect in their work and that they could safely talk about their mistakes with one another.

An important part of keeping your bearings is also knowing where you're heading. One of the simplest ways to achieve a goal is to envision it vividly. You will find that your vision of yourself as an emerging professional will help you to start acting as if you already have achieved that goal. What exactly is a counselor or a therapist? First, he or she is someone who is committed to providing competent, caring, and ethical services. Second, he or she is a professional who engages in a lifelong process of learning and refining these helping skills. Finally, he or she is someone who is actively involved in advancing the profession through research, innovation, training, or service. What particular kind of helper do you want to become? To answer that question, you first must explore who you are *now*. In Chapter 6, we invite you to examine your belief system, your values, your paradigms, and your attitudes toward others who may differ significantly from you.

■ ■ ■
___

EXERCISE 1.1 **Whatcha Gonna Be?**
A Magic Mirror Exercise

The purpose of this activity is for you to relax, reflect, and envision your future. Find a comfortable spot by yourself, away from distractions, and let yourself relax. You may find yourself relaxing by lying down, closing your eyes, letting your muscles unwind, breathing more deeply and evenly, and allowing your mind to drift along. Once you're in a nice state of relaxation, imagine that you are about to step in front of a nearby magic mirror. Like any ordinary mirror, this one shows your reflection, but this mirror reflects how you will look and what you will do in the future. See yourself as you will appear when you have become a professional helper. Look carefully at your face. What does that expression communicate about the person you will become? Notice what you are doing. What skills are you demonstrating? What services are you providing? Pay attention to where you are in the future. Where are you working? Notice the other people around you. Who are your clients? Who are your colleagues? After you have completed this activity, use your journal to describe your vision of the future.

By the way, although you used an imaginary mirror in this exercise, you may be interested in reading how Michael Mahoney (1991) used an actual mirror with clients to evoke powerful emotions and encourage self-exploration.

■■■

Let the Trip Take You

If you surrender to the wind, you can ride it.

—Toni Morrison

As you move along your training journey, you'll also discover that, in spite of all your careful planning, you will find yourself being pulled in surprising directions. In *Travels with Charley*, John Steinbeck (1962) wrote, "We do not take a trip; a trip takes us" (p. 6). Your progress will build its own momentum, and you'll find yourself taking the unexpected turn and discovering new territories. This thriving principle invites you to let yourself be carried along by the flow of your training and to be open to the possibilities of your own transformation.

Learning is one of the most challenging, as well as most fulfilling, of life's adventures. As you examine ideas that may threaten your preconceived notions, as you grope along through your periods of confusion, and as you read, reflect, synthesize, speculate, and brainstorm, you will forge a new personal and professional identity. As a successful graduate, you will not be the person who originally entered the training program.

Along the way, you will gain a sense of self-efficacy, confidence, and trust in your own resources as a counselor or therapist (Sipps, Sugden, & Favier, 1988). Eventually, you'll be "replacing an external supervisor with an internal one" (Granello, Beamish, & Davis, 1997, p. 305). By the time you complete your program, you will be more seasoned and have a greater insight into and a deeper appreciation for the clutter, confusion, and complexity of people's lives. Through this learning, you will do more than acquire knowledge and develop skills—you will transform yourself from a student into a professional. In other words, just as participating in counseling and therapy changes clients, becoming a helping professional changes *you*.

Chapter 8 helps you identify important sources of knowledge and emotional support to help you venture out, take risks, and grow in your practicum, field placement, or internship. These experiences give you the opportunity to translate your theoretical knowledge into effective clinical work and to gain confidence in yourself as an emerging professional.

Always Take the High Road

On life's journey . . . virtuous deeds are a shelter,
wisdom is the light by day, and right
mindfulness is the protection by night.

—Buddha

The final principle for thriving in your training recognizes that the helping professions are based on more than knowledge, skills, and self-awareness. They are also based on values. In fact, you can't become a competent therapist or counselor unless you're also an ethical one (Cohen & Cohen, 1999). As an emerging professional trainee, you'll sharpen your moral compass by learning your professional code of ethics (see the appendices)and following it in *all* situations.

When you become a helping professional, you will have to comply with myriad state and federal laws, follow your profession's ethical standards, and observe the policies of your agency or school. As an enrolled student, you are expected to behave legally, ethically, and honorably in all your course work. Whenever you are unsure about what conduct is allowed by the law, the ethical standards of your profession, or the honor code of your university, immediately consult your trainer or supervisor. A violation can be grounds for failing a course and being expelled from the program.

Finally, taking the high road also means challenging yourself to maintain high professional standards. For example, you need to watch out for the temptation to merely impersonate Hollywood's version of a counselor or therapist—using jargon, spouting simplistic slogans, and blindly following the latest therapeutic fads. At times, you may find yourself being attracted to the certainty and confidence that this posturing seems to offer.

Randy, for example, was a beginning trainee who found himself enamored of his expanding vocabulary of terms culled from courses on counseling theories, interpersonal dynamics, and abnormal psychology. At parties, he would liberally sprinkle these phrases throughout his conversations. Finally, one of his friends took Randy aside, gently pointed out these affectations, and told him how she missed the "real," unpretentious person she once knew. When he brought up this issue in his own counseling, Randy began to recognize how he was harboring serious doubts that he would ever be able to master the complex skills of helping. He discovered that he found some consolation in at least talking like an expert.

Looking back on how she began her training, Zelda realized that she was counting on her trainers to tell her exactly what to say to her clients. She had the notion that doing good counseling and therapy could be reduced to following a script or relying on "chicken soup" inspirational maxims. But then Zelda's supervisor challenged her to discover and develop her own therapeutic voice. Zelda remembered vividly how much she wrote in her journal that night about her doubts of ever becoming a therapist. As she read over her anguished journal entry, she realized that her words rang strong and true. Her voice, and no one else's, was emerging on her journal pages. With a sense of determination, Zelda wrote, "Hey, I'm here to become a therapist—not a ventriloquist's dummy!"

Of course, it's only natural to succumb to some of these temptations as you take on a professional identity. You are, after all, entering a tough, challenging, and nebulous line of work, so taking refuge in jargon, labels, and fads can be very appealing. However, you will come to realize that a true professional speaks and writes with clarity in order to enlighten— not to impress—others. A real helping professional avoids slapping on labels like a grocery clerk and, instead, recognizes the uniqueness and complexity of every client. Finally, a true counselor or therapist is one who thinks critically and develops a healthy skepticism regarding fads, misinformation, and biases in the field. Sure, as a helping professional, you may be softhearted toward people, but you also have to be hardnosed about the evidence needed to validate the effectiveness of therapy and counseling techniques. Taking the high road isn't the easy way, but it's the only way if you plan to be a successful helping professional.

SUMMARY

In this chapter, we presented six principles to follow on your training journey. Observing these guidelines will help you succeed not only as a student but also as a helping professional. The first principle is to pack wisely for the trip. Making provisions to meet basic needs and bringing along important resources are vital for your success. Second, make the journey your destination. Your training is not a rehearsal—it is an integral part of your lifelong commitment to professional development. The third principle of thriving is to have traveling companions. Be open to what your peers, mentors, instructors, supervisors, and clients can offer you because it is impossible to become a helping professional on your own. Fourth, keep your bearings. You will find that the most important discoveries you make in your training—the greatest learning experiences you have—take place when you are truly open to looking at yourself. Fifth, let the trip take you. Allow your progress to build its own momentum and you'll find yourself taking the unexpected turn and discovering new territories. Finally, always take the high road. You can't become a competent counselor or therapist unless you also become an ethical one.

RESOURCES

One of the best ways to begin taking on a professional identity is to join the club. The helping professions have organizations at the state, regional, and national levels. Below is the information you need to contact five of the national associations in the helping professions. All five have developed Web sites that provide excellent information regarding resources, training, and employment opportunities and current issues in the profession.

American Association for Marriage and Family Therapy
1133 Fifteenth Street, N.W., Suite 300
Washington, DC 20005-2710
202-452-0109
http://www.aamft.org

American Counseling Association
5999 Stevenson Avenue
Alexandria, VA 22304-3300
703-823-9800 or 800-347-6647
http://www.counseling.org

American Mental Health Counselors Association
801 N. Fairfax St., Suite 304
Alexandria, VA 22314
703-548-6002 or 800-326-2642
http://www.amhca.org

American Psychological Association
750 First Street, NE
Washington, DC 20002-4242
202-336-5500
http://www.apa.org

National Association of Social Workers
750 First Street, N.E., Suite 700
Washington, DC 20002-4241
202-408-8600 or 800-638-8799
http://www.naswdc.org

Graduate School Survival Guide
http://www-smi.stanford.edu/people/pratt/smi/advice.html

This helpful site includes suggestions for getting the most out of your relationship with your advisor, getting the most out of what you read, finding a thesis topic and formulating a research plan, and avoiding the research blues.

REFERENCES

Campbell, J. (1986). *The inner reaches of outer space: Metaphor as myth and as religion.* New York: van der Marck.

Cohen, E. D., & Cohen, G. S. (1999). *The virtuous therapist: Ethical practice of counseling and psychotherapy.* Belmont, CA: Wadsworth.

Corey, M. S., & Corey, G. (1998). *Becoming a helper* (3rd ed.). Pacific Grove, CA: Brooks/Cole.

Granello, D. H., Beamish, P. M., & Davis, T. E. (1997). Supervisee empowerment: Does gender make a difference? *Counselor Education and Supervision, 36,* 305–317.

Kiselica, M. S. (1999). Confronting my own ethnocentrism and racism: A process of pain and growth. *Journal of Counseling and Development, 77,* 14–17.

Mahoney, M. J. (1991). *Human change processes: The scientific foundations of psychotherapy.* New York: Basic Books.

Malcolm, J. (1982). *Psychoanalysis: The impossible profession.* New York: Random House.

Sipps, G. J., Sugden, G. J., & Favier, C. M. (1988). Counselor training level and verbal response type: Their relationship to efficacy and outcome expectations. *Journal of Counseling Psychology, 35,* 397–401.

Steinbeck, J. (1962). *Travels with Charley.* New York: Bantam Books.

Tournier, P. (1957). *The meaning of persons.* New York: Harper & Row.

Turnbull, C. (1990). Luminality: A synthesis of subjective and objective experience. In R. Schechner & W. Appel (Eds.), *By means of performance* (pp. 50–81). New York: Cambridge University Press.

Watkins, C. E. (1996). On demoralization and awe in psychotherapy supervision. *Clinical Supervisor, 14,* 139–148.

CHAPTER 2

▲▲▲
▼▼▼

Making Your Training Journey

When one travels, the first step is the beginning of the arrival.

—Seng-Chao

Our task is to make ourselves architects of the future.

—Jomo Kenyatta

After receiving his doctoral degree, one of our colleagues described his journey through graduate school as one of taking on the character of each of the Seven Dwarfs. "At the start of my training," he said, "I felt so naïve and shy that I was Dopey and Bashful. By the second year, I felt so sick, exhausted, and frustrated with everything that I was either Sneezy, Sleepy, or Grumpy. Finally, when I got my Ph.D., I was thrilled that I was at last both Doc and Happy."

Although our friend offered this description as merely a cute story, you can expect to undergo profound transformations in your own identity. Whether you pursue a master's, educational specialist, or doctoral degree, you take on distinct roles as you enter and make your way through a program. These roles include applicant, novice, apprentice, and emerging professional. This chapter is organized according to the four roles that you assume as you chart your course along your training journey.

You also encounter important milestones—such as selection, orientation, comprehensive examination, capstone experiences, and graduation—that mark the crucial turning points you face along the way. In this chapter, we describe how you can proceed through a training program's rites of passage. In many ways, the milestones involved in becoming a helping professional parallel your growth from childhood into adulthood. Just as children learn to crawl before they can walk, you learn basic theories and techniques before you can practice counseling and therapy. And just as children discover and explore their unique sense of self as they grow and mature, you also learn about yourself, forging a new identity that emerges and crystallizes at each stage of your own development.

Finally, by thriving in your training, you also go through major changes in how you think. Mark Young (2001) described the successful process of becoming a helper as a personal journey with identifiable developmental stages. Basing his observations on Perry's (1970) research on adult development, Young considered three stages—dualistic, multiplistic, and relativistic thinking—to be applicable to most graduate students learning a new profession (Simpson, Dalgaard, & O'Brien, 1986). These developmental stages can provide a useful framework for reflecting on your own training journey. But do not view this developmental process as a simple sequence of steps that you take. In reality, your development involves much ebb and flow, and at any point in your training, you probably incorporate elements from all three "stages" even though one may dominate.

In the following sections, in addition to offering practical advice about handling the "nuts and bolts" of completing your training requirements, we also suggest ways you can thrive at each stage of your development. For example, by creating a portfolio, keeping a journal, and using rituals, you can support your development, document your achievements, celebrate your progress, and foster a sense of community with your colleagues.

▲▲▲

Why Not Enjoy the Ride?
Cathy's Story

AT THE END of this semester, I'm going to be graduating. Of course, I'm excited about finishing up and a little nervous about finding a job. While I'm pretty busy completing my internship and sending out resumes, at times I've found myself just skimming through the journals I've written over the past three years. It reminds me of when I was a senior in high school. I was excited about all the changes in my life, but I also had a need to look through my yearbooks and relive a little of my earlier high school days.

I'm not sure why, but my reactions to my journals have gone through an incredible change. When I used to read over my entries right after writing them, I would often feel embarrassed and supercritical. I would think to myself, "Those words don't capture my experiences at all. They're so lame, superficial, and trite!" Now when I read over those same entries that I had written at the start of my training, I feel like I'm encountering another person.

Like an indulgent older sister, I now am quick to forgive this person's mistakes, find her awkward phrases endearing, and am charmed by her naïve views. In fact, I feel protective of her, wanting to offer her some nurturance and encouragement, saying something like, "You go, girl!" I'm proud of how that person hung in there through some tough times.

I haven't really counted, but I bet that the number of words I wrote in an entry was a pretty good measure of the turmoil I was in at the time. Last year, there were lots of entries about my comps. I was so afraid that I was going to fail that exam! One week, I had spent every free minute in the library doing this marathon review of all the comps material. When I finally finished, I was convinced that there was no way that I could pass.

When I came home that night, my partner innocently asked me about my day and the next thing I remember is sobbing uncontrollably in her arms, saying that it was no use because passing was impossible. She was great—she didn't give me any silly reassurances or inspirational slogans. She just stayed there with me until I was ready to move on to making a plan of action. Reading that journal entry reminded me of just how lucky I've been to have her and others in my life.

I'm at a different place now—more confident of myself, more seasoned, and on my way to becoming a good counselor. As I reread what I've just written, I recognize that my words still don't capture fully what I'm experiencing right now, but I'm a lot more tolerant and charitable towards myself than I used to be. Sure, I haven't arrived—I still have a long way to go, but why not enjoy the ride?

▼▼▼

BEING AN APPLICANT

Change is not made without inconvenience, even
from worse to better.

—Richard Hooker

With any graduate program, the first role you take on is that of applicant—someone who wishes to become a member of that learning community. As an applicant, you are participating in the phase of your training that is typically called the "admissions process." We prefer, however, to use the term *selection* because it emphasizes that the process involves a *mutual* decision. While a program's selection committee is deciding whether to admit you, you are deciding if that program would help you to meet your personal and professional goals. Just as is true with any committed relationship, one of your most important tasks in graduate training is finding the best match for you.

Here we highlight only some of the major strategies you'll want to pursue to become a successful applicant. There are several fine guides you can read for detailed information regarding program selection. In the "Resources" section of this chapter, we recommend one that is especially relevant to counseling and psychology (Keith-Spiegel & Wiederman, 2000). The selection process is a tough and difficult one that involves literally years of preparation. To succeed, you should follow these steps:

Gain Experience

Your first task is to gain relevant experience. This experience may be volunteer work or paid employment, but any experience in which you were engaged in developing helping relationships would certainly be relevant to counseling and therapy. You may have been, for example, a Big Brother or Big Sister, an advocate for sexual assault survivors, or a volunteer at a crisis hotline service.

Many college graduates work for a year or two before returning to graduate school. There are many bachelor's-level positions in the education, community service, and mental health fields that can offer you invaluable experience to prepare you for graduate training. Some of these positions include teacher, case manager, psychiatric aide, mentor, advocate, and outreach worker.

Gaining experience in helping others is essential to an applicant for a number of important reasons. First, these activities help you develop some fundamental skills in establishing and maintaining a trusting relationship with someone in need of assistance. Second, you get a sense of the realities of a helping profession. Becoming involved in this work can help you confirm your hunch that counseling and therapy may be your life's calling. Third, selection committees look carefully throughout your application materials for evidence of relevant experience. Applicants who have extensive experience, whether it's paid or volunteer work, are more likely to be selected for admission to graduate training programs.

Complete the Academic Prerequisites

One of your fundamental responsibilities is to meet the educational requirements for entering a graduate program. Although academic excellence has not been found to predict counseling effectiveness (Markert & Monke, 1990), selection committees do expect that you have successfully completed academic course work that has prepared you well for graduate training. If you are one of the increasing numbers of older people who have decided to pursue a graduate degree in counseling and therapy, you may need to complete some undergraduate courses before you can qualify.

Explore Your Training Options

Buskist and Mixon (1998) have written a useful guide that lists many training programs in counseling and psychology. Sayette, Mayne, and Norcross (1998) described more than 300 programs and offered helpful advice on selecting schools based on your training goals. Read brochures, check directories, surf the Internet for the Web sites of programs. Be sure to talk to both professors and students in the programs that particularly interest you. You'll soon discover that program descriptions can differ considerably from the reality. Remember that old saying, "You can't tell a book by its cover."

Take the Required Standardized Tests

Another important task you must perform is to successfully take the standardized tests required for the programs to which you are applying.

Although the Graduate Record Examination (GRE) has, at best, only a small correlation with grades in graduate school (Morrison & Morrison, 1995; Sternberg & Williams, 1997), most counselor training programs require the GRE General Test, which has three scores. The Verbal Abilities test items involve analogies, sentence completion, antonyms, and reading comprehension. The Quantitative Abilities items involve arithmetic, algebra, geometry, quantitative comparisons, and data interpretation. The Analytical Abilities items involve logical reasoning problems. Doctoral programs in counseling psychology typically require that you also take the GRE Subject Test in Psychology.

A few programs give you the choice of taking either the GRE or the Miller Analogies Test (MAT) as part of the selection process. The MAT is a fifty-minute test consisting of 100 items, all involving analogies. An example would be

Rose is to flower as chihuahua is to:

A. chalupa.

B. Mexico.

C. dog.

D. Taco Bell.

To help you perform at your best on these standardized tests, you can read preparation manuals, take practice tests, and even participate in workshops to enhance your scores (Finkle, 1999). Many of these practice tests are available as computer software. At the end of this chapter, you will find useful Web sites that can provide you with detailed information about these resources.

Arrange for References

Most training programs expect you to provide at least three references from people who know you well and can confidently comment on your readiness to become a counselor or therapist. These people will need to complete a form or write a letter of support for each school to which you're applying.

For your part, you can help make this task as simple as possible for these people by offering some basic assistance. For example, provide each of them with a cover sheet listing all the schools to which you are applying. You should also organize the reference forms and other materials—and be generous with the paper clips to keep each school's forms together! Provide all the necessary envelopes, appropriately addressed and stamped. These people are already offering you their time and attention to serve as your references—they shouldn't have to worry about details such as postage. It is also helpful to offer them a resume and other specific information about your qualifications and interests. Finally, follow up with a thank-you note and keep them updated on the results of your applications.

Write a Personal Statement

Most programs also require that you submit a personal statement as part of your application. Keith-Spiegel and Wiederman (2000) examined 360 essay questions that were included on the application forms for master's and doctoral programs in psychology and related fields. Typically, the questions concern your career plans, interests, and experiences. The personal statement is the least structured part of the materials that you submit for your application, but be sure to answer the specific question that has been asked. Writing one generic statement to use on all your applications may save you time but can sabotage your chances. Your answer may appear as if you did not pay attention to the question—a bad sign for your potential to be a counselor or therapist!

Be sure that you also use the personal statement as an opportunity to supplement the other information you already have provided. There's no need, for example, to repeat the honors and awards you may have won. Instead, you can make a truly *personal* statement by sharing your own individuality—the experiences that have formed your character, the dreams that you hope to pursue, and the personal qualities that you bring to the program.

Besides providing the content that the selection committee requests, take care to present a statement that is well written. As we discuss in Chapter 4, writing is one of the basic academic skills you need to succeed in graduate school. Selection committee members read these statements to find evidence that you possess this skill.

Participate in a Selection Interview

Many programs include an interview as the final step in the selection process. Some applicants make the mistake of trying to prepare for an interview by developing a script of answers. Keep in mind that you're not interviewing for drama school. In counseling and therapy, there are no scripts. Instead, make a commitment to be open, genuine, and engaged throughout the interview—to be yourself. The interview is also your chance to learn more about the program, so take advantage of your opportunities to ask questions. You need information in order to make *your* selection decision, too.

Consider Your Options Carefully

If you are offered admission to one or more programs, take some time to carefully weigh all the important factors as you come to a decision. Remember that you're investing several years of your life in this training, so don't take this decision lightly.

You need to consider a number of important issues. Two fundamental questions concern the third thriving principle, having traveling companions. Do faculty members personify the helping professional you hope to become? Do you look forward to working with the other students? Other questions, however, are just as important. Are you enthusiastic about the quality, depth, and breadth of the curriculum? Do you like the location of the school? What are the possibilities of financial assistance?

Once you have made your selection, contact the program as soon as possible. After you have confirmed your entrance into the program of your choice, you should quickly notify any other programs that have selected you. These programs can then offer admission to someone on their waiting lists.

BEING A NOVICE

A dream [is] the bearer of a new possibility, the enlarged horizon, the great hope.

—Howard Thurman

When you successfully complete the selection process, your counseling identity makes a major shift from that of an applicant to that of a graduate student. You are now a member—albeit the "new kid on the block"—of a community dedicated to training helping professionals. As a novice, you probably feel a thrilling combination of excitement and worry, eagerness and apprehension.

When you enter the program, you receive information regarding program policies, requirements, options, and procedures. In fact, it is likely that you have access to an overwhelming amount of data. Just sifting through it all, along with skimming through your new textbooks, can leave you confused and intimidated, reaffirming just how little you actually do know—and just how much you still need to learn. But take it easy on yourself. Your basic goal as a novice is to embark on your training journey successfully.

In Chapter 4, we describe in detail how you can enhance your abilities to perform well academically. In the meantime, we invite you to focus on the broader themes of your novice experience—becoming oriented, learning the basics, connecting with others, and becoming fully involved in the training process (McAuliffe & Eriksen, 2000). As you participate in your beginning courses, you begin to develop a foundation—the basic knowledge, skills, and attitudes—necessary for you to move into the apprenticeship phase of your training.

When you first become a novice, you may feel like a kid who has just climbed up the ladder to the high diving board for the first time. You think that everyone is looking at you, while you stand up there wondering what in the world you were thinking when you decided to make this dive. A belly flop would be painful enough, but also, to add insult to injury, everyone would see you fail. Well, if you want to thrive in your training, your best option is to go ahead and dive right into this new endeavor.

To help you dive into your training and succeed as a novice, just remember the thriving principles—come well prepared, live your training, learn from others, explore yourself, be open to opportunities, and always act with character. In the following section, we discuss how you can use rituals to engage deeply in your training experiences right from the start.

Opening Rituals

Rituals are ceremonial activities that give expression to beliefs, values, and concepts. Baptisms, bar mitzvahs, Hindu samsaras, vision quests, walkabouts, and marriage ceremonies are only a few of the countless religious and cultural rituals that enrich people's lives (Bell, 1997). Many counselors, especially those who work with couples and families, have found that rituals can be powerful intervention techniques (Becvar & Becvar, 1996). Rituals can also enrich your own training experience, strengthen your sense of community, celebrate your accomplishments, and give voice to your fundamental values (McKee, Smith, Hayes, Stewart, & Echterling, 1999).

All counselor and therapist training programs have orientation meetings or social gatherings to welcome new students and mark the beginning of a new academic year. These opening rituals are nice ways to introduce everyone to one another and to familiarize newcomers with the workings of their new community. For example, recognizing the emotional and bonding power of rituals, one counseling program added an initiation ceremony to its orientation. The ceremony involved faculty and students forming a circle, lighting candles, declaring personal goals, and pledging support to one another. However, even if your program does not offer any initiation ceremony, you can develop your own ritual to mark this occasion.

■■■

EXERCISE 2.1 **Traditions**
A Reminiscing and Planning Exercise

Rituals that are repeated become traditions. In this exercise, we invite you first to think about two important traditions that have already enriched your life. Select one tradition that is closely connected to your family life and another that reflects your religious or cultural heritage.

Spend a little time reminiscing about each tradition. What were the circumstances? Who was involved? What was your role? When you're ready, go ahead and describe each tradition.

Looking back on this tradition, write about the meaning it holds for you now.

FAMILY

Tradition:

_____

_____

Meaning:

_____

_____

_____

_____

_____

RELIGION OR CULTURE

Tradition:

_____

_____

Meaning:

_____

_____

_____

_____

_____

The second part of this exercise is a planning task. Think of a ritual that you would like to make a tradition connected with your training. It could be a personal ritual that only you would perform, a family ceremony that involves your relatives, or a community activity that includes everyone in the program. Describe the activity and explore its meaning for you.

TRAINING

Tradition:

_____

_____

Meaning:

_____

_____

_____

_____

_____

We encourage you to perform an individual or shared initiation ritual at the start of your training and at the start of every academic year.
Describe your experience in your training journal so that you can refer
to it each year to reflect on your progress. Such an initiation ritual, like
morning rituals of brushing your teeth and taking a shower, can be
invigorating and awakening experiences. Besides, you may be surprised
by the powerful emotions and meaningful discoveries that your ritual
can evoke.

■ ■ ■

Communication

If you are to thrive in your new learning community, you need to be
communicating with others. As you've heard so many times, communication is a two-way street. Be ready to do your part to be both an active
listener and an open communicator in your program. Stay in touch.

Keep your program administrators up-to-date on your current postal address, telephone number, and E-mail address. Be sure to let people know what's on your mind. Both you and the program will be the better for it.

Most training programs have developed a number of ways for their members to share information, ideas, and feedback with one another.

Newsletters A program newsletter provides an overview of recent developments and a preview of upcoming events. It may, for example, introduce you to new members, update you on the accomplishments of students and faculty, and announce program changes. It also offers information on important deadlines, meetings, and conferences.

When you receive a newsletter, take some time to jot down immediately the important dates and times in your calendar. Then keep the most recent edition handy in case you need to refer to it. It is a valuable tool to help you stay up-to-date and involved. Also feel free to suggest items for inclusion in your program's newsletter.

E-mail Electronic mail has become a great way to communicate quickly and easily with others. You can share information about employment possibilities, social events, or other opportunities. Of course, E-mail messages are useless if you don't check your account. If you want to keep in touch, then check and use your E-mail regularly.

Bulletin boards Even the most "high tech" programs still have plenty of bulletin boards in the halls for posting hard copies of announcements, newsletters, brochures, and other information. Check these boards regularly and use them to post interesting and useful information.

Program committee meetings All counselor training programs have regular meetings to review procedures, develop policies, and address concerns. Most programs include student representatives as members of these committees. We encourage you to consider volunteering to be a student representative at these meetings. It's a great way to see how the organization operates and to participate in the planning process.

Meetings with your advisor Every graduate student has an assigned faculty advisor, and you should be meeting regularly with yours. Consider your advisor as a ready and reliable source of information and support. Yes, of course, your faculty advisor is a busy person, but remember that advising is an integral part of teaching—and an essential resource for you.

Progress reviews One accreditation standard is that the faculty must review the overall progress each student is making every semester. Near the end of each semester, you can also conduct your own review by taking some time to think about all that you have discovered, learned, and experienced during the semester. Record these evaluations in your journal and write your ideas for making continued progress. The end of the semester is an especially busy time, but reviewing your progress and planning your future will be time well spent!

Participation in formal assessment procedures All graduate training programs have developed several formal assessment procedures in order to obtain your feedback and suggestions. In your courses, your faculty members will ask you to assess their teaching performance and class activities. We encourage you to offer constructive feedback and practical suggestions when faculty and supervisors request your assessment of training experiences.

Handling Personal Problems

Because you were selected for admission from among many candidates, you will likely do well in your training and make satisfactory progress throughout the program. However, it's also possible that, at some point in your training, you could face serious academic or personal difficulties. If these difficulties threaten to impair your performance as a trainee, then you have the responsibility to take positive steps to address the concerns. You can pursue several practical, specific strategies. These steps may include taking a remedial course, repeating a course, entering personal counseling or therapy, or taking a leave of absence.

If you are dealing with concerns that seem overwhelming, then talk to your advisor about your options. In Chapter 5, we explore in detail how to deal with the stressors of graduate training, and in Chapter 6 we elaborate on the value of receiving counseling or therapy. There's no need for you to be struggling through your training like one of the walking wounded. Take care of yourself and seek help at the first sign of impairment.

Keeping a Portfolio

A portfolio is a collection of your work that tells the story of your efforts, progress, and achievement in your training (Carney, Cobia, &

Shannon, 1996). As part of their evaluation procedures, many programs now require students to assemble certain materials into a portfolio (Baltimore, Hickson, George, & Crutchfield, 1996). However, even if your program does not require a portfolio, we encourage you to begin one in order to take advantage of its many benefits.

Your portfolio offers a composite picture of your professional development. It allows you to demonstrate what you know in a way that reflects the complexity of particular topics and how you have integrated your skills and knowledge to create useful counseling tools. There are no cookbook recipes for what goes into your counseling portfolio. In fact, you can include different items in your portfolio depending on how you're going to be using it. For example, if you need it to document your progress or to evaluate the effectiveness of your program, then certain materials will be required. However, if you are bringing it along for a job interview, then you can custom design your portfolio to fit the position requirements. A third common use of a portfolio is for your personal growth and reflection.

Consider your training journal to be an essential piece of your portfolio, even though you are unlikely to be sharing it with others. Your journal, however, is your personal forum for noting your reflections and observations regarding the other items in your portfolio. What are some other possible items for your portfolio? Obvious choices include written samples of your work, such as assessment reports, diagnostic reports, intervention plans, term papers, handouts for presentations, and correspondence. Of course, you need to take care to protect the confidentiality of the clients you describe in these work samples. You also may want to have a section of works in progress, such as your philosophy of intervention, your evolving counseling and therapy theory, and ongoing projects. It can be useful to include a list of conferences and workshops you have attended, class presentations you have given, professional service activities, and awards. It's also a great idea to add scrapbook items, such as photographs, newspaper clippings, and program announcements, concerning your professional activities. Include drawings and comments by clients, notes from colleagues, and performance assessments from professors and supervisors.

Dualistic Thinking

As a novice, you are likely to be at Perry's first stage of adult development, which is characterized by a dualistic, right-or-wrong attitude

(Young, 2001). At this stage, you tend to approach your learning in a somewhat perfectionistic manner. You may find yourself trying to determine which of the theories of counseling you are learning is *the* correct one. You may, for example, be attracted to a person–centered approach or a cognitive–behavioral theory, and you feel you must choose one or the other. After all, they can't both be right . . . can they?

▲▲▲

The One
Juanita's Story

AS A BEGINNING counselor, I went through a series of infatuations with various counseling fads. The process later reminded me of the series of boyfriends I had had in high school. At first, I was completely fascinated with a particular counseling approach, certain that I had finally found "The One." However, as reality began to set in and I began to notice the imperfections and limitations of the technique, I quickly became disenchanted, "dumped" it, and went on to another counseling approach.

It was only later in my training, when I began to look closely at myself and to value what I brought to the counseling relationship, that I realized that I could set aside my desperate search for "The One."

▼▼▼

Perfectionism

Besides embarking on a quest for the perfect theory, as a novice, you're likely to be demanding perfection from yourself in your performance. You may come to your class in basic counseling skills believing that your performance must be impeccable—otherwise, you will be an absolute failure. With so much at stake, instead of really listening to the person who sits before you as your client, you are focusing on what to say next. You feel queasy as you attempt to make sense of what your client is saying. Nervous mannerisms, such as rhythmically kicking your foot or saying "um–hum," begin to pop up. You're under pressure to come up with the answer to your client's problem, and if you don't, you believe that you have not been helpful at all. So you wind up saying something ineffectual like, "Have you tried talking to your roommate?" As you reflect on your feelings of incompetence at the beginning of your program, you might secretly believe that you are a fraud, and that, sooner or later, you will be found out and excommunicated from the ranks. This is what Harvey and Katz (1985) called the "impostor phenomenon." Don't become too worried about it. Most trainees feel that way at the beginning of their program. In fact, we'll let you in on a little secret in the counseling and therapy training profession. We warn one another, "Be afraid, be very afraid!" about any beginning trainee who is supremely confident that he or she is already a genuine master of the art of counseling and therapy. People who think that they've already arrived see no point in going on a journey—and they make terrible travelers.

BEING AN APPRENTICE

We work to become, not to acquire.

—Elbert Hubbard

When you have completed your basic courses, you are no longer in the role of a novice. As you proceed to the next level of your training program, you begin to take on more responsibilities as you assume a new identity—that of an apprentice. As an apprentice, you are under close supervision, but you now have opportunities to practice your professional skills. For example, you may be assisting a professor on a research project, offering counseling services at a practicum site, presenting a guidance unit at a school, or cofacilitating a personal growth group with an intern.

Once you have demonstrated that you can succeed in a graduate training program, you can, for example, apply for membership in Chi Sigma Iota, the counseling professional honor society. This society recognizes excellence in counseling and helps create an atmosphere of professional commitment. You are invited to apply for membership each semester. Activities often include philanthropic projects, presentations, and social events.

Multiplistic Thinking

As you shift from a novice to an apprentice, you progress from a dualistic to a multiplistic way of thinking. At this point in your development, you begin to give up the idea that there is one correct answer or a single right way to work with people. Furthermore, you begin to see that your standard of right and wrong is not shared by all the people you meet and that their views have merit. You feel less threatened by ideas that once seemed strange—or just plain wrong—to you, and you become more accepting of other lifestyles. Instead of wanting to argue with people who see things differently, you become interested in their way of experiencing the world. Now, you spend less of your energy attempting to figure out what your professors expect of you and begin to operate more on your inner sense of how to carry out a project.

Still, at this stage of your development, you may be overwhelmed by all the new possibilities that are presented to you and a bit suspicious of those who attempt to persuade you to go in new directions. You may find that you become irritable, as well as regularly confused, during this phase of your training. Young (2001) stated that students at this stage

> often report being frustrated and defensive with supervisors who "correct" them because they do not yet know how to select the most helpful course of action. All roads seem to be equally valid (p. 6).

▲▲▲

A Deer Caught in
the Headlights
Bill's Story

"You're the first counseling graduate student I've ever met who's atheoretical!"

After recovering from the initial shock of that statement from my practicum supervisor, I rather dumbly replied, "Oh, I guess I have a theory, I just don't know what it is yet."

"Maybe it's time you found out," he responded. "You are trying to counsel from your personality alone, just being a nice person. I think your clients may be looking for more than that from you," he concluded.

He was right. My secret was out. I was a deer caught in the headlights. I really didn't have a clue about integrating theory into practice. Oh, I had completed several theory and technique classes, even received great grades in them, but somehow the content of those classes had not yet become a reality for either my counseling work or for me. It was time to begin the quest for a theory I could claim as my own.

It was not an easy journey. I had to work more, read more, question more. Being "eclectic" seemed like a cop-out to me. I really wanted to discover a theory that made sense to me, that worked for me in helping relationships and allowed me to be me at the same time. After two practicum experiences and a year-long internship, I landed on what I now call "holistic-integrative" counseling. It includes many aspects from well-known theories, such as those of Carl Rogers, Albert Ellis, Fritz Perls, Salvador Minuchin, and Virginia Satir, yet it also became uniquely mine— an integration of my personality, experiences, and worldview. The really neat part is that it is open-ended, allowing for constant adjustments based on new discoveries I make. In other words, I'm still growing, and so is my theory.

▼▼▼

The "Sophomore Slump"

Gregory Neimeyer (personal communication, March 12, 2001) has observed that many graduate students experience a sense of disillusionment during their second year of training. During your novice year, you probably went through an intensive, challenging time and made some steady progress. However, you may be disappointed you did not make the dramatic advances that you had hoped in your professional development. You also may feel a sense of disenchantment that, although you have gained many insights into yourself, you have not achieved any extraordinary breakthroughs in your personal awareness.

As a novice, you not only demanded a great deal from yourself, you also had high expectations of your faculty and supervisors. Such expectations do not match the realities of faculty life. During your undergraduate days, you may not have worked closely with faculty members.

Consequently, you may not have realized that the average university faculty member works well over fifty hours a week, with direct teaching duties accounting for only a small fraction of this time. Now that you are working more closely with the training faculty, you may notice that they are often heavily overcommitted, with work schedules that are, like a middle-aged man's old blue jeans, dangerously tight.

Certainly, faculty members want to collaborate with you as you progress through the training program. However, they also have to juggle the demands of a challenging teaching load, supervisory meetings, multiple scholarly projects, never-ending committee work, and service to the profession and community. There will be times at which they do not respond quickly to your frantic E-mail messages, seem distracted when you share a concern, or are unavailable when you have an important question. In short, faculty will not always be there for you. However, take care not to assume that they are disengaged or unconcerned about your well-being. The more likely reason is that they are stretched too thin and overburdened—sound familiar?

Whatever you do, watch out that your minor frustrations and disappointments don't crystallize into resentment against the faculty. It's a common dynamic in counseling groups. People are tempted to find a "scapegoat" to blame for their unfulfilled needs. If you find yourself regularly grousing and griping about the faculty with your fellow students, it's time to deal productively with the hostility before it gathers momentum. Recognize that your feelings are normal and that you can communicate your concerns in direct and respectful ways with your teachers, supervisors, and mentors.

Comprehensive Examination

Near the end of the apprenticeship period of your training, you complete a comprehensive examination. Its purpose is to document that you have integrated essential knowledge of counseling theories, research, and practice.

The format of the comprehensive examination differs from program to program. One popular format is the Counselor Preparation Comprehensive Examination (CPCE). The CPCE is a knowledge-based multiple-choice examination that reflects the eight core curriculum areas approved by the Council for Accreditation of Counseling and Related Educational Programs (CACREP). Another common format for the comprehensive examination is a series of essay questions.

Some programs require a portfolio of documents that demonstrate the student's knowledge of counseling theory, research, and practice. In a few programs, students provide a sample of their counseling work, such as a videotape of a counseling session and other supporting documents, for the comprehensive examination. A number of programs use some combination of written and oral examinations. Whatever its format, a successful comprehensive examination involves more than merely passing. Your comprehensive examination serves as an important rite of passage for you. You can use this experience to help you pull together useful information and ideas from your earlier courses and counseling experiences. In meeting the challenge of the examination, you also discover a great deal about yourself, both personally and professionally. The comprehensive examination experience gives you a chance to demonstrate not only to faculty members but also to yourself that you are ready to become a professional. You can thrive during this rite of passage, emerging from this process with a greater sense of personal and professional confidence.

The following strategies can be helpful in preparing for the examination:

- **Train well from the start.** From the start, be actively involved in all facets of your training. The best way to prepare for a successful comprehensive exam is to be a successful trainee in the program.

- **Work long and hard.** There is no quick and easy way to be successful in your examination. It requires intense preparation involving hours of study and review. Once you have laid the groundwork, however, you'll come to the examination feeling equal to the task and confident.

- **Review previous course material.** You will find it helpful to look over all the information, concepts, and issues that you have addressed in your earlier classes.

- **Focus on yourself.** Use the examination preparation to reflect on your own theoretical perspectives, personal issues, competencies, and limitations as a beginning counselor. Take time to explore your own personal and professional development.

- **Link with an informal support group.** Sharing concerns and encouragement can be helpful. It is also reassuring to find out that you are not the only one to have doubts and worries about your performance.

- **Take care of yourself.** You can do this by taking time to relax and rest. On looking back after successfully completing the examination, most students report wishing that they had not worried so much.

- **Be confident.** The comprehensive examination is your opportunity to demonstrate what you have learned from your hard work and long preparation. Come to the examination looking forward to your chance to demonstrate your knowledge and readiness to be a professional.

Although you will only complete this examination once, we encourage you to do your part to make this a thriving experience for other students. You can help by supporting your fellow students as they embark on this rite of passage, encouraging them as they confront their own doubts, and congratulating them on their successes.

AN EMERGING PROFESSIONAL

One's work may be finished someday, but one's education never.

—Alexandre Dumas

The final stage of your graduate training involves the completion of two important capstone experiences—your internship and your research project. *Capstone* refers to the finishing stone of a structure. In your training, your capstone experiences are the culmination of all your work and preparation. You began the program as a novice, progressed to become an apprentice, and have now developed into an emerging professional. Although you will continue to need supervision and advising, you have demonstrated your readiness to successfully complete your formal training and to graduate (Leach, Stoltenberg, McNeil, & Eichenfield, 1997).

Your internship gives you an opportunity to practice an important dimension of your emerging professional role. In Chapter 8, we discuss internships in detail.

Relativistic Thinking

As an emerging professional who is nearing the successful completion of your program, your thinking continues to evolve, from multiplistic to relativistic. At the last of Perry's (1970) stages, you begin to tailor your responses to the circumstance at hand, realizing that there are "different strokes for different folks." During this period of development, you probably use one kind of intervention with people who present with specific phobias and another kind of approach with those who seem "existentially lost." As you learn more about the various theoretical approaches, you begin to see commonalities among them. You may begin to become more eclectic or transtheoretical in your attitudes. Instead of viewing your clients as ignorant or misguided, you begin to understand the circumstances that have brought them to their current situation. You judge your own responses in sessions based on whether they seem to produce the desired effects in the client.

You grow less preoccupied with your own performance and become much more focused on helping your client achieve his or her goals. In your classes, you begin to notice that you are no longer working for the grade as much as you are working for self-improvement. Your learning shifts from "outside in" to "inside out."

As Young (2001) put it, "The main value of thinking about stages of development is that it can help you recognize that your struggles are part of a normal progression" (p. 8). Throughout your program, you are continually progressing. If you are videotaping your counseling work, you may want save your first tape—provided that this is not a breach of confidentiality and that you have the permission of your client. Saving this tape can be helpful to you because your progress is often gradual and imperceptible. If you have a tape, you can look back and be amazed at how much you have improved over the course of your training.

Keeping a journal is also helpful in tracking the metamorphosis you are experiencing. However, no matter how long your training program may be, you must keep in mind that this journey is lifelong (Kottler, 1997). You may have expected that you would graduate and leave your training as a more-or-less finished product. Once you realize just how much more you have to learn, you may at first feel inadequate, disappointed in yourself, or disillusioned with your training. These reactions are simply more of those normal, typical, and common feelings that you'll experience in your professional development.

Keep in mind that in order to become a master counselor, you will need years of practice, intense supervision, and many varied experiences (Etringer, Hillerbrand, & Claiborn, 1995). It has been said that it takes as many as ten years and the accumulation of at least 50,000 bits of information to achieve mastery (Hoffman, Shadbolt, Burton, & Klein, 1995). Right now, that may seem a long time and an overwhelming

amount of learning, but if you are truly committed to the helping profession, you *will* get there. The information in this book will help you
keep your journey in perspective. There will be times, however, when
you judge yourself harshly for not being good enough. Remember to
trust in yourself and in the process. Wherever you are right now in your
progress through Perry's stages, just be there! Go with the flow. You'll
get where you want to go.

Research Project

The purpose of the thesis or dissertation is to provide you with an
opportunity to complete an intensive and comprehensive scholarly
project that makes an original contribution to the profession (Cone &
Foster, 1993). In most programs, you have a wide variety of possible
topics that are acceptable for a thesis or dissertation, as long as you
demonstrate relevance to the field. Your final report will include a review
of the professional literature and a discussion of implications. It may
take one of the following forms:

- **Research report.** The research report involves collecting and
  analyzing quantitative or qualitative data to answer a particular
  research question.

- **Applied study.** An applied study may involve assessing the
  needs of a population or evaluating the effectiveness of an
  intervention or program.

- **Technique or program development.** Your research project
  may involve developing an innovative counseling technique or
  program.

- **Critical review.** A critical review of the literature regarding an
  issue in counseling would be more than merely a summary of
  the literature. The critical review should offer new and creative
  ways of looking at an issue, develop a useful conceptual framework, or give a well-reasoned critique of the material.

You may have been using a journal to explore the emotional nuances of
your training, but you can also use it in your project to jot down your
hunches, speculate on possible topics, or sketch out your research plans.
You can get much more out of keeping a journal if you do more than merely
summarize your experiences. For example, consider what is particularly

interesting, meaningful, unusual, or even puzzling about the research you are doing. Date your entries and write regularly, at least two or three times a week. Use your journal to explore your thoughts, sort through your feelings, recollect memories, and develop ideas. You can use a variety of strategies—questioning, synthesizing, speculating, and brainstorming.

Selecting a Committee You need to select a faculty committee for your thesis or dissertation. Typically, your committee consists of one chairperson and at least two members. You may elect to have an additional reader if this person has expertise relevant to your research project.

As you work on your project, keep in mind that it is your responsibility to keep your chairperson and committee members informed of your progress. Typically, you will have at least two meetings with the entire committee—one at the beginning of the project and another at its completion. At the first meeting, the committee considers your proposal. The purpose of the second is to discuss your final report, recommend revisions, and make a final decision on whether to accept it.

Completing Your Final Draft The format for the final report should follow the guidelines presented in your institution's handbook for theses and dissertations and in the *Publication Manual of the American Psychological Association* (American Psychological Association, 2001). The guidelines impose stringent conditions on the format, such as quality of paper, size of margins, and legibility requirements.

Evaluation Criteria The chairperson and readers of your thesis or dissertation will be evaluating your performance based on several criteria. First, the report must be a thorough consideration of the topic that you have selected. No matter what type of directed research you perform, you must present a comprehensive review of pertinent professional literature. Another criterion is originality. You must offer a contribution to the counseling literature that is based on your own ideas and work. Your report must be more than a summary of the thoughts and efforts of others—it must have the distinction of presenting your individual notions and views. Finally, the most fundamental criterion is the extent to which you are successful in accomplishing what you set out to do in your proposal. Whether it was to perform an empirical study, to develop an innovative program, or to write a critical review, your final report will be assessed in terms of your attainment of that goal.

Graduation and Commencement

The graduation and commencement exercise is a widespread and long-standing tradition. We invite you to personalize this final ritual by saying good-bye to one another as students and professors and greeting one another as professional colleagues. Savor the moment, and soon you will begin to see that the intuition that brought you to the training program in the first place is still valid. You really are a professional helper!

SUMMARY

Your training journey is a metamorphosis from student to professional. This transformation involves much more than gaining knowledge and acquiring skills. You take on new roles, progress through developmental stages, and pass important milestones. Successfully completing this journey sets the stage for launching your career as a professional.

RESOURCES

Several books are available that can help you with your training journey. If you are applying to programs, then read Keith-Spiegel and Wiederman's (2000) *The Complete Guide to Graduate School Admission: Psychology, Counseling, and Related Professions*. It's a comprehensive and practical guide on everything you need to know to enhance your chances, make your choices, and succeed in the admissions process.

Another helpful resource at this stage of your journey is the American Psychological Association's (1997) *Getting In: A Step-by-Step Plan for Gaining Admission to Graduate School in Psychology*. You'll find detailed information on models of training, tips for interviews, and a timetable for planning.

We also recommend Kerr's (2000) *Becoming a Therapist: A Workbook for Personal Exploration*. This workbook includes activities for helping you to experience therapy processes, such as empathy, change, and feelings. Other activities invite you to explore personal topics, such as enhancing your relationships, expressing your feelings, and taking care of yourself.

As its title states, Cone and Foster's (1993) *Dissertations and Theses from Start to Finish: Psychology and Related Fields* helps you plan and complete your research project from beginning to end. The authors offer useful suggestions on getting organized, finding a topic, developing a proposal, and selecting a chairperson. Many Web sites offer information, advice, and access to resources. Following are a few of the best that we've discovered:

Gradschools.com

http://www.gradschools.com

The site offers the most comprehensive on-line source of graduate school information, with links to thousands of program listings. It contains information on graduate programs, on standardized tests, and on financial aid and has discussion boards.

Petersons.Com: The Grad Channel

http://iiswinprd01.petersons.com/gradchannel/

This site has links to information on finding schools, preparing, applying, and paying expenses. It has an on-line newsletter and a bookstore.

On-line *U.S. News*

http://www.usnews.com/usnews/edu/beyond/bchome.htm

The site includes information on America's best graduate Sschools, the latest rankings, interactive tools, and up-to-date articles for particular areas of study.

Kaplan

http://www.kaptest.com/

The Info Center of the world's leader in test preparation, admissions and tutoring has information links for high school, college, business/graduate, law, medical, dental, and professional schools. It has the available option of taking test preparation courses on-line. Information on the site includes class schedules and program information. There is an on-line store, a link for educators, and a planning center with information on parents and children, study skills, financial aid, and career planning.

The Center for Credentialing & Education, Inc. (CCE)

3 Terrace Way, Suite D

Greensboro, NC 27403-3660

336-547-0607 or fax, 336-547-0017

Council for Accreditation of Counseling and Related Educational Programs (CACREP)

http://www.counseling.org/cacrep

5999 Stevenson Avenue

Alexandria, VA 22304

703-823-9800, ext. 301

REFERENCES

American Psychological Association (1997). *Getting in: A step-by-step plan for gaining admission to graduate school in psychology.* Washington, DC: Author.

American Psychological Association (2001). *Publication manual of the American Psychological Association* (5th ed.). Washington, DC: Author.

Baltimore, M. L., Hickson, J., George, J. D., & Crutchfield, L. B. (1996). Portfolio assessment: A model for counselor education. *Counselor Education and Supervision, 36,* 113–121.

Becvar, D. S., & Becvar, R. J. (1996). *Family therapy: A systemic integration* (3rd ed.). Boston: Allyn & Bacon.

Bell, C. (1997). *Ritual: Perspectives and dimensions.* New York: Oxford University Press.

Buskist, W., & Mixon, A. (1998). *Guide to master's programs in psychology and counseling psychology.* Boston: Allyn & Bacon.

Carney, J. S., Cobia, D. C., & Shannon, D. M. (1996). The use of portfolios in the clinical and comprehensive evaluation of counselors-in-training. *Counselor Education and Supervision, 36,* 122–132.

Cone, J. D., & Foster, S. L. (1993). *Dissertations and theses from start to finish: Psychology and related fields.* Washington, DC: American Psychological Association.

Etringer, B. D., Hillerbrand, E., & Claiborn, C. D. (1995). The transition from novice to expert counselor. *Counselor Education and Supervision, 35,* 4–17.

Finkle, J. (1999). *Graduate school.* Seattle, WA: Resource Pathways.

Harvey, C., & Katz, C. (1985). *If I'm so successful, why do I feel like a fake? The impostor phenomenon.* New York: St. Martin's Press.

Hoffman, R. R., Shadbolt, N. R., Burton, A. M., & Klein, G. (1995). Eliciting knowledge from experts: A methodological analysis. *Organizational Behavior and Human Decision Processes, 62,* 129–158.

Keith-Spiegel, P., & Wiederman, M. W. (2000). *The complete guide to graduate school admission: Psychology, counseling, and related professions* (2nd ed.). Mahwah, NJ: Erlbaum.

Kerr, D. R. (2000). *Becoming a therapist: A workbook for personal exploration.* Prospect Heights, IL: Waveland Press.

Kottler, J. A. (Ed.). (1997). *Finding your way as a counselor.* Alexandria, VA: American Counseling Association.

Leach, M. M., Stoltenberg, C. D., McNeil, B. W., & Eichenfield, G. A. (1997). Self-efficacy and counselor development: Testing the integrated developmental model. *Counselor Education and Supervision, 37,* 115–124.

Markert, L., & Monke, R. (1990). Changes in counselor education admissions criteria. *Counselor Education and Supervision, 30,* 48–57.

McAuliffe, G., & Eriksen, K. (2000). *Preparing counselors and therapists: Creating constructivist and developmental programs.* Virginia Beach, VA: Donning.

McKee, J. E., Smith, L. W., Hayes, B. G., Stewart, A., & Echterling, L. G. (1999). Rites and rituals in counselor education. *Journal of Humanistic Education, 38,* 3–12.

Morrison, T., & Morrison, M. (1995). A meta-analytic assessment of the predictive validity of the quantitative and verbal components of the Graduate Record Examination with graduate grade point average representing the criterion of graduate success. *Educational and Psychological Measurement, 55,* 309–316.

Perry, W. G., Jr. (1970). *Forms of intellectual and ethical development in the college years.* New York: Holt, Rinehart & Winston.

Sayette, M. A., Mayne, T. J., & Norcross, J. C. (1998). *Insider's guide to graduate programs in clinical and counseling psychology.* New York: Guilford Press.

Simpson, D. E., Dalgaard, K. A., & O'Brien, D. K. (1986). Student and faculty assumptions about the nature of uncertainty in medicine and medical education. *Journal of Family Practice, 23*(5) 468–472.

Sternberg, R. J., & Williams, W. M. (1997). Does the Graduate Record Examination predict meaningful success in the graduate training of psychologists? *American Psychologist, 52,* 630–641.

Young, M. E. (2001). *Learning the art of helping: Building blocks and techniques.* Upper Saddle River, NJ: Merrill/Prentice-Hall.

CHAPTER 3

Meeting Your Basic Needs

One of the oldest human needs is to have someone to wonder where you are when you don't
come home at night.

—Margaret Mead

M any cultures have addressed the question of what constitutes our "basic needs." A Navajo legend, for example, tells the story of the Spirit Being, who created People to share the beauty of the world with all other living things. The Spirit Being then spent a summer with the People to teach them what they needed to know to survive in the earth world. They were taught how to build shelters, hunt for game, and grow crops. However, according to the legend, the Spirit Being's most important teachings were the songs and chants that would keep the People healthy and in harmony with their world. The lesson here for us is that our basic needs are not confined to food, clothing, and shelter. In fact, our needs for meaning, beauty, and balance are just as fundamental.

The Bread and Roses organization, founded in 1974 by Mimi Farina, is a recent expression of this lesson. The mission of Bread and Roses is to present free, live entertainment to institutionalized and isolated people. Well-known performers, who could demand big money for their talents, have given freely of themselves in hundreds of concerts. On the Bread and Roses Web page (*www.breadandroses.org*), you can listen to a song that Mimi Farina and Joan Baez sing. This song was inspired by a poem written in 1912 by James Oppenheim, who was protesting the miserable conditions in the sweat shops of textile workers. One stanza, in particular, is a powerful statement about fundamental human needs:

55

Our lives shall not be sweated from birth until life closes;
Hearts starve as well as bodies; give us bread but give us roses!

Like those textile workers, you do not live by bread alone. Of course, you must find shelter, feed and clothe yourself, purchase books, and gather the various other accoutrements of academic life. But remember not to neglect your other needs, which will always be present. Be sure to nourish your heart during your time in graduate school. Stop to plant, give, receive, and, of course, *smell* the roses.

In this chapter, we present suggestions and strategies to help you satisfy your basic needs while you are a graduate student. Contrary to the typical view, it is possible to both take care of yourself and succeed in your training program. You don't have to sacrifice your health and well-being in order to become a counselor or therapist. In fact, dealing with your needs with flexibility, creativity, and sensitivity can actually help you to thrive.

As you perceive them, your "needs" are, in part, a reflection of your values. You have acquired these values through your parents and extended family, religious teachings, educational institutions, and the media—in short, your culture. When people move from one culture to another, they often experience "culture shock." You are entering a graduate training program in which you may hear language unfamiliar to you, face situations that seem awkward, and encounter behaviors that were not typical in your own culture. You are likely to feel off balance, self-conscious, and, perhaps, defensive because you find this new environment slightly strange. You are entering the culture of counseling and therapy. As you become acculturated, you will not only begin to feel more comfortable with this new community but also carefully examine and change many of your values and assumptions about human needs.

YOUR PERSONAL HIERARCHY OF NEEDS

The things that matter most must never be at the mercy of the things that matter least.

—Goethe

Any discussion of your basic needs would not be complete without referencing the work of Abraham Maslow. Maslow (1970) identified a hierarchy of needs—usually depicted as a pyramid—that motivate humans to strive toward self-actualization, at the top of the pyramid. Beginning at the bottom of the hierarchy, people strive to satisfy the needs at each level before moving on to the next higher need area. Maslow named the following five levels of need that must be fulfilled for psychological well-being.

> **Physiological.** These needs, which are basic for survival, include such necessities as drinking, eating, and sleeping.
>
> **Safety and security.** This level of the hierarchy includes the need to be safe from physical harm and to have adequate shelter.
>
> **Love and belonging.** These are the needs for affiliation and for giving and receiving love.
>
> **Self-esteem.** This level refers to the needs to have confidence in yourself, to feel worthy of regard, and to believe in your own value and capabilities.
>
> **Self-actualization.** At the peak of the hierarchy are the self-actualization needs, which refer to the fulfillment and real-ization of your potential. Finding ways to express your creativity and feeling a sense of accomplishment are self-actualization needs.

Maslow's hierarchy actually bears a striking resemblance to a model of the soul that Plato proposed more than 2,000 years earlier (Leahey, 2000). The lowest level is the "desiring soul" that resides in the belly and below. This level includes selfish desires for food, money, and sex. Today, you may recognize people at this level on many popular daytime talk shows or court programs. The next level up is the "spirited soul," which resides in the chest. This level of soul is motivated by fame and glory, exemplified today by professional athletes, politicians, or movie stars. The highest form of soul is the "rational soul," centered in the head, which seeks the Good and True, even at the expense of lower desires. People who have achieved this highest level are our spiritual leaders, mentors, and sages.

Our reason for presenting Plato's model is not to put Maslow's theory in a historical context. Instead, we offer it because Plato emphasized a vital point that has been lost in most discussions of Maslow's hierarchy of needs. Although Plato's model is certainly inaccurate in its understanding of human physiology, he does hit the mark regarding our essential human capacity to *choose* what desires we fulfill, to arrange our own personal hierarchy that reflects our fundamental values.

In this chapter, you will explore how Maslow's paradigm can be a useful perspective for coping in graduate school. For example, you can meet your physiological and safety needs by finding and creating a home, investigating options for financial assistance, and maintaining your physical wellness. However, Plato's emphasis on choice can alert you to opportunities for thriving even in times of scarcity. Therefore, we discuss how you can fulfill your self-actualization needs in spite of other deprivations in your life. Let's begin by exploring ways in which you can not only fulfill your needs but also thrive in this unfamiliar culture.

▲▲▲

A Constant Challenge
Ellen's Story

MEETING BASIC NEEDS is a constant challenge! I find I do well for some time, then I look up and realize I've neglected them again. I have trouble remembering to take time for myself. With a husband, kids, and a job, it is easy for me to feel like school is "my time." Even though it's rewarding, it is not the same as having time to myself for meditation, reflection, journaling, or just having fun! My goal is to create some time for ME every day—some days it will be ten minutes, other days an hour.

The other basic need that I often neglect is getting enough sleep. I run close to empty most days of the week. I have come to realize that I often use my fatigue as an excuse—for yelling at my kids, for saying "No" to things, for not being intimate with my husband, and for having an extra glass of wine at night to unwind. I think I have become addicted to the cycle of being exhausted, getting one or two nights of good sleep, then feeling so good I stay up late and begin again.

I realize as I write this that so much of what counseling is about is getting our basic needs met: needs like intimacy and love. I know that having those needs met for me is difficult when I am sleep-deprived and leaving no time for myself. When I am well rested and deeply connected with myself, I am in a good place to give and receive love and to create the kind of relationships I want in my life—relationships that I need to be a healthy, fulfilled person.

▼▼▼

Shirley MacLaine (2000) wrote an account of walking the Santiago de Compostela Camino, a grueling 500-mile pilgrimage across northern Spain that people have undertaken for centuries. Like a true pilgrim, MacLaine traveled alone on her month-long journey and took only the necessities she could carry in her backpack. She discovered that she needed little more beyond water, good shoes, and a floppy hat. By discarding all the distracting unessentials that can clutter our lives and embarking on a demanding quest, she gained an important new perspective.

As you enter graduate school, you are traveling on new terrain, and, as MacLaine's pilgrimage illustrates, you need to decide what is truly essential. You may find that some seemingly pressing needs will fade or even disappear. You may be a little confused and perhaps feel pressured—out of sheer force of habit—to respond to old needs. At the very least, you're likely to be uncomfortable at first, so consider reframing this situation as an invitation to explore your fundamental motivations and values in life. You see, we don't notice when our needs are met. It's only when we believe our needs are unmet that we are motivated to reflect, decide, and act.

BASIC NEEDS AND SELF-ACTUALIZATION

Life is easier to take than you think; all that is necessary is to accept the impossible, do without the indispensable and bear the intolerable.

—Kathleen Norris

In Ellen's story, she engaged in two very important steps toward self-actualization—taking time to identify just what is important to her and then finding ways to address those basic needs. What needs are truly essential to her? How can she organize her day to satisfy them? Most students, faculty, and staff—in fact, most people—face similar challenges in trying to balance needs and demands in their daily lives. At first, juggling all your family commitments, personal needs, and graduate school requirements can seem utterly hopeless.

Remember the old riddle about a farmer who had to figure out how to safely transport a fox, a chicken, and a sack of grain to an island? The farmer could only take one of them at a time in a small boat. However, the fox couldn't be left alone with the chicken, because the fox would eat it. By the same token, the chicken couldn't be left alone with the grain. The farmer solved the problem by deploying resources and manipulating the conditions in a creative way. How did the farmer resolve this dilemma? (One answer to the riddle appears at the end of the chapter.)

Like the farmer in the riddle, you face a similar conundrum of meeting basic needs, personal obligations, and training demands. Leading a reasonably fulfilling life while learning to be a counselor or therapist requires ingenuity, quick wits, and lots of energy. This balancing act is challenging enough, but the idea of reaching the self-actualizing needs at the highest rung seems like a Catch-22. You entered into training to realize your potential, but the stresses and deprivations inherent in your life as an impoverished graduate student seem to make scaling the pyramid impossible.

A quick reading of Maslow may lead you to assume that focusing on self-actualization needs is achievable only when you are well off financially and relatively stress free. Like caviar, self-actualization may seem to be a delicacy that only the fortunate and affluent can afford to experience. How in the world can graduate students—in debt up to their ears with student loans, living in austere accommodations, and trying to cut corners every which way they can—seek self-actualization? And what about people who are returning to school after rearing their children or after a financially successful career in a "dot-com"? Aren't they moving *down* several rungs?

Maslow (1962) himself criticized the simplistic interpretation that sees personal growth as merely "progression toward self-actualization in which the basic needs are completely gratified, one by one, before the next higher need emerges" (p. 24). As Plato pointed out, humans are not slaves to their desires. We can choose to seek self-actualization even though our pursuit may deprive us of basic comforts, take away our financial security, and threaten our personal safety.

■■■

EXERCISE 3.1 **Take That Job And ...**
A Guided Fantasy Exercise

Imagine that, instead of going to graduate school for the next few years, you accepted a job that would offer a huge salary, excellent benefits, a beautiful home, job security, a close-knit group of colleagues, and plenty of recognition for your accomplishments at work. In short, this job would satisfy every conceivable physiological, safety and security, belonging, and self-esteem need. The only catch is that you could not fulfill your personal potential for self-actualization.

As you consider this possibility, write about the needs you would be sacrificing.

_____

_____

_____

_____

_____

Now, write how you plan to ensure that you will address these self-actualization needs in your training.

_____

_____

_____

_____

_____

■■■

CONDUCTING A NEEDS INVENTORY

The hardest thing to learn in life is which bridge to
cross and which to burn.

—David Russell

Below, Renee shares her story of leaving a successful career and
enrolling in a training program in which she had to live away from her
home and family several days a week. In her story, she conducts an
informal needs inventory for herself.

▲▲▲

Touch the Sun
Renee's Story

WHEN TACKLING this portion of my training journey, I first
had to identify what my basic needs were. I cheated a little
and I borrowed my hierarchy of needs from Maslow, as he seemed
to have the right idea. He may not be basic enough for this point
in my life, though.

According to my mother and my kids, I am not doing a good
job meeting physiological needs. Sleep would indeed be a wonderful thing, but I haven't figured out how to work that in, as of yet.

A need for safety has become very important. My family home
is in a nice residential area with regularly spaced signs, proclaim-
ing "neighborhood watch in effect." While at school, I try to handle my fear of living alone by leaving lots of lights on.

Being part of a family fulfilled my belonging and love needs.
However, right now it seems like distance doesn't make the heart
grow fonder—it just makes communication harder. My husband
and I are maintaining a long-distance relationship, and we're sure
our love can stand the test of time, as the songs say. But I really
miss him and my family.

I find I need a social circle here, too. Friendships are beginning
to develop, as I tentatively move past the point of "socialized" hel-
los into the more meaningful depths of knowing someone.

I am working on feeling competent, independent, successful, respected, and worthwhile in order to claim good self-esteem. At the moment, though, I feel I have lost my sense of self, and because I am not successfully satisfying the preceding needs, I have to fall short somewhere. Can a "high maintenance, emotionally needy" person even hope to reach this goal?

Without successfully attaining the needs for self-esteem, I won't even begin to comment on where I stand with self-actualization. Isn't that the thing we're all supposed to be striving for, anyway? I'd hate to touch the sun too soon.

▼▼▼

As you read Renee's story, with what parts did you find yourself identifying? Did you notice that Renee was dealing with needs at several different levels? Assessing your needs and taking action to address them are both effective methods of coping. But what about thriving? Renee suggests that she cannot address self-actualization needs until she has met her self-esteem needs. What do you think? Would Renee be "touching the sun" too soon? How could Renee use her struggle to help her thrive in her training?

Dealing with the challenges of satisfying your personal needs in graduate school can actually enhance your training in two fundamental ways. First, your own strivings are far better than "book knowledge" in helping you to understand and appreciate the struggles that people face in their lives. So, as you try to balance your needs, remain aware of your fatigue, yearnings, and sense of deprivation. These experiences can help you in building an empathic bridge to your clients, who may be seeking counseling to deal with different concerns but who are also struggling. Second, your own successful endeavors to live a full and balanced life can help remind you of the perseverance, creativity, and resilience that your clients have. Even though you have felt overwhelmed at times, you've discovered personal strengths and social resources that have helped you through these difficulties. With your assistance, your clients can also uncover their own hidden abilities and sources of support.

If you stay alert for learning opportunities, you are likely to gain surprising insights regarding your needs. For example, students conducting a parenting group often found that the session they had prepared for the group contained a valuable lesson for themselves, too. Following is one experiential exercise that routinely helped the counseling student group leaders as much as it did the parent members.

■ ■ ■

EXERCISE 3.2 **The Sea Star**
A Balancing Exercise

By watching the sea star, or starfish, you can learn a lesson on being responsive to your needs. The sea star has five distinct arms that work together gracefully. Even if an appendage breaks off, the sea star regenerates its lost arm to ensure that it can thrive in its environment. Your thriving needs, like the sea star's arms, can work together in harmony, but some of your "arms" may be better developed than others. In fact, most people are able to satisfy certain needs more successfully than other needs. This exercise reminds you of the different types of needs and how you can address each of them.

On a large sheet of newsprint, use markers or crayons to draw a sea star and label each arm with one of the thriving needs: physical, mental, emotional, relational, and spiritual.

Consider how well you are currently fulfilling these thriving needs. Draw a line somewhere on each arm to reflect your satisfaction with that particular need—the larger the area within that arm, the greater your fulfillment. Your sea star figure will now have a line at some point across each of its five arms.

Now, using the area that you have set aside in each arm, draw the ways that you are meeting that need. The more you are fulfilling a certain need, the more room you have to draw. Feel free to decorate each area however you would like. For example, you might draw certain people, activities, or symbols to portray how you thrive in that area.

You may be surprised at how successfully you are satisfying some needs and how little you are attending to others. What did you discover about the balance of your thriving needs?

■ ■ ■

One student who completed this exercise found, to her dismay, that decorating the sea star was the most fun she had had in a long time. She realized that she had been neglecting her mental need to engage in creative activities. By the way, you can vary this activity to use with couples and families in counseling. For example, you can encourage them to first come up with a thriving list completely unrestricted by finances, time, family, or work constraints. After the list is generated, they can look over the options and circle ones they can help each other to do, given their current circumstances.

CRAFTING A BALANCED LIFE

Happiness is not a state to arrive at, but a manner
of traveling.

—Margaret Lee Runbeck

A cow is a ruminative animal because it chews its cud but gains no nourishment from the process. When you ruminate, you may obsess or worry for hours on end but gain no benefit from this activity. Well, if you're a ruminator, then it's time to put aside the ways of the cow and bring balance to your life. Fully commit yourself to the task of the moment, but when you have completed it, then set it aside. Returning to reflect on your work, ponder its meaning, and sort through it to find nuggets of success can certainly be nourishing. However, take care not to become so caught up in your work that you can never set it aside and just *be*.

In another ancient Navajo story, when Spider Woman gave Weaving Woman her ability to weave, she also instructed her to walk the Middle Way by keeping her life in balance. Weaving Woman was able to maintain this harmony at first, but then she began to weave night and day until she collapsed, unable to move or speak. She had woven her spirit into her work and could not escape. Like Weaving Woman, you may be learning important skills but may also be having a very difficult time keeping your life in balance. Regularly pulling "all-nighters," ignoring relationships, and never taking any breaks from work means that you are losing yourself in the role of a student. Here is how Beth achieved a satisfying balance and avoided weaving herself into her work.

▲▲▲

We Have Nothing to Fear But . . .
Beth's Story

RECENTLY, I sat down and wrote about my greatest fear. I was afraid that, as a student, mother, wife, teacher, daughter, and friend, I couldn't balance all my roles and responsibilities. I worried that my children would suffer. I was the one who stayed home from my part-time job when they were sick. My part-time job required enormous energy and frequent attendance at meetings. Would there be enough time? My marriage was shaky at best. How much would it suffer? How would I take care of everything? How would I take care of me? Finally, I told myself that if I couldn't keep a healthy balance, I could quit graduate school. Telling myself that it's okay to stop my training if it wasn't working calmed me.

▼▼▼

Beth found that reminding herself that she had the power to bring balance to her life helped her gain a sense of peace. Feeling overwhelmed by unmet needs is a concern that you will hear from your clients, fellow students, and significant others. Why can it seem so challenging to create a balance, to satisfy all these needs? Using your list from the earlier sea star exercise may provide a different perspective.

■■■

EXERCISE 3.3 **Your Needs in Context**
A Systemic Exercise

On a regular sheet of paper, draw three small sea stars. One of the stars represents you, so quickly draw a simple, miniature version of your previous star, by just adding the lines indicating how well you are satisfying the five thriving needs: physical, mental, emotional, relational, and spiritual. Now select two people who have a deep emotional connection to you. You may choose a partner, family member, or roommate. Put their names at the top of the other stars and, using your best guesses, draw lines to reflect to what extent they are meeting their thriving needs.

Draw walls and a roof around the three stars to enclose them in a single house. If you like, you can add other details and decorations to make it more a home. This picture illustrates two important points. First, meeting your needs can sometimes feel overwhelming because you live under the same emotional roof with relatives, friends, and colleagues who have their own needs to address, too. In what ways do their unmet needs complicate your life? At the same time, your picture also portrays the second important point—these people are also excellent resources! You cannot achieve self-actualization by yourself. In fact, you can join with others synergistically to fulfill many of your thriving needs. How can these people help you?

■■■

Pathways to Balance

Paint as you like and die happy.

—Henry Miller

So, what can you do? A useful psychological construct to use in situations such as yours is termed *equifinality*. Equifinality means that there are multiple pathways to the same end. Beth's pathway was to deliberately acknowledge that attending graduate school was a choice to which, for the present, she was saying "Yes." At some time in the future, she may also choose to say "No."

Another pathway to achieving balance is described in the conclusion of the legend of Weaving Woman. According to the story, to free the spirit of Weaving Woman from her work, Spider Woman made the blanket she had woven less perfect. By pulling out a thread, Spider Woman created a pathway for Weaving Woman's spirit to leave the blanket and return to her. Weaving Woman thankfully said she had learned her lesson and began to teach others the importance of not trying to make their weavings perfect. She taught them how to make spirit trails in their weavings so their spirits would not be trapped in their work.

Weaving Woman learned to meaningfully engage in the work of creating beauty, but not at the risk of losing herself in the process. You may notice some similar themes between Weaving Woman's story and your own life. Do you try to make your work absolutely perfect? Who do you ask for help when you feel you may be getting trapped? Who lets you know when you are "weaving" too much?

As you continue to enter the culture of counseling and learn more about yourself, you can periodically conduct an inventory of your needs and, using all of who you are and what you know, create pathways to a more meaningful and satisfying life. In the next section, we discuss the base from which you will operate—your home.

Housing

> Home is where the heart is and hence is a moveable feast.
>
> —Angela Carter

Finding affordable and suitable housing can be a daunting task. You may be tempted to rush this process, but take time to reflect on all the needs you want to address by the seemingly straightforward task of obtaining housing. Are you concerned with safety, convenience to the university, proximity to good elementary schools, or availability of public transportation? Do you prefer to have a roommate? Do you want to keep a pet? What values and meanings are embedded in your selection of a home (Fiffer & Fiffer, 1995)?

Much like producing a research paper, finding housing requires that you first frame your question and then collect data to answer it. In this case, the data collection includes finding listings from the local and university newspapers, the university housing office, other students, or real estate agents. You may find that taking this step is an opportunity to become acquainted with helpful resources in the university and larger community.

Most universities have an office designated to assist students in finding housing. The office typically provides rental information, housing guides, bus schedules, and student directories. Like a Chamber of Commerce, the office can assist you with other aspects of settling in the area, such as finding grocery stores and places for recreation. Find out if the office can help you with potential housing concerns, such as lease difficulties, landlord conflicts, parking limitations, and transportation problems. Many universities also have separate housing available to graduate students. Although living in graduate student housing offers some conveniences, you may want to explore other possibilities.

For example, using information from the off-campus housing office and the advertisements in the local newspaper, Jocelyn and Michael set out to find an apartment that was not "a stack of red bricks that looked like one big red brick." Unfortunately, they discovered that the community's view of students—at least the typical landlord's view—was very negative. They began to feel like second-class citizens. They found their predicament further compounded by their commitment to find a place that would accept them and their three cats. As Jocelyn said, "Evidently, adding a third cat puts you in the 'Crazy Cat Person' category." For Jocelyn and Michael, however, their pets helped them keep a sense of balance in their academic lives.

Other potential sources of housing information for you are your program advisor, peer mentor, and fellow students. They can help you become settled by answering your questions not only about housing but also about the university and the surrounding community in general. They can provide support, encouragement, and some very helpful tips about how to create your base of operations.

After you have collected enough data, you are off to the field to conduct the applied portion of your research project—finding the locations. Once again, equifinality can be a useful idea to keep in mind, because there are many paths to the same end. The following story illustrates a rather casual approach to finding a new home.

▲▲▲

Adventures in Subsidized Housing Land
Chris' Story

L IKE MOST beginning grad students, I needed to visit my school's community well before classes started in order to secure someplace to live. This was not so easy in that I knew nothing of the town. I didn't know where the shortcuts to school were, where the grocery stores hid, where the fast-food joints nested, or where to get a Slurpee at 3:00 in the morning.

I had very specific requirements for the apartment itself. These included walls, floors, and, if at all possible, a ceiling. In other words, I wasn't choosy. I figured I'd be spending a lot of time up at school, so my housing only needed to be comfortable enough for me. So it all came down to cash. I took the cheapest place.

Taking the cheapest place wasn't a bad idea—it's just that there were certain tradeoffs. One was the roommates I got—hundreds and probably thousands of little six-legged tenants. Now I have lived in some rundown places, and I'm okay with that, but marauding armies of roaches were a new experience for me.

Fortunately, the other apartment dwellers (the human ones) are wonderfully diverse—ethnically, racially, and linguistically. As a member of just about every privileged majority there is, I find myself in an interesting position. Here I am, pursuing an advanced degree, while living with marginalized folks who are struggling to get by.

▼▼▼

By living where he did, Chris discovered the striking and vast inequalities in the everyday worlds of his neighbors—an essential lesson for a student of human strivings, challenges, and resilience.

As you make your own decisions about housing, consider what needs your home may help satisfy. Bowlby's attachment theory (Bowlby, 1979) emphasizes the importance of having a "secure base" from which to explore. Bowlby's secure base refers to having an established relationship with someone you feel is emotionally available and responsive to your needs. Although he first developed his theory about the importance of a secure attachment between infants and their caregivers, he has since extended the construct to cross the life span. The protective influence of having a secure base is now considered a prominent factor, similar to the importance of Maslow's needs, for people of all ages.

A primary benefit of this relationship—your home base—is that it helps you successfully explore your surroundings. It is natural to feel both apprehensive and excited when you are in a new setting and with unfamiliar people. You may typically cope with the anxiety by using some combination of defenses—withdrawing into isolation, retreating to your secure base, or "overexploring" the new environment.

When you were a freshman in college, you probably observed students who resorted to these defenses. For example, they may have attended classes, but then they seemed to evaporate into thin air. Other students were homesick and scurried home whenever possible. And then there were the classmates who were always frantically zipping everywhere around campus.

These defensive strategies, however, are neither satisfying, nor, in the long run, successful in fulfilling your needs for safety or belonging. Instead, you can make time to deliberately connect with the people who can provide you with your base for emotional security. By maintaining a firm foundation in those relationships, you will be better able to explore and keep your bearings as you investigate and build your new community.

Jocelyn and Michael helped incorporate their established secure base into their new surroundings in a number of ways. For example, they regularly E-mailed friends and relatives with news about their discoveries, mishaps, and adventures in adjustment. They also relied on generous doses of humor. As transplants from the East Coast to the Midwest, Jocelyn once commented to Michael about driving: "Today, I used my turn signal and someone actually made an opening in traffic so I could get over! Isn't that a sign of weakness where we come from?" They found a farmer's market and made a ritual of going there every Saturday morning and of always frequenting the same little coffee shop.

By taking similar steps to preserve your secure base and build your new community, you are more likely to create a comfortable place—both physically and psychologically—for yourself in graduate school. Give yourself some time to relish your new surroundings and reflect on the changes.

■ ■ ■

EXERCISE 3.4 **It Takes a Community**
An Exercise in Imagination

You've heard the African proverb, "It takes a village to raise a child." Well, it also takes a community to support a thriving graduate student. Because your needs do not remain static during graduate school, it's helpful to spend some time periodically envisioning the ideal community setting for you to continue your development.

Build an imaginary community that would fulfill your needs. Where would you be living? In a house or an apartment? With or without a roommate? Who and what else would be in your neighborhood? What cultures would be represented? What family configurations would be present? Would there be a place of worship? A park, woods, or playground? A vegetarian restaurant? Is the setting urban or rural?

List of the elements or draw a picture of this ideal community. What characteristics of your make-believe community exist already for you? If they do not exist wholly, are there parts you recognize? How can you build you community in reality? Who will you ask to help?

■ ■ ■

Financial Assistance

> Spare no expense to save money on this one.
>
> —Samuel Goldwyn

> Lack of money is no obstacle. Lack of an idea is an obstacle.
>
> —Ken Hakuta

Finkle (1999) pointed out that the enormous financial burden involved in tuition, fees, living expenses, and supplies is the most common reason that students abandon their dream of graduate education. No matter how much financial assistance you are able to manage, you probably need to prepare yourself for a monastic lifestyle. As Hoskins (2000) urged, "Ask yourself, how much macaroni and cheese do I want to eat for the next three to five years?" (p. 32). The financial support available from work, family, savings, university assistance, or government programs will be a significant factor in your decision to enter graduate training. As you explore your financial needs and resources, reflect on the emotional, as well as fiscal, costs and benefits of assistance. If you determine that it would be helpful to obtain a government loan, then, in addition to computing the monthly payments and the years needed to repay the loan, also consider the meaning that receiving a loan has for you. And what is the meaning for your spouse or family?

It is important to realize that the ways in which you address your financial needs can have an impact on your progress through the program. Are you planning to work while you attend graduate school? How will working affect your available study time or commitment to the training? Are you considering borrowing or using funds from family members? How will this arrangement affect your relationships in the family?

It is estimated that about one-half of doctoral students and one-third of master's students receive financial aid (Finkle, 1999). Financial aid is typically available through a program sponsored by the government or your university. There also are a few funds offered by private organizations, businesses, and industry groups.

The awarding of financial aid for graduate school is usually based on financial need, and most aid is distributed in the form of student loans. Keep in mind that funds are sometimes targeted for members of particular groups, such as students with disabilities or international students. If you are a member of a group that is underrepresented in higher education or the helping professions, there may be some funding available for you (Leider & Leider, 1998). Graduate schools also disburse funds on the basis of merit to attract candidates with special talent or knowledge. Typically, merit-based funding support comes in the form of assistantships or scholarship awards.

Assistantships Assistantships typically include both coverage of your tuition and a stipend. You receive this financial assistance in exchange for working about 15 to 20 hours a week during the academic year. To be eligible for an assistantship, you usually are required to carry a specific number of credit hours and to be enrolled in a degree program. Assistantships are generally available in your department, as well as in other academic programs and services across the campus.

Graduate assistantship responsibilities are quite varied and can range from conducting library research and providing laboratory support to photocopying and filing. You may qualify for a teaching or clinical assistantship if you meet specific qualifications. With a teaching assistantship, you may be responsible for teaching an undergraduate class or helping a faculty member with specific course responsibilities. With a clinical assistantship, you may be providing supervision, assessment, and counseling services at a university-based mental health center.

If you are seeking an assistantship, contact your university's financial aid office or the graduate office manager of your department. Most assistantships are one-year appointments, so you will probably need to apply each year that you wish to obtain this form of financial assistance. If you did not receive an assistantship your first year, don't give up! You may be more qualified for one as an advanced student.

Competition for assistantships is often keen, so there are no guarantees that you will be offered one. Graduate school offices report that, depending on funding, there may be three times as many graduate applicants as there are assistantships. These odds may seem tough, but there are some steps you can take to improve your chances:

- **Take care of the basics.** Just like the lottery, you have to play to win. The sooner you complete (and return!) the application form, the better your chances. Also, always make copies of the paperwork you submit, noting dates and to whom it was submitted. You will want to be able to construct a "paper trail" to ensure that your application has not been delayed anywhere.

- **Know how the system works.** Each university will have its own administrative network for conferring assistantships. Some universities have a single clearinghouse; others have more decentralized operations, in which programs operate as separate fiefdoms, with dramatically different application procedures for assistantships. Take care to learn the system and play by its rules.

- **Let people know.** Make certain that your program coordinator, faculty advisor, and student mentor know of your interest in obtaining an assistantship. Ask for their advice and suggestions. While you're at it, give them your E-mail address so they can contact you easily if they hear of an opportunity.

- **Highlight your skills.** The application forms for assistantships typically ask you to list your skills. Keep in mind that computer, research, and people skills are in demand, especially for nonacademic departments.

- **Remember that neatness does count.** Yes, your elementary teachers were right, so be careful when filling out the application materials. People will assume that the care you show on these documents indicates the care that you would take with job assignments.

- **Be persistent.** Faculty and staff members are busy people, so it is important for you to be persistent and not be afraid to ask questions about graduate assistantships.

Student Loans Financing graduate education with a student loan is the most used pathway for students in the helping professions. If you are considering this option, there are many resources that can assist you in finding and evaluating potential loan sources (Leider & Leider, 1998). Again, your university's financial aid office is an excellent source of information about federal loans.

A major source of financial assistance is the Federal Stafford Loan, both subsidized and unsubsidized. You begin the application process by completing a Free Application for Federal Student Aid (FAFSA) and mailing it to the processing center. You can pick up a blank form at your university financial aid office, but the form is also available on-line at:

http://www.ed.gov/offices/OPE/express.html

About a month to six weeks after submitting the application, you will receive a Student Aid Report (SAR) from the processing center. You should review this report, make any necessary corrections, and return it to the financial aid office as quickly as possible. The financial aid office staff reviews the SAR to determine your eligibility for aid and notifies you of its determination. Need is based on a hypothetical student budget, minus any family contribution, that the financial aid office calculates on a yearly basis. If you qualify, you then receive the loan application form. You should complete the application and return it immediately.

If you are an incoming student or have taken a summer class at another school, you also can facilitate the process by arranging for your transcripts to be sent to the university's financial aid office, rather than waiting for the office to request the records. You will help speed up the process if you meet the deadlines for each stage.

One routine interruption of the procedure is the need to verify tax records. Some applicants are chosen at random for verification, and the financial aid office is then required to look at all their tax forms for the past year. If you are chosen for verification, simply provide the information requested. Typically, you are asked to present a signed tax form.

If your need is great enough, you may be offered a work-study job that you can choose to accept or decline. Other possible funding sources are graduate scholarships or fellowships.

Scholarships Scholarships, fellowships, or grant awards may be given on the basis of need, of merit or of membership in a targeted group. They are the most preferred type of financial assistance because they do not have to be repaid. However, they are not commonly available to graduate students, especially those planning to enter the helping professions.

You can be resourceful by looking for financial support from professional organizations and service organizations, such as the Kiwanis. The American Counseling Association, for example, offers a scholarship award to a graduate student who wins its annual essay competition. Assistance is sometimes available if you plan to work in particular areas of specialization, such as autism or death and dying.

Research has consistently identified the presence of a dedicated friend or determined advocate as a crucial contributor to an individual's resilience. Give yourself permission to rely on the help of others as you seek financial assistance, decipher directions on forms, and complete the process. Because financial assistance is an area that can change quickly, we urge you to use the Internet resources listed at the end of the chapter.

Wellness

I'm not into working out. My philosophy: No pain, no pain.

—Carol Leifer

Leisure time is that five or six hours when you sleep at night.

—George Allen

The dominant Western culture spends a great deal of time giving you messages about how to take better care of your body, how to eat healthier foods, and how to be more physically fit. Unfortunately, many of those messages are driven by the desire to promote corporate profits, not personal wellness.

The emerging field of health psychology is reporting important findings about the relationship between your physical and mental well-being. Indeed, many of the results support a more traditionally Eastern concept of the wholeness of your self.

Let's face it. Like most people, you probably know a lot more about healthy exercise and nutrition than you put into practice. In graduate school, however, you are at risk for abandoning even more habits that promote physical well-being. Eating poorly, sleeping fewer hours, and exercising little can quickly become your lifestyle as a graduate student. As one student commented, "Sure, I drink plenty of water every day— if Dr. Pepper, Mountain Dew, and coffee count. And, yes, I also eat a well-balanced diet from the basic food groups—donuts from the round group, tortilla chips from the triangle group, and candy bars from the rectangle group."

As you consider your nutritional and activity needs, reflect on the meaning that eating well and exercising have for you. Here are a few questions to get you started. What messages did you receive about food when you were growing up? In what ways was food part of family and community celebrations? Did you associate nurturance and comfort with food? Did you worry that there was not enough food for everyone?

Was finishing your plate an expectation? Why? What is the relationship between stress and eating for you? Is feeding other people a demonstration of your love?

What does fitness and activity mean to you? What were the models in your family for eating and exercising? Were there gender-related messages about fitness? What messages do you believe about your self-esteem and your wellness? From your spiritual perspective, how do you view the human body?

After you have reflected on these questions, you can come to a deeper appreciation of the regenerative power of eating well and the exhilaration of engaging in physical exertion.

One counseling student, realizing that her physical well-being was being compromised in graduate school, developed a plan. "I made an agreement with myself that I would get at least three hours of exercise a week to release stress, feel better about myself, and fit into my clothes again. My new schedule book would have that workout time in it" (Belcastro, 2000, p. 12). Another student, Martin, entered graduate school with many healthy practices already in place. He had attained a black belt in karate and was extremely careful to protect his practice time. After a while, his classmates learned to refrain from complaining about being tired in front of him, because they knew he would tell them, "You must not be exercising enough!" It was particularly irritating to hear his words because they knew he was right.

▲▲▲

Kicking and Sleeping
Martin's Story

EVEN THOUGH I would like to have maintained a more consistent exercise regimen than I have since entering the training program, I regularly do a Tae Bo routine, a kind of kickboxing/dance-workout video. I make sure to do this whenever I feel stressed and have a need for physical activity. Also, in spite of my demanding schedule, I try to get at least eight hours of sleep a night. Getting a good amount of sleep replenishes my internal drive to tackle the demands and events of the upcoming day.

Finding and Creating Perspective

Compared to what we ought to be, we are only
half awake.

—William James

Martin's observation is consistently supported in the research literature. If you take good care of meeting your physiological needs, you have more energy to use for other pursuits. You may heartily agree but believe that you just can't find the time for exercise. Covey (1989) offered a wonderful example to illustrate the fallacy of not making the time to satisfy your wellness needs. Imagine that, as you are taking a stroll in the woods, you encounter a person laboring frenetically to saw down a tree. The person, who's sweaty and haggard, is obviously worn out but has barely made a scratch in the tree after sawing for hours. Trying to be helpful, you suggest that if the person stopped and sharpened the saw, the work would go much quicker. But the person protests, "I don't have time to sharpen the saw. . . . I'm too busy sawing" (p. 287).

Covey's point is that we truly do *not* have the time to not eat well and exercise. Because we know these are very important activities, why do we often systematically neglect them? He believes it is because we fool ourselves into thinking that the consequences of not fulfilling wellness needs are neither immediate nor significant. We know enough to do the right thing, but we need some help, as the Nike commercials encourage us, to "just do it."

▲▲▲

The Road from Orange Crackers to Rice
Anne's Story

I HAD LIMITED success in eating healthy meals as a graduate student. Nearly every day at lunch, for the better part of three years, I ate frozen raspberry yogurt ("You mean ice cream," a nutritionist finally told me) and those peanut butter and bright orange cracker sandwiches. Fortunately, my body was in good enough health to somehow withstand this simultaneous neglect and assault. My weak defense was that the nearby little grill did not have vegetarian entrees.

What finally helped me was to link my nutritional and exercise needs to my need for belonging. I now enjoy lunch with friends and make sure I eat a healthy meal. I take regular walks with my neighbor. Actually, I *talk* with my neighbor and we move while we do it. The other meaningful context is related to my role as a mother. It is important to me that my children develop good health habits. I know my children will be influenced by what they see me do in these areas, for better or worse.

▼▼▼

As you reflect on your needs and ponder their meaning for you, keep in mind that you are not alone. Linking with others to meet your needs can lead not only to good nutrition and exercise but also to good company. By addressing more than one area of need, you increase your Thriving Quotient (TQ) in ways that are both gratifying and enduring.

These "good habits" are similar to informal rituals observed in healthy families. Research informs us that having meaningful rituals in our lives provides a sense of cohesiveness and security (Driver, 1998; Imber-Black & Roberts, 1992). For example, a group of male graduate students decided to meet each Sunday to enjoy a meal together. First, the eating was paired with watching sports, a dominant interest for them in their pre-graduate-school lives. Over time, they regularly added a study component to their shared meal. Recently, their Sunday ritual has evolved into an informal men's support group—with good food.

■ ■ ■

EXERCISE 3.5 I'll Have the Combo
Meeting Multiple Needs

Think over Maslow's hierarchy of needs and jot down some activities that you want to do that correspond with the types of needs. Look for activities that might naturally combine to meet several needs simultaneously.

For example, to address your safety and security needs, you may want to learn self-defense. You could enroll in a course that would teach you defensive skills, provide an excellent workout, and offer opportunities for developing new friendships. Looking at the need to belong, you might find a camping or hiking club or a gourmet cooking club that could simultaneously address wellness and friendship needs. In addressing self-esteem and self-actualization needs, you might pair yoga, tai chi, or dance instruction with your exercise routine.

_____

_____

_____

_____

_____

Sometimes you hear another perspective and it immediately rings a bell. One student related that the most centering and helpful advice from her advisor was to picture the span of her entire life and then make a ratio of how much time she would actually spend in graduate school—an intense but relatively small part. The reminder helped this student put the challenges of school in a better frame. Like dental work, graduate school does not last forever—and reminding yourself that an ordeal is temporary can make it endurable. You can then focus on how you can use this limited experience to forge a lifestyle of balance, beauty, and well-being.

Although you may focus more energy on satisfying safety and belonging needs at the start of graduate school, you'll find it helpful to regularly tend to these needs throughout your training. For example, you may focus on financial aid more at the start of your training, but you may find that additional support is available later for specific activities, such as funding designated for research or presentations at professional conferences. In the same manner, as you become more familiar with your community and make new friends, you may decide your belonging or safety needs will be better met by changing your living arrangements.

Five hundred years ago, Ficino (Moore, 1992) gave this good advice for staying well: "You should walk as often as possible among plants that have a wonderful aroma, spending a considerable amount of time every day among such things." Sounds good! Maybe you can even invite a friend to join you.

■ ■ ■

SUMMARY

In this chapter, we presented suggestions and guidelines for finding safe and affordable housing, obtaining educational loans, applying for assistantships and scholarships, taking care of your nutritional needs, and maintaining an active and healthy lifestyle. Meeting your needs in graduate school is not easy, but the experience can contribute to your thriving as a trainee. Through your struggles, you build an empathic bridge with the people you counsel. And in your successes, you gain an appreciation for your clients' personal strengths and social resources.

RESOURCES

Finkle's (1999) *Graduate School* assembles an amazing variety of resources to help you research graduate programs, create successful applications, find financial assistance, and excel in your training. These resources include printed materials, Web sites, and on-line services.

The undisputed leader in guidance for finance is Leider and Leider's (1998) *Don't Miss Out*, now in its twenty-third edition. The authors describe the common myths about obtaining aid, steps in completing federal forms, role of the university, and company-sponsored education. It includes information of interest for women and persons of color. The book is comprehensive and has a terrific listing of suggestions and contacts.

The Sage Publications Graduate Survival Skills series offers a comprehensive look at the graduate school experience, including how to apply and finance graduate school. The series has books that address the unique experiences and challenges that some students may confront in graduate school. For example, there are books in the series targeted to women (Rittner & Trudeau, 1997) and African American (Isaac, 1998) graduate students. The series is well written and provides detailed information on a wide range of topics, from studying and taking examinations to dealing with racism and clarifying goals.

Graduate Student Resources on the Web
http://www-personal.umich.edu/~danhorn/graduate.html

Dan Horn, a psychology graduate student at the University of Michigan, has designed an informative and fun site. He has organized the site into three major areas: Getting In, Getting Through, and Getting Out.

Each area has links to other valuable sites. There's even a section of graduate school humor!

Embark

http://www.embark.com/grad

This site includes the steps to making an informed decision about graduate school—research, prepare, apply, finance, and get ready. It also lists schools that have on-line application forms. The site offers application information, free practice GRE's, review classes, a scholarship search feature, and loan applications. A helpful feature is an interactive forum for joining discussions.

The 1999–2000 Student Guide to Financial Aid: Funding Your Education

http://www.ed.gov/prog_info/SFA/StudentGuide/1999-0/index.html

Looking for student aid

http://www.ed.gov/prog_info/SFA/SLA

These electronic guides are published by the United States Department of Education. They provide comprehensive information about applying for federal financial aid. You can also request print versions by calling the Federal Student Aid Information Center at 1-800-433-3243.

REFERENCES

Belcastro, A. L. (2000, February). Finding balance in school and life. *Counseling Today, 43,* 12.

Bowlby, J. (1979). *Separation.* New York: Basic Books.

Covey, S. (1989). *Seven habits of highly effective people.* New York: Simon & Schuster.

Driver, T. F. (1998). *Liberating rites: Understanding the transformative power of ritual.* Boulder, CO: Westview.

Fiffer, S. S., & Fiffer, S. (1995). *Home: American writers remember rooms of their own.* New York: Vintage Books.

Finkle, J. (1999). *Graduate school.* Seattle, WA: Resource Pathways.

Hoskins, C. M. (2000, August). Get a life! Top 10 list for a first-year student. *Counseling Today, 43,* 32, 36.

Imber-Black, E., & Roberts, J. (1992). *Rituals for our times*. New York: HarperCollins.

Isaac, A. (1998). *The African American student's guide to surviving graduate school*. New York: Sage.

Leahey, T. H. (2000). *A history of psychology: Main currents in psychological thought*. Upper Saddle River, NJ: Prentice-Hall.

Leider, A., & Leider, R. (1998). *Don't miss out* (23rd ed.). Alexandria, VA: Octameron Associates.

MacLaine, S. (2000). *The Camino: A journey of the spirit*. New York: Pocket Books.

Maslow, A. H. (1962). *Toward a psychology of being*. New York: Van Nostrand.

Maslow, A. H. (1970). *Motivation and personality* (2nd ed.). New York: Harper and Row.

Moore, T. (1992). *Care of the soul*. New York: HarperCollins.

Rittner, B., & Trudeau, P. (1997). *The women's guide to surviving graduate school*. New York: Sage.

Answer to the Riddle: The farmer first takes the chicken to the island, leaving the fox with the grain. The farmer then returns, picks up the fox, and ferries it to the island. Instead of leaving the fox alone with the chicken, the farmer brings the chicken back on the return voyage, drops off the chicken, and transports the grain to the island. Leaving the fox with the grain on the island, the farmer returns for the chicken once again to make the final transport.

CHAPTER 4

▲▲▲
▼▼▼

Enhancing Your Academic Skills

People get wisdom from thinking, not from learning.

—Laura Riding Jackson

Reason is, and ought only to be, the slave of the passions.

—David Hume

The Chinese character that represents the act of listening combines the symbols of not only ears but also eyes, heart, and mind (Adler, Rosenfield, & Towne, 1989). This wonderful fusion of symbols expresses the essence of successful counseling. As a counselor or therapist, you involve yourself totally—ears, eyes, heart, and mind—in a process of truly encountering your client in a helping relationship. Because counseling is a dynamic and complex process, you need to cultivate not only your observational competencies and emotional sensitivities but also your mental abilities. The purpose of your graduate curriculum is to prepare your mind, heart, eyes, and ears for the challenging work of counseling and therapy.

In this chapter, we discuss how you can use four basic academic skills—reading, researching, writing, and presenting—to make the most of your training. Reading is the original virtual reality—it allows you to broaden and enrich your limited experiences by tapping into the observations, ideas, and discoveries of others. Research skills enable you to observe carefully, collect information systematically, and organize this material into a coherent framework. Writing skills help you give voice to your own experiences, make your thoughts visible, and clarify your vague hunches by putting them into words. Finally, presentation skills enable you to share your expertise with colleagues, clients, and the general public.

You may be wondering how simply improving your academic skills can help you become a better counselor or therapist. Just as these skills are essential during your training, they are no less indispensable throughout your professional career. Staying current, thinking creatively, keeping emotionally engaged, and approaching your work mindfully can help you to maintain your professional vitality and prevent burnout.

▲▲▲

More Than I Had Bargained For
Bonnie's Story

I REMEMBER BEING the first person in the room for the first meeting of my first course in my training to become a counselor. That was a lot of "firsts"! There I sat, a forty-five-year-old woman, successful accountant, mother of two wonderful teenage girls, wife of nearly twenty years in a loving marriage, and now a brand-new counseling student. I had finally decided that, if I really wanted to become a counselor, then it was now or never. Generally, I'm a pretty confident person, but not right before my first class! Every other student entered the room as if he or she belonged there, and I couldn't help noticing how young they were. Some of them looked like they were still in college, and I must have been the oldest student by at least ten or fifteen years. I was even older than my professor! What, I wondered, was I doing here?

Sure, I had been a good student in college. Over the years, I had continued to read voraciously and to write newsletters for a volunteer organization for the mentally ill. I even helped my daughter with her calculus! But my days as a student were a long time ago. Even though I felt a calling to become a counselor, I was worried that I couldn't handle the demands of reading textbooks, writing term papers, and taking tests.

Of course, throughout that first semester of my training, I had to do a personal "crash course" on using the newer research services. I was so out of it that I thought Article Express must be a paper train and WorldCat sounded like a new super hero. Now, I've become an old hand at using the PsycINFO database, and I've discovered I'm still a pretty good student.

My biggest surprise has been how emotionally charged and personally involving the training is. I've found that I cannot be a spectator, detached and disengaged, in my learning. Instead, I've watched my own life unfolding in the course on life-span development. I've noticed all my own symptoms, as well as those of my relatives and friends, in the diagnostics class. And my counseling skills class has stirred up all sorts of personal issues for me.

Early that first semester, we were watching a scene from a documentary, "The Farmer's Wife," which is a powerful account of a woman's courage in enduring all the stresses of modern-day farming. I started crying because that could have been my mother up on that screen. When it was time for the class to discuss the scene, I decided to share the memories and emotions that the scene had evoked in me. One student later thanked me for "enriching" her understanding of these issues. You know, this is more learning than I had originally bargained for, but I'm truly grateful that I'm able to take advantage of the opportunity.

▼▼▼

HEARTS AND MINDS

The heart has its reasons which reason knows not.

—Blaise Pascal

In his autobiography, Carl Jung (1965) described his journey to the American Southwest, where he encountered Ochwiay Biano ("Mountain Lake"), a Native American who was chief of the Taos Pueblo Tribe. Ochwiay Biano shared with Jung his concerns about "whites":

> "We do not know what they want. We do not understand them. We think that they are mad." I asked him why he thought the whites were all mad.
> "They say that they think with their heads," he replied.
> "Why of course. What do you think with?" I asked him in surprise.
> "We think here," he said, indicating his heart (p. 248).

This account is more than just a "Jung at heart" story. In fact, the recent research on emotional intelligence (Goleman, 1995) indicates that we think with *both* our heads and our hearts. According to Antonio Damasio (1994), who is a neuroscientist at the University of Iowa, Descartes made a huge mistake when he left emotions out of the thinking process. Damasio's innovative research has revealed that emotions are actually essential to good thinking.

Like many students who enter graduate programs in counseling, you may have been more of a "heart" person as an undergraduate student. When you first read a poem, you probably responded emotionally rather than thinking about it critically. You may have found yourself passionately involved in projects that captivated your attention. As you enter graduate school, you may view the academic courses in your training curriculum as merely ordeals that you must endure—the hoops you have to jump through—in order for you to qualify for the real learning experiences that take place in your clinical placements. If this brief sketch sounds like you, we invite you to examine carefully your academic skills. You can learn to study better, rather than harder, and make your academic work as personally rewarding and successful as the practice you'll do in your training.

On the other hand, you may be more of a "head" person in your learning style. You may have been a very competent undergraduate student, participating actively in your classes, carefully reading the assigned material, and completing assignments conscientiously. For you, emotions seem to get in the way of thinking objectively. Consequently, you may be less personally engaged and more emotionally detached in your approach to learning. If this description sounds more like you, you may find it challenging to explore yourself, your clients, and the counseling process in your graduate training.

These references to your undergraduate education may feel like ancient history to you. You may be one of the increasing number of "nontraditional" students returning to an academic setting after years of pursuing another calling, such as engaging in a different career or raising a family. As a result, you may have only some vague memories about those distant days as a college student—and some very strong apprehensions right now about entering the academic life once again. Whether you were passive and disengaged or active and involved during your undergraduate years may be irrelevant. After all, you're in a different stage now in your life—more seasoned, mature, and thoughtful. These acquired qualities are going to be wonderful assets for you, but you probably have at least one major worry—that your academic skills may be too rusty.

In this chapter, we describe how you can develop critical reflection by enhancing the core academic skills of reading, research, writing, and presenting. "Isn't this stuff too basic for graduate training?" you may be wondering. "Aren't these just a variation of the three R's—reading, 'riting, and 'rithmetic?" It is true that these are basic skills that you have been practicing for years. However, like many other tasks you'll perform in your graduate training, they'll be a little more complex and a lot more interesting. We share with you here some "tricks of the trade," but more important, we challenge you to commit both your heart and your head to becoming a lifelong learner and successful practitioner.

DEVELOPING CRITICAL
REFLECTION SKILLS

> The function of education is to teach one to think
> intensively and to think critically. Intelligence plus
> character—that is the goal of true education.
>
> —Martin Luther King, Jr.

Put simply, critical reflection is the process of carefully and systemically examining ideas (Meltzoff, 1998). When you think, read, and respond mindfully, you challenge yourself to use higher order thinking skills— to engage in critical reflection. Critical reflection is a requisite skill for you to become a successful counselor or therapist because you must ultimately rely on your own knowledge and judgment. Of course, you should never work without regularly seeking supervision and consultation from others. However, when you are alone dealing with a troubled client in a session, responding on the telephone to a suicidal caller, or even presenting a difficult case in a staffing meeting, you must count on your own abilities. At these crucial times, you have to be able to gather data, analyze complex information, synthesize different factors, present your ideas coherently, and then act on them mindfully.

To begin developing your critical reflection skills as a practitioner, you have to gain a thorough knowledge of theories, develop a repertoire of intervention skills, achieve insight into your clients, recognize their cultural contexts, appreciate the intricacies of interpersonal dynamics, and become more aware of yourself. Mastering all this material is a daunting task, but it's still just the beginning. Once you've gained some familiarity with these components, you need to play with the pieces to see where they fit and then arrange these elements into a complete picture. Ideally, the resulting mosaic will then serve as a working model for successful counseling and therapy.

One way you can facilitate the development of your own critical reflection ability is by striving to be mindful. Langer (1989, 1997) described mindfulness as being open to new information. Mindfulness is to thinking what flexibility is to athletics. Being mindful allows you to reach further, notice connections, and discover parallels that you might otherwise miss.

Bloom and his associates (Bloom, Englehart, Furst, & Krathwohl, 1956) presented a hierarchy that may be helpful to you as you think about how you think. Although an anonymous cynic once insisted, "When it comes to thought, some people stop at nothing," according to Bloom, nearly everyone has at least some skills among six levels of critical thinking. The first skill, *knowledge*, which involves mastering and memorizing, has probably served you well for many a multiple-choice or true-false test. Similarly, *comprehension*, the second skill, is necessary for you to show that you understand the basics and can take them further by interpreting and wondering about them.

Both of these skills are fundamental, but you'll find that graduate education challenges you to move up the hierarchy to other skills, such as application. *Application* requires that you push your comprehension to build new connections and, in some ways, "handle" the material. Application is at work when you try out your skills in your first peer counseling experience.

The fourth skill, *analysis*, involves breaking down information to see how component parts are related and connected. Your analytical skills will be involved, for example, when you compare and contrast psychodynamic and cognitive behavioral approaches to counseling. Analysis is also essential in conceptualizing counseling cases.

Synthesis, the fifth skill, is the process of constructing new ways to integrate information. If your program requires you to describe your personal theory of counseling, chances are you'll use this higher order thinking skill as you put different pieces of information together to create a unified and comprehensive design.

The final skill identified by Bloom, *evaluation*, requires that you form a substantiated conclusion. "Hey, that's easy!," you may think. "I can tell right away if something is good or bad." Perhaps, but what are your criteria? In order to be truly mindful and stretch your critical-reflection muscles, you must be able to establish and apply appropriate criteria so that you can make effective and consistent evaluations. Imagine, for instance, that a peer asks you to evaluate a videotape of her counseling session. What will your criteria be? What are the bases for these criteria? How will you measure performance? Can you ensure that you'll evaluate this videotape and another student's videotape with some degree of consistency?

It's probably obvious to you at this point that evaluation, as well as synthesis, analysis, application, and even comprehension and memorization, are complex skills. You can improve in all these competencies, however, if you practice. As Marilyn vos Savant once said, "My thoughts are like waffles—the first few don't look too good." If that's true for you, then keep cooking!

Stay mindful and stretch your intellectual muscles. Langer (1997) suggested that two ways to improve your mindfulness are to ask good questions and to look for novel distinctions. You can ask your peers, your professors, your texts, and yourself. As you do so, try to expand the ways in which you categorize the answers you receive. Rather than labeling a response as good or bad, for instance, search for a new evaluative description. At the same time, stay open to ideas or tasks that may at first seem unappealing or even boring. Approaching them mindfully by actively seeking novel aspects can actually increase your enjoyment of learning about the concept or performing the activity (Langer, 1997).

LEARNING BY HEART

> There is only one quality worse than hardness of
> heart and that is softness of head.
>
> —Theodore Roosevelt

The underlying assumption of most discussions about thinking has been that it is much better to use your head than to follow your heart. Emotions, according to this orthodox view, only contaminate good thinking. Therefore, the traditional goal of higher education has been to promote dispassionate thinking. However, the recent work of Damasio (1994) and Goleman (1995) have demonstrated that emotions play a vital role in helping us to perform well in academic tasks, engage in effective problem-solving, remain open to new ideas, and think creatively.

In this section, we focus on three important ways in which you can use your emotions to strengthen your academic skills—riding the perturbation wave, finding "the zone," and using the Zeigarnik Effect.

Riding the Perturbation Wave

The word "yes" may bring trouble; the word "no"
leads nowhere.

—Bantu proverb

In any significant learning experience, your mind is in a state of dialectical tension (Presbury, Echterling, & McKee, 2002). On the one hand, you are excited to discover new ways of thinking and to experiment with new ways of acting. On the other, you strive to have some sense of certainty and familiarity. This tension between chaos and order is the essence of learning. If your thoughts have been thrown into chaos, then you feel overwhelmed and confused. However, if you're not experiencing enough challenge, you feel bored and stagnant.

The secret to making the most of any learning opportunity is to ride the wave of perturbation. Just as in surfing, you seek out the situations that make waves and create turbulence. You'll take a tumble now and then, but the adventure is well worth the risk. The learning tasks you encounter under these circumstances will be challenging and may even knock you off balance, but they are rarely overpowering. In contrast to our surfing analogy, the traditional ideal of disengaged, dispassionate thinking is like standing on the shore—you may never be in over your head, but neither do you experience the exhilaration of being carried away with an idea or totally caught up in performing a task.

Mihaly Csikszentmihalyi (1997) describes this invigorating process, in which you find yourself completely immersed in an activity, as "flow." You are more likely to experience flow when several conditions are met. The first condition is that the situation requires specific actions to achieve explicit goals. When, for example, you are weaving, running, playing chess, or studying for a test, you are more likely to "become" that activity and achieve flow. Another condition for flow is that you receive immediate feedback on your efforts. You can see the pattern emerging as you weave, the route you are completing as you run, the new positions of your chess pieces as you move them, and your understanding enhanced as you continue studying. The final, and most important, condition is a manageable challenge. You can achieve flow if successfully completing a task requires that you make the most of your emerging skills. When the weaving pattern is particularly complex, the running route especially demanding, the chess game intriguing, and the subject matter challenging, you have the opportunity to immerse yourself in the productive and satisfying experience of flow.

If you are a new student, you may not realize just how challenging your training experiences will be. Of course, like other graduate programs, the intellectual content of your curriculum will involve some difficulties, and the workload will be heavy. But graduate training in counseling and therapy may seem to you to be much more manageable than other programs. The textbooks, for example, appear much more readable than those in physics, medicine, or law. Your counseling professors may seem nice—after all, they're also counselors—so you may initially assume that they won't be so demanding. However, you'll soon find that your counseling faculty, curriculum, readings, and learning experiences will all work together to consistently challenge you to deal with emotionally charged material, face your own personal issues, and learn painful lessons. Your training is more than hard work; it's *heart* work. The ride may turn out to be much more turbulent than you thought!

One of the common sources of turbulence you'll encounter as a counseling student is questioning your assumptions about yourself, people, and life in general. These familiar assumptions that you have developed over the years are like an old pair of comfortable shoes—you're reluctant to give them up, even though there are holes in them. Particularly when you first begin to question your assumptions about cultures, gender, and values, you are likely to feel confused. As Milton Erickson pointed out (Erickson, Rossi, & Rossi, 1976), people have a powerful need to resolve confusion. Because you can't rely on automatic thinking anymore, you become attentive, focused, and mindful. At these times, you will embark on an intense search for new ways to view yourself, others, and the world. Embrace your confusion! Out of this chaos, you can create a deeper, richer sense of order and harmony.

Relying on automatic thinking can cause you to see other people as stereotypes instead of mindfully noting the unique qualities of those you encounter. Such a reliance can also blind you to the often subtle forms of oppression that others must endure every day.

■ ■ ■
_____

EXERCISE 4.1 **The Bird Cage**
Encountering Oppression

Frye (1995) offered a powerful metaphor to perturb our thinking about oppression. Take a couple of minutes to read the following brief fantasy.

Imagine that you are seeing a bird cage for the first time. However, the bird cage is so close to your face that you can only focus on one of the wires. With the wire right before your eyes, you can see minute details—the gleam of light on its shiny surface, the texture of the paint, and its cylindrical shape—but not the other wires. If your conception of a bird cage was based only on this close examination, you could continue to examine it carefully and be incredulous to hear that a bird could not escape from it. Why couldn't a bird simply fly around this wire anytime it wanted? What's wrong with this bird? Lack of initiative? Some personal flaw?

It's only when you have an opportunity to step back and gain a macroscopic view of the bird cage that you can begin to appreciate how this systematic network of barriers works. Alone, each wire presents no obstacle to the bird's freedom, but together, these slender threads are just as effective as any prison made of solid stone.

Consider the meaning of this fantasy for you and write your reflections below.

Finding "The Zone"

Life loves to be taken by the lapel and told: "I'm with you kid. Let's go."

—Maya Angelou

Goleman (1995) found that a moderately elated, or energized, emotional state is best for thinking flexibly and solving complex problems more readily. The classic Yerkes-Dodson Law shows how your state of emotional arousal affects your performance. You perform poorly when your emotions are at either extreme—disengaged or highly aroused (Martindale, 1981). At a moderate level of emotional arousal, you're at your best—adrenaline pumping, memory enhanced, neurons firing, and attention focused. When you're in "the zone," you can do your finest work.

Most guides on academic success emphasize the importance of managing your time, but more crucial is managing your emotional arousal. If you led with your head as an undergraduate student, encourage yourself to follow your heart more in your graduate training. Become a passionate scholar! Psyching yourself up can become part of your preparatory ritual before you open a book, attend class, or start an assignment. You may want to remind yourself of the goals you are working to achieve, to visualize yourself as a successful counselor, or to ask yourself important questions that your academic work can help you answer. Get personal with the material. Explore, for example, how you can use a particular concept to gain insight into yourself. How have you experienced enmeshment in your relationships? When have you used denial? How has modeling influenced you? Engaging with these concepts in such a personal way is like playing a sport—you're a participant in the process, not a spectator.

If you've followed your heart throughout most of your previous education, you may be more likely to hit the higher end of the Yerkes-Dodson curve when you are facing important tasks in a counseling graduate program. In that case, your routine for preparing for a challenging assignment or test may include practicing relaxation and focusing activities. When it comes to engaging your emotions in the learning process, you need to follow the "Goldilocks Principle"—not too hot and not too cold.

Using the Zeigarnik Effect

The suspense is terrible. I hope it will last.

—Oscar Wilde

Did you ever follow one of the "soaps" on TV? No matter which program you may have watched, it never seemed to fail that just as someone was disclosing a dramatic piece of news, the episode ended with this new plot twist left unresolved. If soaps never interested you, perhaps you've read an adventure comic book that ended with the aggravating notice, "to be continued," just when it looked like the hero was facing certain doom. Remember how badly you wanted to know how things were going to turn out? You may have replayed the events over and over in your mind, speculated about the possible consequences, and talked about the circumstances with friends. Until the program's next episode or the comic book's following issue, your curiosity continued to nag at you. At those times, you were experiencing the Zeigarnik Effect.

Hergenhahn (1992) described how Kurt Lewin, the famous Gestalt psychologist, hypothesized that a person who has not finished a task or achieved closure on a topic will remember the material better. Bluma Zeigarnik, a student of Lewin, tested this hypothesis in an experiment in which participants were permitted to finish some tasks but not others. As predicted, she found that participants later remembered many more of the uncompleted tasks than the completed ones.

What the Zeigarnik Effect means for you is that if you want to "chew" on an idea, rather than forget it immediately, you should not rush to make up your mind about it. Similarly, because no graduate class ever resolves all the issues you will face in your counseling career, there is always naturally "unfinished business" in your personal and professional development. If you allow yourself to leave a classroom holding on to least one suspenseful note, you are more likely to keep reflecting on it as you seek a richer and deeper understanding of the subject matter. In fact, we have a multitude of unresolved issues that face us in the counseling profession, unanswered questions that confront us in our personal lives, and vast unexplored territories that beckon us in our own psyches. Invoking the Zeigarnik Effect could be a great daily ritual to stay open, curious, and engrossed.

As you read the following material about the basic academic skills, keep in mind that you can enhance your abilities in each of them by using your emotions to help you learn by heart.

THE CORE ACADEMIC SKILLS

Reading

Reading is a means of thinking with another
person's mind: it forces you to stretch your own.
—Charles Scribner, Jr.

Literacy is a fundamental skill for elementary school students, and the same is true for you in your graduate training. "Hey, reading is no big deal!" you may think. "I already read E-mails, newspapers, magazines, novels, and nonfiction books. I read all the time—what's so tough about the reading I'll do in a graduate training program?"

Well, the reading that you will encounter in graduate school will differ in significant ways from the reading you've done so far. In addition to course textbooks, you'll be expected to read seminal works in the field, manuscripts by your professors, drafts of collaborative papers by your fellow students, psychological assessment reports, client files, program evaluations, counseling protocols, and the most recently published professional literature. Some books and articles have become such standards in the field that they are often considered unofficial required readings for all counselors. The "Golden Oldies" in Appendix A lists a few of these counseling classics.

Although the material you read in graduate school will vary tremendously in its content, style, and purpose, it has several common characteristics. First and foremost, the sheer weight of material you will be reading will seem intimidating. You may not be able to prevent eyestrain, but many graduate students do invest in backpacks that can manage heavy loads without straining their backs. Second, unlike a book you might take to pass the time on the beach, this reading is not "fast food for the mind." The material is likely to be challenging in several ways—it may be difficult, complex, provocative, demanding, or even emotionally painful to read. This material requires a commitment from you to give it your full attention. Otherwise, you are likely to miss subtle nuances and crucial details. You also need to read the material critically—with an inquiring mind. And afterward, you need to reflect on what you have read. This material is not something you can swallow in one quick gulp. You need to take the time to digest it.

Successfully handling both the breadth and depth of the reading material you will encounter in your graduate training is like baking a cake—you just have to combine a few basic ingredients.

The Place First, take some time to determine what environment is best for helping you engage in productive, intensive, and extensive reading. Do you concentrate best in silence? With others around? With or without music?

Karen, a graduate student with two children, found that she did her best reading and reflection in a coffee shop near school. The smell of the coffee, the arrivals and departures of others, and the piped-in classical music were soothing to her. She could sit for hours, occasionally getting a refill of coffee or a biscotti, without being interrupted by family members. The others in the shop served as a welcome distraction when she needed to take a break, and she enjoyed getting to know the coffee shop employees, who occasionally inquired about her school work.

Rae, on the other hand, found that she was most able to read with depth and comprehension when she was at home, in total silence, sitting on a folding chair at a plain card table tucked in a small monastic-like alcove of her apartment—no coffee, no food, no distractions, and no visitors.

You may want to experiment to determine where and how you do your best reading. Once you've discovered what environment works for you, then find and claim it.

The Time Second, you need to set aside plenty of time for reading. This suggestion, like the first, will depend on you and your preferences. Many students find that when they begin graduate school, they have enough opportunities to handle the assigned texts and articles. As they become more involved in their classes and other activities, however, they find that the extra time has slipped away. They then struggle to keep pace, if not one step behind, with their reading assignments. After you've found your ideal place to read, figure out the best time to do it. Then claim this time, like you did the place, as yours. Kelly, for example, found that the only way he was able to protect the time he had set aside was to schedule appointments for R.T.—"Reading Time."

Yourself Of course, you have to put more than time into your reading—you have to put yourself into it, too. Read mindfully, asking questions of the material and of yourself. What does this information suggest to you? If you had to explain the information to someone else, or perhaps defend it to someone else, what would you say?

Whenever you read a text, consider yourself to be entering into a partnership with the author. Your role is to custom-design a personalized book based on the generic one that the author has provided. As a collaborator, you will be jotting down comments in the page margins, outlining the material in your own way, drawing visual representations of the ideas, critically evaluating the book's arguments, and even engaging in a dialogue with the author. In your own journal, you can also write at greater length about your own epiphanies—"aha experiences"—as you read the book. You'll find that this collaborative approach to reading is much more engaging than simply highlighting your text.

■ ■ ■

EXERCISE 4.2 **What? So What? Now What?**

We mentioned the three R's earlier, but the three W's can serve you well, too. Choose a chapter in a text and take notes while you're reading it. Pay particular attention at first to capturing the salient points of the content—the "What?" Then think about what you just read and figure out what it means—the "So What?" For example, you may want to jot down some of the implications of these ideas for counseling. Finally, now that you understand this material, consider what you are going to do with it—the "Now What?" How are you going to apply it? How are you going to connect it to material from other courses? Write about this experience in your journal. Keep using the "What? So What? Now What?" approach with all your reading until it becomes second nature to you.

■ ■ ■

When the material is so challenging that you are having problems concentrating on it, you can use two strategies. First, remind yourself of the similarities between reading and counseling. Both involve an encounter between people through the medium of words. You certainly don't expect to completely understand any client in one session. You may have trouble at first reading your client's emotional state, deciphering the meaning of comments, or even comprehending important motives. In spite of these difficulties, you can remain committed to working with your client because the payoff for a successful counseling experience makes it all worthwhile. You'll find that you're much more successful in your reading when you bring this same level of commitment to understanding an author. When you read, you don't have to fully comprehend every intricacy of the author's theory or be able to articulate each nuance of an argument. Nevertheless, you can do your best to engage with the author by mindfully attending to the written word.

Another strategy you can pursue when you feel overwhelmed by your class readings is to remember that you are not alone in this endeavor. As one counseling student recommended, "Do not be afraid to ask for help or for what you need. No one gets through this on his or her own" (Hoskins, 2000, p. 36.) You can ask a colleague to read or study with you. Together, you can support and encourage one another, helping each other read and reflect. When you're tackling particularly tough material, you can discuss it with your reading partner.

▲▲▲

I Learned How to Read All Over Again
Brian's Story

THIS WEEKEND, I learned how to read all over again. Last week I kept facing my textbook with my highlighter in my hand, trying to find the motivation to keep going. As I read, I realized that my book was starting to almost glow with all the yellow marks in it, but I couldn't recall a word. There seemed to be too much information and I couldn't prioritize it, so I wasn't retaining anything. I'm new to this field, so I don't know enough yet to recognize the important concepts!

I finally asked my professor how to read this text. She told me to take my time. Pay attention to the organization of each chapter. Then figure out what points the authors were trying to make and pay particular attention to anything that didn't make sense to me. If I don't understand something, it's important that I take note of it and ask for clarification in class. I started taking notes when I read, and now I feel like I'm not only retaining more, but I'm starting to see the internal structure of the material. I'm starting to see how concepts relate to each other. Wow, I was really starting to feel worried for awhile that I couldn't do it.

▼▼▼

Researching

To ask well is to know much.

—African proverb

The Need for Research Skills You may be wondering how research is relevant to becoming a competent helping professional. You came to a graduate training program to learn how to help people, not to crunch numbers—right? Well, there are several important reasons for integrating research into your training experience. First and foremost, if you're going to be a competent helping professional, you have to develop good research skills. In order to design successful interventions, you must be able to make careful observations, systematically collect relevant and comprehensive information, and organize this material into a coherent framework. Research is not limited to the laboratory. When you gather background information on a school or community, when you review recent studies on a particular problem, and when you read about a new theoretical perspective in therapy, you are doing important research. The knowledge you gain from these research activities is essential to being a capable professional who stays current in the field.

Second, research experience itself will hone your critical thinking skills. You are entering a complex, challenging, and ambiguous line of work. When you are confronted by the obvious pain of troubled clients, it may be tempting to latch on to highly touted but untested techniques. However, you need to maintain a healthy skepticism regarding fads, cure-alls, and biases in the field. Research experience reminds us softhearted helpers to be hard-nosed about the evidence we need to validate therapeutic effectiveness.

Third, throughout your training, you will be learning to plan, design, implement, and evaluate programs that meet the therapeutic needs of communities and schools. Once again, you will need to rely on your research skills in order to assess people's needs accurately and to evaluate programs carefully.

A fourth important reason for integrating research into your training is that it is one of the major ways that you can advance the profession. As an emerging professional in the counseling field, you have an obligation to contribute to our growing knowledge base through your scholarly activity.

Fifth and finally, an immediate and practical training benefit of research is that it provides excellent opportunities for you to collaborate with faculty members and other students on important and stimulating projects. As you become more comfortable engaging in research activities now, you'll be more likely to continue to reach out to others in collaborative research efforts later. After you've graduated, you are likely to find that practicing as a counselor can feel isolating at times. Unfortunately, it's likely that you will not have the benefit of a peer group that's always available to you. Working with others to explore areas of interest is a great way to build and maintain a community of supportive colleagues.

If you're still not sold on the importance of research, consider this scenario. You've graduated and have a position in a school, mental health center, community agency, or hospital. You begin to work with a client who has a problem that's more complex than those you've worked with before. The situation may not necessarily demand that you refer the client to someone else, but you realize that if you're going to work effectively with this person, you'll need to find out more. The process of finding out more is essentially research. The more skilled you are at researching now, the more resourceful you'll be later when your client's well-being is on the line.

Learning Research Skills So how do you become skilled at research? This question may be especially pressing if you're nervous about, or slightly afraid of, research methods and statistics. Perhaps you're one of the many who read only the beginnings and ends of journal articles, casually skipping over the method and analysis sections in the middle. Heppner and his colleagues (1999) stated that both the graduate school environment and the personality styles of the students themselves cause some trainees to struggle with research. The implication is that students who have investigative interests or statistics skills or who are in research-oriented graduate programs may have an advantage over other students.

However, certain activities in graduate school can increase your comfort with research and improve the chances that you'll continue to engage in research efforts after graduation. Participating in research teams with other students can help you identify what aspects of research come more easily to you (yes, there will be some things you do quite well!) and which areas are more challenging for you. Then you and your colleagues can pool your expertise and help each other. In the process, you become not only more comfortable with research but also more critically reflective.

You can gain valuable research experience by joining faculty members' research teams or volunteering to work individually with a faculty member who is investigating an area that is interesting to you. Consider asking if you can assist, even if your help would consist primarily of literature review or library searches. If you're able to watch the research process from beginning to end—problem identification to manuscript completion—you'll likely increase your research self-efficacy.

■ ■ ■

EXERCISE 4.3 **Doing a Little Detective Work**

Think about the helping profession—what interests you right now? What would you like to know about counselors or therapists? Clients? Problems? If you were to formulate one question you want to explore, what would it be? Remember that note pad you keep handy to jot down ideas and questions while you are reading? Use it now to write down your question. Now think about ways in which you may go about answering it.

At this point, imagine that you're a detective, either a sophisticated British variety or a tough American private eye. Whichever you choose, what would you want to know about your question (your subject)? Who would you ask? What would you ask? If you had to prove that there is a connection between two things, how would you do it?

Spend a little time thinking about this scenario. Don't worry right now about exact measurements, procedures, or instruments. Just try to expand your mind and become fully engaged and interested in your subject. After you've gotten to know your question, go to the library and engage in a literature search.

■ ■ ■

You may find that a literature search, which typically occurs early on in the research process, is an intimidating task. It may seem overwhelming to find so much information on so many facets of your topic available in so many places. If you keep the detective metaphor in mind, you may feel like you're looking for clues in a hall of mirrors and doors. Which doors are real and offer you access to important information? Which doors only look real? The following tips may help you choose wisely.

- Ideally, your undergraduate education provided you with training in library search skills. If so, then you'll feel fairly confident going to the library and using your school's search system or staying at home and searching the library via the Web. (We'll talk more about Web searching shortly; for now let's focus on general library searches.) If you feel rusty or underprepared, sign up for a workshop or ask the reference librarian for help. Most libraries use common databases, such as ERIC or PsycINFO, but the manner of accessing those databases may vary. Don't hesitate to ask for help, and when you do, take notes! You don't want to try to replicate a search on your own and find you can't remember what to enter when you want to expand or limit your search. Similarly, don't limit yourself to one database. If you're truly stretching your thoughts and thinking critically, you may find that interesting connections exist with fields such as social work, biology, sociology, philosophy, anthropology, literature, medicine, and theology.

- Be organized. Even if you're not organized as a rule, take on some "obsessive-compulsive" traits when you work on your research. Keep your note pad with you so that you can keep track of your searches. You'll want to remember what keywords you used to initiate your searches and what databases you used. You may want to download, print out, or E-mail yourself your search histories so that you won't have to start from scratch the next time you go to the library or sit down at your computer.

- As you find materials that relate to your topic, read the abstracts available on the databases and identify which articles you would like to read. Then find those articles. It'll help if you can remember to take your copy card (if your library uses these types of debit cards) or money with you when you go to the library. You'll probably need to make copies of the most relevant articles. Since no library's collection is complete, you will also want to take advantage of interlibrary loan services.

- Learn how to use copiers, microfiche, and microfilm readers. Again, ask for help if you're not familiar with these tools. Make sure that your copies are clear and complete before you leave the library.

- Save yourself lots of headaches by making sure you have complete citation information for each article you may use.

- Keep copies of articles or chapters that interest you in a labeled folder or binder.

- Don't go to the library when you're exhausted, unless the idea of a couple of hours of searching is just what you need to wake yourself up!

- Take time to read what you have, and don't skip the middle section. This tip leads us to the next exercise.

■ ■ ■
_____

EXERCISE 4.4 Critiquing

Use your critical reflection skills to analyze the articles, chapters, and books you gathered in the first exercise. Maybe you have assumed that if research is published, it must be of good quality. We hate to disillusion you, but as blues singers often point out, "It ain't necessarily so."

Check this out by looking at how the articles are written, from beginning to end. How are research questions phrased? What hypotheses are presented? What information is gathered, and by what method? How does this information relate back to the hypothesis? If particular instruments are used, are these instruments reliable and valid? How are participants chosen? Are sampling procedures adequately described? Do you see any inherent complications in the sample or procedures? How are data analyzed? Look at your statistics textbook and see if the researchers' data match the assumptions of their analysis.

_____
                                                            ■ ■ ■

One advantage of doing research is that the process itself tends to use higher order critical thinking skills. As you practice and gain experience with research, you may find that you are more mindful in general. You'll have a broader knowledge base from which to draw, and your ability to make thoughtful conclusions will improve.

Remember that your research should be related to concepts and issues that you find truly intriguing. If you focus on what's captivating to you, you'll find that the process is not only easier but also that it can be genuinely exciting. Some students opt to choose one primary area of interest at the start of their program. They read about that area, investigate it, and focus in on it whenever possible in course assignments. Those students generally go on to write theses or dissertations that build on their initial investigations. Other students find that they have several areas that call to them. They may focus on play therapy when working with children in a practicum and then explore substance abuse issues when they take an addictions course. Advantages and disadvantages exist with both of these approaches, so don't worry that there's one right way to begin your research efforts. The key is just to begin!

Writing

> Writing is not what the writer does after the
> thinking is done; writing is thinking.
>
> —D. Murray

The third core academic skill is writing. Writing is a little like eating raisins. People tend to love it, to dislike it intensely, or to enjoy it in small doses, as long as it's mixed with something good—like oatmeal cookies. If you belong to one of the latter groups, then the bad news is that you're going to have to write a great deal throughout your graduate training, and do it well. The good news is that you can not only improve your writing but you can also develop a taste for it—even if you don't care for raisins.

The Need for Writing Skills At first, you may be tempted to assume that whatever writing skills have brought you this far in your academic career will be sufficient to carry you through your program and professional career. After all, how frequently are people actually called on to write during their everyday activities? Actually, if you become a counselor, you'll be writing more than you think, especially if you plan to contribute to the field by sharing your research and clinical experiences.

Even if you decide not to pursue a career in academia, you'll be writing case notes, treatment summaries, reports, and correspondence on a regular basis. Your case notes must be clear and accurate in describing what occurred in the session. Likewise, your treatment summaries and reports must be thorough and complete, ensuring that another professional will be able to understand your words and use them to design an appropriate intervention strategy. Similarly, correspondence is another important way you will be representing yourself as a professional.

▲▲▲

Learning the Hard Way
Susan's Story

I N MY FIRST INTERNSHIP as a school counselor, I had the chance to present a guidance unit for students in the third grade. I decided, with the approval of my supervisor, that I would send a letter home to the students' parents introducing myself and explaining the purpose of the guidance unit. Like many interns, I was always busy, so I frantically wrote the letter late one evening, quickly showed it to my supervisor, and then sent the letter out to parents. Within three days, the school had received two telephone complaints about the misspellings and grammatical errors in my letter. In addition, one parent returned the letter with each of the three mistakes circled in red, along with a written note admonishing me to review basic grammar rules and improve my writing skills before sending another letter on school stationery.

I felt humiliated! My supervisor was embarrassed, the principal was angry, and the parents were concerned about the quality of their children's education. I realized that I had made several foolish and serious mistakes here. First, I didn't take seriously my responsibility as a writer. Instead, I assumed that people would understand my meaning and give me the benefit of the doubt because I cared so much about the students. My second mistake was relying on my computer spell-check program to catch all the misspelled words. Finally, I had imposed on somebody else to carefully proofread my writing for me. As a result of my carelessness, my professional reputation suffered.

Fortunately, my story didn't end there. My internship instructor urged me to take that parent's advice and referred me to the campus writing lab. At first, I felt ashamed about going to the lab, especially because I was near the end of my school counseling training. Now I'm glad that I went. If I'm going to be a good counselor, I need to communicate effectively in writing, as well as in speaking.

P.S. One reason that I've written this story is to share with other students an important lesson that I learned the hard way. Another reason is to show you that I can write clearly and spell correctly!

▼▼▼

As a trainee and professional, you will be expected to express yourself clearly and to write in a style appropriate for your audience. Those conventions may feel stifling or rigid, but they are the minimum requirements for professional writing. When you write a term paper, research report, thesis, or dissertation, you'll want to have handy a copy of the *Publication Manual of the American Psychological Association* (5th edition, American Psychological Association, 2001). Baird

(1998) has written an excellent resource for writing effective case notes and summary reports.

"Oh, how boring!" you might think. "Where's the opportunity for me to express myself as a creative person?" Don't despair. You'll probably find that using the *APA Manual* will actually help you improve your ability to express yourself. Another helpful and much more entertaining guide is *The Elements of Style* (3rd edition, Strunk & White, 1979). Writing well, in a manner that is engaging and comprehensible to the reader, doesn't require you to be boring—just clear.

■ ■ ■

EXERCISE 4.5 Writing Twice-Told Stories

Take a few minutes to write down a story about yourself that you have often told others. For instance, you might have told others how you met your significant other, the way your family spends its vacations, or how you acquired your nickname. A friend's favorite story is how he was lost for several days in the Everglades! No matter what your story is, write it down. Write it out completely, imagining a listener hearing the words as you write them, anticipating the questions a listener might ask you, and providing enough detail so that the event or memory is captured as vividly as possible (Metzger, 1992).

In a couple of days, make the time to write down another story. Then, a couple of days later, write down another. As you practice, you'll find that writing comes more effortlessly. Expressing yourself through the written word, finding your own voice, and saying what you want to say will become second nature.

■ ■ ■

Learning Writing Skills   Earlier, we said that writing is like eating raisins, so now we'll present you with another metaphor. (Metaphor, by the way, can be a great way for you to express yourself.) Writing is also like playing a musical instrument. When you're learning to play an instrument, you have to focus on the mechanics under the careful guidance of an instructor. Where do I put my fingers? How do I hold the instrument? How do I read music? The answers to those questions come with regular instruction and diligent practice.

The same answers apply to writing. If you haven't mastered some of the basics of composition and grammar, seek instruction and begin practicing. As you practice, you'll find that soon you no longer worry about the basics. A musician progresses from struggling to reach the high notes to striving to improve his or her tone and phrasing. As a writer, you move from attempting to write transition sentences to focusing on being more concise, vivid, and engaging. Along the way, you set higher expectations for yourself as a writer, and you probably find that writing becomes easier and more enjoyable.

If you haven't already done so, consider asking other students to join you in your writing exercises. Read each other's work and talk about it. As you read one another's writing, focus on what stands out for you as particularly vivid, clear, and organized. Take risks with your attempts to express yourself, stretching yourself to engage fully in the process and reaching to pull out of the air the words to give voice to your experience.

■ ■ ■

EXERCISE 4.6 Reading
A Writing Exercise

Read. Read novels. Read newspapers. Read journals. Read the backs of cereal boxes. Read. Now go back and improve one of the "Twice Told Tales" that you wrote.

■ ■ ■

You've probably guessed by now that this section on writing focuses primarily on practice. Of course, the practice can take a variety of forms. In Chapters 1 and 2, we recommended that you keep a journal to document your training journey. The habit of keeping a journal is not only a wonderful way for you to reflect on your experiences but also a great technique for practicing the craft of writing. As the process of capturing your thoughts and expressing your feelings becomes a daily ritual, you can then read back over your journal to hear the emergence of your own voice and to recognize when it's particularly authentic and clear. Those are the occasions that you'll want to pay attention to and build on as you work on improving your writing strengths. The journal has the added benefit, by the way, of allowing you to discover things for yourself in your own time and place. Many students report that writing a journal, especially during their practicum and internship experiences, helped them see not only important issues regarding their clients but also vital information about themselves as counselors. If Chapters 1 and 2 didn't convince you to keep a journal yet, we hope that this third time is the charm.

Structuring So far, the writing exercises we've offered have had the feel of narratives, or stories, that take form as you're writing them. Now you're ready for a different type of skill. The next exercise is to put some structure into your writing.

■ ■ ■
_____

EXERCISE 4.7 Structuring
A Writing Exercise

Remember the topic that you investigated in the section of this chapter on researching? Imagine that you will be writing a paper about it. The paper may be expository, or it may be a research project. You choose. Then develop an outline for the paper. What are the most important areas to cover? How do those areas arrange themselves into headings and subheadings? Is there a natural or implied sequence in the headings and subheadings? Write down possible transition sentences you would use to connect the various components of the paper.

_____
■ ■ ■

When you've finished this exercise, applaud yourself. Organizing your material can be tough, but it's essential if you want others to be able to understand what you've written. Even when you write case notes, you may find that your supervisor asks you to follow a specific organizational structure. The ability to organize, along with your understanding of the writing conventions mentioned earlier, will help you appropriately frame your writing.

Mindful writing—taking care to give voice to your experiences and ideas through the written word—is a skill that you can develop with practice and feedback. We think you'll find that it's well worth the effort because the improvements will not be limited to your writing. You'll find that you will also know yourself better, think more clearly, and trust your creative hunches more.

Presenting

A speech is like an airplane engine. It may sound
like hell but you've got to go on.

—William Thomas Piper

The Need for Presentation Skills The fourth core academic skill is presenting. "Presenting?" you may be saying. "What do you mean? I want to be a professional helper—somebody whose career is listening and responding to clients." Although it may be true that you will do most of your therapeutic work with individuals and small groups, sooner or later you'll be asked to share your expertise with others, and that process will often take the form of a presentation.

Many graduate courses require that you gain some experience in presenting your ideas to other students. As a matter of fact, in one graduate program, the last two weeks of all courses were devoted to student presentations. Some cynical students claimed that the instructors were simply tired of teaching. There may be some truth to that idea, but it's more likely that the instructors realized the importance of effective presentation skills.

If you're wondering why counselors and therapists need presentation skills, keep the following in mind. School counselors are regularly asked to present guidance units for classes, educational programs for parents and community members, and training sessions for school personnel. Family therapists are often called on to present educational programs to the public, psychoeducational programs to groups, and reports to boards, funding agencies, and local governments. In addition, many counselors and therapists find that presenting at state, regional, and national conferences enhances their own professional development while building a community of colleagues that can extend across the country. For counselors and therapists in private-practice settings, offering mental health-oriented programs to community members is often an effective strategy for finding appropriate clients and referral sources.

Learning Presentation Skills Presentation skills are undoubtedly essential for succeeding as a practitioner. Like many important skills, though, successful presenting is a craft that takes time to master. One obstacle to overcome is the common fear of public speaking. Another barrier is that you may not view yourself as a public speaker. If you don't have a dramatic flair or enjoy being the center of attention, you may assume that you're not cut out for public speaking. However, being a "good counselor" and a "good presenter" are not mutually exclusive. In fact, people who are successful in both roles have several important characteristics in common:

- **Focus.** They give an endeavor, whether it's counseling or presenting, their complete attention.

- **Preparation.** They take the time beforehand to ensure that they know what they need to know. They also stay current and use appropriate resources and technologies to provide the best service.

- **Competence.** They may not always feel comfortable, but they believe in their own abilities.

- **Tolerance for ambiguity.** They understand that few things in life are concrete and that nothing is static. They allow themselves to trust the process and stay immediate.

The list could go on. Presenting, like other skills, requires that you practice and be open to feedback if you are to improve. The good news is that Heppner and his colleagues (1999) found that practicing increased students' self-efficacy ratings and thereby increased their confidence in presenting. Some students who participated in practice presentations also found that they felt more confident that they could contribute important information to the field. Furthermore, students evaluated practice presentation sessions as a useful educational tool. The researchers found that presentations not only were an effective way to learn public speaking but also promoted higher order thinking skills. (These findings provide vindication for those instructors who require student presentations.)

It's likely that there have been many times when you have been practicing your presentation skills without even realizing it. We're talking about being in class, being fully present, and participating in the learning process in as many ways as possible. Class participation (the two words that stir great dread in students who are a little shy) can help you read mindfully by improving your comprehension, keeping you focused, and helping you synthesize and build unique connections between concepts. Furthermore, if you assume that you'll be participating in class, you're more likely to read the reading assignments carefully and systematically, preparing questions in advance.

Participation Anxiety For you, the idea of class participation may be rather unpleasant. Deborah, for instance, found that when she started to share an idea or respond to a professor's question in class, she would immediately flash back to the time she threw up in front of her fourth-grade class. Of course, she knew that she was very unlikely to repeat that scene, but even recalling her sense of profound embarrassment would make her recoil and flinch. By the time Deborah regained some composure, the opportunity for participating had passed. Over time, she simply quit trying to contribute her comments.

Similarly, in Chris's first graduate classes, he found that his face would feel hot whenever he spoke in class. He began to fear that he was blushing, and although he couldn't identify what would make him feel so self-conscious, he decided to stop speaking in class.

Unfortunately, both Deborah and Chris taught themselves not to participate. In doing so, they not only deprived themselves of opportunities to connect more deeply with the course material but they also created an additional stressor for themselves. Every class period became stressful because they dreaded that they would have to speak in class.

Certainly, some faculty members can be intimidating when they put on their "game faces" and challenge students in class. Keep in mind, however, that if you're having a problem with a particular faculty member, your first and best option is to make an appointment to discuss the issue directly with the person. If that doesn't help to address your concerns, then by all means contact your advisor, another faculty member, or the program coordinator.

In many cases, though, students who are worried about participating in class are apprehensive regardless of the instructor. If you're plagued by participation anxiety, consider that all of the following are actually forms of participation:

- asking questions
- summarizing to ensure comprehension
- reflecting critically while in class, either by taking notes or writing down questions to ask later.

The class experience is yours—you're entitled to it. You can do with it what you please. If you walk out of class not understanding something because you didn't ask, you've made a choice to accept less than you deserve. You can also choose to push yourself to improve your participation habits. For example, you can set a goal for your participation. Maybe this week you'll ask one question. Next week you can make a connection between two different concepts. Another strategy is to ask your instructor for help. If you have an instructor with whom you feel relatively comfortable, ask her or him for some time to talk about class participation. The two of you can identify some ways to ease you into participation.

■ ■ ■

EXERCISE 4.8 Preparing and Practicing

Take the topic you've been investigating as you've read through this chapter. You now have an outline for a paper, so use it to formulate a ten-minute presentation. Ask your study group if you can present it to them for their feedback on your presentation style.

■ ■ ■

This exercise worked for Adrian, who was very apprehensive about public speaking. She asked her statistics study group if they would listen to her presentation on human development and give her suggestions for improvement. The students not only listened and gave advice but also shared their own fears of public speaking. Soon, all the students in the group were sharing tips, encouraging each other, and providing general support. If you don't have a study group yet, ask your roommates or classmates to serve as an audience for you.

Improving Your Presentations When preparing for your presentations, remember that you want to challenge yourself and your audience. Ideally, you and the people to whom you're speaking will come together to share ideas and look at your topic in new ways. You can help your audience reflect critically on your topic by deciding what points you want to make and identifying the most effective ways to do so. People enjoy being challenged if you provide sufficient support.

Borrowing from Yoder (1999), we offer the following practical tips for improving your presentations.

- **Organize the presentation.** Decide how you want to present the information (for example, lecture, discussion, group activities) and how much time you want to spend on the various parts of your presentation. Some people follow the presentation rule, "Tell them what you're going to tell them. Tell them. Then tell them what you told them." You can use that rule if it helps. The "tell 'em, tell 'em, tell 'em" approach does tend to be systematic and can help you stay organized. If the idea of planning out minutes seems too rigid, then you may just want to plan approximately how much time you'd like to spend on each area.

- **Know the audience.** Does your audience consist of other students whose knowledge base on the topic is similar to yours? Or are your audience members relative newcomers to your topic? You'll present differently based on the audience's needs. Similarly, if your audience is a class of third-grade students, you'll likely present differently (be more active, use different words and expressions, have a shorter time frame) than if your audience consists of national conference attendees.

- **Practice.** Practice more than once. If you can't find an audience with whom to practice, practice in front of the mirror. Go through the entire presentation more than once so that you develop a sense for timing, clarity, and organization.

- **Prepare for pitfalls.** You might expect 30 people to show up and find 5 in the room. Or 150! You might reserve the last ten minutes of your presentation for a question-and-answer period and find that not one person has a single question. You might plan to use Power Point and then realize there is no equipment in your room. What do you do in these situations? Try to anticipate what might throw a kink into your works and have a backup plan. Better yet, have several backup plans. A favorite professor used to always carry several case studies with him whenever he presented. He said:

  > If all else fails, no one talks, the electricity goes out, no one understands my points, or I forget everything I was going to say, I can pull out these case studies, pass them around, and say, "Okay. What do you all think?" I rest easier the night before the presentation knowing that I have that to fall back on.

- **Know your subject matter.** We recently attended a presentation in which the speaker consistently described her research findings incorrectly. The result was confusing and frustrating. Be sure to know what you're talking about, including understanding the meaning of figures and graphs that you use to supplement your talk. Similarly, have plenty of examples ready to help the audience understand your point.

- **Keep it lively.** Many people use technology (Power Point, videos) in their presentations so that they won't have to carry the ball alone in lecture format. Other options include role plays, group activities, panel presentations, and just about anything else you can imagine. Thinking creatively about how you can best communicate your ideas will likely improve your presentation and keep audience members interested. One caution: try to avoid being too cute. Some examples or metaphors can only be carried out so long before the audience starts to grow bored or (worse) groan.

- **Ask for feedback.** Receiving feedback on your presentation can be enormously valuable, but remember that you may be your own best evaluator. As Rogers (1961) wrote, "People can trust their own experiences; evaluation by others doesn't have to be our guide." In class, as well as conference, presentations, the presenter typically receives some type of evaluation. Occasionally, especially at conferences, the evaluations will provide information that is not necessarily helpful. Some unhelpful comments include: "room was too cold," "room was too crowded," "I thought this was something else," "I work with the elderly, so this topic didn't really pertain to me." At times, though, an insightful participant will make a comment such as, "The section on unique characteristics was especially helpful. The part about the relationship could have been more thorough."

  Frequently, presenters will find that the evaluations are consistent with their own take on the presentation. They know, for instance, that they rushed the ending or lost their focus a little in the middle. The point is, then, to read the evaluations, but don't be crushed if one of your audience members didn't like your presentation. Pay attention to your own evaluation of your performance and set goals for next time.

- **Watch others present.** Attend presentations whenever possible and critique them for yourself. What worked? What didn't? Learn from the successes (and mistakes) of others.

- **Use your emotional arousal.** Finally, and perhaps most important, use your emotional arousal by channeling that energy into productive work. Whenever you find yourself starting to tense up and worry, decide what particular task you can carry out to prepare for your presentation. Perhaps the task is to design your handout materials, develop your Power Point presentation, imagine yourself successfully articulating your major points, practice your delivery, or just enjoy a relaxing run. Whatever the specific task, you're transforming that worry and tension into positive and productive preparation—and the more prepared you are, the less anxiety you'll feel.

■ ■ ■

EXERCISE 4.9 Imagining Success

Prior to giving a presentation in class, take time to imagine yourself as successful. Find a quiet, private place and sit or lie comfortably. Close your eyes and imagine that you're in the classroom and that it's time for you to go to the front of the class. You have all your materials ready, your name is called, you pick up your materials and walk confidently to the front of the room. You feel just excited enough to be sharp and energetic. You know your material. You're confident in your ability to present it effectively. Continue to go through your presentation, anticipating questions and feedback, and see yourself as you plan to be. Don't stop the imagery until you have finished the presentation, received applause or acknowledgement, and returned (triumphantly!) to your seat.

■ ■ ■

The tension related to public speaking can be unpleasant and distracting, but as you gain experience in using your arousal, you'll find that you're not just feeling more relaxed, you're also feeling more confident. One technique that we're certain will not work for you is avoidance. Unless you develop your presentation skills now, the anxiety will remain, lurking and waiting for the chance to emerge. Then, when you're called unexpectedly to present, you'll be less prepared to handle it.

■ ■ ■

EXERCISE 4.10 Breathing

Lie on your back with your hands on your stomach. Breathe in and out, paying attention to how your stomach rises and falls with each inhalation and exhalation of breath. Do this for several minutes until you have a sense for what this feels like. Now sit up and continue to breathe in the same manner. Breathing diaphragmatically will help ease your tension and slow you down. It will also improve your voice tone!

■ ■ ■

Take time now to practice this breathing, and remember, many of your peers are just as nervous as you are. You can be great resources for each other, so make the most of this time together and support each other as you try your hand at presenting.

SUMMARY

Being a successful counselor relies, at least to some degree, on your ability to think mindfully about the helping process, your clients, and yourself. Through reading, researching, writing, and presenting, you can savor the pleasures of pursuing knowledge, refining your skills, and gaining personal awareness. Academic skills do so much more than just help you earn good grades—they help you succeed as a counselor.

RESOURCES

For a lively and comprehensive guide to enhancing your academic skills, we recommend Santrock and Halonen's (1999) *Your Guide to College Success.* Don't let the reference to "college" fool you—this book has exercises, tips, and information that's appropriate for academic success in graduate school, too. You can focus on the particular areas, such as writing or taking tests, that are especially challenging to you.

The Company Therapist
http://www.thetherapist.com/Introduction.html

What a fun site! This site is a Web-based drama about the fictional world of a computer company therapist. The story is written by the audience. "The Company Therapist" is an entertaining way for you to improve your writing skills.

Virtual Classroom

http://www.enmu.edu/virtual/virt.html

This site offers assistance in integrating technology into K-12 instruction. It includes course templates, examples of Web courses, and instructional issues. This is a great site for school counselors.

Study Skills Self-Help Information

http://www.ucc.vt.edu/stdysk/stdyhlp.html

This site provides information on developing good study habits. It covers skills in scheduling time, setting priorities, and taking notes and has many other helpful study guides for students.

Guide to Selecting Statistics

http://trochim.human.cornell.edu/selstat/ssstart.htm

This site walks you through a simple question-and-answer process to select the proper statistics for your research design. This site is especially useful to students new to the area.

REFERENCES

American Psychological Association (2001). *Publication manual of the American Psychological Association* (5th ed.). Washington, DC: Author.

Adler, R., Rosenfield, L., & Towne, N. (1989). *Interplay: The process of interpersonal communication.* New York: Holt, Rinehart & Winston.

Baird, B. N. (1998). *The internship, practicum, and field placement handbook* (2nd ed.). Upper Saddle River, NJ: Prentice-Hall.

Bloom, B. S., Englehart, M. D., Furst, E. J., & Krathwohl, D. R. (1956). *Taxonomy of educational objectives: Cognitive domain.* New York: McKay.

Csikszentmihalyi, M. (1997). *Finding flow: The psychology of engagement with everyday life.* New York: Basic Books.

Damasio, A. (1994). *Descartes' error: Emotion, reason, and the human brain.* New York: Putnam.

Erickson, M. H., Rossi, E. L., & Rossi, S. I. (1976). *Hypnotic realities.* New York: Wiley.

Frye, M. (1995). Oppression. In M. L. Andersen & P. H. Collins (Eds.), *Race, class and gender: An anthology* (2nd ed.; pp. 37–41). Belmont, CA: Wadsworth.

Goleman, D. (1995). *Emotional intelligence.* New York: Bantam Books.

Heppner, P. P., Rooney, S. C., Flores, L. Y., Tarrant, J. M., Howard, J. K., Mulholland, A. M., Thye, R., Turner, S. L., Hanson, K. M., & Lilly, R. L. (1999). Salient effects of practice poster sessions on counselor development: Implications for research training and professional identification. *Counselor Education and Supervision, 38,* 205–217.

Hergenhahn, B. R. (1992). *Introduction to the history of psychology.* Belmont, CA: Wadsworth.

Hoskins, C. M. (2000, August). Get a life! Top 10 list for a first-year student. *Counseling Today, 43,* 32, 36.

Jung, C. G. (1965). *Memories, dreams, reflections.* New York: Vintage Books.

Langer, E. (1989). *Mindfulness.* Reading, MA: Addison-Wesley.

Langer, E. (1997). *The power of mindful learning.* Reading, MA: Addison-Wesley.

Martindale, C. (1981). *Cognition and consciousness.* Homewood, IL: Dorsey Press.

Meltzoff, J. (1998). *Critical thinking about research: Psychology and related fields.* Washington, DC: American Psychological Association.

Metzger, D. (1992). *Writing for your life: A guide and companion to the inner worlds.* San Francisco: HarperCollins.

Presbury, J., Echterling, L. G., & McKee, J. E. (2002). *Ideas and tools for brief counseling.* New York: Merrill/Prentice Hall.

Rogers, C. (1961). *On becoming a person: A therapist's view of psychotherapy.* Boston: Houghton Mifflin.

Santrock, J. W., & Halonen, J. S. (1999). *Your guide to college success: Strategies for achieving your goals.* Belmont, CA: Wadsworth.

Strunk, W., & White, E. B. (1979). *The elements of style* (3rd ed.). New York: Macmillan.

Yoder, B. R. (1999, September). How to survive a presentation and be successful. *Counseling Today, 42,* 22.

CHAPTER 5

▲▲▲
▼▼▼

Embracing Your Stress

There were only two times when I felt stress in graduate school—night and day.

—A colleague

What man needs is not a tensionless state but the striving and struggling for something worth longing and groping for.

—Viktor Frankl

By this stage of your life journey, you've probably heard a lot about stress management. You may even think you already know all you need to know about stress and the need to take care of yourself. However, before you are tempted to skip this chapter with the assumption that you've heard it all before, please read on. Have you ever considered *embracing* your stress? Yes, we're serious! After all, this book is a manual about thriving in graduate school. Developing resilience under stress is an excellent way to thrive throughout both your training and career.

Let's be honest, training is stressful. In fact, all forms of training—athletic, academic, or occupational—are designed to involve increasingly demanding and challenging tasks. Physical exercises, essay examinations, and field placements are all different forms of stress. Of course, successful training also includes plenty of support and guidance as you gradually progress through achievable steps. As an athlete, you can overstress your body by exercising too much or too quickly. If you don't take care, you can put yourself at risk for fatigue, injuries, and physical breakdown.

As a trainee in a helping profession, you can also become overstressed. You may often feel as if you are living by the law of supply and demand. You have limitations regarding your "supply"—resources such as time, energy, money, and information. Meanwhile, your training, as well as life in general, continues to place seemingly limitless "demands" on you— tests, reading assignments, work obligations, and family responsibilities. It's no wonder that you may feel overwhelmed and depleted! As stress is an essential part of your training, why not learn how to welcome your stress? Like an athlete relishing a vigorous workout, you can be enthusiastic when you are engaging in the challenging experiences that help you to grow stronger as a counselor and therapist.

In the first half of this chapter, we offer specific tips for successfully managing the stressors that you will face in your graduate and professional life. We also present important principles for dealing with stress. Balance, harmony, pacing, and a healthy perspective are important components of keeping your bearings along your journey. Remember that although many of our recommendations may appear to be commonsense advice, if you—and indeed most people—fail to practice these steps regularly, then how common are they? Isn't it ironic that, as counselors and therapists, we want to help *others* deal with stress, but we're often reluctant, unwilling, or unable to address our own?

Once we have covered these practical approaches to managing stress—the "how" questions—we turn to the meaning of stress—the "why" questions. In the second half of this chapter, we encourage you to do much more than merely manage your stress as you follow your calling to become a helping professional. We invite you to make your stress meaningful. In his book, *Psychotherapy and Existentialism*, Viktor Frankl (1967) asserted, "What man really needs is a sound amount of tension aroused by the challenge of a meaning he has to fulfill" (pp. 87– 88).

What meaning do *you* have to fulfill by completing a challenging and rigorous training program? You're going to graduate school because you feel a calling to become a helping professional. You know it is not an easy journey, but how meaningful is it to you right now? Certainly, you realize that attending graduate school adds stress to your life. You have made a public commitment by embarking on this adventure, but you have no guarantee that you will succeed. How will you make that stress worthwhile? What point is there to the struggles and frustrations you must encounter in your training?

You might be wondering how your life experiences would change if you actually expected—even looked forward to—the stress that is inevitably part of a productive training and professional career. We believe your outcome would be considerably different! Like an oyster that transforms an irritating grain of sand into a pearl, you have the chance to embrace stress and eventually create something beautiful.

▲▲▲

Stressed Out
Bill's Story

THE YEAR 1991 was a very stressful time in my life. I had just returned home after serving several months in Saudi Arabia with the Air National Guard during the Persian Gulf War. My mother died very suddenly of a massive stroke. My marriage of eleven years was crumbling. On top of all that, I had just started a graduate program in counselor education. The demands on my life were overwhelming!

By October of that year, I was completely stressed out. I began the painful journey of a separation and divorce, moved into an apartment, started visitation with my son every other weekend, and watched helplessly as my bank account dwindled into nothingness. I found myself feeling isolated and alienated from others and quite depressed and lifeless.

How did I survive? Faith and hope helped tremendously. I believed that the stressful time would not last forever and that I would become stronger, wiser, and more compassionate from enduring the pain of those life events. A few very close friends and family members also enabled me to keep going because they accepted my situation, supported and encouraged me, and truly lightened my load as I made this difficult journey. I am very thankful for the people who allowed me to vent my anger, shed my tears, and express my fears. I am also grateful that I had the courage to seek professional therapy, and the therapeutic relationship empowered and strengthened me to move on with my life.

I learned to take responsibility for my own life (and my thoughts, feelings, and actions) and became intentional about eating better, sleeping more, and exercising regularly to regain my energy and relieve some of the pressure in my life. The people who really cared about me never gave up on me, and as a result, I learned to never give up on myself.

▼▼▼

STRESS

We learn the rope of life by untying its knots.

—Jean Toomer

Do you ever watch nature programs on television? It seems like every one of those shows features some hapless insect, bird, or mammal being eaten by another animal. On a recent program, a narrator calmly explained how the world is divided into predators and prey. To illustrate the concept, a mink was shown dragging along a reluctant muskrat to dinner—presumably as the main course, rather than a companion. While a cow was shown grazing, the narrator pointed out that some creatures are herbivores. The program went on to present a sampling of carnivores—a weasel enthusiastically chewing on a mouse—and omnivores—a raccoon eating a fish and, for dessert, a plant. The narrator concluded by asserting that at the top of nature's food chain are humans, who are the only species on the planet without a natural enemy.

So humans have *no* natural enemy. Well, isn't that interesting news? If that's the case, why are so many of us dying before our time every year? For Americans, the answer is a line from "Pogo," a comic strip from years ago—"We have met the enemy and he is us." Suicides and murders are among the top ten killers. Our own behaviors—smoking, poor nutrition, and lack of exercise—are also major contributors to our early deaths. One factor, however, is a common thread among all the major causes of death. That factor is stress. Many researchers now believe that stress is involved in more illnesses than any other single contributor known to science. Our problem as human beings is that even though we are at the top of the food chain, what seems to be eating us is stress.

In this section, we discuss stress and recommend some practical ways you can prevent the negative physiological consequences of stress reactions.

In the second half of the chapter, we move beyond these coping strategies to explore what you can learn and gain from your encounters with stressors to thrive in your training.

In a very real sense, stress is a natural part of living. Stressors are any demands placed on you by life events and circumstances that require your attention, time, or energy. Not all stress is bad. In fact, you may feel bored, empty, and unfulfilled without enough stress in your life. As we mentioned in Chapter 4, a certain level of stress can enable you to perform at your best, but too much may deplete and overwhelm you. Would you ever study for a big test and put in all the necessary time for an important paper if you didn't feel some stress about your performance? Yet when examinations, papers, relationships, and work are clamoring for your attention all at once, you can quickly feel overwhelmed. At these times, you are in a state of distress. Your life demands are far exceeding your personal resources, and the results may feel anything but positive.

The Stress of Helping

> One cannot be deeply responsive to the world
> without being saddened very often.
>
> —Erich Fromm

Helping professions are very stressful occupations. The responsibility inherent in counseling and therapy, combined with the professional isolation that often occurs, can cause many practitioners to become so physically and emotionally distressed that they burn out. The promising results of one study (Sowa, May, & Niles, 1994) show that, although counseling is a stressful endeavor, practitioners don't have to feel overly stressed. The researchers found that people with higher levels of coping resources, such as self-care activities, recreation, and social support, reported lower levels of occupational stress. Furthermore, graduate students who had completed stress management courses reported greater coping resources than those students who had not completed such training. This research suggests that graduate school is an ideal time for you to improve your stress-related skills. This is the time for you to take positive steps to handle stress and prevent burnout.

Distress

> The process of living is the process of reacting to stress.
>
> —Stanley Sarnoff

When you begin to feel overwhelmed by particularly stressful events or circumstances, you may notice some signs of distress. First, you may observe any of these physical symptoms: faster heartbeat, dry mouth, and increased sweating and urination. You may also develop indigestion, feel nauseous, develop migraine headaches, and sense pain in your neck and shoulders. You may discover that you are sick more often with colds and viruses. Then you may observe, on an emotional level, that you feel more irritable, fatigued, sad, or apprehensive. You may discover that you laugh nervously or that you have the urge to cry, scream, hide, or argue more than usual. On a cognitive level, you may find that you have more difficulty concentrating and making decisions. Finally, on a behavioral level, you may notice that you act more impulsively, are more prone toward accidents, or feel tempted to smoke, drink, or medicate yourself. You may find it difficult to relax or sleep.

Prolonged symptoms of distress may also include increased blood pressure; fainting; increased secretion of stomach acids, leading to ulcers; and decreased immunity protection against other diseases. The more of these signs you notice in yourself, the more assertively you will need to respond with healthy stress management strategies.

Stressful Events

What you can do is learn to take better care of yourself, now and in the future. Life is filled with events, both large and small, joyful and tragic. Any of these can lead to stress or, when multiplied together, distress. An on-line adaptation of the Social Readjustment Rating Scale (Holmes & Rahe, 1967) measures some of these life events and their impact on us. Take a few moments to visit this Web site:

http://www.teachhealth.com/#stressscale/

and take the inventory. As you monitor the number of stressful life events you have encountered over the past year, ask yourself how you've handled all these events. These researchers suggest that unresolved stress may accumulate over time, multiplying the pressure on your life. Please note that the higher your score, the more attention you'll want to give to healthy stress approaches.

▲▲▲

When It "Hurts Good"
Rachel's Story

WHEN I ENTERED my graduate counseling program, I anticipated a great deal of stress. However, in a smug sort of way, I thought that I was prepared for it. As a massage therapist, I was already in the business of dealing with stress. I ate well, exercised every day, and practiced deep breathing and meditation. I wrote in my journal, sought solitude, prayed, listened to soft music, and all while the sweet fragrance of aromatherapy dispensed itself throughout my house.

These stress reducers worked very well for a while. What I did not foresee was the stress that was to come out of getting to know myself in a more in-depth and revealing way. That first semester, not only did I worry and stress out about the normal things—grades, finances, and relationships—but also my program required me to take a very close look at myself. "This is not what it's supposed to be about," I thought, "I'm here to help *other* people."

Later, a professor explained to me, "You can't expect clients to confide in you their flaws and imperfections, if you are not willing to do the same work yourself." This made sense, but I thought, "I'm not sure that I'm prepared to deal with this AND worry about writing papers."

I stopped exercising because I felt that the time would be better spent studying. I started eating a lot of those little snacks from machines to quell my anxiety. Meditating was out because statistics problems kept popping into my "white space." The stress was beginning to consume me.

Fortunately, in my second semester, as I became more familiar and in tune with the therapeutic process of counseling others, I also benefited. I began to discover better ways of looking at things and more effective ways of expressing myself. I was also learning, through my experiences, all of the things that I would want to provide for my potential clients. Of course, there were growing pains, but they were like the soreness that is felt when I am getting a massage and the therapist is working directly on the painful spot. It is a hedonistic pain that hurts—but it "hurts good." I was gaining more from my counseling program than just a master's degree; I was gaining the ability to function more productively in the world.

All this is not to say that I have no more stressful days—for there are plenty. I have come to learn how to balance my schoolwork with exercise, meditation, and time for myself. However, it has been the personal growth through the trials and tribulations of my program that has helped me to become a stronger, healthier person.

▼▼▼

RESPONDING TO STRESS

The ability to effectively respond to stress, like many other skills, varies tremendously among individuals. Some people feel they're falling to pieces if they break a fingernail, but those people are not likely to be admitted to graduate programs in the helping professions. It's a safe bet that you've been able to manage stress pretty well. In fact, you probably can face looming deadlines, car breakdowns, and financial woes without being overwhelmed. However, you cannot put your life "on hold" when you enter training, so the added pressures of graduate school can be a tremendous strain. Now's the time to consider specific steps you can take to better handle stress.

Recent research has suggested that there may be differences in the ways in which women and men respond to stress (Taylor et al., 2000). The "fight or flight" response, which has been a widely accepted model for depicting reactions to stress, may now be supplemented by the "tend and befriend" response. This response describes the tendency of many women to reach out to others during stressful times. The researchers realized that previous research on stress focused primarily on men, and the "fight or flight" response may be an accurate description of most men's reactions to stress. However, women are more likely to reach out to others in their social network and care for others around them during times of stress.

This research does not necessarily suggest that men should respond to stress in one way and women should respond in another. You may want to think about the ways in which you typically respond when stressful situations confront you. The "tend and befriend" response can remind you that you do have options in how you choose to react, live, and be. If you've maximized your "fight or flight" responses, perhaps those perpetual butterflies in your stomach are a reminder of just how good you've gotten at this reaction. Maybe it's time to look at new ways to make the most of the energy that stress might provide you. Reaching out to others, drawing strength from relationships, and contributing to your community are fine ways to transform your stress into connections and creativity. The key is to recognize the possibilities and then take advantage of your own ingenuity to adaptively respond to stress.

■■■
_____

EXERCISE 5.1 Your Success with Stress

You cannot have made it as far as you have in your life without encountering a variety of stressors. Take a few minutes to reflect on how you have successfully dealt with stress by answering these questions.

1. What were the major stressors you faced during the past year?

_____

_____

_____

_____

2. What reactions did you notice yourself having to these stressors?

_____

_____

_____

_____

3. How did you manage to handle your stress?

_____

_____

_____

_____

4. What important lessons did you learn from these experiences?

_____

_____

_____

_____

Keep your stress successes in mind as you read the following suggestions on managing stress. Like Rachel in the preceding story, you may need to remind yourself of the strategies you have already successfully used.

Whether you worry, fight, flee, tend, or befriend, you can develop a wide range of adaptive responses as you manage stress. Consider the following suggestions, recalling the personal examples illustrated in the stories earlier in this chapter. As you read through this section, assess your own stress response strategies.

- **Resting.** This may not be as easy as it seems, but find ways to relax and "let go" of each day's events so that you can get the rest you need. Many people under stress may say they are sleeping "like a baby," but what that really means is that they are waking up crying every couple of hours!

  Adult human beings need between seven and nine hours of sleep to function well. In many cultures, there is also a rest or "nap" time during the middle of each day. Perhaps our parents, caretakers, and kindergarten teachers were on to something. You are, after all, human, and your body must rest to replenish your energy supply. Yet you may be sleep deprived at the most critical times, when you need rest the most. Are you getting the rest you need?

- **Eating well.** Good nutrition is important because it provides your body with the fuel it needs to deal with the daily hassles and struggles of life. Especially because you're leading a hectic life, you need to eat more fruits and vegetables to function well.

  When under stress, you may be tempted to grab quick foods on the run or to skip meals altogether, but eating nothing or foods with little nutritional value, such as Pop Tarts, potato chips, and pizza, will not provide you with critical energy when you need it most. Also, carefully monitor your consumption of drinks with caffeine and alcohol, which you may be using to become alert in the morning and to calm yourself at night. Moderation and balance are the key. How do your nutritional habits measure up?

- **Exercising.** Walking, jogging, biking, swimming, aerobic classes, and weight training are fun ways to improve your fitness level and sense of well-being. However, they also relieve stress and provide you with additional energy to persevere in your training. People who exercise regularly find that they usually rest better at night. Make it a part of your daily routine to exercise moderately for at least 30 minutes.

  Have you ever noticed that when you're under stress, you find it hard to remember things? Studies of people who have suffered prolonged stress show a marked degeneration of the hippocampus, which can lead to poor memory (LeDoux, 1996). The good news is that recent research has suggested that new cells can actually be generated in the hippocampus through physical exercise (van Praag & van Praag, 2000). Spending time in the gym can do much more than relieve stress and improve muscle tone. It may also improve your memory and help you "bulk up" your brain!

  Of course, what you do for exercise is up to you, but make sure that you have some fun with it. A word of caution here— if you have not exercised for quite some time, getting a health screening is the best place to start. And take care! A few precautions, such as stretching your muscles and wearing safety gear, can help you avoid injuring yourself. Remember that your primary goal is to feel better, not tear yourself up. How would you assess your physical fitness at this time?

• **Using humor.** You've heard the expression, "Laughter is the best medicine," haven't you? Well, there is much truth to that sentiment. Laughter releases endorphins in your brain that help to relax and calm you. Humor can also be a powerful therapeutic tool for developing rapport with your clients and promoting their resilience (Goldin & Bordan, 1999). Being able to laugh at yourself is probably the best single sign of a healthy self-concept.

Of course, you can add some humor to your life by renting a comedy movie, watching a situation comedy on television, reading the comics in the newspaper, or reading humorous literature. You can also make a point of being with people who add laughter to your life. Even more important than appreciating humor is actually creating it yourself. You're probably not a professional comedian, but you definitely have the potential to see the humor in the daily aggravations, nuisances, and hassles you encounter. By putting a funny "spin" on such annoyances, you can "thumb your nose" at them and laugh some of your stress away. As Langston Hughes said, "Humor is your unconscious therapy." How's your humor quotient?

• **Relaxing and renewing.** Do something just for *you*—a trip to the hairdresser or barber or a therapeutic massage can work wonders when you are under a lot of pressure. Yoga, prayer, meditation, tai chi or biofeedback classes can help promote relaxation responses. Learning to breathe deeply and slowly can enable you to slow yourself down and allow your soul some time to replenish itself.

• **Seeking professional help.** Talking with someone you can trust, whether it is a therapist, nutritionist, or personal trainer, can provide you with some guidelines for leading a healthier lifestyle. If you're feeling overwhelmed by stress, consider asking for help through the counseling or health center on your campus. Professional helpers can guide and support you through this difficult time. Seeking help for prolonged stress, anxiety, or depression should not be postponed indefinitely. An added benefit to seeking professional help is that you get the experience of knowing what it's like to be a client, which will enhance your empathic skills once you begin working with others.

- **Reflecting.** Confucius once said, "The person who wants too much will always be in need." You may find that much of your stress comes from wanting too much. Monitor carefully what you may merely want and what you really *need* in order to live well. For too many Americans, enough rarely seems to be enough. Watch what you are striving for and keep tabs on your thoughts and attitudes. Negative attitudes can drain you of valuable energy and add insult to injury when you are under duress. An anonymous writer once cautioned, "Watch your thoughts; they become your words. Watch your words; they become your actions. Watch your actions; they become your habits. Watch your habits; they become your character. Watch your character; it becomes your destiny."

  Reflect on your definition of success to determine if it may be driving you toward perfectionism. Compare your definition to this one commonly attributed to Ralph Waldo Emerson:

  > To laugh often and much; to win the respect of intelligent people and the affection of children; to earn the appreciation of honest critics and endure the betrayal of false friends; to appreciate beauty; to find the best in others; to leave the world a bit better, whether by a healthy child, a garden patch, or a redeemed social condition; to know even one life has breathed easier because you have lived—this is to have succeeded.

- **Managing your time.** Set realistic goals and prioritize your life events. Because you cannot do everything or please everyone in your life, you must learn how to say "No" to some things and make room to say "Yes" to your higher priorities (Covey, Merrill, & Merrill, 1994). You can practice ways of saying "No" and "Yes" in the following exercise.

■■■

EXERCISE 5.2 Ways of Saying "No" and "Yes!"

Saying "no" to others is probably difficult for you. After all, you want to become a professional *helper*. Here are some different variations on the theme of declining requests.

- **The polite no.** "I'm sorry, but I really have to pass on your request."

- **The postponement no.** "I might be able to do this in the future, but I can't right now."
- **The considerate no.** "It was very nice of you to think of me and I'm honored you asked. However, I won't be able to help you with that right now."
- **The backpedaling no.** "I'm sorry, I made a mistake. I shouldn't have committed myself so soon. I must either reschedule or back out this time."
- **The forthright no.** "I'm sorry, but I have no desire, time, energy, or inclination to do anything like that. Catch you later!"

Let's face it, saying "no" can be disheartening if you don't consider what priorities you're also affirming when you turn down a request. Each time you say "no" to an opportunity, you're saying "yes" to another, so be sure that every "no" counts for something important. Here are some ways to remind yourself of the positive values and goals you are pursuing.

- **The committed yes.** "I'm determined to do my best in my practicum class."
- **The dedicated yes.** "I want to be sure that I stay a vital contributor to my family's well-being."
- **The playful yes.** "I'm making time for some recreation in my busy schedule."
- **The spiritual yes.** "I'm preserving my time for meditation, reflection, and prayer."
- **The compromise yes.** "Instead of what you're requesting, I can help out in a smaller way."

Think about the last time that somebody made a request that you wished you had declined. In the space below, write out a couple of answers you could have given by combining one type of "no" with one type of "yes."

_____

_____

_____

_____

■ ■ ■

Beyond Stress

Life is at its best when it's shaken and stirred.

—F. Paul Facult

The idea of stress has inspired a great deal of productive thinking, fruitful research, and useful interventions in the helping professions. However, the concept does have its limitations. For one thing, its physiological emphasis fails to capture the complexities and depth of the human experience. When we must confront challenges or endure difficult conditions, we do have physiological reactions. But, as human beings, we are also reaching out to others, creatively coping with threats, courageously sacrificing ourselves, or experiencing spiritual transcendence. Labeling these responses as merely reactions to stress is like using the concept of arousal to capture the essence of romantic passion. It's foolish to reduce our mysterious strivings and deeply powerful emotions to only physical functioning.

Another limitation to the concept of stress is that it does not take into account the creative, transformative powers that human beings can demonstrate under challenging and difficult circumstances. This mechanistic model suggests that humans may be able to reduce the negative impact of stress but can never actually gain positive transcendence through stress. Think about the most important achievements you have accomplished, the greatest lessons about life that you've learned, and the times in your life that you went through the most dramatic positive changes. Our bet is that you did not make these gains without some stress.

Rather than running from stress, consider turning to face it and learn from it. Taking this action now, while you're in graduate school, will strengthen your ability to take good care of yourself later in your career. You'll find that the personal exploration that you engage in during your training experience will remind you of your own resilience and strengths. Embracing your stress can lead to surprising discoveries and delightful rewards. After all, "stressed" spelled backwards is "desserts"!

Resilience Under Stress

Life does not happen to us, it happens from us.

—Michael Wickett

Resilience, the ability to bounce back from life's blows, has been the subject of recent exciting research. By focusing on those people who can be amazingly resilient in times of stress, researchers have uncovered promising results that question the traditional views of stress. For example, some children have been found to be incredibly hardy and to actually thrive under very severe circumstances, such as grim poverty, domestic violence, and negligent institutional settings (Masten & Coatsworth, 1998). In fact, resilience is the rule, rather than the exception, for people who encounter stressful circumstances. When Antonovsky (1990) observed so many people learning how to devise such successful strategies to handle stressful adversities, he coined the phrase "learned resourcefulness" to describe this valuable trait. Marilyn Bowman (1997) made a convincing case that even most traumatic stress survivors show remarkable resilience.

Another promising line of research offers even more encouraging news regarding our resilience during times of stress. Many people actually achieve a positive transformation as they make their way through difficult and threatening situations. Tedeschi and Calhoun (1995), as well as other writers, have documented the dramatic changes and significant personal growth many people achieve under stressful circumstances. As Grotberg (1999) affirms:

> Being resilient does not protect you from pain and suffering. Pain and suffering, however, can trigger resilience responses that help you face, overcome, and be transformed by . . . adversity. (p. 26)

The important implication of these findings is that you are not merely the product of your environment—even if the environment is stressful and challenging. You have the potential not only to survive hard times but also to actually thrive and prosper under stressful conditions.

Of course, when you're feeling overwhelmed by stressors, you're less in touch with your own personal strengths and not as aware of the resources available to you. These feelings can undermine your confidence, sap your motivation, and cloud the once-clear vision you had of your future. At these times, you need to make a special effort to consciously look for your strengths and resources—to search for those clues that point to a successful strategy of thriving.

Making Meaning of Stress

Meaning, not raw facts, is what humanity seeks.

—Alvin Kernan

What makes you resilient under fire? Why aren't you a passive victim of your environment? Fundamentally, you are the master of your own fate because you can choose how to make meaning of your circumstances. Even if you lose everything else, according to Frankl (1969), you still have "the last of human freedoms—the ability to choose one's attitude in a given set of circumstances" (p. 73).

If you decide to find positive meaning in your stress, then you are likely to prevent its typical negative consequences. Thompson (1985) found that survivors of a variety of traumas who identified some positive meaning in their traumatic stress were able to cope better. In another study, those people who were able to find meaning in the death of a loved one reported less intense grief reactions (Schwartzberg & Janoff-Bulman, 1991). Likewise, those who report a greater sense of meaning also experience less distress (McIntosh, Cohen, & Wortman, 1993).

Telling Your Story

You are the hero of your own story.

—Mary McCarthy

What makes humans unique is our ability to create meaning by weaving the raw material of our lives into a fabric of stories (Atkinson, 1995). But your narratives do much more than organize your experiences. The stories that you spin to give coherence and meaning to your life also help form your own identity. They encourage you to take on certain roles, play out particular expectations, and choose some options over others. Yes, you have stories to tell, but your stories also tell you.

Recently, researchers have found that writing about the stressful events you have experienced can produce a wide range of benefits (Smyth, 1998). People who wrote about some traumatic stress experience had significant improvements in their health, emotional well-being, and physiological functioning compared with control participants who wrote only about neutral events.

Once again, we find support for the tremendous value of keeping a journal of your training experiences. The process of telling your story helps you to find some meaning in the challenges you are enduring. One student, Steph, noticed that the length of her journal entries were an accurate barometer of the stress she felt. The more stressful her day, the longer her journal entry. She also found herself returning to write about particularly stressful times.

The mindfulness you bring to your studies can be especially helpful in seeking understanding and insight into your own experiences. As you shift through the rubble of a setback or failure, be on the lookout for those golden nuggets of strengths and resources among the disappointments and mistakes. By looking carefully, you can find plenty of examples of your own resilience, determination, creativity, and courage. Remember, it's also okay to compliment yourself in your journal. When you're under stress, your self-esteem and confidence may suffer, so at these times you can benefit from some reminders of your strengths and abilities.

■ ■ ■

EXERCISE 5.3 The Embracing Attitudes
A Quick Check Exercise

Here are some quick tips for embracing stress successfully along your journey:

- Look for puzzles that intrigue you.
- Involve yourself in meaningful causes.
- Strive for progress—not perfection.
- Forgive yourself and others.
- Take the Serenity Prayer to heart: "Grant me the serenity to accept the things I cannot change, the courage to change the things I can, and the wisdom to know the difference."
- Start a "feel good" file. Keep encouraging notes, cards, letters, and E-mails people send you. Even if you don't have immediate access to these important people in your life, you can find consolation in their words. When you're having a particularly difficult day, pull out your file and read the words these persons have written about you. It will amaze you how uplifting a few of these can be on a stressful day!

■ ■ ■

THRIVING UNDER STRESS

Power is the ability to achieve purpose.

—Martin Luther King, Jr.

Most approaches to managing stress begin by assessing your stressors. For example, Sowa (1992) developed a process by which you carefully list all the stressors in your life, assess how much each is under your control, decide how important each stressor is, and then consider your options. But focusing on all your stressors at once can seem both daunting and disheartening—especially for counseling trainees, who feel demoralized too often already (Watkins, 1996).

Envisioning Your Goals

To truly thrive under stress, begin on a positive note by envisioning your goals. Remember, you are always a work in progress—extending, evolving, and expanding. Therefore, you want to regularly orient yourself to where you are heading—especially when you are going through stressful episodes. During these dark times, your goals can serve as beacons to light your way and keep you on track.

■ ■ ■
_____

EXERCISE 5.4 Mission: Possible
An Exercise in Envisioning

What do you hope to accomplish as a result of completing your graduate program? Reflect on your training hopes and dreams. Once your vision of the future has come into focus, write down your training mission statement. Be sure to develop goals that are positive, specific, and achievable. Knowing why you are going through stressful times can enable you to thrive under stress.

My Training Mission

_____

_____

_____

_____

_____

_____

_____

■■■

Using Your Strengths

You are going to be relying on your personal talents to succeed in your venture. Now is the time to bring your positive qualities to the foreground as you begin planning your strategies for thriving under stress. Earlier in this chapter, for example, you reflected on your success experiences in dealing with stressful events and circumstances.

■■■

_____

EXERCISE 5.5 Panning for Gold:
Uncovering Strengths and Resources

Recalling your accomplishments is a great way to recognize special talents that you may be taking for granted and to remember important people that you may be forgetting. Write an inventory of your strengths and resources.

_____

_____

_____

_____

_____

_____

_____

_____

■ ■ ■

Connecting with Others

Over and over again, researchers have found that social support serves as an important buffer against stress (Sarason, Sarason, & Pierce, 1990). Having traveling companions, the third principle of thriving, is particularly valuable if you're feeling overwhelmed with stress.

A supportive network of friends, relatives, peers, and others can make a world of difference when you're going through an ordeal. In fact, one of the surest ways to thrive in tough times is to reach out to others and face the stressors together. Cultures throughout the world have developed rituals in which family members and friends congregate to deal with difficult events—everything in life from births to deaths.

Talking to a trusted friend or family member, sharing time together, or joining others for a meal can lead you to the truth of the proverb: "A sorrow shared is half the sorrow; a joy shared is twice the joy." Even if your stressful circumstances involve only you, by telling your story to others, your experience becomes an episode of your network's shared history—a piece added to the communal mosaic. Sharing your turmoil helps to reconnect you, during a time when you may feel all alone and alienated, to others who can offer support.

■ ■ ■
_____

EXERCISE 5.6 **The Sea Star II**
A Revisiting Exercise

Returning to the image of a sea star, we invite you to take another look at how well you are thriving on each of these five dimensions: relational, spiritual, physical, emotional, and mental. Using a scale of 1–10, with 1 representing the absence of any sense of thriving and 10 representing your highest level of thriving, rate your current level in each area.

Whatever rating you give to each dimension of thriving, take some time to consider carefully what you can do to move from your present score to the next higher number. Describe the specific steps you can take. As you imagine possible strategies, you may discover that you have more capabilities and resources than you realize. Share your ratings and plan with a friend.

RELATIONAL THRIVING

My current level is a _____. I can move higher by . . .

_____

_____

_____

SPIRITUAL THRIVING

My current level is a _____. I can move higher by . . .

_____

_____

_____

PHYSICAL THRIVING

My current level is a _____. I can move higher by . . .

_____

_____

_____

EMOTIONAL THRIVING

My current level is a _____ . I can move higher by . . .

_____

_____

_____

MENTAL THRIVING

My current level is a _____ . I can move higher by . . .

_____

_____

_____

_____

■■■

STRESS AND CHARACTER

> Character cannot be developed in ease and quiet.
> Only through experience of trial and suffering can
> the soul be strengthened, vision cleared, ambition
> inspired, and success achieved.
>
> —Helen Keller

Loosely paraphrasing Buddha, life is not for sissies. You get knocked around quite a bit by just trying to get on with living, much less striving to realize your cherished dreams. Though advertisements would have you believe otherwise, many of life's bruises and stresses cannot be avoided. Advertisers try to sell the idea that, with the right car, the right body, the right *something*, you will magically be insulated from stress, loss, disappointment, and discomfort. For example, in a recent luxury automobile ad, the caption under the car said simply, "Fire your therapist." For many people, particularly in Western society, the ideal of personal happiness implies that life must be free of any suffering and stress.

It is likely, because you are attracted to the helping professions, that you do not believe personal fulfillment can be found either in static, Eden-like bliss or in a double overhead cam V-8 engine with a turbocharger. It is also likely that your journey toward becoming a counselor began as you struggled to respond to difficulties and painful stumbling blocks in your own life. You are interested in what makes you "tick," and curious about how you are "put together." Perhaps there is something that draws you to looking at your own life head on—even the stressful and unsettling experiences that you sometimes would just as soon forget.

Regardless of how well you may have been shielded by benevolent circumstances, you have faced stressors and endured pain in growing up. Each of us has experienced injuries that originate in important caregiving relationships, in traumatic stress experiences with peers, in unanticipated losses that seemed overwhelming or unbearable. Sometimes, our injuries are not so discrete or identifiable but emerge from a long and repeated experience of unsatisfactory interpersonal relationships or stressful environmental circumstances.

One of the themes that appears again and again in your counseling training is the idea that, though you can never expect to be completely free of painful life events, you can choose how you will respond to them. It is not the particular trauma and wound that determines the person you become. Rather, it is your response to these painful experiences that shapes your process of "becoming" (Rogers, 1961). Even the pains and times of suffering can be seen as rewarding, for they are enabling you to mature and sensitizing you to the anguish of others. As Frankl affirmed, "Through the right attitude, unavoidable suffering is transmitted into a heroic and victorious achievement" (1969, p.88).

The work of converting your sufferings into wisdom and the possibility for new choices is the work of personal transformation. Booker T. Washington once said, "Success is to be measured not so much by the position that one has reached in life as by the obstacles . . . overcome while trying to succeed." Always hard won, never trivial, the process is metaphorically represented by the structure and color of the yin-yang symbol. One side represents crisis, the other side opportunity. The dot in the center of each side means that each experience is embedded in the other. Our personal wounds are such an expression of crisis and opportunity. As a counselor in training, you will find that they are a two-ingredient recipe for transformation and change.

Of course, this transformation is a lifelong project. The work of fully integrating and understanding yourself is never finished, and you have sustained injuries and faced difficulties in life that are still "alive" for you now. These experiences are often well hidden, but sometimes they become open wounds that show up in your relations with others, in your particular sensitivities and needs, and in your unique ways of protecting yourself from new painful events.

Your graduate training will include many courses with a variety of academic and experiential exercises to give you a firm understanding of the counseling field. You may find, however, that your training evokes a parallel process of self-examination and exploration that more fully reveals your areas of sensitivity and defensiveness. These are the "sore spots" that seem to keep getting nudged as you move through your program, especially in work with clients and supervisors. If it's any consolation, you can be sure that you are not the only one whose old wounds are resurfacing during this intensive training. If you are able to skate through your program without the experience bringing up charged issues in your own life, then you haven't fully engaged in your training.

STRESS INTO STRENGTH

> Life is a grindstone. Whether it grinds us down or
> polishes us up depends on us.
>
> —Thomas L. Holdcroft

The poet William Stafford once observed in a personal conversation that, unless one had experienced difficulty and personal distress in life, it would be impossible to be a poet. The same can be said of becoming a counselor. The trick, he observed, was to suffer intelligently and then to share that suffering with others. By this, he meant that you can mine the experiences of your own life for the valuable images, feelings, and responses that characterize you as uniquely human. You can then communicate with others about a shared human situation. In this sense, the particular psychological and emotional stresses that have attended your own growth and development and through which you have suffered intelligently represent personal strengths. These are your true areas of expertise. One form of communicating in the counseling situation is by understanding these areas in others.

The idea that your personal struggles have the potential to be your areas of greatest strength is not some cozy notion that we offer to reassure you. The words "What does not kill you makes you stronger" express something of the experience of having to develop some new talent or strength in response to a particular life wound. History is replete with examples of persons whose genius and wounds were inextricably linked. Winston Churchill, whose oratorial skills galvanized the Allies against Hitler's aggression, stuttered as a child. Django Rheinhart, the first great jazz guitarist, known for his astonishingly unique phrasings, had only two working fingers on his left hand (Hillman, 1996). Maya Angelou, the lyrical writer of transcendent prose and poetry, was mute for nearly five years after she was raped as a child. She transformed her struggles into works of beauty, such as her first work of literature, *I Know Why The Caged Bird Sings* (1970), and has become a marvelously powerful and inspirational speaker.

Carl Rogers, whose work changed the practice of counseling and therapy by emphasizing interpersonal authenticity, warmth, and empathy, observed that his early years were characterized by an "unconscious, arrogant separateness" that emerged from his family's strict religious conservatism and fear of outsiders (Rogers, 1980, p. 28). Reflecting on his inauthentic relationships with other family members, Rogers admitted that "it would never have occurred to me to share with them any of my personal or private thoughts or feelings, because I knew these would have been judged and found wanting" (p. 28).

Think about your own life. In what ways have you transformed the "slings and arrows of outrageous fortune" into your personal character? Perhaps you have used your stress as a teacher. You may have learned valuable lessons about life as the result of these experiences. It may be that you have used your stress as an empathic bridge to help you connect with the anguish and suffering of clients. Or you may have used stress to gain an appreciation for the creativity, resourcefulness, and resilience of humans. However you have used stress, you have done so by embracing it, engaging in the struggle of making it meaningful, and finally emerging from that encounter as a better person and counselor.

SUMMARY

In this chapter, we discussed how stress is an essential part of any successful training program. We described a variety of strategies, such as relaxation and exercise, that you can use to manage stress. We also encouraged you to embrace stress as a means of thriving in your training. Relying on your resilience, connecting with others, making meaning of your stress, and envisioning your goals are ways in which you can transform stress into wisdom, empathy, and character. Finally, we end this chapter as we began, with a thought from Viktor Frankl. You are "called upon to make the best use of any moment and the right choice at any time: it is assumed that [you know] what to do, or whom to love, or how to suffer" (1967, p. 93).

RESOURCES

Because we quoted him so frequently, it should come as no surprise that we recommend the writings of Victor Frankl as a wonderful resource for reflecting on the meaning of your stress and suffering. We suggest you start with *Man's Search for Meaning: An Introduction to Logotherapy*. A survivor of Nazi concentration camps, Frankl describes his harrowing experiences. In this painfully honest and unsentimental account, Frankl (who had intended to write it anonymously, using only his prison camp number) explores the psychology of suffering and our struggle to find meaning. His approach to therapy, which is an outgrowth of his concentration camp experiences, leads us to confront the essence of our existence and challenges us to create a meaningful life through faith and love.

The Medical Basis of Stress
http://www.teachhealth.com/#stressscale/

At this site, you can take either the adult or youth forms of an updated version of the Holmes and Rahe Stress Scale. Steve Burns and Kimberley Burns, who are health educators, also provide helpful and basic information about stress.

ASGS Association for Support of Graduate Students
http://www.asgs.org/

This site provides the following services for graduate students: thesis news, DOC-Talk, professional consultant directory, and computer template disks for APA style.

ResilienceNet
http://www.resilnet.uiuc.edu

This site offers access to the most recent information on resilience, including guides and teaching materials, program descriptions, and evaluative reports. There is a virtual library with full-text publications of articles and reports. An on-site discussion group gives you an opportunity to interact with others interested in resilience.

REFERENCES

Angelou, M. (1970). *I know why the caged bird sings.* New York: Random House.

Antonovsky, A. (1990). Pathways leading to successful coping and health. In M. Rosenbaum (Ed.), *Learned resourcefulness: On coping skills, self control, and adaptive behavior* (pp. 31–63). New York: Springer-Verlag.

Atkinson, R. (1995). *The gift of stories.* Westport, CT: Bergin & Garvey.

Bowman, M. (1997). *Individual differences in posttraumatic response: Problems with the adversity-distress connection.* Mahwah, NJ: Erlbaum.

Frankl, V. E. (1967). *Psychotherapy and existentialism: Selected papers on logotherapy.* New York: Pocket Books.

Frankl, V. E. (1969). *The will to meaning.* New York: New American Library.

Frankl, V. E. (1984). *Man's search for meaning: An introduction to logotherapy.* New York: Simon & Shuster.

Goldin, E., & Bordan, T. (1999). The use of humor in counseling: The laughing cure. *Journal of Counseling and Development, 77,* 405–410.

Grotberg, E. H. (1999). *Tapping your inner strength: How to find the resilience to deal with anything.* Oakland, CA: New Harbinger.

Hillman, J. (1996). *The soul's code: In search of character and calling.* New York: Random House.

Holmes, T. H., & Rahe, R. H. (1967). The social readjustment rating scale. *Journal of Psychosomatic Research, 11,* 213–218.

LeDoux, J. (1996). *The emotional brain: The mysterious underpinnings of emotional life.* New York: Simon & Schuster.

Masten, A. S., & Coatsworth, J. D. (1998). The development of competence in favorable and unfavorable environments: Lessons from research on successful children. *American Psychologist, 53,* 205–220.

McIntosh, D. N., Cohen, R., & Wortman, C. B. (1993). Religion's role in adjustment to a negative life event: Coping with the loss of a child. *Journal of Personality and Social Psychology, 65,* 812–821.

Rogers, C. R. (1961). *On becoming a person.* Boston: Houghton Mifflin.

Rogers, C. R. (1980). *A way of being.* Boston: Houghton Mifflin.

Sarason, B. R., Sarason, I. G., & Pierce, G. R. (Eds.). (1990). *Social support: An interactional view.* New York: Wiley.

Schwartzberg, S. S., & Janoff-Bulman, R. (1991). Grief and the search for meaning: Exploring the assumptive worlds of bereaved college students. *Journal of Social and Clinical Psychology, 10,* 270–288.

Smyth, J. M. (1998). Written emotional expression: Effect sizes, outcome types, and moderating variables. *Journal of Consulting and Clinical Psychology, 66,* 174–184.

Sowa, C. J. (1992). Understanding clients' perceptions of stress. *Journal of Counseling and Development, 71,* 179–183.

Sowa, C. J., May, K. M., & Niles, S. G. (1994). Occupational stress within the counseling profession: Implications for counselor training. *Counselor Education and Supervision, 34,* 19–29.

Taylor, S. E., Klein, L. C., Lewis, B. P., Gruenewald, T. L., Gurung, R. A., & Updegraff, J. A. (2000). Biobehavioral responses to stress in females: Tend-and-befriend, not fight-or-flight. *Psychological Review, 107,* 411–429.

Tedeschi, R. G., & Calhoun, L. G. (1995). *Trauma and transformation: Growing in the aftermath of suffering.* Thousand Oaks, CA: Sage.

Thompson, S. C. (1985). Finding positive meaning in a stressful event and coping. *Basic and Applied Social Psychology, 6,* 279–295.

Watkins, C. E. (1996). On demoralization and awe in psychotherapy supervision. *Clinical Supervisor, 14,* 139–148.

van Praag, F., & van Praag, H. (Producers). (2000, November 21). *Scientific American Frontiers.* New York and Washington, DC: Public Broadcasting Service.

CHAPTER 6

Exploring Yourself

One of the most profound ways in which I can
change myself is to change the story I tell myself
about myself.

—Jerome Levin

If you don't stand for something, you'll fall for
anything.

—Country Song

MAKE PERSONAL GROWTH
YOUR GOAL

As you make your training journey, you need time alone to check
your bearings, process your experiences, and reflect on the discoveries you are making. Like a photographer in a darkroom, you have
been developing a more vivid picture of who you are. And like a novelist, you have been constructing a life story with yourself as the protagonist. Your self-concept, identity, and personal beliefs about the world and
other people are beginning to emerge. The "who I am," "where I stand,"
and "what I stand for" make up the person you have so far come to know
as yourself.

Your training experiences will challenge many of your developing ideas
about yourself. Your first reaction to these challenges might be to hunker
down and defend your self-image and your beliefs. Instead, we invite you
to remain open to new possibilities and ideas. The one certainty about

your journey is that you *will* be changed by it. In fact, a personal transformation is essential to becoming a successful professional helper.

In this chapter, we offer some guidelines for coping with the dramatic changes that you will experience during your training. Even when you're making positive changes, you'll find that they can feel uncomfortable, unfamiliar, and strange. At some level, you may even fear that you're turning into a stranger whom you won't recognize. At these times, remind yourself that you can become a new person while also preserving your basic integrity. Though you may be altering your beliefs, trying out new ways of acting, and challenging your experience of yourself, you can trust that this change process is part of your fundamental identity. Your essential being is always "becoming." Making personal growth your goal is the best way to stay vital, both in your training and in your career.

Whether you realize it or not, you are changing all the time. This change is the unfolding story of your life. The only difference during your graduate training program is that the change will be enormous— like the "growth spurt" you may have had as a child. You'll find yourself rewriting your life story as fast as you can. You are in training to make yourself into a helping professional, and you will find it an exciting process. At your center, you already have the basic ingredients to become who you wish to be. But you need to go through a metamorphosis to fulfill this potential. Such change is always stressful, but you have chosen to undergo this process. Welcome the change! Enjoy the journey!

▲▲▲

Thanksgiving Leftovers
Edna's Story

THANKSGIVING, I recently discovered, can involve other kinds of leftovers besides the turkey, dressing, and pumpkin pie. This year, I was really looking forward to Thanksgiving because it was my first visit home since entering a program to become a therapist. I desperately needed a break and was excited about going home again. It was weird, though—it didn't seem like home anymore. I felt like a stranger in a familiar place. As an undergrad, I had gone to a nearby college and was home nearly every weekend—you know, so Mom could do my laundry and I could talk my parents out of a little more money for the upcoming week. So you might say that I was really never away from home before.

Now I find that playing the role of my parent's little daughter is getting harder for me to carry off like I used to be able to do. I'm just not that girl any more. As we sat at the table on Thanksgiving, I was hassled to "eat up," my uncle was getting drunk, and my father told a racist joke. When I refused to laugh, he accused me of being "politically correct," and later, when I tried to tell people about what I was learning in school, they dismissed it as "psychobabble."

My mother scurried around like a servant and was up and down from the table so many times, filling people's glasses and offering second helpings, that she hardly ate a bite. She claimed not to be hungry because she had sampled so much while she was cooking the meal.

My cousins talked incessantly to each other as we ate and seemed to ignore me. We had been so close when we were younger, but now we didn't seem to have much in common. Then there was my best friend Jeannie, who's going to Tech and studying computer science. She kept talking about how much money she's going to make when she graduates. Dad said, "You see, Edna? You could be making the big bucks if you changed programs. You'll never get rich as a therapist."

I sat there watching these people with whom I had always been so close, and after a while all I could hear was "blah, blah, blah." "Who are these people?" I asked myself. When I was a small child, I thought that when I finally got to sit at the big table on Thanksgiving, I would officially be a successful grownup. But somehow, I felt like I was still at the kids' table. Then it hit me, "I don't know who *I* am! I've been changing so much, I seem to have lost *me* in the process." I realized that I have a lot of leftovers here!

▼▼▼

Why is it that understanding and keeping track of yourself is one of the most difficult tasks you have to do? Perhaps it's because a "self" is not a thing that you can observe and contemplate. Your sense of self is so close and yet so far. As Levin (1992) put it, "The self to which we think we are so close eludes definition and, indeed becomes more elusive as we attempt to grasp it" (p. 1).

Because your self is not a material substance, but rather an experience that is constantly with you, it may seem like an illusion. Part of your self is pure feeling or sensation. When you are "on top of the world," this feeling is vivid, but when you are ill or sleepy, the feeling is vague. Another part of your self is your concept of who you are—your identity. In large part, this self-concept is an active determiner of your behavior and your feelings (Rogers, 1942, 1951). In addition, who you consider yourself to be is shaped by cultural influences. Your family, your gender, your race, and your location on the planet have all contributed to your conception of self. You have entered a training program for helping professionals in which you will be asked to be authentic—to be the self you really are. But, at the same time, you are being asked to change. It can all be pretty confusing.

Your identity is really the story you tell yourself about yourself. You update your identity as new experiences alter your beliefs, your values, and your worldview. Usually, this process is slow and difficult to notice. But now, with your entry into graduate school, you have been thrown into chaos, and you are developing your new identity more rapidly than ever before. It is your goal to become the best counselor or therapist you can become. Goals such as this become a part of your self-concept and then act like magnets that draw you toward your future, helping you to focus your energies and activities. However, your current self is different from the self you hope to become as a counselor. This disparity is probably causing you some distress because you're feeling as if you are a page or two behind in your story.

■■■

EXERCISE 6.1 "I Am . . . " versus "A Counselor Is . . . "

On a piece of paper, write "I AM . . . " at the top. Then take a little time to consider the qualities and characteristics that define who you are, what you believe, and what you can do. Finish the statement by writing the twelve words or phrases that best describe yourself.

Then, on a separate sheet, write "A COUNSELOR IS . . . " at the top. Reflect on the traits and qualities that characterize a successful counselor. Write a dozen words or phrases that describe the person you are training to become.

Finally, do the following task. On a scale of 1 to 10, with 1 indicating that you currently possess none of the attributes of a successful counselor and 10 meaning that you already possess all the traits of a successful counselor, rate where you are now.

Obviously, you would not give yourself a 1. If you had thought you possessed none of the characteristics of a counselor, you would not have entered a training program. You already have many of the attributes you will need to be successful as a helping professional. On the other hand, neither are you a 10. If you thought you had already arrived, you would not have embarked on this training journey.

Whatever number you assigned yourself to show where you currently are, ask yourself this question:"What changes will I notice in myself that will let me know I am on the way to the next higher number?" Instead of immediately trying to get to 10, you'll be taking this process one step at a time. So what do you need to do to get to that next higher number? As soon as you answer that question, you have begun your journey.

■■■

Ontological Security

> You really have to spend time with yourself to
> know who you are.
>
> —Bernice Johnson Reagon

R. D. Laing, in his 1969 classic, *The Divided Self,* created a vivid picture of what it means to have a secure base in life by contrasting this security with an uncertain experience of the world. According to Laing, "an *ontologically* secure person will encounter all the hazards of life . . . from a centrally firm sense of [one's] own and other people's reality" (p. 39). If someone does not achieve this secure base, then the person grows up ontologically insecure, and everyday life seems threatening. Such an individual "cannot take the realness, aliveness, autonomy, and identity of . . . self and others for granted . . . [and] has to become absorbed in contriving ways of trying to be real" (pp. 42–43).

You may believe that in order to be a successful helping professional, you must first attain complete ontological security. But most of us have only achieved an ontological security that is "good enough," and we usually can recognize a small glimmer of our insecurity in the dark corners and recesses of ourselves. Furthermore, when we are in circumstances in which our self-esteem is on the line, we feel this insecurity intensely. Your training program will require you to practice your skills in front of other students, on videotape, or while being observed through a one-way mirror. At these times, you're likely to feel insecure.

You may find yourself so focused on what you are going to say next that you hardly hear what your client is saying.

You may find it reassuring to know that mistakes are unavoidable in such training situations. At first, you may be motivated by the need to preserve your self-esteem by acting as though you know what you are doing. After a while, as you begin to truly listen to what the other person is saying, you will get into the sense of "flow" we described in Chapter 4. In flow, you "lose yourself" and become absorbed in what is happening. The paradox here is that when you get to the point at which you really listen, rather than wait for your turn to talk, you will lose your self-consciousness, but you also will be more ontologically secure.

"I" and "Me"

Your self-system is inherently divided between the core of your self (the "I" awareness) and the contents of your self (the "me" and those experiences that seem to happen to "me"). William James (1890) has been credited with making this distinction between the "I" and the "me." Deikman (1996) said that the "I" is what gives us our subjective sense of existence.

> [S]elf-image, the body, passions, fears, social category . . . are aspects of our persona that we usually refer to when we speak of the self, but they do not refer to the core of our conscious being . . . the "I" is identical to awareness. (pp. 350–351)

The "I" is the center of your existence, whereas the "me" is the object of your perception—the part of yourself you can observe. Erikson (1968) articulated the concept of "identity," or that observed part of us. There is some evidence that we do not begin to form an identity until we are about eighteen months of age and that we do not consolidate our identity until we are in our twenties. If you are recently out of undergraduate school, then you may still be in the process of putting yourself together. On the other hand, if you are a nontraditional learner—someone who has returned to school after years of establishing your identity—then you will be opening up your view of yourself to make room for the new you. In either case, there will be times when your sense of yourself will be less vivid and you will be experiencing ontological insecurity. At other times, you will be observing aspects of yourself that may be surprising and that must be incorporated into your identity. This experience will be what Erikson called "self-uncertainty." You will find that these experiences are way stations on your journey. They mean that you are on course to stabilizing your "I" and consolidating your "me."

THE NEED FOR PERSONAL GROWTH

The battles that count aren't the ones for gold medals. The struggles within yourself—the invisible, inevitable battles inside all of us—that's where it's at.

—Jesse Owens

Being a "Do-Gooder"

You are in a training program for helping professionals because you wish to prepare yourself to relieve the suffering of others. You are altruistic. Perhaps some of your more cynical acquaintances regularly accuse you of being a "touchy-feely type," a "bleeding heart," or a "do-gooder." By these terms, they mean that you are too softhearted for your own good. In an age in which it seems that self-interest and competition are essential to survival, someone with altruistic feelings for others may appear to be unnatural or naïve.

Jeffery Kottler (2000) investigated why animals and humans "do good," and he discovered that it is not only natural but essential to the survival of a species that individual members act altruistically for the good of others. Animals often do it to the point of self-sacrifice. For example, Kottler found that birds will often sound alarms when predators are near. This behavior warns the other members of the flock but also calls attention to the bird giving the warning, placing that individual in danger (Trivers, 1971). Squirrels often give warning while risking their own safety (Sherman, 1980). Bees, termites, and ants have developed societies in which certain members sacrifice themselves to save the rest of the group from attack (Thomas, 1983). Higher order species, such as monkeys and apes, engage in similar behaviors for the benefit of the troop (Gould & Marler, 1987). One adult member of a wolf pack forgoes mating and its own territory in order to help the alpha male and female raise their brood (Masson & McCarthy, 1995). So you see, there is nothing unnatural or rare about altruism.

Of course, we can never be absolutely certain about the meaning of such behavior among animals. However, you certainly have witnessed many instances of self-sacrifice among your fellow human beings. What is even more remarkable about the altruism of humans is that they consciously choose to perform these acts and obviously display tremendous empathy for the plight of others (Kottler, 2000). Charles Darwin considered empathy to be not only natural but also the very basis for an ethical society.

If you had chosen to be, say, an engineer, a physicist, or an accountant, you would expect your training to be centered largely on content and skills. You would be surprised if you were asked to work on who you are. But you have chosen to be a counselor, and the fact is that your success in this field will center largely on your personhood and the way you use who you are. Truax and Mitchell (1971) reviewed more than 100 studies of counselor effectiveness and found that counseling techniques are useful only when the counselor's personality is inherently helpful. Others (Perez, 1979; Seligman, 1995) found the counselor's personality to be the most important criterion for effectiveness with clients. Like members of the clergy who follow their vocation, successful helping professionals have somehow been called to their life's work and are ready to fully give themselves to it. The more willing you are to make such a commitment, the more likely you will be to experience joy and success in the work of helping others.

Having Empathy for Others The journey that has brought you to this training program has taken many years. It is likely that negative experiences in your life have sensitized you to the misfortune of others and stimulated in you the desire to be helpful. Henry (1977) found that, as children, counselors often had experienced illness, loneliness, or bereavement. Counselors were likely to have endured more traumatic events, and their families of origin were often in turmoil. Not surprisingly, counselors were likely to have been clients themselves before entering their training. Such findings have led to the "wounded healer theory" (Guggenbuhl-Craig, 1971; Rippere and Williams, 1985), which suggests that the healer's history of misfortune or trauma confers the power to heal.

Firsthand experiences of loss and suffering are certainly helpful in understanding what life might be like for clients. A counselor trainer of our acquaintance often says, "I wouldn't give you a nickel for a counselor who hasn't suffered." Such painful events in the counselor's life are, however, a two-edged sword. Although they may aid in the establishment of empathy, they could also result in the counselor overidentifying with the client's pain. One thing you will need to check in yourself is how strong your "rescue fantasy" might be. A rescue fantasy is the urgent need to fix the client's situation and then to be appreciated for the extraordinary intervention.

Handling Difficult Topics You also need to explore your value system in order to become more aware of what "pushes your buttons" and what makes you uncomfortable. For example, you may have strong opinions regarding abortion, incest, infidelity, physical abuse, or alcohol and drug use. It's okay for you to have these opinions, but it is important that you work on respecting and accepting clients, even when their opinions or behavior are different from your own.

Often, your discomforts and prejudices may lie beyond your awareness. In such cases, you may communicate to your client, without realizing it, that talking about such subjects is out-of-bounds in the counseling relationship. For example, when he was a graduate student, Jack once met with an admired professor who later that day committed suicide. Although he retained feelings of guilt at having been the last person to see this man alive, Jack subsequently graduated and entered practice. Two years later, while discussing a particularly vexing case with a supervisor, Jack was asked if the client had talked of suicide. At that moment, Jack realized that none of his clients had ever spoken of suicide. Somehow, he had subliminally communicated to all his clients, "Don't talk about suicide—it makes me uncomfortable." After that epiphany, Jack's clients often spoke of suicide.

Like Jack, you may unconsciously hope that your clients do not bring up certain topics in counseling because they might make you feel threatened or helpless. Do you know what those topics are?

■■■
_____

EXERCISE 6.2 Things I Hope My Clients Never Say
An Aversion Exercise

Listed below are some of the things clients have said to us. As you read them, imagine that the client is speaking directly to you. Try to identify the feelings you have as you read these quotes. Write your immediate reaction in the space below each quote, then think about what you could say that would be useful to the client:

1. "You look awfully young. I'm not sure you could understand a problem as deep and complicated as mine."

_____

_____

2. "I was raped last night."

_____

_____

3. ". . . and Goddammit! I'm so fucking pissed off at her that I just can't think about anything else!"

_____

_____

4. ". . . I don't know, they just told me I had to be here. I don't have a problem."

_____

_____

5. "I come in here week after week and spill my guts and all you do is listen. I don't think this is helping."

_____

_____

6. "I've been to lots of counselors, but they were the pits! They had no idea how to help me. But I get the feeling that you are the one who can solve my problem."

7. "How about meeting me this evening at that bar down the street? I'd like to get to know you better."

8. "I've tried everything to get past this problem. I'm pretty discouraged. If you can't help me, I guess it's all over."

9. "You don't really care about me, you're just paid to listen—but you don't really care."

10. "There is something I have been wanting to tell you, but I am not sure you would understand . . . I'm gay."

11. "You remind me of someone I knew in college that I really hated."

12. "I was sexually abused as a child."

_____

_____

As you read some quotes, you may have found yourself hoping that your clients will never say something like that to you. To which statements did you have greater confidence responding? How did you develop this self-assurance? Which quotes were most threatening to you? How will you go about developing the confidence to respond to these statements?

■ ■ ■

Consider Counseling for Yourself

The key to understanding others is to understand oneself.

—Helen Williams

The importance of counselor self-knowledge and self-awareness cannot be overstressed in the counseling relationship. You "must be able to differentiate between counter-transference reactions that are triggered by client transference, and those that are projections of unresolved personal conflicts" (McLeod, 1998, p. 364).

Although none of us will ever be problem free, it is our responsibility as counselors to always work to maintain "personal soundness." After reviewing the evidence, McLeod (1998) concluded that successful counselors "are people who exhibit higher levels of general emotional adjustment and a greater capacity for self-disclosure" (p. 351). Many counseling programs advocate personal counseling for their trainees. Besides being a great way of learning more about yourself and the therapeutic process, participating in counseling for yourself can be a powerful means to a more deeply empathic understanding of your clients. According to McLeod, there is also considerable evidence that participating in your own counseling can enhance your effectiveness. Personal counseling can give you "a reliable basis for the confident and appropriate 'use of self' in relationships with clients" (p. 351).

Of course, you don't have to be a paragon of mental health in order to be a successful counselor. All of us have our ups and downs, and counseling is useful for everyone. It helps you "clear the circuits" and stay in touch with yourself when the trials of everyday life make you begin to feel as though you have been "nibbled to death by ducks." Working with troubled clients costs you a great deal of psychic energy and can result in a residual confusion and burnout unless you continually process your experiences. National surveys have suggested that at least three-fourths of all practicing counselors have had at least one sequence of personal counseling (Norcross, Strausser, & Faltus, 1988). Remember, you don't have to be sick to get better!

▲▲▲

It Feels Weird for a Counselor to Be a Client
Robert's Story

I ENTER THE COUNSELING CENTER and take a seat in one of the empty chairs in the waiting room. People are coming and going, counselors are greeting their clients and then disappearing with them down the hall. The only sound following them is the squeak of the hinge as the door closes.

I know this feeling that is permeating my insides. I have had this reaction before, but not for some time. Because I am in my third year of counselor training, I thought I should be past this feeling by now. As I sit in the waiting room, the realization hits me that I have absolutely no doubt that this is what I needed to do and where I needed to be. This is a wonderful feeling! I am proud of myself for taking this step because it contradicts some very unconscious stereotypical masculine notions. By making the phone call and following through with my appointment, I was able to feel good about this decision and not let my internal "critic" voice itself in derogatory ways about my manhood.

Each of us has a personal story to tell and somehow I had lost or forgotten part of my story—what being a client was like. Books can convey a wealth of information and insight about counseling, but actual experience can be the door to true understanding. As my counselor appears in the waiting room, I realize that I have been so focused on learning how to be a counselor that I forgot how much was involved in being a client.

As soon as I sit down in the counselor's office, I am uncertain of my role. All at once, I feel entangled in a psychological web—confused as to whether I am a client or a counselor. I am immediately struck by my focus on the man sitting across from me. I am exploring every facial expression, scrutinizing each of his words, and making mental notes of his every move. I cannot help but compare and make judgments about what my counselor is doing and saying. "How dare you write down what I am saying? Where is the rapport building? I was taught to be present with the client and taking notes was not encouraged. Where are the eye contact, the head nods, and the empathic reflections? I have taken risks to be here and you are scribbling old historical stuff about me on a note pad. What's going on?"

I have learned to deal with a fair amount of ambiguity in my training program and have been challenged to think outside of my traditional gender and cultural mindset, but how to be a client again? I guess that if I expect my clients to make an honest self-assessment, I must be committed to this same quest for self-awareness. I think I am ready to do this.

▼▼▼

Allow Yourself to Mess Up

Life is very interesting if you make mistakes.

—Georges Carpentier

As a new counselor, you may tend to focus on the mistakes you are making with clients. You may even consider these mistakes to be evidence that you were wrong to think you could be a successful counselor. This is your crisis of faith. Be assured that such crises come with the territory. Counselors always make mistakes.

You are probably more sensitive to your mistakes because you really want to be good at this work and you somehow have had the idea that good counselors can do it perfectly. In the book *The Imperfect Therapist: Learning From Failure in Therapeutic Practice*, Kottler and Blau (1989) suggested that it is not mistakes that cause us problems. It is our attempts to avoid acknowledging mistakes that can undermine our confidence and effectiveness. As Kottler and Blau point out, therapeutic "failures" can lead to positive results because they can:

promote reflection, stimulate change, provide useful information, give feedback on the impact of action, encourage flexibility, teach humility, increase resolve, improve tolerance for frustration, and foster experimentation. (p. 163)

Maybe you have been shown videotapes in which master counselors are modeling their approaches to counseling. You are probably in awe of some of them. You may also feel overwhelmed and doubt that you could ever do counseling with the skill level they display. Please remember that these people have been at this work for a long time. Besides, do you think you would ever see the videos in which they really screwed up? No chance!

Explore Your Assets

When you decided that you had what it takes to be a counselor and applied to graduate school, you intuitively felt that aspects of your personality seemed to fit the role. Perhaps over the years, people regularly came to you with their problems, and you wanted to learn how to be more helpful. Hold that thought. You have obviously been able to establish warm and empathic relationships, and several studies have shown that the desire to be helpful to others is perhaps the most indispensable aspect of a counselor's personality. You were correct to think that you had the right stuff.

However, if being a good listener were all there was to successful counseling, then you would already be an accomplished helper. Besides learning the theories and practicing techniques of counseling, you have to liberate "the authentic you" to use in the therapeutic relationship. As Parrott (1997) put it, "A counselor cannot fake authenticity; it is not something you do, but something you are" (p. 28). Being authentic is not easy. We have all been taught to be less than forthright in our social relationships, often to the point of feeling as though we have lost our way. The good news, however, is that under our social veneer, we are all authentic. Underneath is who we really are. During your training program, you will need to find your way back to that person you are. Socrates admonished each of us to "know thyself." In order to do this, you sometimes need to uncover experiences that you have sealed over or put out of your awareness. Socrates also said that the unexamined life is not worth living. Make a commitment to examine your life and find the real you. Although it is often exhausting work, you will find it exhilarating at the same time. And it certainly will make you a better counselor.

Avoid the "Groucho Paradox"

The term "Groucho paradox" (Swann, 1996) comes from a statement made by the famous comedian Groucho Marx, who explained his reason for withdrawing his membership from the Hollywood chapter of the Friar's Club by saying, "I just don't want to belong to any club that would have me as a member" (p. 18). When we are in the midst of a negative self-evaluation, we cannot accept positive feedback from others. When something good happens to us that we feel may be undeserved, our level of self-esteem can actually drop.

As you make this journey through your training program, at times you will find yourself plagued with self-doubt (Egan, 1986). Because you have such high standards for yourself, you will occasionally feel vulnerable and incompetent, discouraged and confused. Your trainers expect this to happen, and they know that because you are being asked to change in ways that no educational experience has previously demanded of you, there will be times when you need to escape. Consult Chapter 5 on caring for yourself during the training experience to keep your balance.

There is the story of a woman, blind from the age of six, who had her sight miraculously restored by a new medical procedure. Prior to this surgery, the woman had done well in school, obtaining a doctoral degree. She married, had two teenage daughters, and held a responsible position in a rehabilitation clinic. With her sight newly regained, she first felt ecstatic, then ambivalent, then depressed. Her whole life, once happy in spite of her disability, began to deteriorate. She alienated friends and family, and her job performance suffered. On the face of it, something wonderful had happened, but the results were feelings of confusion and emptiness. She had undergone a profound change, and she just didn't know how to "act sighted." All aspects of her behavior had to be relearned, and she felt as if she had lost something terribly important in her life (Swann, 1996).

One would think that a positive change, such as suddenly being able to see, could yield nothing but good feelings. But think about your own situation. You were accepted into a graduate program of your choice. The day you got the letter was probably a major milestone in your life. You initially felt great. You entered your professional training with positive expectations and a little nervousness. Then, because you were expected to change in so many ways, you began to have your crisis of faith: "Maybe I can't do this," "Maybe I was deluding myself to think I had what it takes," "Maybe they made a mistake when they accepted me," "Maybe I don't want to belong to a program that would have me as a member!" It's the Groucho paradox that some have called the "impostor syndrome." You begin to feel as though you put something over on the admissions committee members who believed you were a good candidate for this work.

It is important for you to know that you can expect, from time to time, to have major misgivings about becoming a helping professional. It is part of your developmental process. Despite the fact that you are finally preparing for the profession that has felt like your life's calling and that you are at last able to focus all your course work on this goal, the resultant feelings will not always be positive. You will question your decision to become a member of the helping profession, and you will probably have times when you are really down in the dumps as a result of the changes you are going through. No matter how much you may desire to become the "new you," there will be times when you long for the "old you" and feel you have lost something very important. Gloria Steinem (quoted in Swann, 1996) put it this way:

> Change, no matter how much for the better, still feels cold and lonely at first..because it doesn't feel like home. Old patterns, no matter how negative and painful . . . have an incredible magnetic power—because they do feel like home. (p. 147)

BE A BEGINNER, NOT AN EXPERT

When you forget the beginner's awe, you start decaying.

—Nobuko Albery

As an undergraduate, you probably spent a great deal of time ingesting information to later regurgitate on a test. You may have memorized definitions, names, dates, formulas, or scientific principles without truly understanding them or being able to apply them. You became expert in how to beat the system and make grades, often perhaps at the expense of truly learning. Now you are in a program in which you must go beyond mere information and begin to use concepts to guide your behavior. The test becomes whether you can actually do it, not whether you can talk or write about it.

Your current problem may be that you have spent so many years going through the motions of learning that you have forgotten how to truly learn. You find yourself in a situation in which many of your former strategies will not apply. You are a rank beginner, and you are confused by this new environment. These circumstances certainly make you feel insecure, and you may attempt to cover your feelings of inadequacy by acting as though you know more than you do and by sticking to those areas of knowledge in which you are expert.

However, we are suggesting that you allow yourself to know nothing—to be a beginner. The Zen philosopher Suzuzi (quoted in Kosko, 1993) said, "In the beginner's mind there are many possibilities. In the expert's mind there are few" (p. 44). The Zen master teaches students by confusing them, sometimes using a koan, such as asking them to answer the question, "What is the sound of one hand clapping?" The Zen method of the koan is the way the master convinces students that expertise is precisely what keeps them from understanding fully the truth of a situation. The koan throws the student into ambiguity so that the problem at hand must be approached naïvely. Creative thinkers always behave as if they were naïve beginners, never as if they are experts. There is a freshness and awe to creative discovery that, as Bruner (1973) has said, surprises and delights the onlooker, as well as the creator.

An expert knows how to do things and how to think about things. Expert thinking often proceeds automatically as a convergent problem-solving process. On the other hand, someone who is not an expert must approach each circumstance as novel and must discover fresh ways of adapting to its demands. It is much harder work to stay fresh than to behave automatically. You have to burn a lot of calories dealing with something you have never encountered before. Be careful about becoming an expert at helping, because every person you are helping and every situation in which you will find yourself *will* be novel.

Assimilation and Accommodation

Piaget (1970) stated that there are two major processes by which we develop our knowledge schemas—assimilation and accommodation. You're involved in *assimilation* when you route new information into knowledge structures that you already have in place. The process involved in this type of learning is a mere addition of information or elaboration of previous knowledge. In order to assimilate any new information that does not fit precisely within your existing schemas, you may be tempted to distort it. If you can't hammer the new data into some form that fits your knowledge structures, then you can either reject the information or accommodate it. You engage in *accommodation* when you actually change your own schemas and create new knowledge structures to take in and process new information.

Someone who assimilates but refuses to accommodate tends to become rigid and narrow in dealing with information. Chances are you know people like this. They claim to be experts on everything, but they seem to you to be merely prejudiced and biased in their opinions. They suffer from hardening of the categories. Believe it or not, there are counselors who are like this! You can avoid becoming an expert by remaining open to new information, willing to accommodate—to change the way you see the world—as you encounter new experiences.

Clearly, you must be flexible to accommodate. If, however, you believe yourself to be expert with regard to the new information, you are likely to deem accommodation to be unnecessary. As children grow older and develop what they consider to be a sufficient set of categories or cognitive schemas, they sometimes become refractory or resistant to much of the new information that challenges them to accommodate. After all, accommodation can feel uncomfortable. Everyone knows how insufferable adolescent experts can be and how at this stage parents suddenly lose at least 30 IQ points in their teenager's eyes. Probably the motivation for the adolescent striving for expertise is the feeling of security that comes with the belief that one has everything under control and that no new disquieting mysteries are on the horizon. Adolescents become rigid in their beliefs as a defense against their rapidly changing world. Unfortunately, it is a transparent and pathetic sort of expertise.

Accommodating Information About Yourself

Certainly, you have enjoyed the "aha!" exhilaration of discovering an accommodation that offers new and exciting breakthroughs in your ways of thinking. This is not always the case, however, when it comes to accommodating new information about yourself. Sometimes being open to learning about yourself results in jarring and confusing results. According to some reports, when the astronomer Galileo asked the College of Cardinals to look through his telescope, which was pointed toward the heavens, they refused because they were afraid they might see something contrary to their beliefs. All of us are reluctant to look at ourselves too deeply, because we fear that we will find aspects, beliefs, or values that we didn't know were there and that we didn't want to be part of us. Like the adolescent, we may like to think we know everything about ourselves that there is to know. We can then have the sense of false security, that we are completely in control of our behaviors and attitudes.

In the training program in which you find yourself, you have the opportunity to indeed discover who you are. You will realize that the ambiguity of the koan is rampant in your experiences. Many of your discoveries about yourself will make you uncomfortable, but that happens only because you are human. Humans are not perfect. Karen Horney (1970) said that if we erect for ourselves an "ideal self" and attempt to maintain it, the result will be neuroticism. The only way to be mentally healthy is to accept yourself as you are. Approach the challenge of knowing yourself as a beginner, not as an expert.

HOLD TO YOUR CENTER

> There comes a point when you really have to
> spend time with yourself to know who you are.
>
> —Bernice Johnson Reagon

Graduate school is, to say the least, a demanding venture, and you can easily feel overwhelmed by all you have to do. You certainly need to keep a calendar of your appointments, a daily "To Do" list of your assignments and chores, and maybe even a personal digital assistant, such as a Palm Pilot, to help you set your life in order. Dealing conscientiously with each of the tasks you have scheduled is a fine idea, but take care to hold to your center through all the distractions of your days. It is easy to pay so much attention to the demands of your world and to focus so much on the expectations of others that you begin to disappear. You then become, like Lewis Carroll's Alice, unreal—a thing in the Red King's dream.

> "He's dreaming now," said Tweedledee, "and what do you think he's dreaming about?"
> Alice said, "Nobody can guess that."
> "Why, about *you*!" Tweedledee exclaimed, clapping his hands

triumphantly. "And if he left off dreaming about you, where do you suppose you'd be?"

"Where I am now of course," said Alice.

"Not you!" Tweedledee retorted contemptuously. "You'd be nowhere. Why, you're only a sort of thing in his dream!"

"If that there King was to wake," added Tweedledum, "you'd go out—bang—just like a candle!" . . . "You know very well you're not real" (Carroll, 1896/1991, pp. 173–174)

The Demands of Others

Carroll's message to all of us is that we should take care not to let ourselves be defined by others or allow our self-esteem to be dependent on the approval of others. In these situations, which Carl Rogers (1961) called "conditions of worth," we become acceptable to other people only when we measure up to their standards. If we try too hard to be what others want us to be, we become existentially ill. Ironically, when we feel ourselves losing ourselves and becoming ontologically insecure, we often try harder to validate who we are by seeking the approval of others. We may also distract ourselves by plunging into relentless motion so that we will not notice that we don't feel well. When we become so immersed in our activities that we lose contact with our center—our true self—we fear that the Red King may be waking and we will disappear.

In *The Roman Spring of Mrs. Stone*, Tennessee Williams (1958) described a character's futile attempts at self-distraction by constantly pursuing diversions: " 'the hairdressers at four o'clock, the photographer at 5:00, the Colony at 6:00, the theater at 7:30, Sardi's at midnight . . . she moved in the great empty circle. But she glanced inward from the periphery and saw the void'" (as quoted in Gergen, 1971, p. 86).

Having an impossibly full appointment book and frantically attempting to run a marathon distance at a sprinter's pace can quickly make you feel overwhelmed, but it can also be a way to keep you from looking at yourself. A demanding educational environment requires time management on your part and a more refined vigilance to the cues of professors. So go ahead and buy the personal digital assistant and make sure that you are fulfilling the requirements of your courses. But remember, when you find yourself feeling like you are being hit from all sides by the expectations of others, don't just do something—*be* there. There is much wisdom in that old cliché about stopping to smell the roses.

▲▲▲

Learning from the Inside Out
Teresa's Story

A T THE END of my first year in the counseling program, I felt like I was walking around inside out. I was certain when I started that I wanted to become a counselor, but I didn't know that this would entail such microscopic self-examination. In my classes, outside my classes, in conversations with my fellow peers, I explored so many crevices, dark holes, files that had been shoved away—even those that wanted to remain hidden. It was a relentless process, and many days I came home feeling a mix of exhaustion and exhilaration from uncovering layers of meaning and emotion.

One of the most important discoveries that I made is that I have a great need for people to be happy with me; so much so that I lose myself and my needs in striving to be ALL for everyone. Because of the intensive focus on MY thoughts, MY feelings, MY contributions, and MY beliefs, I embarked on a slow process of change—of wanting to become my authentic self and to shed the self that I THOUGHT others wanted me to be. This process is not easy, and it felt, and still feels, strange—like I had entered into the Land of Fog, and everything in my life became murky. Nothing was clear until I accepted the strangeness and the realization that ambiguity is a state that can be traveled through.

As I muddle through my second year, this is by no means a resolved challenge, but I have learned how to read my own map. And, at least now, I am aware of what I am doing and can forge ahead in hopes that the result of this journey will be to emerge as the self that I am genuinely happy and comfortable being.

▼▼▼

Honor, But Modify, Your Style

Here's a news flash for you—no one has had a perfect childhood. Even when parents have tried to do right by us, we all came into adulthood with unmet needs. To the extent that our needs were not satisfied, we developed compensating strategies or styles in order to avoid the anxiety that arose out of our unique situation (Teyber, 1997). Karen Horney (1970) identified three prominent coping styles that people adopt. She called them the "moving toward," the "moving against," and the "moving away" strategies. These coping styles served to reduce anxiety when our needs were not met as children, but they can prove to be a liability in adulthood because we tend to enact them over and over, even though modifying them would be much more productive.

The *moving-toward* style manifests as the need to please people. Someone with this strategy is compliant and wishes to be seen as unfailingly nice and good (Teyber, 1997). This style results in the need to be approved of by others and in the attempt to meet their needs in an almost servile way. Those with the moving-toward style "suffer under the self-imposed demands that they should be the perfect lover, teacher, spouse, and so forth" (p. 203).

The person with a prominent *moving-against* compensatory style developed an aggressive or rebellious attitude toward parental authority and protects against feelings of vulnerability by attempting to control self and others. Such people are strongly assertive, sometimes to the point of aggression, and they demand of themselves that they should quickly overcome all obstacles and difficulties. They try to control their feelings and to overcome their "bad moods" quickly by an act of will.

The person with a *moving-away* style compensates in situations that produce anxiety by physically withdrawing, avoiding, and attempting to become self-sufficient. Those who employ the moving-away strategy pay for this "by believing that they should be able to work tirelessly and always be productive. They demand that they should be able to endure anything without becoming ruffled or upset and that they should never need help or reassurance from anyone" (Teyber, 1997, p. 203).

■■■

EXERCISE 6.3 Toward, Against, or Away?
A Moving Exercise

Obviously, the three coping styles of Horney (1970) are not mutually exclusive. You employ each of them at different times. All of them serve to ward off your feelings of anxiety. Because of this, you should be respectful of your need to use these compensatory strategies in your life.

STEP 1.

Look at the circles representing the three styles and think about which one you employ most often. Put the number "1" in that circle. Then put a number "2" in the circle that represents your second most favored style, and a number "3" in the remaining circle.

An Exercise in Self-Reflection

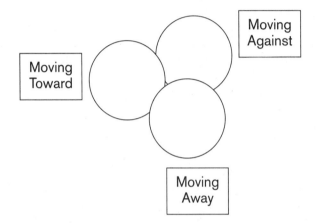

The first thing to think about, after you have completed this ranking, is what purpose your dominant style serves in your life. How is it *helpful* to you? Reflect on recent stressful experiences in which your dominant style successfully dealt with the circumstances. Self-acceptance is a fundamental part of your personal growth. Just as you must honor resistance in your future clients, you must also honor it in yourself.

STEP 2.

There is, however, an annoying paradox involved in these defense styles. They help you to cope with anxiety-producing situations, but they also sometimes get in your way. The paradox is that, although you have adopted these styles in order to compensate for unmet needs of childhood, they sometimes deprive you of getting your needs met as an adult. So the next step in this self-exploration exercise is to think about how this style *interferes* in your life, how it compels you to act in certain ways, and how your style may sometimes be off-putting to others.

STEP 3.

The next time you are in a stressful situation, you have the opportunity to complete the final step of this exercise. Use that opportunity to deliberately refrain from using your favored style. For example, if moving toward is your dominant style, instead of immediately considering how to impress and please others, focus on your own needs and desires in this situation. Practicing a new style will seem strange and uncomfortable, but it will allow you to become more flexible in how you respond to challenges.

■ ■ ■

COUNTERTRANSFERENCE

It's déjà vu all over again.

—Yogi Berra

Inevitably, you have sensitive areas of emotional injury that you have not fully explored, that are hidden and sequestered by protective layers of emotional shielding. Sometimes these unresolved injuries become activated in your present relations with others. Someone "touches a nerve," a sensitive issue that provokes in you a reactive response that may seem out of proportion to the current situation with that person. Or perhaps you may find yourself responding very negatively toward someone, but you are unable to identify why you experience that person as so obnoxious. In other words, the ways in which you have been injured, frustrated, or disappointed in your past relations with others can affect how you perceive and respond to new relationships in the present.

This is particularly true if you have not yet fully explored and understood how past injuries or interpersonal problems with others have influenced you. Part of your journey of self-exploration will include becoming more aware of these areas of unresolved conflict. The less you are motivated by protective and defensive efforts designed to shield you from emotional pain, the more you will be able to engage others with full awareness of your authentic thoughts and feelings.

Playing out unresolved personal issues in your current encounters with other people is a human tendency that Freud (1924) called "transference." In the therapeutic relationship, Freud observed that a client often acted as if the therapist were a sort of stand-in for another important person in the client's life. The client may express emotions toward and assign motivations to the therapist that rightly belong to that patient's experience of someone else. Gaining insight into the origins and meaning of the client's transference constitutes one of the main goals of psychoanalytic therapy.

Although you're not in training to become a classic psychoanalyst, you will encounter transference in your clients. What's more, you will find that clients will evoke in you certain feelings and reactions that touch on your own personal conflicts and unresolved issues. Freud called the counselor's reaction in this situation "countertransference." He cautioned that it has the potential to derail a productive therapeutic relationship because the counselor's own unresolved feelings and conflicts get in the way of the client's self-expression. In other words, the therapist distorts the client's behavior to conform to the counselor's own expectations or biases.

Freud's concept is not a relic that is irrelevant to either counseling or interpersonal relationships. Most modern forms of counseling include some variant of the concepts of transference and countertransference. You can probably think of times that stand out as examples of your having had a strong transference reaction to someone. Of course, you will introduce your biases, distortions, and interpretive schemes in your subjective and unique fashion. The important point to remember is that self-awareness about how your past injuries become expressed in your interpersonal behavior is critically important to both your personal relationships with fellow students and teachers and to your future work with clients.

It is difficult to lift up bandages to look at old wounds and even more difficult to go poking around when they are not fully healed. But as you can see, those wounds that are still "alive" will invisibly influence your behavior toward others. Shoving painful life events down into a cellar of forgetting just makes you afraid to go down to the place in which your deepest, richest feelings may live. It is a natural human tendency to want to "move on" from painful life events. How you choose to move on becomes vitally important to whether you become an integrated and fully alive person or whether you surround yourself in a shroud of insulating forgetfulness. As Freud observed, it is what we forget that we repeat.

GETTING CLEAR

When one is a stranger to oneself then one is
estranged from others too. If one is out of touch
with oneself, then one cannot touch others.

—Anne Morrow Lindbergh

As should be obvious to you by now, becoming a successful counselor is
not merely a matter of veneering a set of techniques and theories onto
yourself. A counselor is someone whose very personhood is therapeutic,
and honesty is the counselor's most powerful asset. But in order for you
to be honest with your clients, you must first be honest with yourself. As
Carl Rogers put it, the counselor must be authentic, congruent, and
transparent in the counseling relationship.

Most people, in everyday social situations, cannot trust that they are
receiving feedback from others that is not veiled in some way. As a result,
most of us are uncertain about how others truly see us. This is why honesty is one of the things that differentiates the counseling relationship
from other situations. One of the most refreshing and therapeutic aspects
of the counseling relationship for clients is that they can rely on the counselor to give them straight talk. However, certain criteria must be met for
such feedback to be effective. The client must be convinced that your
honesty is meant to be helpful and not to humiliate him or her or to be
self-aggrandizing. Your feedback must be timely and given in ways that
the client can accept. But most of all, you must be clear as to your own
motives for offering the feedback. Staying clear on your motives and values is a constant struggle that does not end with counselor training.

Trying to get a clear picture of your clients is like taking a photo with
an old camera with slide-in glass plates. If the plate is clear, then the picture you have of the client will be reasonably accurate. On the other
hand, if you have marred the surface of the plate with your fingers, then
it will be hard to tell which part of the picture belongs to the client and
which to you. Striving to stay as clear as possible is a lifelong effort, and
it requires that you commit to continually work on yourself. As
McConnaughy (1987) affirms, the actual techniques you use as a counselor are not as important as your unique personhood. Moreover, "the
more a therapist accepts and values himself, or herself, the more effective he or she will be in helping clients come to know and appreciate

themselves" (McConnaughy, 1987, p. 304). The clearer you stay about yourself, the more room the client has to get clear on his or her concerns.

Finding Your Roots

> Those of us who attempt to act and do things for others or for the world without deepening our own self-understanding, freedom, integrity, and capacity to love, will not have anything to give others.
>
> —Thomas Merton

Exploring or knowing yourself goes deeper than trying to *understand* who you are. While this statement may, on first consideration, seem confusing, there are really two parts to knowing yourself. Complete self-exploration also means that you must come to understand how other people may regard you. Look into the mirror. What do you see? That person in the mirror may not be the same person that others are responding to. How do you appear to others? They will see your ethnicity, gender, age, mannerisms, and many manifestations of your upbringing and values that are so much a part of you that you have failed to even notice them as being important. Who you are for others creates an image that must also become part of your total self-understanding. Each time you encounter your clients, they will be responding to an image of you that may or may not be alignment with how you see yourself. Moment to moment you must attempt to view yourself through their eyes and deal with their misgivings about whether you can be trusted, whether you can care, and if they will be safe in your company.

▲▲▲

I Need to Pay Attention to Who I Am
Michelle's Story

PRIOR TO MY FIRST practicum experience, I thought I knew myself pretty well. I had spent a good deal of time during my classes exploring my values and getting in touch with my beliefs. In one class we completed an exercise in which we imagined how it might be to counsel a pedophile, a substance abuser, or a wife batterer. I convinced myself that I would be able to transcend the "differences" of my clients and, as long as I treated each person with respect, my work as a counselor would be relevant and effective. Then I sat down with my first actual client. The client seemed nervous, which helped me overcome my own anxiety and assume what I believed to be a true helper role. I did my best to help the client feel at ease. After a few minutes of small talk and tentative "starts and stops," the client looked at me with a kind smile. "You know, I don't want to hurt your feelings, but I have to tell you I'm a little uncomfortable." No problem! I thought. I started to internally formulate a soothing reflective statement when my client continued. "I have a feeling you're probably Christian, and I really don't think I'll feel comfortable talking to a Christian counselor."

I can't begin to accurately express my reaction. All I can remember is a sinking feeling while I chanted to myself, "What do I do now? What do I do now?" I'll admit that in addition to feeling shocked, I was a little hurt that anyone would not want to talk to a Christian. What's wrong with Christians? I wanted to protest.

Later, after discussing this session with my supervisor and peers and experiencing a range of emotions, I discovered a few things about myself. During all my thinking about difference and what I can "tolerate" about other people, I never realized that the "different" one in the counseling room might be me. I also started to see that prior to that session I had never consciously explored my own ethnicity, religion, or socioeconomic status. As a person who sits squarely and comfortably in mainstream society (white, Anglo Saxon, Protestant, middle class), I've never had to think about these things. Unlike my peers who are Latina or African American, for instance, I've taken my identity and its implications for granted. Thanks to my sensitive client, I've begun an exploration of myself and my identity as white, female, Christian, and middle class. All of those identities mean something to me, and they obviously mean something to my clients. I need to pay attention to who I am.

▼▼▼

Michelle had a variety of options available in response to the client's expressed concerns. She could have acknowledged the client's concerns, addressed the religious differences, offered a referral, and so forth. In your training you will be developing skills in handling situations such as these, but our emphasis here is on your own self-understanding. As you can see, Michelle used this situation as a catalyst for her own growth experience and she came away from the session with a much greater sense of who she was. Such awareness is much more useful to her than learning a new counseling technique.

Find the "I AM" Experience

Rollo May (1983) wrote of a client who had rediscovered what he called the "I AM" experience. When asked what this experience was like, the client said:

> [I]t feels like receiving the deed to my house. It is the experience of my own aliveness. . . . It is my saying to Descartes, "*I Am, therefore I think, I feel, I do*" (p. 99, emphasis in original).

As you continue through your training program and discover the new you, you will find that it is also the old you that is discovered. Somehow, your "I" and your "me" become united. Your confidence in yourself increases, and your trust in who you are becomes solid and confident. This does not mean that you will never again feel insecure about who you are. We all experience times when we lose touch with ourselves. But once you get hold of that "I AM" feeling, you always have the deed to your house, and, contrary to what you have heard from Thomas Wolfe, you can go home again.

SUMMARY

In this chapter, we have hammered home the point that, in order to be an effective counselor, you must first be committed to your own "personal soundness." Being personally sound does not mean that you must be free of all wounds and troubles. In fact, the very program that you are going through will create new troubles for you and expose old wounds that must be dealt with. The main thing you must do is remain open to the changes that are happening in you. The Greek philosopher Heraclitus said that a person cannot step in the same river twice. But because the person cannot remain constant either, he might have gone on to state that the same person cannot step in the same river twice. You are always changing. You are different today than you were yesterday. As you make your journey through your training program, be sure to keep up with yourself!

RESOURCES

Two books were cited in the text of this chapter that we think merit a thorough reading. They will be helpful to you as you explore yourself and navigate your own process of change. The writing style of both authors is quite readable and lively. Many of our students have reported that these books spoke to them and were personally reassuring during their "dark night of the soul."

Rollo May's book, *The Discovery of Being* (1983), is devoted to the explanation of existential psychotherapy and its history. You may find this information interesting. But beyond gaining a better understanding of this way of working with clients, you will find that May has much to say about your "existential condition" as you become a helping professional. We especially recommend the chapter entitled, "To Be and Not To Be."

Edward Teyber's book, *Interpersonal Process in Psychotherapy*, also describes a particular approach to working with clients and contains many useful examples of what to say in counseling sessions. The chapters that will be most helpful to you as you attempt to make sense of your own formative experiences in life will be Chapter 6, "Familial and Developmental Factors," and Chapter 7, "Inflexible Interpersonal Coping Strategies."

Each of these books can also serve as a very good source as you develop your own counseling theory. They are very evenhanded and nondogmatic texts, and the ideas within each book can be incorporated into many approaches to counseling.

Following are two Web sites that you may find useful in your self-exploration process. One is a Web page from the United Kingdom, and the other is a resource for books and software.

Psychnet-UK

http://www.psychnet-uk.com

An interesting site containing links to articles, jobs, chat rooms, games, MP3s, and "humour." You may find it interesting to see how the

United Kingdom treats issues of personal growth and psychology. There is a special section on this Web page for students in the mental health professions.

Room 42

http://www.room42.com/store/health_center/selfgrow.shtml

This site is associated with Amazon.com. You can review videotapes, books, and software, and then order from Amazon. Each listing contains star ratings from consumers as to the quality of the item. You can read what they have written and be better informed before you buy. Of course, you are not obligated to purchase anything from this site. By the way, we don't know why they call it "Room 42." You may recall that in *The Hitchhiker's Guide to the Galaxy*, "42" was the answer to the question about the meaning of life.

REFERENCES

Bruner, J. (1973). *Beyond the information given: Studies in the psychology of knowing.* New York: Norton.

Carroll, L. (1991). *The complete illustrated Lewis Carroll.* New York: Gallery Books. (Original work pulished 1896)

Deikman, A. J. (1996). "I" = awareness. *Journal of Consciousness Studies: Controversies in Science and the Humanities, 3*(4), 350–356.

Egan, G. (1986). *The skilled helper: A systematic approach to effective helping* (3rd ed.). Belmont, CA: Brooks/Cole.

Erikson, E. (1968). *Identity: Youth and crisis.* New York: Norton.

Freud, S. (1924). *A general introduction to psychoanalysis.* New York: Washington Square Press.

Gergen, K. J. (1971). *The concept of self.* New York: Holt, Rinehart & Winston.

Gould, J. L., & Marler, P. (1987, January). Learning by instinct. *Scientific American,* 74–85.

Guggenbuhl-Craig, A. (1971). *Power in the helping professions.* Dallas, TX: Spring.

Henry, W. E. (1977). Personal and social identities of psychotherapists. In A. S. Gurman & A. M. Razin (Eds.), *Effective psychotherapy: A handbook of research.* Oxford, England: Pergamon Press.

Horney, K. (1970). *Neurosis and human growth.* New York: Norton.

James, W. (1890). *Principles of psychology.* New York: Holt, Rinehart & Winston.

Kosko, B. (1993). *Fuzzy thinking: The new science of fuzzy logic.* New York: Hyperion.

Kottler, J. (2000). *Doing good: Passion and commitment for helping others.* Philadelphia: Brunner-Routledge.

Kottler, J. A., & Blau, D. S. (1989). *The imperfect therapist: Learning from failure in therapeutic practice.* San Francisco: Jossey-Bass.

Laing, R. D. (1969). *The divided self.* New York: Pantheon Books.

Levin, J. D. (1992). *Theories of the self.* Washington, DC: Hemisphere.

Masson, J. M., & McCarthy, S. (1995). *When elephants weep.* New York: Delacorte.

May, R. (1983). *The discovery of being: Writings in existential psychology.* New York: Norton.

McConnaughy, E. A. (1987). The person of the therapist in therapeutic alliance. *Psychotherapy, 24,* 303–314.

McLeod, J. (1998). *An introduction to counselling* (2nd ed.). Buckingham, England: Open University Press.

Norcross, J. C., Strausser, D. J., & Faltus, F. J. (1988). The therapist's therapist. *American Journal of Psychotherapy, 42,* 53–66.

Parrott, L., III (1997). *Counseling and psychotherapy.* New York: McGraw-Hill.

Perez, J. F. (1979). *Family counseling: Theory and practice.* New York: Van Nostrand.

Piaget, J. (1970). Piaget's theory. In P. H. Mussen (Ed.) *Carmichael's manual of child psychology* (Vol. 1, 702–732). New York: Wiley.

Rippere, V., & Williams, R. (1985). *Wounded healers: Mental health workers' experiences of depression.* New York: Wiley.

Rogers, C. R. (1942). *Counseling and psychotherapy.* Boston: Houghton Mifflin.

Rogers, C. R. (1951). *Client-centered therapy.* Boston: Houghton Mifflin.

Rogers, C. R. (1961). *On becoming a person.* Boston: Houghton Mifflin.

Rogers, C. R. (1980). *A way of being.* Boston: Houghton Mifflin.

Seligman, M. E. P. (1995). The effectiveness of psychotherapy: The *Consumer Reports* Study. *American Psychologist, 50,* 965–974.

Sherman, P. W. (1980). The meaning of nepotism. *American Naturalist, 116,* 604–606.

Swann, W. B. (1996). *Self-traps: The elusive quest for higher self-esteem.* New York: Freeman.

Teyber, E. (1997). *Interpersonal process in psychotherapy: A relational approach* (3rd ed.). Pacific Grove, CA: Brooks/Cole.

Thomas, L. (1983). *Late night thoughts on listening to Mahler's ninth symphony.* New York: Viking Press.

Trivers, R. L. (1971). The evolution of reciprocal altruism. *Quarterly Review of Biology, 46,* 35–57.

Truax, C. B., & Mitchell, K. M. (1971). Research on certain therapist interpersonal skills in relation to process and outcome. In A. E. Bergin & S. Garfield (Eds.), *Handbook of psychotherapy and behavior change* (pp. 299–344). New York: Wiley.

Williams, T. (1958). *The Roman spring of Mrs. Stone.* New York: Atheneum.

▲▲▲
▼▼▼

CHAPTER 7

Being with Others

All real living is meeting.

—Martin Buber

It takes one kind of mind to absorb facts, and another to absorb the presence of another human being.

—Abraham Maslow

As you begin your training as a counselor, you quickly become aware that you are entering a whole new educational environment, one much different from your undergraduate experiences. You are no longer thrown in with other students as a matter of chance—you share a dream with those around you of becoming a counselor. There is a different feeling as you join with others to pursue not only training goals and a degree but also a new concept of who you are. Together, you are reaching for something that is not entirely known but that you sense has wonderful possibilities for your own growth and your relationships with others. You are suddenly part of a new community.

This chapter is about being with others in the community formed by your peers, faculty members, support staff, mentors, and supervisors. It is also about how changes in you—as you evolve as a person and forge a new identity as a counselor—influence important others in your life. These important others may be relatives, friends, romantic partners, and fellow students. One thing is sure—you are taking a journey that will change you. Because you have such close-knit ties with others, your journey affects them all, and, in some measure, they are taking the trip with you.

Changes in you are inevitable because you are entering into a new kind of interpersonal environment, one you have never experienced before. You notice that, in your new community, you are called on to respond in fresh ways, to take risks, to collaborate with others, and to be open and flexible to a degree that might be unfamiliar to you. You're expected to be "game" for new ventures, such as role-plays and experiential exercises. You become used to seeing yourself on videotape when learning and practicing counseling skills. You also find that, to really engage in a learning dialogue with others, you welcome the productive critique of supervisors and peers. Above all, being fully invested in forging an identity as a counselor requires you to be open, accessible, and collaborative with others, throwing your whole self into the experience.

Don't worry—though you might feel that you don't know how to swim, you won't drown! Others are there to buoy you when you need it, and you can discover secret resources you never knew you had. At the same time, you find yourself learning new ways of relating to others that will serve you, not only with those who will one day seek your counseling but also with anyone whose life touches your own.

This chapter addresses the ways in which these new relational opportunities can test your ability to adapt and can provide memorable and joyful experiences. When you finally enter the fellowship of healing professionals as a full-fledged member, you may look back on your training and say, shaking your head, "What a long, strange trip it's been!" But you will be gratefully alive with a new capacity for relating to others that is at the core of what it means to become a counselor. The question to ask yourself now is, "Am I open to this experience?"

▲▲▲

Being "Processed"
Rebecca's Story

I CAN STILL RECALL how strange it felt sitting in a circle with my classmates and thinking, "Who *are* these people?" It was my first experience in a "process" group. I wasn't sure what that meant, but whatever it was, I sure was leery of being "processed" by this bunch. They were so different from what I had expected. Looking back on it, I think I assumed that they would be more like me— you know, normal! Now, I can really appreciate the diversity in my classmates, but back then it felt like entering another world. I was disconcerted and a little scared. Later, I wondered how my earlier social world could have been so uniform. But at the beginning of that group, I felt a sense of being out of place.

Apparently, "process" meant that we were supposed to share our thoughts and feelings about stuff that we were experiencing as new graduate students. Some students seemed fine with this and openly talked about their excitement, as well as their frustrations. An older guy talked about being disoriented now that he's a student again. Somebody else talked about how her boyfriend felt threatened by her going on to graduate school. One African American woman described how it felt to be the only person of color in the class, especially because she was from a "black" university. Her words about being in the minority stirred a guy to talk about his sexual orientation. Just when I was feeling like the most conventional person in the world, a young neohippy-looking guy, Robert, talked about "body-mind" stuff. He related how important yoga and meditation were to him. I thought to myself, "What a flake!"

I tend to be very private, so I felt like, "What am I doing here?" When it came to be my turn to share my experiences, I mentioned a few things that were not particularly deep, but nobody seemed to mind. It creeped me out that some people in the group talked so freely, especially about personal stuff. I gravitated to Alicia, who was more quiet, like me, and who was also nervous about being processed. We stuck together like we had been cast adrift and were clinging to the same life preserver.

Over time, though, I started to feel a little left out of the group. I began to be interested in the experiences my classmates shared and felt like I wanted them to know me better, too. I started to open up a little, and it wasn't so bad! This kind of dragged Alicia along, too, and she began to loosen up around the others. By the time I was really feeling comfortable with everyone—well, almost everyone—we started our practicum.

This change set me back a little. It was hard because we had to show our work with clients and talk about our personal responses to client's issues. I was afraid of being criticized and felt somewhat exposed again. Strangely enough, Alicia, who had complained about all this personal disclosure, seemed to really like the process group for our casework, and eventually I enjoyed it too because it helped me develop my counseling skills. It seems like second nature now to discuss my personal responses to client issues or relate how a particular experience affects me. I now realize that appreciating diversity is not just about ethnicity or race.

Now I look back on how strange it felt to be thrown in with people who are so different from me, and I can't understand what I was nervous about. I am not as drawn to some of the people in the program, but I have been surprised that even they have something valuable to offer me. Sometimes it is the person who is most different from me that has helped me see things in a new way with my clients. Now the neohippy guy, Robert, is one of my closest friends, and I've almost got the inverted swan position in my yoga repertoire!

▼▼▼

WHAT'S IN YOUR BACKPACK?

Remember that thriving principle about packing for the journey? Well, your counseling journey is the most recent adventure in the larger journey of your life. You have things in your backpack already, and a lot of what is in there influences how you relate to others. You may be fully aware of some of what is in your pack, and you pull it out all the time in your relationships. But there is probably a lot in the backpack that you forgot—or never knew you had!

Like everyone else, you have a long history of interpersonal experiences that have helped to contribute to who you are and how you relate to others. It's nice when you discover in your backpack a quality or skill that helps you connect well with others. It's like when you were a child on the bus heading off to camp. Just as you were starting to get hungry, you found that peanut butter and jelly sandwich your mother packed for you. Now in your backpack, you may discover your ability to take risks and encounter people authentically in your new program. However, in addition to finding something nice in your sack, you may also discover that you've been carrying around a bunch of rocks—dead weight from old relationships that holds you back from engaging with others the way you long to. You wonder, "What is all this junk that I've been lugging around?"

SELF AND RELATIONSHIP

It takes two to know one.

—Gregory Bateson

You are answering that question about lugging junk as you begin to participate in counseling, therapy, supervision, and other relationships that are essential for your development into a helping professional. Even if you are skilled at forging new relationships, the chances are that you will gain new perspectives as your counseling identity evolves. As you discover new insights, you will want to reevaluate your assumptions about how you interact with others.

In any profession, the practitioner has a set of tools. In the helping professions, the most valuable tool that you will have at your service is your ability to form a variety of interpersonal connections and relationships. Learning how your own experience manifests in your communications and becoming aware of the effect these communications have on others are the major challenges you face in becoming a helping professional (Natterson & Friedman, 1995).

During the early phase of your graduate training, your interpersonal awareness and skills are most relevant to developing relationships with your peers and professors. Later, awareness of how you structure your relations with others influences how you interact with your first clients. In your training, you learn new techniques, master new methods, and bring newfound knowledge to bear as you seek to help your clients. It is important to understand, however, that all of these are secondary to the interpersonal context in which you practice these skills. For this reason, your professors and supervisors encourage you to become more aware of how you encounter them as you work together. These relationships, as well as those with your new peers, are the laboratories in which you can develop your greatest counseling tool—yourself.

Exploring Your Relational Worldview

We are here to hand one another on.

—Walker Percy

You have become who you are, in some part, because you developed in a unique psychological environment with people who are important to you. In that shared participation, especially with early caregivers, you forged a unique sense of self, as well as an awareness of how others behave in relation to you. It was in your early important relationships, for instance, that you learned to feel, regulate, and express emotion. The very structure of the way you experience your emotional life took shape in a relational system (Stolorow, Brandchaft, & Atwood, 1987).

During that time, you learned to make sense of people's behavior. You also discovered how your own actions, feelings, and expressions affected others (Stern, 1988). In these countless encounters that took place every day of your young life, you developed a working model for structuring interpersonal relationships. More important, in the context of others, you became a self.

Building on this early formative matrix of relational experiences, you had to accommodate new interpersonal events as you grew and developed, sharing a psychological environment with friends, relatives, peers, and intimate partners. Emerging out of this participation, you developed an interpersonal style that reflects certain experiences, values, needs, traumas, motivations, and fears. All of these experiences are like features on a map showing where you have been in the past and where you are likely to go as you navigate new relationships.

Your unique map records all the relational terrain you traversed as you grew into a person. This map is an enormously complex collection of interpretive categories that take shape from your unique interpersonal history, which you bring to bear in each new relational event. These interpretive categories, with which you make sense of interpersonal encounters, are not often the focus of your conscious and deliberate examination (Stolorow & Atwood, 1992). Without even realizing it, you use these meaning-making templates all the time. You assume that they are accurate and reliable representations of some external reality because you have a fundamental need to make sense of your interpersonal life.

However, one reason for the success of your assumptions is that you develop relationships with people whose interpersonal assumptions are similar to your own. When you encounter someone with roughly similar sets of interpretive categories, you naturally feel that you understand the other person. You feel in familiar territory, and because you sense a connection, a relationship is more likely to grow out of the encounter.

Your new learning community, however, is not a freely selective social environment. Instead, you are thrown in with a wide assortment of people with whom you might not normally associate. Even though they may share a common commitment to a helping profession, your colleagues, professors, and supervisors can have vastly different organizing frames of reference for interpersonal interaction. It is in this diverse and unfamiliar personality "salad bowl" that you are challenged to explore your own assumptions and expectations about others. In your class discussions, supervision meetings, and counseling sessions, you will be regularly stretching your capacity to accept alternate experiences of the same event. Like a prism that transforms a single ray of light into a spectrum, people can have a colorful range of reactions to a single, shared episode. In this psychological environment, you'll come to truly appreciate that others' subjective experiences of interpersonal events are as real for *them* as your experience is for you. By accepting and valuing these alternate perceptions, you can not only enrich and broaden your own perspective but also become a successful helping professional.

For example, facing the issues of racism and sexism can be very perturbing. White people, in particular, can be hesitant to bring up these concerns with others. In your conversations, you may find yourself avoiding the topics of affirmative action, inequality, immigration, and race relations because you fear these will stir up strong emotions. One of the unfortunate results of this avoidance, however, is that you never become genuinely engaged in deep discussions about the pain of these social problems—and the ways of addressing them. Now, more than ever, is an excellent time for you to explore yourself as a gendered, ethnic individual.

■ ■ ■
___

EXERCISE 7.1 **Visitor from Another Planet**
A Guided Fantasy

For the next few minutes, imagine that you're from another planet where people are androgynous. Your spaceship lands in the United States, and you are met by several government officials. After determining that you pose no threat, the officials decide to educate you regarding U.S. culture. They suggest that you watch an evening of prime-time television and read national magazines and newspapers. Imagine what you see and read. What impression do you have about men and women? Women who are racial or cultural "minorities"? People who are Asian American, Latino/a, Native American, of African descent, or white? People who are gay, lesbian, bisexual, or heterosexual? People with disabilities or special needs? Take a few minutes to write your impressions.

___

___

___

_____

_____

Now, imagine that the officials tell you that the United States is a meritocracy in which people get what they work for and deserve. Imagine that the officials tell you that the principles of the country's government state that all men are created equal. What are your opinions now?

_____

_____

_____

_____

_____

To reflect on the meaning of this exercise for you, consider your opinions and assumptions that you've taken for granted. What do your findings imply about how different people may feel about their place in society? How might this information apply to your clients?

_____

_____

_____

_____

_____

■ ■ ■

A central goal of your training is to gain a thorough understanding of how you structure your interpersonal experiences in the unique way that you do. In other words, as you make explicit your organizing frames of reference for understanding relationships, you become a more effective helper. As part of this process, you also discover how you respond to relational events. In your learning community, you can be open to revising your map, exploring your own relational assumptions, and becoming more aware of the impact you have on your fellow traveling companions.

Growing in Relation

When we are listened to, it creates us, makes us unfold and expand.

—Karl Menninger

Most students new to counseling programs are a little startled, and later excited, by how much their programs are structured around not only training but also personal growth, especially in relation to others. Alberta, for example, was having trouble with the emphasis placed on interpersonal self-awareness in her counseling program. Once she remarked with exasperation that her training felt "more like personal therapy." Alberta was striving to accommodate to how her interpersonal style, habits, and assumptions were challenged and made more explicit as she participated in forging new relationships with peers and supervisors. These relationships were centered on the cultivation of the person, as well as the skills, of the counselor.

Day after day, Alberta felt compelled to examine her interpersonal style and its effects on others much more closely than she would if she had chosen some other profession. However, at the end of her program, Alberta shared her feelings with her colleagues: "I thought that I could just come here and learn what to do, and not have to change myself. I guess I had this idea that I would only 'do something to' others, rather than 'be someone with' others. Giving up that sense of control, and being open to change, and to all of you, was the hardest thing about the program."

One of the rocks that Alberta was carrying in her backpack was the desire to be in control all the time in order to feel safe with others. It was difficult for her to try new things or to be frank about her own thoughts and feelings because she reserved trust only for lifelong friends. Being open to helpful guidance, productive evaluation, collaboration, or mentoring was difficult, because she felt threatened not being the one directing the show.

Quite different relational issues may be more troublesome to you. Claire had always been the "star" in her academic pursuits. She proudly declared that she had a "high need for achievement." As her relationships with supervisors and peers developed, however, Claire began to realize that she actually harbored a strong and unrealistic desire for perfection. At first, she had a hard time trying new skills because of her fear of making a mistake—and of not being the star. As others watched her videotaped sessions, Claire felt overly sensitive to criticism. Her unrealistic aspirations hit a brick wall when her competitive desire to outshine her peers and win accolades began to disrupt her supervision group. It was difficult for Claire to accept that her interpersonal style, rather than her external achievement, was fair game for discussion in this setting. However, as she began to understand how her interpersonal and counseling effectiveness were related, Claire's desire to become a good counselor eventually enabled her to be open and receptive and to accommodate the feedback that others gave her. She discovered how her competitive behavior reduced, rather than elevated, the esteem with which others regarded her. Claire was also able to explore these interpersonal dynamics in terms of the family dynamics in which they had formed.

Like Alberta and Claire, you have a complex mixture of talents, fears, and interpersonal assumptions that serve as either peanut butter and jelly sandwiches or rocks in your backpack. Your expectations about relationships influence your defenses, fears, and hopes. Some of your habits of relating and communicating can work well, but some get in the way of being open, honest, and fulfilled in your relationships. Unlike the latest diet fad, which can offer you no guarantees, we offer you two assurances about your training experience. First, whatever your interpersonal style, you can discover its strengths and limitations as you continue on your journey. As you explore the baggage you bring to training, you can spread your backpack's contents on the ground so you can examine everything carefully before deciding what you want to keep carrying with you. Our second guarantee is that, as you successfully make your way through training with a lighter load, you will relate to others in new and more fulfilling ways.

Mirrors

Your important relationships are like mirrors (Kohut, 1971). You see yourself reflected back through the experience of those with whom you are in contact. Your professors, supervisors, peers, and clients form the relational laboratories in which you will forge your professional identity.

Undoubtedly, there will be times when you see yourself reflected back in a way that seems familiar and confirming to you. But it is just as likely that there will be times when the reflection you see looks strange, unnerving, or disconcerting. As you ponder the many opportunities for growth that emerge out of these encounters, keep in mind that you are a work in progress and that the journey itself—not the destination—is most important.

▲▲▲

The Childlike Feeling of Possibility
Antoinette's Story

IT IS A BEAUTIFUL morning, so I decide to lie in the grassy arms of the campus quad. Sunlight speckles down on the noisy undergrads walking off the effects of last night's festivities. I am right near the sidewalk. I wonder, "Is this somehow symbolic? In my life, do I dare not stray too far from safety?" I'm lying in a rare, unnatural pose of openness—bared arms, black skin shimmering in the fall sunshine, making me truly rainbow-like.

I feel the damp ground through my jeans. My black braids are long and soft. They comfort me as they sway in the breeze against the goose bumps on my skin. I sense the green, the wind, and the childlike feeling of possibility that I am often too scared to embrace.

I am almost 23 and I still fight the feeling of being alone. I can handle every day before I look in the mirror. No, I used to feel that way. But it still isn't a good idea to look for too long. Still, I see a life proposed again—one lived beyond mere survival. I am with these others, strangers and friends, different and the same. Now they are mirrors, too. I do not get the answers, but I ask the right questions, and I know there are options. I don't feel like I have to always question if I can live this life like somebody people know. And I don't feel like I am left alone with the world balanced between teeth and tongue. I can't help but wonder how long today will last inside of me. But today . . . maybe today, I am strong and beautiful and confident enough to dare and say, "I belong."

▼▼▼

THE COUNSELING QUALITIES

Our fate is shared.

—Susan Griffin

Pondering what is in your interpersonal backpack is good preparation for having traveling companions on your journey. To really get the most from your program, you need to join with others to navigate your way through the variety of experiences designed to foster your growth as a helping professional. These important persons are your professors, mentors, supervisors, clients, and fellow students. Some of your student traveling companions will be farther along in the program and can help and guide you when you feel disoriented or lost. With your new companions, you can discuss new ideas, practice your emerging skills, observe one another, and give feedback as you seek to apply what you are learning. You can practice therapy skills by watching one another's role-plays, as well as actual counseling sessions, on videotape. You can become comfortable with giving and receiving constructive criticism and helpful observations. These activities can stretch your capacity for being "out there" and exposed to professors and fellow students in your learning process. If you open yourself to others, your companions can be there to encourage you when you need it—as well as challenge you to explore your potential to the fullest.

Two very important criteria must be present for these relationships to truly have a profound impact on your growth as a counselor. First, you have to cultivate these relationships in an interpersonal climate of honesty and understanding. You need to really know and appreciate your traveling companions for you to fully trust and respect them. The good news is that your advisors, supervisors, and learning companions are very likely to value openness. However, you also have to let others truly get to know you, too.

The second criterion for successfully creating dynamic and profound relationships is for you to be a vital and engaged participant. Go out of your way to offer your animated interest, sincere curiosity, and unique perspective to the people who form your new learning community. By sharing your ideas and experiences, expressing your doubts and confusion, and communicating forthrightly, you help promote an environment that encourages discoveries and facilitates growth for everyone.

Many of the qualities that are essential to becoming a helping professional are equally relevant to fostering your relations with your traveling companions. An attitude of respect and acceptance for persons different from yourself will enable you to reach outside your normal comfort zone and create connections with others whom you would not typically encounter.

For example, Hannah grew up in a close-knit community, all of whom shared her religious views. Until she learned to appreciate value systems different from her own, Hannah found it particularly difficult to create close and productive relationships with fellow students who were not religious. Her initial practicum experiences further challenged her to accept persons whose worldviews, values, sexual orientations, and religious beliefs were very different from her own. Hannah later acknowledged, "When I first started, I assumed that I would help people find answers to their problems. What I really assumed is that they would want *my* answers! It's still difficult for me sometimes to remember that my way of seeing things is not the only way."

Cultivating mutuality and interdependence means that you have to be open to give and take, to stand on an equal footing with others, and to be responsive to opportunities for engagement at a meaningful level. Many persons attracted to the helping professions enjoy the role of the "helper" but have a harder time with mutual relationships that require reciprocal self-disclosure and trust. Such reciprocity implies a willingness to be vulnerable at times and to take a chance that others will afford you the same acceptance that you are willing to show them. For example, Deaken's peers celebrated him for his thoughtful and sensitive listening skills. Over time, however, his fellow students noticed that Deaken rarely revealed much when it was his turn to participate in counseling exercises and role-plays. They also noticed, as friendships developed, that though he was supportive and caring to his fellow students in time of need, Deaken did not disclose his own struggles or feelings. When confronted about his one-sided relational style, Deaken acknowledged that he found it difficult to open up to others. His companions let him know that for mutual trust to develop, Deaken had to take the same risks that they did.

Mutuality implies that you are willing to be genuine with others, not merely pretending to show your real thoughts and feelings. For example, when his supervision group discussed his counseling tape, Elias remarked that everyone complimented him on his strengths and commented on only what he was doing successfully. How could he improve his skills if everyone was merely being polite? Elias's candor and lack of defensiveness showed his peers that he was trying to grow and that they could respond forthrightly to him without creating ill will. When the other members pointed out where he had missed some important client expressions, Elias began to trust the integrity of the group process and to feel he was getting his peers' real reactions. You must do your part in helping to create a community of learners by sharing yourself, supporting and respecting others, and by being invested and engaged with all those whose lives are joined with yours in becoming helping professionals.

"TRUTH" WITH A CAPITAL "T"

> Truth is always what a person believes privately
> and emotionally.
>
> —Hergenhahn

Postmodernism suggests that multiple truths exist. Therefore, you can only truly encounter others when you realize that your "Truth" may not be someone else's "Truth." The bottom line is that in order to be both a successful and ethical professional helper, you have to be able to accept others who are different from you.

Certainly, you have values that are sacred to you, but it's likely that you also consider yourself pretty understanding about different beliefs and lifestyles. However, it's also just as likely that there are times when you react to certain differences with a "hard belly." Nothing about that different perspective seems to penetrate—everything bounces right off. When you hear people talk about their life circumstances, it's as though you suddenly have "abs of steel." At that particular time, you are unable to absorb the experience. When do you have a hard-belly response? The best way to figure that out is to look at what purpose it serves.

Your hard belly is an example of distancing behaviors, those reactions and protests that may arise when you're faced with challenging ideas about diversity. Distancing behaviors include statements such as, "We don't have those kinds of problems around here," or "I don't see color," or "We've certainly come a long way in race relations/gender relations/accepting diversity." Although these statements may contain some element of truth, they're directly linked to the hard belly. These reactions protect you from feeling the intense emotions of others and genuinely connecting with their experiences. You may even recognize this pattern in yourself, but how do you move beyond that? Simple insight isn't enough.

The video "The Color of Fear," showed several men of different races and ethnicities who spent the weekend together to discuss their experiences of themselves and others. One white man, David, consistently listened to the other men's stories with a hard-belly attitude. He rejected the legitimacy of the other men's experiences, tried to convince them that racism isn't as bad as they think, and actually attempted to teach them to be more like himself in order to get along. Finally, Wah, a Chinese man who facilitated the group, quietly asked David what stops him from genuinely hearing the other men's experiences. David's reaction was startling. He began to cry, saying that if he believed the other men's stories, then he would have to face the fact that not everyone has the privileges that he has had as a white man.

As a future professional helper, you can learn from David's decision. These hard-belly behaviors do indeed protect you—not only from painful emotions but also from change and growth. You can make the commitment to engaging with others authentically by being open to and respectful of the reality of their experiences. The next time you feel yourself becoming rigid when encountering another person's experience, ask yourself, "What do I fear? What am I protecting myself from? What am I preventing myself from learning and experiencing?" This exploration is a vital part of your ability to be with others. In fact, it's a vital part of being an ethical practitioner. You are expected to know yourself and your own prejudices well enough to be able to practice effectively and refer appropriately.

■■■

EXERCISE 7.2 Your Hard-Belly Response
A Quiz

Recently, the American Psychological Association adopted guidelines for therapy with lesbian, gay, and bisexual clients. You are expected to recognize how your own attitudes and knowledge about lesbian, gay, and bisexual issues influence your ability to assess and work with your clients. Let's test out your hard-belly response regarding this issue. If you are heterosexual, take the following quiz:

1. What do you think caused your heterosexuality?

2. When and how did you first decide you were a heterosexual?

3. Isn't it possible your heterosexuality is just a phase?

4. How does it feel to hear that heterosexuality doesn't offend me?

5. If you should choose to nurture children, would you want them to be heterosexual, knowing the problems they would face? (e.g., sexism and inequality in intimate relationships; high rates of divorce)

6. Why must heterosexuals be so blatant, making a public spectacle of their heterosexuality?

7. Heterosexual marriage has total societal support, but why are there so few stable heterosexual marriages?

Did you feel the hard-belly response? If so, take time now to explore what you were protecting yourself from. What would you give up if you set aside this response?

■ ■ ■

GIVING AND RECEIVING FEEDBACK

If you don't risk anything, you risk even more.

—Erika Jong

Let's explore this idea of giving feedback to others a little further. As you can see, your psychological health and personal well-being depend greatly on the manner in which you conduct your interactions with others (Johnson, 1981). The ability to create and maintain cooperative and interdependent relationships is also fundamental to your success as a helping professional. Engaging in intimate communication with others is a personally nourishing experience, and such relationships help you to become more self-aware. There are two ways in which you can become more self-aware. The first is to listen to yourself and be sensitive to how you are feeling. The second is to seek feedback from others about how you are affecting them.

You are in a training program with other people who are very special. Like you, they recognize the value of authenticity in relationships, and they are also seeking to understand themselves better. You can help each other toward greater self-awareness—and thus greater psychological health—by engaging in truly honest discussion together. In such encounters, you not only disclose yourself to other people but you also give and receive honest and authentic feedback.

When you think about it, this may be the first time in your life when you have the opportunity to be in such a special setting, with colleagues who are acting in good faith to be helpful to you. Before, you may have been blind to the impressions and opinions others had of you. It is very hard to understand how the person who says, "Thanks for shopping at Wal-Mart" or asks, "Do you want fries with that?" actually feels about you. Even worse, you have been in situations in which other people talk behind your back, withhold information from you, or deliberately try to deceive you in order to serve their own ends. Even in some of your close relationships, there have sometimes been so many hidden agendas that you couldn't fully rely on what significant others said to you. They may not have wished to hurt your feelings, or they may have been afraid that you would stop loving them if they told you what they really thought.

So this is your chance. While you are with other people who understand the value of straight talk, take advantage of the opportunity to use them as honest feedback sources. It's a bit scary at first, but also quite exhilarating, to learn how other people see you.

Giving Helpful Feedback

Given the right conditions, people can learn to trust that what others say to them can be accepted as given with good intentions. Such conditions need rules. Johnson (1981) suggested some guidelines for establishing a trusting environment in which feedback is helpful to you and others. We have modified these guidelines somewhat.

- Focus your feedback on the person's actions, not on his or her being.
- Describe the behavior, rather than labeling it. For example, if you say, "You talked a lot in today's group," rather than, "You've got diarrhea of the mouth today," the person will be less defensive, and you will still get your point across.

- Focus your feedback on descriptions rather than inferences. Instead of something like, "Just now I noticed that you were angry," you might say, "When Jane said that, your face got red and your lips narrowed." Leave the explanation of the behavior to the owner.

- Focus feedback on current happenings, rather than on history. If you say, "Last month when I said 'Hello' to you, you blew me off," the person may not remember the incident or may not be able to recall the mood of the moment. Keep your feedback as close to the "here and now" as possible.

- Share your perceptions, rather than giving advice. Advice always comes across as a one-up–one-down relationship. "Shoulds," "oughts," and other admonitions always communicate that the person is not doing it right. Advice also makes you come off as an expert on the other person's life.

- Make sure the other person is open to your feedback—don't force feedback on people. You might ask, "Would it be okay with you if I said something about that situation that has you upset?" Conversely, you don't have to take feedback from others if you don't want it at the moment. Just hold up your hand for them to stop if someone is giving you more that you can process.

- Focus your feedback on something the person can change. Calling attention to the fact that someone blushes easily or that each of their eyes is a different color may be interesting to you, but it is probably not helpful. If the person does or says something that is bothersome to you, then it may be something the person can change.

- Make sure that the feedback you are giving is motivated by your desire to improve your relationship with that person rather than to "cut" the person down. Obviously, any feedback that is intentionally hurtful or vengeful is not in the proper spirit. Such feedback can destroy a trusting relationship.

- Feedback should never be given lightly. Timing is always important as well. "Excellent feedback presented at an inappropriate time may do more harm than good" (Johnson, 1981, p.25). When given in a respectful manner and received with an open mind, feedback can help each of us become more socially skillful, more self-aware, and more comfortable in the presence of others.

The Johari Window

Known Only to Self	Known to Others, Not to Self
Known to Nobody	Known to Everybody

The Johari Window, named after the originators Joe Luft and Harry Ingham (Luft, 1969), is a way of looking at the four areas of the self.

"Known to Everybody" represents the "public self" that is known by others and ourselves. This area would be expanded as we disclose things about ourselves to others.

"Known to Others, Not to Self" is the so-called bad breath area that is unknown to us but is known by others. This area would be reduced as we encourage feedback from others, while the area of free activity in "Known to Everybody" would be increased.

"Known Only to Self" is the "avoided" or "hidden" area that is known by ourselves but not by others. This area would be reduced by self-disclosure, and "Known to Everybody" would be expanded.

"Known to Nobody" is the area of "unknown activity," as it consists of material that is not known by ourselves and not known by others. According to Luft and Ingham, this area stays constant.

■■■

EXERCISE 7.3 Giving and Receiving Feedback

Briefly list four things that you would be comfortable disclosing in a training session with a colleague. These disclosures do not have to be deep, dark secrets but things about you (accomplishments, ideas you have, things about your family) that you usually would not share with anyone but a friend.

List four things that you have noticed about your training partner or significant other that you would be comfortable sharing with him or her as feedback. Even though this area is called the "bad breath" area, for the purposes of this exercise, we would like to have you offer observations that would fall into the "good breath" area, too. Remember to follow the guidelines for giving good feedback that appear earlier in the chapter and in subsequent sections.

Allow five minutes for one partner to give the other feedback. When you are finished, receivers describe what it was like for them to receive feedback in such a manner. Switch roles and repeat the exercise. Join the larger group and discuss if applicable.

■ ■ ■

AUTHENTICITY

You don't have to be right. All you have to do is be candid.

—Allen Ginsberg

All of the qualities we have been discussing are embedded in a concept that you will fully explore in your counseling studies—authenticity. The personal quality of authenticity is essential, not only to your relations with peers and professors but also ultimately to your work with clients as a helping professional. You probably have an idea what authenticity means in everyday language, but as you delve deeper into your studies, you will discover that the word *authenticity* has a very specialized meaning in the helping professions.

Social Masks

To some degree, you wear a mask in your relations with others. You manage an impression of yourself that represents how you would like to be seen and that you hope others will find acceptable, likable, and appealing. Your social mask also helps you negotiate the complex demands of a variety of interpersonal encounters by making a "version" of yourself available to others. At the same time, you protect and preserve more intimate aspects of your own experience from others' view. Your social mask is very useful.

The problem with your social mask is that sometimes it ends up getting stuck to you. Your mask, designed to be removable when you wish to encounter another closely and intimately, becomes a hindrance to deeper and more sustaining interpersonal connections. When your mask is stuck, you fail to authentically show yourself as you really are to others. Carl Rogers (Kirschenbaum & Henderson, 1989) argued that to truly encounter another person means to demonstrate a sense of transparency. By transparency, he meant that you allow your outer presentation to be completely congruent with your inner world of thoughts and immediate feelings.

Being and Seeming

The philosopher Martin Buber (1958) described these dimensions of interpersonal experience as the difference between "being" and "seeming." When you connect with another from the "being" dimension of yourself, your relations with others are characterized by all the qualities that we have been discussing. These qualities include immediacy, mutuality, acceptance, openness, and a willingness to access another person's inner world, while being anchored in one's own experience.

Buber argued that when persons encounter one another authentically, they can participate with each other at the deepest levels of human experience. Buber described this interpersonal event as an "I-Thou" encounter and argued that something is created that is bigger than each of the persons. That is to say, in such a meeting, the whole is bigger than the sum of the parts. Something new and vital emerges that does not reside in either person but that exists *between* them. Buber said that this ability to "meet" one another authentically is really what defines us as human. Without it somewhere in our lives, we would live in an impoverished and shrunken interpersonal world. "All real living is meeting," Buber (1958, p.93) said, as a testament to the importance of our "I-Thou" connections with others. Carl Rogers (Kirschenbaum & Henderson, 1989) acknowledged his debt to Buber when he made a variation of this idea the cornerstone of his theoretical and therapeutic model.

In contrast to relationships grounded in "being" with others authentically, you may sometimes settle for the poor substitute of "seeming" to others, as a counterfeit for real connection. To protect you from encroachment or injury, you may develop a layer of protective shielding around your inner life. At the same time, however, your defenses also work against you by keeping you from being nourished and sustained by others at deep levels of engagement.

Of course, the needs you have for such nourishment and affiliation do not diminish just because you are unable to meet them in relationships. You still wish to be approved of, accepted by, and cared for by others. Instead of being authentic, you may seek connection without real engagement by managing an impression, cultivating a "seeming" self that you present to others to gain favor and approval. Usually your "seeming" mask is successful, and you can elicit from others a response that looks accepting and approving. Unfortunately, even when you get the reaction that you are looking for, it fails to sustain or nourish you because it does not reach beyond the mask to touch your authentic self. "If Sara really knew me," you might say, "she wouldn't say such nice things about me." The self that needs that response was not the self that was shown to others. Therefore, the approval, acceptance, or praise fails to stick and merely bounces off the mask. Buber called this false and self-conscious presentation the "I-It" way of relating to others, because it is designed to objectify and deflect real encounter with others.

The greatest asset that you can bring to your studies in the helping professions is the ability to form interpersonal relationships and connections with others. To the degree that your relationships are characterized by the aforementioned qualities, you are likely to become a successful healer and helper. As you move through your program and become knowledgeable about different approaches to counseling, you will study these concepts in more depth. Do not simply learn them. Make them *come alive* for you. Examine your own assumptions, stretch your empathic abilities, celebrate diversity, and discover a new willingness to take some interpersonal risks. (What? Did you think it was just going to be multiple choice?)

IMPORTANT PEOPLE IN YOUR TRAINING

> No matter what accomplishments you make, somebody helps you.
>
> —Althea Gibson

Always keep in mind that when you successfully complete your graduate program and launch your professional career, your professors and supervisors, as well as your fellow students and clients, go with you. Throughout your training, you are internalizing the important and most significant others you encounter. You already have had experiences with others that have changed your life and have stayed with you through time. In fact, the constellations in your mythological sky are populated by the figures of those who have had the most profound influence on you. At this very moment, you can easily recall someone whose presence and interest in you made a difference in who you are today.

Mentors

Most myths involving journeys have the hero setting out on a quest that is a metaphor for self-discovery. The "hero cycle" goes something like this. The hero sets out with high hopes, full of confidence and courage. He or she has many adventures that test the hero's strength and determination. In the end, after many trials and tribulations, the hero prevails and discovers or achieves something of great value. Not content to selfishly possess the thing of great worth, the hero brings it back to share with the greater community (Campbell, 1973). But there is one important part to this hero cycle that we have not mentioned. That part, paradoxically, seems to be the most important pivotal event. At some point between the idealistic setting out and the returning in wisdom and accomplishment, the hero gets hopelessly lost.

At this point in the story, the hero's weapons are broken, the food is gone, the horse is dead, and the reason for setting out in the first place is no longer clear. The hero is lost in an impenetrable forest, waterless desert, or endless night or is cast up on a desolate shore. It seems as if the journey is a failure, and the hero is a goner.

But then something happens. Out of the deepest part of the forest, a person appears unexpectedly. This mysterious person always seems to be expecting the arrival of the hero and possesses some knowledge or secret that he or she shares with the hero. Sometimes this guide helps the hero understand, in a new way, something the hero already knows. At other times, the guide gives the hero a new tool or weapon that the hero's courage and determination have made him or her worthy to receive. The hero, fortified with new knowledge, self-understanding, and resources, eventually prevails, completing a journey that is perhaps less glamorous, but much more profound, than the one on which the hero began with naïve hopes of easy success.

There are plenty of epic myths—both ancient and modern—that feature mentors rescuing and guiding the lost heroes. Theseus, for example, went into the depths of the labyrinth, slew the Minotaur, and followed Ariadne's silver thread back into the light of day. Arthur had Merlin's magic to help and protect him. Luke Skywalker had crashed into a swamp, his spaceship—the horse equivalent—was nonfunctional, and he was out of options. It was then that Yoda appeared to guide his Jedi training. And when Dorothy crash-landed in Oz, she had the Good Witch to direct her to "follow the yellow brick road."

Believe it or not, your graduate school experience has a lot in common with the hero cycle. Just as there are times of adventure, achievement, and clarity, there are also times when you feel confused, depleted, and unsure which way to turn. In these bleak valleys, you may even forget the reasons why you even began the journey. It's at those times that you especially need mentors and faculty members who can serve as guides for you. Of course, you can't just count on your mentors appearing, as in the myths—you must cultivate a relationship with them.

Seek out the help, guidance, and experience of a supervisor or professor whose values, personal qualities, research interests, or professional activities appeal to you. Working closely with such a mentor who possesses the skills and knowledge you wish to acquire gives added meaning and dimension to your journey. A mentor is someone who not only teaches you what you want to know but who is the embodiment of what you wish to become. These are lessons that you cannot learn from a book. Rather, by modeling yourself after persons who have gone before you on the adventure, you can discover the things of value that you wish to bring to your own community. When you near the end of your hero journey, you will have developed a professional identity and philosophical orientation that represents and structures your work in the helping professions. In your undergraduate experience, you probably found that, if you attended class, studied hard, and took your exams, you did pretty well. There was likely not as much opportunity—or demand—for you to become involved more directly with your professors. Fortunately, in most graduate programs, you can find faculty members who take a special interest in you. They can guide you to the kinds of experiences that stay with you long after you may have forgotten exactly what the Zeigarnik Effect is.

If you are wondering how you might connect with a faculty member whom you would like to have as a mentor, we'll let you in on a little secret. Professors, supervisors, and advisors love to work with sincerely committed, fully engaged, and curious trainees. Even mentors have a need to feel that what they do is meaningful and important—they like it when students want what they have to offer. Trainers of helping professionals are more than willing to really get to know you, to understand your needs and interests, and to help you in your journey by mentoring you along—if you are responsive. It is enormously gratifying to professors and supervisors when they feel that their investment in, and devotion to, the helping professions is being passed on to students who are their future peers. Your strategy is simple—let your passion show!

Perhaps the faculty member you want to get to know seems busy, preoccupied with other projects, or simply hard to approach. That's okay. Just show how intrigued and fascinated you are by what your potential mentor is teaching, researching, or sharing. It is likely that he or she will make time for you. Then you can make the most of this opportunity to form a productive learning partnership—and a meaningful, lasting relationship.

In your graduate program there is someone waiting, just as in the myth, for you to stumble into their forest. He or she will help you understand what it is you need to discover in yourself and to carry back with you as you continue your journey. Your mentor won't be wielding a light saber, like Obiwan Kenobi, or waving a magic wand, like the Good Witch. But your mentor, whoever he or she may be, will help you recognize and realize your unique potential.

Support Staff

We have been discussing your relationships with peers and professors. It is worth noting, however, that your program's support staff members are essential to having a successful training experience. They are often the first persons you speak with when you are in the application phase, and they help you with all the practical details of getting oriented. These staff members are typically underpaid and overworked but truly devoted to making your experience a good one.

You would be wise to cultivate the goodwill of the program support staff. The kindness that you show them will be returned to you in many ways. Every seasoned graduate student knows that, in a practical sense, it is really the secretaries who most often know what is going on. They have the power to facilitate your progress—and to prevent it from becoming a living hell! These support persons can assist you in negotiating the various technical and bureaucratic hurdles that are an inevitable part of any training program.

As you progress through your training, regularly drop in on the program secretaries and offer them your thanks for their help and support. They are vital members of your learning community.

Significant Others

No one enters a graduate program alone. You have significant others in your life who are, in some small or large way, partners in your new undertaking. You may have been away from school for some time and have an established family or another career. If you are entering your graduate training with the support of someone important to you, the chances are that you have had many discussions about what this commitment means to your relationship. Perhaps you have to move to a new city, give up a good job, strain the family finances, or renegotiate family responsibilities. Perhaps your partner is concerned that you will not have enough time to spend taking care of your relationship or nurturing other family members. Whatever your unique circumstances, you have had to take into account the needs, views, and feelings of important others in your life.

Graduate school often places new and unique stresses on intimate relationships. The amount of time and energy that you pour into your studies may reduce the personal resources you have to give to others in your life. How will your significant others feel about you being frequently absorbed and preoccupied with your projects? In the economy of your relationship, what redistribution of time, energy, and attention will need to occur for your intimate connections to be preserved undamaged? Will you spend less time at the gym, with friends, or with the kids? How will you carve out a space in your life that is reserved exclusively for you and your partner to renew and nourish your love? Discuss these issues with your partner as you launch into your program. Once you begin your training, keep your "relationship antennae" up to stay sensitive to the shifts and changes in your partnership. Devise ways in which you can communicate to each other when things are getting too far out of whack.

Your intimate partner may not realize the degree to which he or she will be called on to adjust and to accommodate to your graduate school commitments. In very real ways, your significant other takes the journey with you but may, for some time, receive less gratification from the experience than you do. After all, graduate school was probably your idea. If you are embarking on the hero's journey, your partner may be the unsung hero, the one standing in the background holding the reins of the horse while you take on the world—the Sancho Panza to your Don Quixote. Just remember—as you are tilting at windmills, you'll need your significant other to be there to celebrate your victory when it comes. Discuss with your partner some of the challenges you are likely to struggle with as you move into a demanding and time-consuming phase of your training.

Graduate school, especially in the helping professions, also introduces a more subtle challenge to your intimate relationships. There is no doubt that if you truly throw yourself into the adventure of becoming a healer and a helper to others, you also gain new insights into yourself and your relationships with others. These insights and experiences can dramatically change you. You have a new lens with which to view yourself and others. You look at your life differently and begin to question your values, assumptions, and motivations. As you gain understanding of individual development and family systems, you may reevaluate your own history in the light of a new perspective. As you come to understand relational dynamics, you may find yourself realizing how certain themes play out in your own intimate relationships. You may begin to question the status quo and to ask your partner to take into account your new perspective and feelings. You will be excited to share and apply what you are discovering with others in your life.

Of course, your partner does not automatically share your newfound perspective and is not looking through the new lens on relationships that you have discovered. The changes you are experiencing may not be entirely welcome to your significant others because they upset the homeostatic balance of your relationship. Your newly discovered insights may be disorienting or even threatening to your partner's sense of connection with you. The context that you take for granted in the culture of your program and that makes certain kinds of interpersonal engagement possible may be unfamiliar to your family and friends. In your eagerness to share your new perspective on interpersonal dynamics, you may find yourself approaching intimate others in the same way that you communicate with your graduate school companions. One minute, for example, your partner is quietly eating corn flakes and reading the paper. The next moment, your significant other is being asked to consider the passive-aggressive implications of hiding behind a newspaper every morning!

You want to make real what you are learning by applying new insights to your life and relationships, but this can be disruptive. People grow and change, and relationships must accommodate to this change if they are to be vital and dynamic. Keep in mind, however, that one facet of empathy is to be sensitive to the degree to which others can adapt to new experiences. Your partner probably expected that you would go to graduate school, learn many new things, and later get a rewarding job. But, like it or not, he or she signed on with you to a program that influences you profoundly and has implications for your growth together.

We offer one last consideration for you to ponder regarding how your graduate school journey affects your intimate connections. Remember that you are gaining a new community in which you make new friends, share very personal aspects of yourself, and create a new identity as a helping professional. You engage with others on a level that may have been reserved only for your most significant others. You are, perhaps, even fostering a sense of family with others in your program and forming bonds that may last a lifetime. Your partner, though you may include him or her in social activities outside of school, may have a sense of being excluded from an area of your life that has become profoundly important to you. Your partner may have mixed feelings about you forming close bonds with others who are not in your normal circle of friends. Because your partner may not be involved in the helping professions, it may seem as if you are learning a foreign language and talking with others in a manner unfamiliar to your "normal" way of being with others. Remember that change is good but also destabilizing. It is likely that you will need to make extra sure that you and your significant other find a new balance as your relationship seeks to keep up with the changes you experience as you become a helping professional.

SUMMARY

Have you ever had the experience of fondly remembering an event and realizing that your original experience of the event was entirely different from the feelings you now have? It seems that our lives and the events in them involve multiple layers of meaning that are not revealed all at once. A sailor may battle through a storm, cursing and fearing it, but later describe it almost with affection. The yarn the sailor tells is about the crashing waves, the tossing boat, the howling wind that drowns out everything else, and finally reaching the calm water. Such a story is so exciting to tell, and to listen to, because it describes a person in an extreme situation, mustering every resource to rise to the challenge. The sailor is never more fully alive, all senses keen, than when the challenge is the greatest.

Graduate school is a lot like surviving a storm at sea. It calls on you to bring to bear all your talents and abilities. At times you feel overwhelmed and challenged to the utmost. Perhaps you wish that you had never left the safety of the harbor. Later, when you have reached calm water, you will recall things differently. People and events that were, at the time, simply part of the changing scene stand out as important. What you are most likely to remember are those times when you felt fully engaged, striving, connected, and open to the experience itself. At the center of this memory will be all of the traveling companions you had along the way. The most enduring, life-changing events always involve your encounters with others—those who share some part of your life journey.

RESOURCES

COUNSGRADS: Counseling Student Listserv

listpro@lists.acs.ohio-state.edu

The Ohio State University and American Counseling Association have formed a listserv to meet the needs of counseling graduate students. COUNSGRADS is an active listserv that enables graduate students from across the country to communicate with one another. You can talk about classes, internships, papers, and ideas about the profession. Darcy Haag Granello, a counselor educator at The Ohio State University, is the list owner. Questions regarding the listserv can be sent to her at *granello.1@osu.edu*. To sign up for the listserv, send an E-mail to *listpro@lists.acs.ohio-state.edu* with the following in the body of the message:

subscribe COUNSGRADS (your first name) (your last name)

REFERENCES

Buber, M. (1958). *I and thou* (R. G. Smith, Trans.). New York: Scribner's. (Original work published 1923)

Buber, M. (1988). *The knowledge of man: Selected essays*. Atlantic Highlands, NJ: Humanities Press International.

Campbell, J. (1973). *The hero with a thousand faces*. Princeton, NJ: Princeton University Press.

Johnson, D. W. (1981). *Reaching out: Interpersonal effectiveness and self-actualization* (2nd ed.). Englewood Cliffs, NJ: Prentice-Hall.

Kirschenbaum, H., & Henderson, V. L. (1989). *Carl Rogers: Dialogues*. Boston: Houghton Mifflin.

Kohut, H. (1971). *The analysis of self*. New York: International Universities Press.

Luft, J. (1969). *Of human interaction*. Palo Alto, CA: National Press Books.

Natterson, J., & Friedman, R. (1995). *A primer of clinical intersubjectivity*. Northvale, NJ: Aronson.

Stern, D. N. (1988). The dialectic between the "interpersonal" and the "intrapsychic": With particular emphasis on the role of memory and representation. *Psychoanalytic Inquiries, 8,* 241–250.

Stolorow, R. D., & Atwood, G. (1992). *Contexts of being: The intersubjective foundations of psychological life*. Hillsdale, NJ: Analytic Press.

Stolorow, R. D., Brandchaft, B., & Atwood, G. (1987). *Psychoanalytic treatment: An intersubjective approach*. Hillsdale, NJ: Analytic Press.

Wah, L. M. (Producer). (1944). *The color of fear* [Videotape]. Berkeley, CA: Stir-Fry Productions.

CHAPTER 8

Thriving in Your Practicum and Internship

> Until you are willing to be confused about what
> you already know, what you know will never grow
> bigger, better, or more useful.
>
> —Milton Erickson

As any traveler knows, preparing for a trip and actually taking it are two very different experiences. Your course work in counseling and therapy has prepared you well, and now you have the opportunity to put your skills into action with real clients. Your practicum and internship represent the next step of your journey to become a full-fledged helping professional.

As you embark on these experiences, you may want to look into your training backpack again—just to double-check that you have all you need. At first, you may not see anything that appears useful. You may have overpacked with a lot of "just in case" items that now do not seem very helpful. Or you may feel as though you have left behind some important utensils and valuable supplies. In either case, you will want to take time to reflect on your preparedness, review the knowledge and skills you bring to this experience, and take stock of your readiness.

When you are poised to begin counseling with actual clients, the responsibilities and complexities of clinical practice can seem overwhelming. In this chapter, we offer practical information and concrete suggestions for completing a practicum or internship. We also invite you to thrive in these settings by creating a secure base from which to venture out, take risks, and grow.

YOU ARE READY, ALTHOUGH
YOU MAY HAVE DOUBTS

We are the hurdles we leap.

—Michael McClure

During your practicum, you will face predicaments that challenge your sense of readiness. Coming in a variety of shapes and sizes, these dilemmas will, in fact, continue to confront you later on in your internship. That's the point—these training experiences are demanding because you must be prepared to enter the challenging profession of counseling and therapy. Of course, there are other purposes to your practicum and internship. At these training sites, you will have plenty of opportunities to try out intervention approaches to see what fits your personal style and professional aspirations. While experimenting with different perspectives and techniques, however, you may be faced with issues of "fitting in" as a professional. And, even though it is likely that you will be successful, you may sometimes feel as though you are playing a part or acting—rather than actually being yourself.

Along the way, it's also likely that you will encounter people—(besides yourself, of course!) who will question your abilities and decisions. For example, if you are a practicum student in school counseling, a parent may confront you with questions such as, "What do you know about children?" and "Are you a parent?" If you are a young intern, some client will be sure to ask, "How old are you?" If you are an intern at a substance abuse treatment center, clients may want to know if you're in recovery. Although no one looks forward to being questioned and confronted, you can quickly realize how exciting it can be to be able to think on your feet and make some discoveries about yourself in the process.

You may think that, because you are dealing with "real world" clients, you should possess more skills and knowledge than you do. But give yourself a break. You have not been at this for a very long time. You are, after all, here to learn.

Someone has said that counselors and therapists—no matter how many years of experience they may have—are always guilty of not being good enough. This adage is even more true for your professors and supervisors. We must be willing to work constantly at improving ourselves and yet also to forgive ourselves for not being further along than

we are. Keep your expectations of yourself reasonable, and when someone implies that you should be older, wiser, or more skilled, don't feel as
if you have been "found out."

▲▲▲

How Old Are You?
Grace's Story

THE FIRST CLIENT I ever saw during my master's program was
a woman in her mid-thirties. I can still remember how nervous and excited I was to be actually working with a real live client!
Although I felt relatively prepared for this first encounter, her first
question for me threw me for a loop. After reciting my well-
rehearsed informed-consent speech, I asked her if she had any
questions before we started. Without hesitation, she asked, "How
old are you?"

It was a simple question. It had a simple answer if I were anywhere but in my first counseling session with my first real client. I
was flustered. I felt as though she saw right through me and
wanted to expose my lack of experience. I tried to gain my composure and decided to fall back on the classic evasive maneuver
that counselors resort to in a pinch.

I asked, "I find it interesting that you want to know how old I
am. How is that important to you?" I hoped that would suffice!
Surely this redirection would prove my professional competence. I
was wrong. She was neither impressed nor satisfied with the reply
and responded, "You just look so young!"

I somehow managed not to answer the question and steered
her off the topic. Much to my surprise, the following week's session started off in an equally unsettling way. Though I hoped that
she didn't have any more "bombs" to throw at me, when I asked
her where she would like to begin, she said, "Since you never
answered my question last week, I'll ask it again. How old are
you?"

Off balance, without another counseling cliché, I meekly con-
fessed, "Twenty-two." I felt like I was raising a white flag in defeat.

After a pregnant pause—which I'm sure was not as long as it
felt—she replied with an off-handed "Oh." She did not get up and

leave. She did not laugh. She did not have a look of horror on her face. All along, I feared that she needed qualities that I did not possess. Much to my surprise, all she really wanted was honesty.

▼▼▼

Like Grace, you will find yourself making valuable discoveries about clients, the helping process, and yourself. You'll be developing a conceptual framework that makes sense to you, that works for you in helping relationships, and that allows you to be natural. Your practicum and internship experiences are special times in your training when you can consolidate everything you learned in your classes—and everything you've learned about your own personhood. A theory is only as good as the person practicing it. Explore how you can bring your theory alive by making it your own.

YOUR PRACTICUM

The great end of life is not knowledge but action.

—T. H. Huxley

The practicum is your first "hands-on" learning opportunity to work with actual clients. The services you may be providing include assessment, individual and group counseling, crisis intervention, consulting, education, and promotion of growth. Although the number of hours required for practicum varies across training programs, you will be expected to provide counseling and therapy services to both individuals and groups.

Your practicum is the first bridge for connecting the knowledge you've acquired in courses to the practical realities of working with clients. At times, this bridge may seem long, high, and precarious. To cross, you might avoid looking down, take a deep breath, and keep your eyes fixed straight ahead. You may even occasionally fear that if you venture a look to the left or to the right, you'll feel dizzy or off balance. In other words, you may fear trying new things or making mistakes. At these times, you can remind yourself that you're not alone. You have an instructor, supervisor, colleagues, and staff to guide, support, and help you along. Just remember, not only does this bridge help you reach your destination, but it also provides a terrific view!

Accommodating to Your Practicum

There are a couple of points you need to keep in mind as you begin your practicum. First, most sites have the dual mission of serving clients and providing a training ground for those entering the helping professions. Therefore, you may need to make significant accommodations, especially in the early phases, as you become oriented to the schedule and demands of the site. Clients, for example, may need to be seen at times that do not fit conveniently into your lifestyle. As a representative of your program, you will want to present yourself in a professionally appropriate manner. For instance, in your classes, you may have found that students, as well as faculty members, dress very casually. Your practicum site, on the other hand, is a different culture. You'll want to fit in and meet the site's expectations of how a professional should look and act. It's not that difficult to figure out. Ask questions, observe, and don't forget the old saying, "When in Rome, do as the Romans do."

▲▲▲

Pipe Dreams
Lennie's Story

EVEN THOUGH it was over 25 years ago, I still remember vividly how insecure and unprepared my fellow students and I felt as we started our practicum course. To make matters worse, our professor looked like he had been chosen by Central Casting to play the role of the experienced and wise therapist. He was middle-aged, had distinguished graying hair, was impeccably dressed in suit and tie, and, most importantly, smoked a pipe. Now keep in mind that my training was back in the days when there were no restrictions on smoking in offices and classrooms. Many professors and graduate students smoked cigarettes during classes, meetings, and counseling sessions. However, a pipe was considered a cultural icon of authority and wisdom.

One evening, when we were behind a one-way mirror watching our professor conduct a counseling group, I was entranced by how he used his pipe as a counseling tool. On one occasion, he pointed with his pipe stem to indicate the interpersonal dynamics between two members. Another time, while packing his pipe bowl with tobacco, he began a compelling commentary, "Well, the real issue that this group is struggling with is. . . ." Then, when he had everyone's rapt attention, he paused dramatically to light his pipe and take a few puffs before finally finishing his pronouncement. I can't remember what he said, but it sounded really profound! The other male students in my practicum immediately took up smoking pipes. As a nonsmoker, I truly felt disadvantaged in my counseling because I couldn't use that talisman of insight and sagacity.

▼▼▼

Your practicum will challenge you in unexpected ways. At times, you may feel aggravated, insecure, and uncertain. Entering the subjective world of your clients and participating with them at this deep level of engagement will expose you to troubling events and disturbing circumstances. You may find it painful to deal with clients who are impoverished, drug addicted, or sexually abused. These encounters will provoke you emotionally and perhaps even disorient you at times.

Clients are not the only ones who will be stirring up your emotions. The staff members at this site may intimidate you because they seem so competent and knowledgeable. You may doubt that you'll ever reach their level of professionalism. At times, the staff may also appear to you as less than caring in how they deal with clients. And no matter how supportive your supervisor may be, your sessions with him or her will bring up issues that will be challenging and perturbing. Many of these encounters with clients, colleagues, and supervisors have the potential to leave you reeling and confused.

At some time during your practicum or internship, you may even wonder if you're cut out to do this line of work. When you have these doubts, use your journal to explore your concerns and take time to reflect on their meaning. Talk to your supervisor and friends. The trick is not to ignore your doubts but to use them to seek deeper answers. After all, you will face "crises of faith" regularly throughout your career. You'll be surprised how you can emerge from such an experience as a stronger and more resilient counseling professional.

Taking Pictures Along the Way

Many programs use videotape recordings of your counseling and therapy sessions to help you refine your skills. If you are like most people, you may feel self-conscious and embarrassed reviewing your videotapes when you are by yourself. However, watching these sessions with your supervisor, professor, or fellow students also viewing can produce real terror! Of course, you're not alone in feeling this way. Over time, you will discover how valuable it can be to revisit your sessions, both by yourself and with others.

Your tapes are wonderful resources for exploring, discovering, and refining your skills. Because practicum is so busy and hectic, you may be tempted to move along to the next session before you have mined a tape for all its treasures. Baird (1999) recommended that you return to your tapes several times to view them from different perspectives. Each time you review the session, you can notice elements that were not apparent to you while you were participating in it. You can focus on the subtle nuances of phrases, emotional shadings, and minute gestures that offer a more textured and vivid understanding of the dynamics and themes of your therapeutic relationship. With each encounter, ask yourself, "What do I experience now as I focus on this element of the interaction?" Also ask yourself, "If I could do this session over again, what would I do that would be different?" This question will help you think about how to conduct the next session with your client and will increase your general knowledge of how to make all future sessions more productive. Involving yourself fully in the process can help you get the most from your experience.

▲▲▲

Sometimes the Therapist Learns More Than the Client
Jane's Story

I HAD MY FIRST practicum assignment in graduate school at an inner-city agency that worked with low-income clients. I was really excited when I heard my first client was ready for me. But was I ready for my first client? My actual involvement with therapy was strictly what I had acquired in my own reading. I hadn't taken any formal therapy course work prior to being thrown into the deep end of the pool. But I assumed that my supervisor knew what he was doing, so I reported at the scheduled time.

My client turned out to be a soft-spoken, moderately depressed young woman who complained about a conflictual, unsatisfying marriage. She detailed a fight she had with her husband about access to the only key to their house. We discussed some options that she might have to reduce the tension, including getting copies of the key made. She left my office feeling some optimism about ways to assert herself in their relationship. She returned to my office with bruises and scrapes. The formerly verbal antagonism between them had shifted to physical abuse. There was an ominous sense that something much worse was possible.

By the second therapy hour, I had already learned some very valuable lessons. Therapy is not advice. Human systems are complex; tinkering can produce unexpected results. Clients can be very forgiving. Sometimes the therapist learns more than the client.

▼▼▼

INTERNSHIP

First to know, then to act, then to really know.

—Bishr al Hafifi

As we described in Chapter 2, during the final stage of your training, you participate in an internship that serves as a capstone of your training. It is during this time that you undergo a major transformation. Your internship experience involves a change in your self-concept—you enter as a trainee and you leave as a professional.

One of our counseling colleagues, John, remembers a moment during his internship when his concept of self was suddenly reframed. After a particularly stressful day in the clinic where he was doing his internship, John went to a local restaurant for dinner. He struck up a conversation with a server who asked him, "What do you do?"

Without thinking, John replied, "I'm a counselor." Immediately, he felt a rush of pride and thought to himself, "I really *am* a counselor!"

John recalled how wonderful it was to consider himself in this new way—as a counselor. Almost imperceptibly, he had metamorphosed into a new person. As a result of your internship experience, you also will find yourself developing a new identity. You really will be a helping professional.

Choosing a Site

Internship sites include community mental health centers, counseling agencies, programs for survivors of sexual assault, university student counseling centers, and elementary, middle, and high schools. The counseling services you may be offering within these settings include assessment, individual counseling, group counseling, family or couple counseling, emergency or crisis services, outreach services, consultation and education programs, prevention programs, and health promotion activities.

Training programs use a variety of methods for making decisions regarding internship placements. In your program, you may be responsible for contacting sites and obtaining a possible placement. In other cases, faculty members take responsibility for placing you while considering your interests, goals, and skills. In most situations, you have input into the placement decision (Simon, 1999).

When you explore your internship site options, you'll want to consider the services offered at the site, the client population, the reputation, the location, and, most important, the quality of supervision offered. According to Kiser (2000), the heart of your internship is the supervision you receive. Ask yourself this fundamental question about a possible supervisor: "Is this someone I think I can work with and who would be interested in helping me learn?" (Kiser, 2000, p. 5). Because selecting a field placement is to be one of the more important training choices you must make, it is important not to take the decision lightly.

■ ■ ■
_____

EXERCISE 8.1 Refreshing Your Memory and Plotting Your Course
A Decision-Making Exercise

Gather all the materials you have from all the classes you have taken so far—handouts, textbooks, notes, counseling and therapy videotapes, journals, and papers you have written. Mariners have navigated their courses by the stars since ancient times, so as you revisit each class, put a star by an activity you really liked—a written passage you found particularly meaningful, a microcounseling segment in which you excelled. Be careful not to let any preconceived notions get in your way. Pretend you are lost and are searching for directions. Even if you think you have a pretty good idea of where you are headed, completing the activity will be a good test of your reckoning.

Now go back through everything and see how your stars line up and converge on one or two clusters of common themes. You can use these clusters to chart your internship course.

■ ■ ■

Writing an Internship Agreement

Once you have located an internship site and have spoken with a helping professional who has agreed to be your supervisor, you are now ready to formalize your relationship. Your training program develops an agreement about what the internship will include. Two types of agreements should be created before you begin an internship. First, there should be a written agreement between your academic institution and the internship site. Next, together with your instructor and supervisor, you should formulate an agreement that describes the specific details of your individual internship experience. Establishing such agreements in writing at the outset will help avoid any misunderstanding or confusion about what the internship site and supervisor expect of you and what you expect of them.

Because no two internship sites or academic programs are identical, there is no single model for institutional agreements. There are, however, a number of common ingredients (Faiver, Eisengart, & Colonna, 2000; Thibadeau & Christian, 1985). Gelman (1990) identified four types of training agreements. These ranged from what he described as "friendly" agreements that are not legalistic to a more technical agreement that focuses on avoiding liability. Cooperative/joint agreements include the mutual benefits and responsibilities of the academic institution, student, and field placement.

Professional Liability Insurance

Being a student does not exempt you from being sued. You need protection from the financial devastation that you would face in a lawsuit. Even if your program does not require it, we strongly advise you to obtain your own professional liability insurance. Both the American Psychological Association and the American Counseling Association have professional liability insurance programs for graduate students. You will need to be a student member of the organization, but the application process is simple, and the insurance rates are economical. In this chapter's "Resources" section, you will find information on how to contact these insurance trusts.

Adhering to Ethics Codes

Competence The first and most important principle of most ethics codes is to operate within one's level of competence. Pope and Brown (1996) pointed out that the work you will be doing requires both "intellectual" and "emotional" competence. Recall from Chapter 4 that you think with both your head and your heart. Intellectual competence refers to knowledge and skill, but emotional competence refers to your ability to manage the emotional challenges of working with clients.

No counselor is competent to work with every client or problem. You may find that there are certain clients who "push your buttons" or overwhelm you. Don't try to fake it. Consult your supervisor and talk about these feelings. You will not be expected to work effectively with everyone. Furthermore, burnout, stress, family problems, and personal matters can impair your performance, regardless of your intellectual or technical skill. You can't take care of your clients unless you can take care of yourself.

Informed Consent Another important ethical principle is informed consent. Clients have a right to be informed about the treatment, assessment, or other services they will receive before they agree to participate in those activities. In order to ensure informed consent, you must give certain information in a manner and language that clients can understand. At a minimum, inform your clients about each of the following subjects (Harris, 1995):

- **Qualifications.** Clients should know that you are an intern and will be supervised. You should also explain your educational and training background.

- **Supervision.** Clients should be given the name and qualifications of your supervisor, should have an opportunity to meet with your supervisor if they desire to do so, and should know how they can contact your supervisor if they have any questions or concerns in the future. Your clients should understand the nature of your supervision, including the frequency of supervision and the activities it will entail (e.g., reviewing case notes, listening to tapes of sessions).

- **Services.** Your clients should be apprised of the nature of the counseling or assessment to be provided, including a brief description of the approach to treatment or the purpose of an assessment and the instruments that will be used. The frequency and duration of treatment sessions and a reasonable estimate of the typical number of sessions involved to treat a given concern should also be discussed.

- **Client Responsibilities.** The client is expected to attend scheduled appointments, to notify you in advance to cancel or change an appointment, and to follow through with any therapeutic assignments.

- **Fees.** Information should include the costs for services and whether or not there are charges for missed sessions. Your client should understand how and when payments are to be made, as well as the procedures that will be followed if payment is not made. Your discussion should also cover how insurance provider contacts will be managed and how this relationship affects confidentiality. If a client's insurance policy limits the number of sessions the insurance company will pay for, an agreement must be reached about how to proceed if more sessions are needed and the client is unable to pay without the assistance of the insurance.

- **Confidentiality.** The nature and limitations of confidentiality, including what is said in treatment, as well as what is contained in the client's records, should be included.

- **Questions.** You should encourage your client to ask questions at any time.

Confidentiality The essence of confidentiality is the principle that clients have the right to determine who will have access to information about them and their treatment. In clinical settings, clients need to feel that the information they share will stay with you and not be released without their permission. Without this assurance, your clients are less likely to explore and express their thoughts and feelings freely. Such a situation is likely to restrain the client's willingness to share certain information and may distort the treatment process (Nowell & Spruill, 1993). It is important to keep in mind that there are five instances in which absolute confidentiality does not hold and in which information must be shared. These exceptions are (1) dangerousness to self, (2) intent to harm others, (3) legal proceedings, (4) court orders, and (5) insurance company inquiries. Be sure to let your clients know the limits of confidentiality before they share personal information with you.

Putting It All Together

Most agencies and schools probably have photocopies of an informed consent document that they give to their clients as soon as they walk in the door. Clients are supposed to read, sign, and date the document as if they have completely understood everything they just read. Right!

When most of us are given a legal document that begins, "Whereas the party of the first part, heretofore known as the . . . ," our eyes glaze over as we search the page for some clue as to the meaning of what we are about to sign. Nevertheless, before they can enter into a therapeutic relationship, clients have to understand their rights and responsibilities. In most cases, the job of informing a client falls to the counselor.

Before every flight, all airplane pilots are required to perform a preflight check. A detailed list of "must do" procedures is performed and checked off before the aircraft ever enters the runway. Just like a pilot, you need to be sure that your client understands the essentials before the session ever begins. Let's tune in as Eduardo, a counseling intern, is beginning the first session with his client.

Counselor: Before we get started, there are a few things I'd like to discuss with you. You've probably heard the term "informed consent" before, right?

Client: Yes, I think so.

Counselor: You have heard of it, good. As you know, "informed consent" means you have a right to know everything about the services you will receive here at the counseling center. We go through this procedure with everyone who comes to the center. It is the policy of the counseling center and our ethical responsibilities as service providers. Speaking of responsibilities, you and I also have responsibilities in our work together. I'll go over mine first, then yours, and then we can discuss anything you may have questions about. How does that sound?

Client: All right, I guess.

Counselor: There are quite a few things we have to cover, so I'll be using this checklist to make sure I don't leave anything out. First off, as you know, my name is Eduardo and I'm a graduate student in the School of Psychology at the university. I have been working as a counseling intern since September and I'll continue working here until summer. Because I'm still in training, I am being supervised by two licensed professional counselors. One is on the staff here at the counseling center and the other is my professor at the university. I meet with them both at least once a week and I confer with them about my clients. Sometimes I show a videotape of a counseling session. Both of my supervisors' phone numbers are on this sheet I'll give you so you can talk to them any time you want about any concerns you have about our work together. OK so far?

Client: OK, I guess

Counselor: Good. In addition to my two supervisors, two other graduate students will view the tapes and . . .

Client: Oh, great, that's all I need. Now everybody in town will think I'm a weirdo.

Counselor: Don't worry—they are mostly focusing on my counseling and giving me feedback about my skills rather than sitting around analyzing every word you say. Plus, you are protected by confidentiality. I know you have heard that term also, but let's talk about it again, just to make sure. Essentially what confidentiality means is that you have a right to say anything you want to say in our sessions without having to worry about it being repeated. What is said in this room stays in this room except for a couple of exceptions.

We have already discussed my supervisors and my classmates at the university watching videotapes of sessions. In addition, if someone I'm counseling tells me that he or she plans to hurt himself or herself or someone else, I have to report that to my supervisors and to the proper authorities. Also, if I am subpoenaed by the courts or a client's insurance company, the confidentiality of our counseling relationship may no longer apply.

Client: So as long as I don't threaten to hurt myself or someone else, get in trouble with the law or with the insurance company, everything will be OK.

Counselor: Yes, that's right. We were told that it is standard practice pretty much all across the country.

Client: What else?

We aren't going to go through everything that needs to be covered in dialogue form, but we encourage you to develop your own "preflight checklist" for your site. Feel free to use what we've presented as a guideline.

Taking the High Road

In matters of style, swim with the current; in
matters of principle, stand like a rock.

—Thomas Jefferson

The Principles of Ethical Conduct As we discussed in Chapter 1, the sixth principle of thriving in your training is to always take the high road. To succeed as an intern, you need to practice the highest values every single day. Ethical conduct requires more than having good intentions and merely "following the rules." You will need to have a thorough understanding of the ethical standards that serve as the guiding principles for professional conduct (American Counseling Association, 1995; American Psychological Association, 1992). Both the ACA and APA codes are included in the appendix. Accepted ethical standards help you to structure the counseling relationship, place boundaries on its activities, and define aspects of its character that help you to promote client welfare.

Understanding your own values becomes especially important to your conduct as a professional when you confront ethical problems that require you to interpret or apply ethical principles in an ambiguous situation. Being ethical involves learning to make moral decisions based on criteria that emerge out of the goals and context of the helping relationship. As you read through the ACA and APA ethical guidelines, you will notice that they constitute a body of regulations and rules that you are expected to apply in your work with clients. But they do not apply to all situations. You must become an ethical person who can make judgments that will benefit your clients and remain within the general ethical guidelines for counselors.

Dual Roles An important ethical consideration is avoiding a dual role with clients. This means that you should not provide professional services for someone with whom you have another, nontherapeutic relationship that might interfere with your ability to function effectively. For example, according to the guidelines, it is unethical for you to provide counseling services to someone whom you employ. This employee may be your tax accountant or secretary or anyone with whom you have an ongoing relationship based on provision of goods or services. In relation to this person, you would assume a dual role because you interact with him or her in a specific context unrelated to the goals of your professional "helping" role. It is easy to see how this outside relationship, involving the exchange of money, the expectation of quality labor, the clear structure of power, and the difference in function of each of the persons involved can undermine the intent of a separate helping relationship.

Consider, however, a slightly different scenario that is not so clear-cut. Suppose you are one of only three mental health professionals living in a small town. Your son's seventh-grade history teacher seeks your help in addressing her problems with depression. You have expertise in this area, and she says she would feel comfortable with you as her therapist. In making a decision as to whether to accept this client, you must evaluate the situation in light of the ethical guidelines on dual relationships but also take into account other relevant information in making a moral decision.

For instance, is there someone else who has similar expertise to whom you can refer her, or will she go without services otherwise? How acute is her need for intervention? How much contact are you likely to have with the teacher regarding your son? How might unforeseen events, such as after-hours emergencies or a hospitalization, influence whether the relationship is contained in the counseling sessions? What effect might these potential complications have on the teacher-parent relationship?

These are the kinds of questions that you need to consider when the ethical issue falls in the gray area of decision making. Therapists in very small towns face these sorts of ethical dilemmas frequently, and they quickly understand that ethical questions are often complicated and usually involve more than a "cut and dried" application of rules. As an aside, the good news about avoiding dual relationships is that, should your family and friends seek counseling from you because of your professional training, you can tell them that your ethics prevent you from being their counselor—and you are off the hook!

As you can see, to be an ethical practitioner, you cannot simply rely on "going by the book" without examining the values that influence how you apply accepted ethical standards. In the preceding scenario, it may be unethical *not* to accept the teacher as a client, at least temporarily, especially if she were depressed enough that other harm may result in her not receiving services promptly. The application of ethics requires you to examine your own value construction. It is a vital part of knowing yourself as a person and a professional and understanding the process by which you interpret information in making moral decisions. A developed sense of moral reasoning, especially in response to an ambiguous situation, is essential in becoming a truly ethical professional.

Handling Ethical Dilemmas Ethical theory has long been of interest to philosophers and thinkers who are working to understand how persons may distinguish between what is morally right and what is wrong. According to Aristotle (Cohen & Cohen, 1999), the ancient Greek philosopher, moral virtues are character states that pertain to rational control and direction of emotions. However, recent discoveries in neuroscience have suggested that good social judgment depends as much on emotion as on reason (Damasio, 1994). Sometimes you have to rely on your gut feelings in situations that pose ethical dilemmas. Ethics are dependent on both head and heart. Examine the situation carefully, explore your motives, and be aware of your emotions. Taking time to reflect on your choices and staying committed to developing your personal character can also help you form an ethical worldview.

Because of your desire to help others, you are way ahead of the game. Our greatest reference points are the principles that form the basis of the therapeutic relationship itself. When you choose actions that best honor and actualize the goals of the counseling relationship, then you remain faithful to an important set of organizing concepts that define ethical values. Thus your choices are based on values that reflect your use of your skills to foster growth and to communicate respect and acceptance of the person. Authenticity of expression, responsibility in actions, and courage to change become guiding principles when making ethical decisions. Fostering well-being and advancing the best interests of clients become touchstones for structuring your interventions and making your decisions. Although your goals may be clear, their application in practice is often complex.

▲▲▲

Eric's Story

WHILE I WAS a practicum student, I counseled a man seeking help for depression. In the course of treatment, the man revealed that, though he was married with two children, he promiscuously engaged in unprotected heterosexual and homosexual activities with many partners. This client learned that one of his frequent homosexual partners had recently tested positive for the HIV virus. The client had not informed his wife of his secret life, nor of his own HIV status. He continued to have unprotected sex with his wife. When I encouraged him to get tested for HIV, he declined, saying he did not want to know, though he felt guilty about his wife's potential exposure. When asked whether he was willing to discuss these issues with his wife, he protested, saying that she would leave him, take his children away, and ruin him financially.

▼▼▼

Clearly, the ethical dilemma in this case is between maintaining the trust of client confidentiality or invoking the principle that states that when a client is a serious threat to him- or herself or others, confidentiality may be breached. To keep client confidentiality may result in significant harm to a third party. At the time, the legal precedents relevant to such cases did not encourage informing a third party if a sexually transmitted disease were the only identifiable indicator of harm. The case illustrates that sometimes what is law and what is viewed as ethical may be in opposition. New provisions by the American Counseling Association (1995) include a "Fatal, Contagious Diseases" clause that allows disclosure in some cases.

In this case, if the counselor had instantly broken confidentiality, the client would have left therapy feeling betrayed, and the therapist's ability to influence the situation would have been lost. The client would continue to have unprotected sex with other partners who would also be at risk. On the other hand, even though the HIV status of the client was undetermined, the counselor felt compelled to protect a third party from potential harm out of an ethical duty that transcended his relationship with the client.

Drawing on the principles discussed earlier, the counselor resolved to change the course of the therapy to address this central issue. First, the counselor secured an agreement from the client to cease sexual relations with his wife until the problem could be explored in therapy or until the client was tested. The client agreed to this provisional arrangement. The counselor concentrated on helping the client take responsibility for his choices, to be honest and authentic in his communications both inside and outside of the consulting room, and to rigorously examine the issues that led to such passive-aggressive behavior toward his wife and others. The frequency of sessions was increased, and within weeks of the initial discussion, with the strong support of the therapist, the client invited his wife to one of the sessions and disclosed the truth to her. He tested positive for HIV (his wife tested negative), and the couple divorced. The client continued to pursue therapy and to examine his sexual choices in regard to his HIV status, choosing to take more responsibility for protecting others. The client's wife was assisted in finding a counselor for herself as she sought to put her life back together.

Obviously, there are sometimes no happy endings, even when the counselor takes a proactive ethical stance. Cohen and Cohen (1999) provide a five-stage framework for conceptualizing and resolving ethical dilemmas. The following suggestions may be helpful to you as a template for resolving ambiguous situations.

- **Defining the moral problem.** The first stage involves identifying and defining the moral problem. How are the needs, interests, or welfare of the client or others threatened? The problem may be an intellectual one, such as "What should I think or believe?" The problem usually involves a practical question, such as "What should I do?" Defining these issues requires a developed moral sensitivity, insight, and awareness.

  In the preceding example, the counselor, rather than coercing the client, temporarily "stood in" for the client's lack of sensitivity by protecting the welfare of others. He emphasized the nature and scope of the moral problem by raising the central issue of responsibility for choices, a fundamental principle of the counseling relationship.

- **Identifying morally relevant facts.** The second stage focuses on identifying the morally relevant facts. How will the welfare of the client or others be affected by any decision? Morally relevant facts include such variables as the likelihood of suicide, test results from a medical examination, or history of violent behavior. In other words, what real factors impinge on the process of choosing a course of action?

- **Analyzing the issue.** This gathering of information leads to the third stage, which is to analyze the issue philosophically in light of all the morally relevant facts. Facts by themselves are insufficient to reach an ethical outcome. The goal is to clarify key organizing moral principles. Examining values, reflecting on effects of choices, exploring frames of reference, and meaning-making help formulate an ethical principle. This principle should have the central value of mitigating harm and promoting the welfare of all involved. As shown in the preceding case vignette, the counselor's ethical action may protect all parties from injury or pain.

- **Reaching a decision.** The fourth stage involves reaching a decision that is reasonable in light of the philosophical analysis. In the case vignette, the client initially refused to seek medical testing or to address the issue of his hidden life with his wife. He was making a decision by not making a decision. If the counselor had gone along with the client's denial and procrastination, then the counselor would have colluded with the client in this avoidance behavior. The counselor reached a decision to address the moral issue through the therapeutic process only after securing from the client agreements that satisfied the counselor's imperative to protect the third party.

- **Acting ethically.** The fifth stage concerns implementing the decision in action. For the counselor whose moral compass is responsive and accurate, this implementation is often the hardest part of ethical functioning. For instance, most helping professionals eventually encounter a situation in which their client is at risk of harming himself or herself. The intensity and timing of intervention in such cases is often not clear. Deciding to break confidentiality or hospitalize clients for their own protection—and against their will—may severely or irreparably damage the therapeutic bond. Not to act in such instances also may have harmful consequences.

Ethical conduct involves many other issues that are delineated in the codes. These principles include practicing within your scope of expertise, being sensitive to cultural differences, obtaining informed consent, and the nonsexual nature of the counselor-client relationship. The codes also address more practical matters, such as advertising, fees, bartering, and record keeping. Learn these ethical guidelines well. But remember that you must seek to implement these guidelines wisely, in consultation with your supervisor, keeping in mind the welfare of those who have sought your help and counsel.

Making Rest Stops Along the Way

In addition to performing your duties at your internship site, you will participate in weekly supervision sessions and may meet regularly with other interns. The internship class provides opportunities to share your internship experiences, explore the many opportunities for your professional development, look at your counseling work, learn from one another, clarify your professional goals, and help everyone to achieve those goals. It is also the time to exchange support and encouragement with your peers. It is a designated time for you to "fill up your tank" so you can continue on the journey. Reflecting on the internship experience, students have commented that they "didn't feel so isolated and alone after talking with other interns." Others described the experience as a "support system that cheered" them on throughout the semester.

▲▲▲

Nathaniel's Story

I WAS SEEING my first family in my practicum experience. In they trooped: father, mother, daughter. Then another woman came in who was introduced as an aunt. "What's she doing here?" I thought. "Is this okay?" I was thinking about confidentiality and consent and trying to figure out what kind of family this was! Pretty soon, I found out. The mother was on "house arrest." She wore an ankle monitor and was allowed to leave her house only for work and counseling. The aunt was with us in the session because she had assumed primary caretaking responsibilities while the family was adjusting to Mom's situation. The father seemed stunned. He reported that he and his wife had been fighting frequently. The daughter was bright and hopeful, but I was uncomfortable with the banter and teasing that went on between her and her mother.

"These poor people," I thought with sympathy. "They have no money and this is their lifestyle. They probably don't know any better." As I listened to their stories I judged every one of them. I remember vividly how I left the session shaking my head and telling my supervisor there was little potential for progress with this "family."

My supervisor seemed confused. What was the evidence for my gloomy prognosis? The entire family had come in—all had expressed dissatisfaction with their current situation. Everyone present claimed a desire to work. What obstacles did I see to their progress and growth in counseling? I fumbled for words. "Well, you know, they're . . . Well, it seems limited." My supervisor looked at me inquisitively, patiently, and silently. Those were the longest few minutes of my life. It seemed as though my supervisor could see and hear every stereotype and prejudice that I had ever had. Furthermore, I started to suspect that I had been equally transparent to my clients.

My face began to feel as if it were on fire, and believe it or not, I started to get teary-eyed. I was so unprepared to face the ugly stuff that lies within me that I had avoided it until that moment. When it came, it came in a rush. I had always believed that prejudice was a given in our lives, and that I was in touch enough with my own "stuff" that it wouldn't interfere with my work. I was wrong. My supervision helped during that time, as did my own counseling. I've also come to appreciate the need to continually check on my own attitudes and beliefs and be responsible for my own growth. Even if prejudices really are a given, that doesn't mean I have to be satisfied with my own.

▼▼▼

You may believe that you've effectively confronted your prejudices, only to be smacked in the face with a nasty reminder of old messages and beliefs that you learned as a child. Facing your prejudices and stereotypes can be painful and make you feel guilty. If you avoid doing so, however, you're bound to find yourself feeling like Nathaniel—ashamed and disappointed. Take time now, before you enter practicum or internship, to again examine your own beliefs and attitudes about difference. Recognize that guilt is the great silencer, and don't let it stop you from being honest right now.

■ ■ ■

EXERCISE 8.2 First Thoughts
An Exploratory Exercise

Consider this mix of different people. Read through the following list and write down the first thoughts that come to your head. Don't censor yourself. Just write down your thoughts. Now, imagine what might go through your mind if you were to counsel a member of each group.

Men

_____

_____

Sex Abusers

_____

_____

Elderly

_____

_____

Athletes

_____

_____

Women

_____

_____

Whites

_____

_____

Alcoholics

_____

_____

African Americans

_____

_____

Disabled

_____

_____

Latinos

_____

_____

Rich

_____

_____

Asians

_____

_____

Of course, presenting people as members of groups is always tricky. You run the risk of denying or ignoring individuality for the sake of categorization. Typically, however, you learn your prejudices and stereotypes about groups, not about individual people. That's why stereotypes are so specious—they erase your pictures of unique individuals worthy of respect and replace them with faceless images that create fear or contempt.

This exercise is a chance for you to explore how you really feel about yourself and others. Look over what you've written and work to identify your prejudices and stereotypes. Where did these messages originate? How have these beliefs affected you over time? After you've given some time and thought to this exercise, talk with your supervisor and peers about how you approach and accept difference.

We offer one caveat regarding this exercise. You may find that you have to confront—at least in your mind—beloved members of your family. Your uncle Joey, for instance, who always took you sledding and gave you the most perfect birthday presents year after year, may now appear to you to be a first-class bigot. This realization need not be the end of your relationship with Uncle Joey. It may, however, cause you to evaluate your expectations of others and to consider how you want to handle differing opinions. Furthermore, attempting to understand where Joey got his ideas and what motivates his clinging to them might be a very illuminating exercise for you. Merely labeling him as a bigot and writing him off is contrary to the values in counseling and therapy. We try our best to understand how everyone sees the world. Good luck in your continued explorations.

■■■

Stages in the Journey

*The real voyage of discovery lies not in seeking
new landscapes but in having new eyes.*

—Marcel Proust

Kiser (2000) suggests that internships progress through specific developmental stages that include preplacement, initiation, working, and termination.

Preplacement Stage During your preplacement stage, you work with your professors to decide on internship locations. You spend time carefully matching your needs, along with the program's expectations, to an appropriate site. Activities include writing a resume or introductory letter to potential sites, visiting schools and community agencies, and interviewing. You may be discouraged if you are not able to find a perfect match. However, keep in mind that what you *want* in an internship may not necessarily be what you *need* in an internship. It is important to keep an open mind during this stage.

Initiation Stage Once the internship is under way, you begin the initiation stage. During this stage, you meet new people and become familiar with the site's procedures. It is during this time that you begin to develop a trusting relationship with your supervisor. You may "shadow" your site supervisor at this time to help familiarize yourself with your surroundings. This stage of your internship is the "look" before the "leap" into counseling and therapy on your own. You may be asked to observe procedures, sit in on meetings, and take extensive notes. Remember, this stage does not last forever.

Working Stage In the working stage, you are focusing your energy on reaching the goals that you developed during the preplacement stage. At this stage, you begin to feel more settled and confident. A key element of this stage is taking advantage of learning opportunities that are available at the internship site. Kiser (2000) warns that you should not become too independent and urges that you continue seeking all the supervision, feedback, and teaching opportunities that are available.

The working stage is the point in the journey at which you may turn on the car's cruise control. Feeling confident about where you are, where you are headed, and the rate at which you are traveling, you can relax a little. This is not necessarily a bad thing—travelers cannot maintain a high level of stress and anxiety throughout such a long journey. But it is important to remember that you are still responsible for keeping the car on the road and headed in the right direction.

Final Stage The final stage of internship is the termination stage. During this time, you begin planning for the completion of the internship, which includes saying good-bye to supervisors and colleagues, and terminating with clients. Don't be surprised if you feel some sadness during this period. Be sure to take time during this hectic period to review your internship, to contemplate on what you have learned, how you have changed, and what you have discovered. And give yourself permission to feel proud of your accomplishments!

Juggling

Once your internship is under way, you may feel overwhelmed at first. You may feel like you have one foot in "student life" and the other foot in "professional life." As classes start and supervisor's expectations become clear, you will begin to realize that this is an exciting time. You are given opportunities to try things out while still receiving support and direction from your professors and peers. Once you begin to feel that you are standing on solid ground, take the time to explore. This is your time to ask questions, gather opinions, and formulate your professional identity. If your internship class size is small, take full advantage of the opportunity to use class time to share with your classmates. Although your professional career is only a few months away, you may begin to wonder if you are ready for it, and you may begin to mourn the loss of the community in your training program. Vow to stay in touch with your professors and your colleagues. They will want to know how you are doing, and they will be proud of your future accomplishments.

Making the Most of Your Internship

It is important that you remember to collect "postcards" along your journey. There are several different types of postcards you can gather to make the most of your internship. Your internship experience is a time for you to acquire as much information as possible from supervisors, peers, clients, professors, and other professionals. Although it is your time to put theory into action, it is also a time for you to make the most of the resources that surround you.

One way to do this is to "pick the brains" of your colleagues at your site. If you are interning in a school, for example, make a point of setting meetings to learn from educational specialists, classroom teachers, principals, and students. It is important that you develop and maintain a group of professional peers.

Your internship is also the time to attend as many workshops and conferences as possible. Use these opportunities to see, hear, and talk about techniques, approaches, and interventions that are currently being tried in the field. Take advantage of the cheaper student membership fees and join professional organizations and affiliations.

Internship is also a time to meet other professionals and develop a networking system. Rather than loading down your backpack with mementos from the journey, you can keep a journal of your personal reflections.

SUMMARY

Your practicum and internship experiences are unique opportunities to apply what you have learned. Each experience offers an opportunity to put your knowledge and skills into practice in a supervised setting. With careful planning and consideration, you can learn what it takes personally and professionally to thrive as a counselor. When you complete your internship, you will become a professional helper. Along with the opportunities for employment in the field will come many responsibilities. You will be well prepared for your new career, but remember that becoming an successful counselor or therapist is a lifetime pursuit. Commit yourself to be the very best you can be.

RESOURCES

One of the most helpful books for general internship questions is Baird's (1999) *The Internship, Practicum, and Field Placement Handbook*. The author includes such topics as preparing for an internship or field placement, getting started, and legal and ethical considerations. The book also provides many helpful lists and forms that will come in handy during your internship.

Kiser (2000) also provides another type of workbook for the counseling intern. It offers a variety of opportunities to reflect on your internship experiences. A list of "myths about internship" is included and is worth a look.

If you are concerned about paperwork, Boylan, Malley, and Reilly (1995) do a great job of providing every possible document you will need for your internship and beyond. It is a great resource to keep nearby when you are starting out.

If you are interning in a school setting, you should take a look at Van Zandt and Hayslip's (2001) *Developing Your School Counseling Program: A Handbook for Systemic Planning*. Once your school counseling internship is under way, check out Blum's (1998) book of lists. The author provides sample letters, activities, and definitions that are practical and useful.

Many practicum and internship supervisors require you to have personal liability insurance prior to working with clients. The American Counseling Association and the American Psychological Association both offer liability insurance at very reasonable rates for graduate students enrolled in training programs. The addresses are provided below:

American Counseling Association Insurance Trust
5999 Stevenson Avenue
Alexandria, VA 22304-3300
800-347-6647
www.acait.com

American Psychological Association Insurance Trust
750 First Street N.E., Suite 605
Washington, DC 20002-4242
800-477-1200
www.apait.org

REFERENCES

American Counseling Association. (1995). *Code of ethics and standards of practice*. Alexandria, VA: Author.

American Psychological Association. (1992). *Ethical principles of psychologists and code of conduct*. Washington, DC: Author.

Baird, B. N. (1999). *The internship, practicum, and field placement handbook* (2nd ed.). Upper Saddle River, NJ: Prentice-Hall.

Blum, D. J. (1998). *The school counselor's book of lists*. West Nyack, NY: Center for Applied Research.

Boylan, J. C.; Malley, P. B., & Reilly, E. P. (2001). *Practicum and internship: Textbook and resource guide for counseling and psychotherapy* (3rd ed.). New York: Brunner/Routledge.

Cohen, E. D., & Cohen, S. P. (1999). *The virtuous therapist: Ethical practice of counseling and psychotherapy*. Belmont, CA: Brooks/Cole.

Damasio, A. (1994). *Decartes' error: Emotion, reason and the human brain*. New York: Putnam.

Faiver, C., Eisengart, S., & Colonna, R. (2000). *The counselor intern's handbook* (2nd ed.). Belmont, CA: Brooks/Cole.

Gelman, S. R. (1990). The crafting of fieldwork training agreements. *Journal of Social Work Education, 26*, 65–75.

Harris, E. A. (1995). The importance of risk management in a managed care environment. In M. B. Sussman (Ed.), *A perilous calling: The hazards of psychotherapy practice* (pp. 247–258). New York: Wiley.

Kiser, P. M. (2000). *Getting the most from your human service internship: Learning from experience.* Belmont, CA: Brooks/Cole.

Nowell, D., & Spruill, J. (1993). If it's not absolutely confidential, will information be disclosed? *Professional Psychology: Research and Practice, 24,* 367–369.

Pope, K. S., & Brown, L. S. (1996). *Recovered memories of abuse: Assessment, therapy, forensics.* Washington, DC: American Psychological Association.

Simon, E. (1999). Field practicum: Standards, criteria, supervision, and evaluation. In H. Harris & D. Maloney (Eds.), *Human services: Contemporary issues and trends* (pp. 79–96). Boston: Allyn & Bacon.

Thibadeau, S. F., & Christian, W. P. (1985). Developing an effective practicum program at the human service agency. *Behavior Therapist, 8,* 31–34.

Van Zandt, Z., & Hayslip, J. (2001). *Developing your school counseling program : A handbook for systemic planning.* Belmont, CA: Brooks/Cole.

CHAPTER 9

Launching Your Career

To love what you do and feel that it matters—how
could anything be more fun?

—Eileen Nelson

The top of an advertisement page in a recent *U.S. News and World Report* proclaimed, "Take this job and *love* it!" Why does this phrase capture our attention? Besides the fact that it was an obvious takeoff on a country music hit, "Take This Job and Shove It," it is the audacity of declaring that you can feel passionate about your work!

A newspaper cartoon that appeared a while ago explored a similar theme. The first frame showed a man working at his desk with a sign hanging prominently behind him—"Seize the Day!" The second frame had the same man sitting in the same position, yet the sign behind him had changed to "Survive the Day!" The caption stated, "Today's corporate philosophy." What a sad commentary on the contemporary employment world.

Why can't you both love your job *and* thrive each day at work? We believe you can. In this chapter, we discuss how you can forge a passionate and successful career in the field of counseling. As you prepare to become a professional helper, you'll want to consider five specific goals: (1) gaining employment, (2) obtaining licensure or certification, (3) becoming more involved in a professional network, (4) staying creative in your work, and (5) continuing your personal and professional development. This chapter offers you guidelines for developing an effective resume, designing vigorous job-search strategies, writing persuasive correspondence, and participating in successful job interviews. You'll also learn how to obtain information about the different licensure

243

and certification requirements for counseling and therapy across the United States, and you'll discover opportunities to become more involved in professional organizations. You'll learn ways to stimulate and keep your creativity. Finally, you'll explore ways to maintain your professional vitality through a variety of continuing training experiences.

Above all, you'll see that your career can be an exciting adventure, another thrilling phase of your journey. You can make a difference through your work—and one way to start is by being opportunistic. Carpe diem! Seize this moment to make positive career choices that will make a difference for yourself and others.

▲▲▲

Around the Next Corner
Bill's Story

AT THE AGE of thirty-six, following three years of graduate school and twelve years of experience in one career, why would I make a change? I was in the midst of a promising career and financially stable. Why would anyone in their right mind leave an annual income of $64,000 for a life of financial worry and stress for a period of three to five years? (For the record, my average annual income was around $16,000 during three of the five years of my doctoral program.)

Most of my family and friends thought I was crazy! I thought that of myself a few times. But I wanted to be a counselor and make a difference, and I needed more training and experience to get to the place I wanted to be. For years, I had been doing "counseling" and "crisis intervention" without the expertise, and I was tired of pretending. I needed instruction, more experience, and a sense of personal and professional integrity. So I studied for and took the GRE. I applied for a Ph.D. program and was accepted. I began the journey toward becoming a professional counselor.

Little did I know that, along the way, I would have the opportunity to teach counseling and discover my true life passion—teaching! Now I have the best of all worlds. I am a lifelong learner of the trade I teach, and I have the honor of teaching counseling among some of the brightest minds and most caring people in the world!

My best advice for you as you continue along your career journey is to be prepared for, and open to, the unexpected turns in the road, for around the next corner you may discover a surprising opportunity that may lead you toward discovering your life passion.

▼▼▼

How do you discover your true passion in life? How can you make your work meaningful and successful? As you conclude your training and prepare to launch your career, perhaps you can identify with Laura Cornely (1999), who reflected on her own training journey:

> Look around and you will see that the road from student to professional is well traveled. Your peers, supervisors, and professors have each traveled the professional development road for various distances (p. 16).

Some of the signs that Cornely mentioned are what we would like to call to your attention now.

■■■

EXERCISE 9.1 Life-Span Time Line

Think about all the career options you have considered pursuing in your life. As a child, you may have fantasized about becoming a professional actor, dancer, or athlete. As an adolescent, you may have seriously explored several other career options. When you became a young adult, you probably experimented by taking a variety of jobs. Now you are at a point in your life at which you are focusing on a few career options.

Describe your career fantasies, experiences, and plans at different points in the past, present, and future along your life-span time line below. Note the persons, places, or events that influenced your decisions. Look for emerging themes, crucial turning points, and future aspirations. How do you get from the present to a successful future?

■■■

FROM STUDENT TO PROFESSIONAL

It is good to have an end to journey towards; but it
is the journey that matters in the end.

—Ursula K. Le Guin

As you prepare to make the transition from student to professional, you begin to think more seriously about the specific career path you want to follow. New possibilities and opportunities are constantly developing in the fields of counseling and therapy. Before exploring your options, you can consider your values and family background, your unique interests and abilities, your personality traits, and the needs of others to whom you are committed. You will also want to know where to go to discover the career possibilities open to you. You'll need to develop your resume, prepare for interviews, and make plans for the professional writing and correspondence that will be required of you. And finally, you'll want to make plans for continuing your personal and professional thriving journey through licensure, certification, and continuing education. Let's address these issues more specifically now.

Exploring Your Values

A great way to start your career development journey is by assessing your values—what you see as truly important—and the unique perspective you bring to life and work. Here is an exercise to get you started.

■ ■ ■
_____

EXERCISE 9.2 **Building a House**
A Values Exercise

All of us have values and beliefs that govern who we are and the decisions we make in life. Rarely, however, do we take the time to examine these values. For the next few minutes, think about the following questions and then draw a symbolic representation of your answers in the form of a house. You don't need to be an artist to complete this exercise. Just go ahead and let yourself have some fun with it!

Foundation

In Chapter 5, you wrote your training mission. Now take a much broader perspective and consider your *life* mission. What would be your life motto? What is the guiding principle that you live by every day? Draw the base of your house and write your answer inside the space you've drawn.

Walls

Where do you get your support in life? Who or what provides you the support you need? Draw some walls for your house, and write your answer on your walls.

Roof

Certainly some storms come in every person's life. Who or what provides you the protection you need when difficulties arise? Write your answer on the roof you've drawn.

Chimney

How do you vent when life gets hard for you? What outlets do you turn to for a safe place to let off steam? Place your answer inside your chimney.

Windows

What accomplishments or experiences are you most proud of, and what in your life are you most willing to let others see? Put your answers in the windows you have drawn.

Door

Who are the most significant and influential people who have entered your life? What have you learned from them? Write their initials on the door to your house.

Trees

What are you planting and nurturing that you hope will outlive you? Draw one or more trees to represent your legacy.

What have you learned about yourself and your values from this exercise? Share your drawing with a trusted colleague or mentor.

As you gain insight about the role of your values in your career choices, you may feel greater confidence about the choices you are making.

Exploring Your Roots

Sooner or later, thinking about where you want to go leads you to consider where you've been. As you try to make sense of your career choices, keep in mind that you can best be understood in context and that your context includes the influences of your family of origin. Family can be defined in a number of ways, so don't excuse yourself from this part of the chapter if your caretakers were actually grandparents, foster parents, or older siblings. You can define your family however you like. The important issue to consider at this point is how your heritage affects your career and lifestyle decision making.

You can begin to answer this question in a number of ways. Think about what you learned from your family about work and career. Were certain jobs considered acceptable and others not? Did your family have different expectations for men and women? Did they value higher education? How did your family balance love, work, and play? How are your current choices similar or dissimilar to those of your family? Finally, are you where you want to be?

Give yourself some time to ponder these questions. The answers that arise can be illuminating—and maybe even surprising.

▲▲▲

The Legacy of My Parents
Gabe's Story

I GREW UP in a blue-collar household and was the first member of my family to receive a college degree. As a matter of fact, my pursuit of a doctoral degree was primarily driven by my desire to prove that I could do it. I hadn't really given much thought to the type of lifestyle I would have after I graduated.

In my first job as an assistant professor in a counseling program, I couldn't believe how much my colleagues grumbled about their work. I kept thinking, "These whiners don't realize how lucky they have it!" I kept imagining my mother and father and the hard physical work that they had done for years—and continue to do even now! I started to have doubts about my career choice, and I also felt distant from my colleagues. At first, I felt like an impostor. Deep down, I didn't believe that it was okay for me to have a good-paying job in which I didn't physically exhaust myself. Although my efforts in school had earned my current position, I felt guilty. I also didn't feel comfortable with aspects of my job that required administrative or committee work. I knew I could teach and do research, but the rest of the job seemed like uncharted territory to me. I chose not to participate in many university activities for fear of being rejected, labeled ignorant, or identified as an "outsider."

As I continued to think about my family, though, I began to realize a few things about myself. I came to understand that I do work very hard and that I can be proud of my accomplishments. One strength that I now can acknowledge is that I easily empathize with the first-generation college students in my classes. Although I still feel like an outsider at times, I'm working to make a place for myself in my job while honoring the legacy of my parents.

▼▼▼

A career genogram can help you identify your worldview, perceived barriers, role conflicts, intergenerational patterns, and beliefs about work and roles (Gysbers & Heppner, 1997). Constructing one and reflecting on what you find can be an important step for you in this stage of your journey.

Putting yourself in the context of your family, you can explore patterns and influences that have helped and hindered your progress so far. You can then decide what to do with this information in order to make the most of your experiences.

■ ■ ■

EXERCISE 9.3 **Career Genogram**

Begin by constructing a genogram of three generations and include occupations for each person. See *Genograms in Family Assessment* by Monica McGoldrick and Randy Gerson (1985) for information on constructing genograms. Now spend some time responding to the questions below.

Who are you most like?

What were the dominant values in your family?

Did any family members have obvious vocational callings?

What roles did different family members play?

What values did you learn from your family about work?

How are love, work, and play balanced?

What do the vocational patterns that you see suggest to you?

What did you learn from your family about education?

If each person were to provide one word about work, what would it be?

As you notice any patterns, what do you want to do with that information?

■■■

USING THE CAMPUS CAREER CENTER

A good place to begin your career path is at your college or university career center. Most campuses have great resources available, with a professional staff ready and willing to assist you. Undergraduate students flock to these centers for help, but you may be surprised to discover that the center is available to graduate students, also.

The career counselors and advisors can assist you with resume questions, interview preparation, job openings in your area, and contacts with alumni. Many colleges and universities have established wonderful career networks among alumni. Consider contacting graduates from your program through your college or university alumni network. Your career center may regularly sponsor a career fair and probably has many resources available for you to read. One such resource is the annual edition of *Planning Job Choices*. This magazine has excellent tips about the current job market, writing outstanding resumes, interviewing successfully, and thriving in your first year of employment. See the list titled "Top 10 Personal Characteristics Employers Seek in Job Candidates," taken from *Planning Job Choices* (National Association of Colleges and Employers, 1999) for information about what employers want most in job candidates.

Top 10 Personal Characteristics
Employers Seek in Job Candidates
Honesty/integrity
Motivation/initiative
Communication skills
Self-confidence
Flexibility
Interpersonal skills
Strong work ethic
Teamwork skills
Leadership skills
Enthusiasm

Source: National Association of Colleges and Employers, 1999.

SEEKING CAREER COUNSELING

You may want to consider seeing a career counselor to explore the numerous areas of specialization in the counseling field. Bolles (1999) listed possible contacts from every state in his annual resource guide. Career counselors can help you sort through your concerns, and many offer testing and assessment services to further enable you to gain clarity about your career options. Possible career interest inventories include the Self-Directed Search (SDS), the Strong Interest Inventory (SII), and the Values Scale (VS). Personality instruments, such as the Myers-Briggs Type Indicator (MBTI) or the Sixteen Personality Factor Questionnaire (16PF), and cognitive scales, such as the Career Beliefs Inventory or the Career Decision Scale, may also be useful.

CAREER POSSIBILITIES BY DEGREE
Careers with a Master's or Ed.S.

With a master's or educational specialist degree in counseling, you can meet the course work requirements for licensure and can work in a variety of settings, including businesses, hospitals, schools, community mental health centers, and many other public and private institutions. However, these professional opportunities vary considerably and depend to a large extent on the type of training you receive. You may be involved in assessment, providing intervention services, counseling, consultation, health promotion, vocational rehabilitation, or behavior management.

Licensing and Credentialing Licensed professional counselors may provide psychological services without supervision by other professionals. Currently, forty-six states, including the District of Columbia, license professional counselors. Most of those states issue a general credential for a licensed professional counselor. All fifty states and the District of Columbia regulate school counseling through their state school boards.

Licensure and credential requirements vary from state to state. Typically, states have course work, supervised experience, and examination requirements for licensure. The course work requirements are generally based on the Council for Accreditation of Counseling and Related Educational Programs (CACREP) accreditation model for a counseling curriculum. The curriculum usually involves forty-eight to sixty semester hours of graduate study in the following areas: human growth and development, social and cultural foundations, helping relationships, group work, career and lifestyle development, appraisal, research and program evaluation, and professional orientation. The supervised experience requirement often involves up to 4,000 hours of work following the completion of your training. And the licensing examination requirement typically includes passing the National Counselors Examination. Also, the National Board of Certified Counselors nationally certifies CACREP graduates who successfully complete this examination.

For information on the licensing of professional counselors in your state, you can consult your telephone book's blue pages for the state regulation board's telephone number and address. For information regarding your state's regulations for credentialing as a school counselor, contact your state's department of education. You can go to the American Counseling Association Web site at *www.counseling.org* or call 1-800-347-6647, extension 222, and ask for the publication, *A Guide to State Laws and Regulations on Professional School Counseling.*

Other Helping Professions If you are seeking employment in school psychology, you probably hold an educational specialist degree, which usually requires at least sixty semester hours of graduate study. Most professionals in school psychology work primarily in the schools and are concerned with a variety of psychological and educational issues.

If you are seeking a general, research-oriented degree and you are not planning on pursuing further study at the doctoral level, you may find employment in teaching or research. Without a doctoral degree, however, you may find that your opportunities for employment or advancement in higher education are limited. You may discover that you are seldom able to provide services without supervision.

As a graduate of a professional master's degree program in industrial/organizational psychology, you may find employment opportunities in private businesses and government organizations. You may devote much of your time to the selection and training of employees. You may also focus on human resource development, employee assistance programs, and other programs related to personnel management and employee relations.

Careers with a Doctorate

Counselors and counseling psychologists with doctoral degrees assume many different occupational roles. You may work as a teacher, researcher, mental health service provider, administrator, or consultant. Doctoral-level counselors and counseling psychologists are employed in a variety of settings, including universities, elementary and secondary schools, hospitals, human service agencies, private business and industry, and government organizations. In addition, many helping professionals with doctorates maintain independent practices for the provision of counseling and psychological services. The doctoral degree offers you the most professional flexibility and leads to many career opportunities in counseling and psychology.

Obtaining a doctorate requires a deep commitment to academic training. The successful completion of a doctoral program entails at least four or five years of intensive graduate study. You must also pass a set of comprehensive examinations and write and defend a dissertation. If you wish to provide counseling and psychological services, you need to complete a year-long internship plus at least one additional year of supervised practice.

Admission to doctoral programs is highly competitive. The average acceptance rate for doctoral programs is approximately 11 percent; some programs in clinical psychology accept less than 2 percent of all applicants. Still, a doctorate in counseling or psychology is a very appealing option for students who are willing to make a substantial personal investment in order to achieve high academic and professional goals.

Counselor education is centered on the goal of training successful counselors who will be prepared to assume leadership roles in the field of counseling. A doctoral degree in counselor education is accredited by the Council for Accreditation of Counseling and Related Educational Programs (CACREP). CACREP emphasizes the training of professional counselor educators and counselors who will have competence in the core areas of counseling, teaching, research, and supervision. Counselor educators often fill multifaceted roles but are most often distinguished as helping professionals who work from a developmental and health perspective.

The majority of counselor educators and counselors who complete the doctoral degree will work in educational settings such as colleges, universities, public and private schools, technical schools, and a broad spectrum of human service agencies. Professional activities usually include counseling, assessment, diagnosis, casework, consultation, referral, and research.

PLANNING YOUR CAREER

Being Intentional

Selecting and pursuing your career goals are obviously important matters that will have a profound effect on your life. Explore your career options thoroughly, not only to improve your chances for eventual employment but also to choose paths that will lead to personal and professional satisfaction. Because of their extensive involvement in the field, faculty advisors and other helping professionals are in an excellent position to help you weigh your career alternatives. Rewarding professional experiences seldom happen by chance alone. You will need to carefully consider your options and to be intentional with your plans in order to achieve a happy, fulfilling career.

Where to Look for Jobs

The best way for you to discover an available employment opportunity is still the old-fashioned way—through other people. So it is still vital that you stay connected with your professors, fellow students, professional contacts in the field, and alumni of your program. In many, if not most, helping professions, job opportunities are found through personal contact—through someone you know or people who know you. So maintaining your personal contacts is essential. This does not mean that *what* you know is less important than *who* you know; however, counseling and other helping professions are less likely to advertise positions in more traditional ways, such as through newspapers or Web sites. You may discover a good job that way, yet we cannot tell you how often we have found our students receiving job opportunities through word of mouth or an E-mail. Keep this in mind.

■ ■ ■

EXERCISE 9.4 Interviewing Two Masters
A Journal Exercise

Schedule interviews with two professionals who are well established in the career field you hope to enter. Ask them their reasons for going into this profession to begin with and what keeps them in it. Inquire as to what they like and dislike most about their jobs. You may even want to ask them what they would do differently if they had it to do all over again. Finally, you might ask what they see as future trends in their particular fields.

After each interview, write a reflective entry in your journal about the personal meaning and insight you gained. Sometimes it helps to compare or contrast your journey with those of others whom you deeply respect. This exercise may even emerge as the beginning point of a mentor/protégé relationship, as it has for many of our students.

■ ■ ■

Local newspapers are still a good resource for finding specific jobs in your geographic area. Most newspapers now have Internet sites available, allowing you access to almost any conceivable job market. Many Web sites are also maintained simply to provide employers with a means of reaching the largest possible audience of prospective employees. We have listed some of these popular Web sites at the end of this chapter. There are thousands of jobs available on any given site. Some sites charge minimal fees for their services, and some are free to the public. Other services, such as resume posting, are also available on many sites.

Professional organizations related to counseling, psychology, and other helping professions also advertise current position openings. The *APA Monitor* and *ACA Counseling Today* are outstanding resources in this regard. The *Chronicle of Higher Education* posts jobs in academic environments weekly. These professional newspapers also have Web sites with job listings, and these sites are included at the end of this chapter.

Remember to use your university's alumni office and career center. These centers often maintain binders with thousands of job opportunities that have been targeted for students about to graduate. Networking through professional organizations is also a great way to discover job leads.

Becoming Professionally Involved

As you consider your career options after graduation, you may be preparing to seek a position or to continue your education. Regardless of your current intentions, become involved in professional organizations. These organizations, such as the American Counseling Association, American Psychological Association, Association for Counselor Education and Supervision, and their regional, state, and local divisions, offer options limited only by your imagination and initiative. The student membership rates for professional organizations are much cheaper than they are for professional members, so take advantage of this opportunity while you can.

Through professional organization involvement, you can attend conferences, offer presentations, participate in workshops, serve on committees, find a mentor, lobby state and national politicians, keep abreast of current research, or simply meet and socialize with other professionals. Beginning this type of involvement now, while you're a student, will increase your network, perhaps enhance your capability to find an excellent job that matches your interests, and improve the likelihood that you'll stay connected and relevant in your own professional development.

When imagining such involvement, some students may immediately ask, "Yes, that sounds good, but how do I get involved?" You may feel intimidated by the idea of approaching strangers and asking if you can join a committee—especially if those strangers are well-known authors or researchers. Meeting a favorite author at a conference can feel like meeting a celebrity! One of the many advantages of being a student is that you can reasonably expect your professors to introduce you to "movers and shakers" in the field. In fact, you'll probably find that your professors and other mentors would love to "show you off."

As you meet people who are involved in professional organizations, ask them if there are ways that you can help. Most conference committees rely on graduate student assistance. Trainees who volunteer to work at national or international conferences usually receive compensation in the form of reduced or waived conference registration fees. They also enjoy the opportunity to see how professional organizations are administered and have the chance to meet colleagues from across the country. Some of these interactions fall into the category of networking—a skill that may seem more appropriate for business and the corporate world. Actually, networking is essential for an active and successful professional in almost any field.

If you're trying to decide how to go about becoming more involved in professional organizations, consider the following tips (Huddock, Thompkins, & Enterline, 2000):

- Research organizations by visiting their Web pages and then consider joining as a student member.

- E-mail or telephone leaders to see if their committee needs your assistance. Don't be surprised to find that they do. Handle your shyness or nervousness by starting small. Contact local or regional divisions of professional organizations first. Ask a professor to introduce you to a committee chairperson via e-mail or telephone prior to making your first contact.

- Submit a proposal for a state, regional, or national conference. Ask a few peers to present with you. When you attend the conference, participate in the entire experience. Make the most of the opportunities that exist for you to meet people and become involved.

- Don't stop yourself with excuses. Just do it!

CONDUCTING YOUR SEARCH

Designing an Effective Resume

As you begin the process of preparing your professional resume, keep in mind the following basic tips. Choose high-quality paper, staying with basic colors such as white, beige, or gray. Use a font style that is easy to read, such as Courier or Times New Roman, and a size that is legible, such as 11 or 12 points. Limit the length of your resume to two or three pages.

Place your current personal data at the top of your resume, because this basic information is essential for the employer to contact you. Include your name, permanent and local addresses, telephone number, and E-mail address. Immediately below your personal information, offer a career objective statement that clearly reflects your interest in the position. Then list your undergraduate and graduate educational experience, highlighting specialized training, awards, and your grade point average—if it will be a good selling point!

Below the education section, present your employment experience, beginning with the most recent jobs. Don't forget to add your relevant volunteer, practicum, internship, and field placement experiences. You may also want to list any additional skills that seem relevant, such as Web design, Power Point presentation, and word processing skills. Following this section, include any professional presentations, publications, and research projects.

On a separate sheet, list the names of your references, along with the necessary contact information. Your references should be respected, responsible individuals who can describe in detail your personal qualities, work habits, and professional qualifications.

Be sure to ask someone to read and edit your resume before sending it. Most colleges and universities offer this service to students through the career development office. There are also many resume writing services available on-line. Choose this resource carefully, however, because some can be costly. There are also many Internet sites that will post your completed resume.

Writing Persuasive Correspondence

Carefully construct your resume cover letter to make it brief, yet informative. Again, use high-quality paper with a basic color scheme, rather than something flashy and gauche. Remember that the basic color schemes will please almost everyone, but a unique paper may offend some personal tastes. It is best to stay conservative with paper choice, font style, and size.

Your cover letter should be brief—rarely longer than three paragraphs. In your introductory paragraph, write a clear, personal statement about your desire to apply for this particular position. In your middle paragraph, communicate succinctly several skills you possess that qualify you. Finally, express appreciation for being considered and respectfully request a personal interview.

Successful Job Interviewing

Before the Interview Find out all the information you can about your potential employer. Research the history and mission of the company, organization, or institution. These efforts not only demonstrate your personal initiative but also help you determine if this position is a good match for you. As a result of your research, you can speak with greater confidence and ask informed questions during your interview. It will be obvious to the employers that you've done your homework. Practice a "mock interview" with a trusted peer or professor before you head out. Again, many campuses offer this service through the career development office.

At the Interview Dress appropriately, wearing only business or professional attire. Be prepared to offer several questions to the interview team. Remember that every interview involves finding the best match for a position, so seek to find the answers to your questions about this position, your potential colleagues, and the work environment.

You may want to bring along the portfolio that you have developed during your training. It can be a great way to showcase your experience, accomplishments, and developing areas of expertise.

Finally, make sure you remain energized and focused on the interview. Eliminate any possible distractions by turning off your cell phone or beeper. Above all, be yourself. You'll waste your energy and everyone's time by trying to be someone you are not. Trust who you are and the valuable experiences you've had.

After the Interview Following an interview, write a personal note of appreciation to all key persons who participated in the process, especially those on the search committee. If you are offered the position, in addition to responding with a formal letter, write notes of appreciation once again—even if you decline the offer. These personal touches will go a long way toward establishing you as a thoughtful person determined to excel in all aspects of the position.

If you are offered the position, be prepared to negotiate salary and benefits. This is often the most difficult part of the hiring process, but it is essential that you prepare yourself for this crucial piece of the process. Research the salary range and benefits for this position. In other words, you must stay within the realm of possibility, but do not shortchange yourself, either. Remain confident in your abilities and experiences!

YOUR CAREER AND YOUR LIFE
Lifelong Learning

Be a lifelong learner. Even after you land your dream job, consider the importance of continuing your personal and professional growth journey. Take additional courses at a nearby university, participate in professional development workshops, and regularly attend conferences. If you are seeking licensure or certification, you will be required to receive additional training after you complete your degree. Enthusiastically embrace these opportunities as they come your way.

Fitting In and Standing Out

> Become aware of what is in you. Announce it,
> pronounce it, produce it, and give birth to it.
>
> —Meister Eckhart

So far, we have offered you advice on how to become a professional in your chosen field. Of course, in order to belong to any group or organization, you must engage in the behaviors deemed appropriate to qualify you for membership. To the extent that you can do this successfully, you will be fitting in. But conforming to the standards and conventions of your field will also tend to make you ordinary—someone who is just like all the others.

Thriving as a counselor is much more than fitting in—it's standing out. Lefrancois (1982) asserted that "just as very low intelligence is stupidity, so very low creativity is ordinariness" (p. 264). So to become extraordinary in your profession, you must exercise your innate creativity. Being creative is simply seeing things in ways that others might miss and coming up with new ideas.

E. Paul Torrance conducted a twenty-two-year longitudinal study of people in various professions who had been able to maintain their creativity (Millar, 1995). From this research, Torrance (1995) identified certain important factors and offered a seven-point "manifesto" to preserve your creativity.

- Fall in love with something and intensely pursue it. Staying fascinated with your work is only possible when you really love what you are doing. Of course, your interests will change, and if you are not paying attention to yourself, you may not even notice. As a result, you may go on doing something that you have long since "chewed the flavor out of" and, not surprisingly, finding that it bores you. Make sure that what you are doing continues to bring you joy. If it doesn't, do something else.

- Know, understand, take pride in, practice, develop, exploit, and enjoy your greatest strengths. Sometimes families seem to divide talents as if they were a scarce resource among the children. You've heard people comment about brothers that "John is the shy one, James is the confident one." Or they may contrast sisters by asserting, "Jane is the artistic one, Jill is the scholarly one." Or they simply slap on a label by saying that "Brad is athletic, Bob is bookish." Perhaps, because of this allocation-of-talent phenomenon in your own family, you believe that there are certain activities you can't do well or domains of endeavor you should avoid. Think again. Try your hand at everything that might interest you. You will be surprised at the many latent talents that you have.

- Learn to free yourself from the expectations of others. Free yourself to play your own game. All of us are raised under what Rogers (1961) called "conditions of worth." As children, we received the message that we would be lovable only if we behaved in ways that significant people endorsed. As a result, some of the ways in which you regard yourself are not truly you. Furthermore, you may harbor the belief that, in order to preserve your self-esteem, you must continue to please teachers, bosses, spouses, and all others who can withhold approval from you. Liberate yourself from the expectations of others. This does not mean that you must become an outlaw and ignore the wishes of people. It simply means that you can't please everyone, so you must first please yourself.

- Find a great teacher or mentor who will help you. Seek out someone who "knows the ropes" in your profession. Only veterans truly understand the many subtle dynamics of counseling that, as a novice, you are only beginning to grasp. In every setting, there are older people who are in the stage that Erikson (1975) called "generativity." They are eager to be helpful to fledgling professionals like you. Search carefully for such a person.

- Don't waste energy trying to be well rounded. Do what you love and can do well. Although you should explore everything that attracts your interest, don't feel that you must know and be able to do everything. In this era of information explosion, it is impossible for anyone to be a complete "renaissance person." Focus on those activities with which you have fallen in love, and refine your abilities in those areas.

- Learn the skills of interdependence. Remember that your professional development is not a journey that you have to take alone. Collaborate and cooperate. Share your talents and borrow talents from others. You will notice, for example, that this book was written by eight authors. We each contributed in the areas of our expertise, wrote the sections with which we were most familiar, and benefited from the contributions of our colleagues. Being a team player has many rewards. Give up the notion that you must be competitive in order to stand out. You will be more respected if you generously give of your creativity and seek the contributions of others in the work that you do.

Think You're Not Creative?

There is a vitality, a life-force, an energy, a quickening that is translated through you into action and because there is only one of you translated in all time, this expression is unique.

—Agnes de Mille

Perhaps you're thinking that you are not a creative person. If so, you are either confusing creativity with the ability to paint a picture or play music or you have buried your creative spark somewhere along the way. When you were a child, you were constantly creating, inventing new games, allowing yourself to be enchanted by imaginary play, and proposing all sorts of fabulous ideas. But something happens to many children as they grow older and become formally educated. "Many people with the potential for creativity probably never realize it. They believe that creativity is a quality they could never have" (Sternberg & Lubart, 1995, p. vii).

What happens to these creative children? Why do they arrive at adulthood having misplaced their potential? What happened to you? In their book, *Defying the Crowd*, Sternberg and Lubart (1995) state that creativity can be developed, but they suggest that one reason that we are all not more creative is that creativity is generally undervalued and overlooked in our culture. Critics of our educational system, such as Gardner (1991) and Goleman (1995), view school as a place that values only certain kinds of learning. The traditional cognitive, convergent, and conforming biases of school make it difficult for students to develop their creative thinking.

Compulsive conformity is the antithesis of creative thinking. Imagination, a precondition for original thought, is often given up as a liability early on. One study found that, in preschool children, the percentage of original responses on ideational fluency tasks was about 50 percent. However, this percentage dropped to 25 percent during elementary school. Whether you entered adolescence equipped to preserve your creative thinking depended on whether your home and school environments valued the thought processes that support creativity.

Along about the fourth grade, you began to face increasing expectations that your thinking should be free of emotion and concerned only with facts, not fantasy. Torrance (1967) identified what is called the "fourth-grade slump." At about this stage of education, an alarming number of children display a marked decline in their creative production. It is at this stage that male and female roles become important, peers become significant evaluators, children are expected to behave in more adultlike ways, and the school curriculum changes:

> Children, it is thought, need to learn that the world isn't all roses, that animals don't talk, that competition is keen, and that the rewards of life go to persons who are alert, practical and realistic. (Strom & Bernard, 1982, p. 309)

Torrance (1963) studied teachers from several countries regarding their attitudes toward creative behaviors in their students. He found that, of sixty-two student behaviors listed, conforming behaviors, such as being courteous and obedient, handing work in on time, and accepting the judgment of authorities, were most prized, but creative behaviors were consistently listed as least desirable. Teachers and parents complain that highly creative children don't pay attention and get off task.

Does any of this sound familiar to you? If you remember yourself being criticized for your daydreaming or off-task behavior, you were probably targeted as someone who needed to be less creative. But the good news is that your creative ability is still *there*, buried under layers of conventional behaviors, and you are past the fourth grade now. You are in a program in which you can once again exercise your creativity. Your professors will appreciate it, and you will feel the exhilaration of rediscovering a part of yourself that you had carefully packed away in elementary school.

Clock-Watchers and Workaholics

Some people work to live, and some live to work. Those who see their work only as a means to an end are the clock-watchers. They live for the time when they are no longer at work. Perceiving their jobs as boring and the time they spend at work as endless, clock-watchers are under-committed to the work they do.

On the other hand, people who seem to have no time for anything but work are workaholics. Their cell phones and briefcases are their constant companions. Instead of enjoying pleasant midday meals, workaholics "do working lunches." Regarding vacations as merely inter-ruptions of their jobs, they are overcommitted to their work, and their time is experienced as fleeting and frantic.

Both of these extreme attitudes toward work pose dangers. Worka-holics tend to burn out, whereas clock-watchers tend to rust out. The philosopher Aristotle preached the "golden mean" in all things and was among the first to say that you must find balance in your life. You want to be able to enjoy work and also to enjoy your free time. Unless you are independently wealthy, you must work to live, but don't be a clock-watcher. If you truly enjoy your work, you will live to work, but don't be a workaholic. Be careful to find the proper ratio of work and play for yourself. The only test as to whether you are accomplishing this balance is how you are feeling at the moment. Consult that inner voice.

By the way, if you are being a clock-watcher during your counselor training program—marking time until you graduate—you are not get-ting the most from your classes and practicum experiences. Conversely, if you are being a workaholic who is trying to get better grades than anyone else in your program, you need to lighten up and have more fun. See if you can turn your work into play, so that it becomes a joy rather than a grind.

Leaving the Nest and Making Mistakes

> Do not fear mistakes. There are none.
>
> —Miles Davis

No matter whether your training has been a joy or a grind, as you near graduation, you may be surprised to find that you are approaching it with mixed emotions. You are excited about finally reaching your training goal, but you likely also feel some sadness about what you are leaving behind—and even some dread about what lies ahead. You now have to go out into the real world, leaving behind the safety and comfort of your learning community. Looking for just the right opportunity and interviewing for the "dream job" can lead to disappointment and rejection. However, thinking creatively about this phase of your journey will give you a good start.

Of course, being only creative will not ensure your success. Creativity may be essential for thriving in your career, but other personal qualities, such as determination and perseverance, are also necessary. This little ditty below clearly makes that point:

> *Reflective on Creative*
> While I am very receptive
> To your urging convective,
> My experienced perspective
> Leaves me somewhat skeptive,
> 'Cause most of my inventive
> Is a little bit not productive.

John Irving, author of several critically acclaimed novels, including *The World According to Garp* and *The Cider House Rules*, described writing as "one-eighth talent and seven-eighths discipline"(Gussow, cited in Amabile, 2001). That claim brings to mind Thomas Edison, holder of more than a thousand patents and widely described as one of America's true geniuses, who said, "Genius is 1 percent inspiration and 99 percent perspiration."

Edison also showed an amazing passion and positive attitude. A reporter once asked him what it felt like to have failed 10,000 times in searching for the right material needed to make a light bulb. Edison replied, "I have not failed. I've just found 10,000 ways that won't work." He was also wonderfully opportunistic because some of his greatest inventions were accidental or resulted from failed experiments (McAuliffe, 1995). For example, when a large supply of chemicals was ruined in storage, Edison stopped all his experiments and used that calamity to invent new techniques for storing and combining chemicals.

No one in your graduate program requires you to write like John Irving or to be as inventive as Edison, but in order to make the most out of your professional career, we offer four cliched but important reminders:

- Think outside the lines.
- Walk the extra mile.
- Accept your mistakes as "practice."
- Seek clues for success in your failures.

■ ■ ■

EXERCISE 9.5 Putting It All Together
A Balancing Exercise

We are sure you have noticed the pictures of loved ones and vacation postcards that most professional people have sitting on their office desks or bookshelves. You have probably also observed that most people also have little mementos, souvenirs, and knickknacks sitting around in conspicuous places. Just as these photographs of friends and family serve as reminders, sources of inspiration, or metaphors, so may the knickknacks have more meaning than mere "conversation pieces."

One of our colleagues has this interesting structure (pictured in the figure) resting on his desk to remind him of how the important things in his life must remain in harmony. As you can see, six larger nails are balanced on one smaller nail, which is anchored to a solid foundation of oak. The structure is freestanding. That is, the nails are not magnetic and they are not held together with any type of adhesive, yet the figure remains intact, connected, and balanced.

The themes of becoming connected and maintaining balance in your personal and professional lives have been addressed throughout this book. As you prepare to launch your career, it can be valuable for you to construct a personal reminder or symbol that you could take with you on the next part of your journey.

Make a list of things that would make up your foundation (the oak block), the fulcrum (the smaller nail) and six elements in your life (the six larger nails) you would like to remember from this book and from your training that must always be balanced and connected.

FOUNDATION POSSIBILITIES:

_____

_____

_____

FULCRUM POSSIBILITIES:

_____

_____

_____

POSSIBILITIES FOR SIX NAILS:

_____   _____

_____   _____

_____   _____

It's fun to construct one of these structures, but maybe you lack the time or inclination. If so, you have our permission to copy the picture and use it instead. Perhaps you would like to invent your own connecting and balancing structure. Let us know what you come up with!

■ ■ ■

SUMMARY

In this final chapter, we discussed how you can begin exploring strategies for gaining employment, obtaining licensure or certification, becoming more involved in your professional life, and continuing your personal and professional development.

ONE FINAL POINT

Leap, and the net will appear.

—Julia Cameron

Remember the Zeigarnik Effect that we discussed in Chapter 4? It refers to the fact that you're more likely to remember and take with you the lessons that are still ongoing and not fully resolved. We therefore leave you with one final point. Your most important discovery about thriving in your training is an emerging insight, unfolding before you like a rose on a spring day. You are discovering that thriving is. . . .

_____

_____

_____

_____

_____

RESOURCES

Some books we recommend to you are: Bolles's annual edition of *What Color Is Your Parachute?* (2000), Lamarre's *Career Focus: A Personal Job Search Guide* (1998), Leider's *Life Skills: Taking Charge of Your Personal and Professional Growth* (1994), and Naylor, Willimon, and Osterberg's

The Search for Meaning in the Workplace (1996). Each book provides a wealth of resources and current ideas, including exercises for self-discovery, questionnaires that providing insight on your work values, and tips to assist you with resume writing and interview preparation.

American Counseling Association Job Listings
www.counseling.org/ejobs

This is the official job listing site of the American Counseling Association. Job offerings are updated weekly.

American Psychological Association Classified Ads
www.apa.org/ads/

This is the official job listing site of the American Psychological Association. Employment opportunities are updated weekly.

Monster Board
www.monster.com/

Billed as the largest Web site for career searchers, Monster is a great place to find job openings, to post your resume, to read career-related articles, to research organizations you're interested in, or to contact prospective employers. Monster often has nearly half a million job openings posted!

Career Magazine
www.careermag.com/

Career Magazine is similar to Monster, just a little less overwhelming. There are often some wonderful articles posted there, as well as the same services listed by Monster.

Chronicle of Higher Education Job Listings
http://jobs.chronicle.com/free/jobs

The Chronicle is the primary publication of higher education, so college and university jobs are updated weekly.

Occupational Outlook Handbook
http://stats.bls.gov/ocohome.htm

The Occupational Outlook Handbook is a nationally recognized source of career information, designed to provide valuable assistance to individuals making decisions about their future work lives. Revised every two years, the *Handbook* describes what workers do on the job, working conditions, the training and education needed, earnings, and expected job prospects in a wide range of occupations.

REFERENCES

Amabile, T. M. (2001). Beyond talent: John Irving and the passionate craft of creativity. *American Psychologist, 56,* 333–336.

Bolles, R. N. (2000). *What color is your parachute?* Berkeley, CA: Ten Speed Press.

Corona, J., & March, P. A. (2000, June). Into the real world: Moving from school to work. *Counseling Today, 43,* 31–32.

Cornely, L. (1999, October). Travels from student to professional: Signs along the road. *Counseling Today, 42,* 16.

Erikson, E. H. (1975). *Life history and the historical moment.* New York: Norton.

Gardner, H. (1991). *The unschooled mind.* New York: Basic Books.

Goleman, D. (1995). *Emotional intelligence.* New York: Bantam Books.

Gysbers, N. C., & Heppner, M. (1998). *Career counseling process, issues, and techniques.* Boston: Allyn & Bacon.

Huddock, T. J., Thompkins, C., & Enterline, C. (2000, May). Counseling students need to get involved in networking, conferences. *Counseling Today, 43,* 16, 23.

Lamarre, H. M. (1998). *Career focus: A personal job search guide* (2nd ed.). Upper Saddle River, NJ: Prentice-Hall.

Lefrancois, G. R. (1982). *Psychology for teaching: A bear rarely faces the front.* Belmont, CA: Wadsworth.

Leider, R. J. (1994). *Life skills: Taking charge of your personal and professional growth.* San Diego, CA: Pfeiffer.

McAuliffe, K. (1995). The undiscovered world of Thomas Edison. *Atlantic Monthly, 276,* 80–93.

McGoldrick, M., & Gerson, R. (1985). *Genograms in family assessment.* New York: Norton.

Millar, G. W. (1995). *E. Paul Torrance: The creativity man. An authorized biography*. Norwood, NJ: Ablex.

Morrison, T. (Summer, 1998). Generate opportunities: The latest in resume writing trends. *The Quill of Alpha Xi Delta*, 11–23.

Naylor, T. H., Willimon, W. H., & Osterberg, R. (1996). *The search for meaning in the workplace*. Nashville, TN: Abingdon Press.

National Association of Colleges and Employers (1999). *Planning job choices* (42nd ed.). Bethlehem, PA: Author.

Rogers, C. R. (1961). *On becoming a person*. Boston: Houghton Mifflin.

Sternberg, R. J., & Lubart, T. I. (1995). *Defying the crowd: Cultivating creativity in a culture of conformity*. New York: Free Press.

Strom, R. D., & Bernard, H. W. (1982). *Educational psychology*. Monterey, CA: Brooks/Cole.

Super, D. E., & Super, C. M. (1982). *Opportunities in psychology* (4th ed.). Skokie, IL: National Textbook.

Torrance, E. P. (1963). The creative personality and the ideal pupil. *Teachers College Record, 65,* 220–226.

Torrance, E. P. (1967). *Understanding the fourth-grade slump in creative thinking*. Washington, DC: U.S. Office of Education.

Torrance, E. P. (1995). *Why fly? A philosophy of creativity*. Norwood, NJ: Ablex.

Our Favorite Counseling and Therapy Books

We have compiled a far-from-comprehensive list of favorite books to recommend to you. Avoiding textbooks and the recent literature in the helping professions, we have focused instead on classic books that influenced our personal and professional development by inspiring, provoking, or touching us in some powerful way.

Reading a great book is like any other profound experience. You do not understand completely when you first encounter it, but the experience is so rich and intriguing that you find yourself returning to it again and again—and discovering more each time. There have, of course, been many books that you may not have understood, but you were able to dismiss them as irrelevant to your life. However, a great book compels you in some ineffable way. It convinces you of its truth while revealing its message only bit by bit. It is a frustrating but challenging pursuit. A great book, like a great friend, is never superficial, sometimes surprising, and always there for you when you need inspiration.

As you look through the list, we invite you to select titles that intrigue you. You can easily see how our recommendations reflect the diversity of the counseling and therapy profession.

Bateson, M. C. (1989). *Composing a Life.* New York: Atlantic Monthly Press.

This is a study of five women engaged in the shaping of their lives. Bateson uses comparative biography to inquire into the creative potential of complex lives in which energies are continually refocused and redefined. Each of the women has faced discontinuity and divided energy and has been rich in professional achievement and

272

personal relationships. The conclusion affirms that discontinuity and conflicted priorities are part of our lives and should be seen as a source of wisdom.

Belenky, M. D., Clinchy, B. M., Goldberger, N. R., & Tarule, J. M. (1986). *Women's Ways of Knowing*. New York: Basic Books.

The authors discuss the differences in the ways women and men acquire knowledge. Belenky et al. develop a five-stage model of intellectual growth and development of women that parallels Perry's model of intellectual development. They believed that Perry's model, with its emphasis on the objective, analytical model of thinking, was more reflective of the male experience. Their model focuses on the qualities of intuition, empathy, and connectedness with others as the ways of knowing that are favored by women.

Berman, M. (1981). *The Reenchantment of the World*. Ithaca, NY: Cornell University Press.

This wonderful book was written by a historian. He traces the history of human thought from its beginnings in an enchanted world of participating consciousness through the dawn of scientific consciousness. His general thesis is that we threw out the baby with the bathwater when we denied the value of (primary process) participating consciousness. His ideas appear to be vindicated by constructivism—a form of scientific thinking, which seems to be emerging in all the sciences at once.

Carkhuff, R. C., & Berenson, B. G. (1977). *Beyond Counseling and Therapy*. New York: Holt, Rinehart & Winston.

An excellent background for beginning students, as this book was one of the first attempts to translate counseling theory into workable methodology and to include the notion of stages and phases in the counseling process. The book served as a harbinger for Gerald Egan's *The Skilled Helper* and other works on training counselors and therapists.

Frankl, V. E. (1967). *Psychotherapy and Existentialism: Selected Papers on Logotherapy*. New York: Washington Square Press.

Frankl elaborates on his special brand of existentialism and logotherapy, discusses paradoxical intention at length, and offers powerful case studies. He explores other topics, such as meaning, values, and self-actualization.

Gilligan, C. (1982). *In a Different Voice*. Cambridge, MA: Harvard University Press.

Gilligan documented her research on the moral development of women. Based on interviews of women from diverse samples, Gilligan discovered that the stages in Kohlberg's theory of moral development described the development of white, educated, middle-class males. She found that women place much more emphasis on contractual arrangements and moral principles in making their moral decisions. She developed a three-stage model to describe the moral development of women.

Helms, J. E. (1992). *A Race Is a Nice Thing to Have: A Guide to Being a White Person or Understanding the White Persons in Your Life*. Topeka, KS: Content Communications.

This book is essentially a primer for understanding racial identity. Written with whites in mind, but certainly helpful for others as well, the book contains activities and descriptions that are intended to help you understand the role that race plays in all of our lives. Many whites don't consider themselves as having a racial identity, so this book, although brief and very "user-friendly," actually has the potential to offer profound insights. In addition, Helms avoids guilt and shame by affirming the possibility of a positive white racial identity. This is a quick but powerful read.

James, W. (1990). *The Varieties of Religious Experience*. New York: Vintage Books. (Original work published 1902)

Long before the recent interest in integrating spirituality and psychology, William James took on this challenging task. His insights are still as fresh and vivid as ever. The book is full of wonderful quotes, such as James's charming example of the impossibility of a psychological science capturing the unique and ineffable experience of an individual's spirituality: "Probably a crab would be filled with a sense of personal outrage if it could hear us class it without ado or apology as a crustacean, and thus dispose of it. 'I am no such thing,' it would say; 'I am MYSELF, MYSELF alone.'" (p. 17).

Jung, C. G. (1965). *Memories, Dreams, Reflections*. New York: Vintage Books.

As the title suggests, Jung's autobiography is unique because, instead of describing the external events and circumstances of his life, he explores his rich inner world. As the eighty-three-year-old Jung says in his prologue, "My life is a story of the self-realization of the unconscious." Our most original theorist describes his intellectual struggles, personal epiphanies, and even a dramatic near-death experience with power and clarity. Near the end of this wise book, Jung concludes that "the sole purpose of human existence is to kindle a light in the darkness of mere being."

Karen, R. (1994). *Becoming Attached: First Relationships and How They Shape Our Capacity to Love.* **New York: Oxford University Press.**

This is a wonderful resource for understanding early attachment problems and the subsequent difficulties we all have in adult relationships. No one gets out of his or her family completely intact! We all have some residual unmet needs and defensive strategies that get in our way. We all experience shame, self-consciousness, and occasional difficulties in relationships. This is not to say that we have problems that would approach a diagnosis of personality disorder, but everyone has stylistic quirks that can probably be traced to early attachment failures. This book is written from an object-relations and self-psychology standpoint, and it contains interesting bios on such famous people as John Bowlby, Mary Ainsworth, and Harry Harlow. Besides being a good primer on the post-Freudian approach to understanding personality, it will also cause you to reflect on your own experiences in your family of origin.

Katz, J. H. (1978). *White Awareness: Handbook for Anti-Racism Training.* **Norman, OK: University of Oklahoma Press.**

As you embark on your career, you'll likely find that your attitudes and beliefs about yourself and others are frequently challenged. This book, which contains exercises that can help you explore your views of yourself and others as racial beings, may be especially helpful for you. In particular, Katz encourages us to take responsibility for change—personally and socially—and to expect to make a difference in how we relate to one another. Many of the exercises can be designed to capture our beliefs about issues, such as classism and sexism, that influence and complicate our attempts to be multiculturally competent counselors.

Kopp, S. B. (1976). *If You Meet the Buddha on the Road, Kill Him!* **New York: Bantam.**

After about four years working as a counselor, I read this book, and it had a tremendous impact on me. It helped me understand what I was doing as a counselor, and it kept me going when I became discouraged. Kopp is an existential therapist who relates stories about his clients and about his reactions to working with them. His self-disclosures and his vulnerability were a comfort to me as I struggled with my own questions about being a counselor.

Kozol, J. (1991). *Savage Inequalities: Children in America's Schools.* **New York: Crown.**

If you're considering working in public schools, then we encourage you to read Kozol's view of the reality of public schools for many children across the country. The disparities that Kozol describes as existing between the "haves" and the "have nots"—schools in suburban or wealthy areas versus schools in Latino, African American, and less wealthy communities—are shocking and at times hard to read. This book serves as a clear call to action for justice and equality.

Maslow, A. H. (1962). *Toward a Psychology of Being.* **Princeton, NJ: Van Nostrand.**

A pioneer in many ways, Maslow studied self-actualizing people instead of the psychologically disordered, used qualitative research methods before that term came into vogue, and served as a major catalyst in the "Third Force" of the profession. His book is still fascinating to read.

May, R., Angel, E., & Ellenberger, H. F. (Eds.) (1958). *Existence: A New Dimension in Psychiatry and Psychology.* **New York: Basic Books.**

This is an exposition of the human condition and a consideration of Daseinanalysis—an existentialist version of psychoanalysis. The first ninety pages are by Rollo May and are a good, and readable, introduction to existentialism. A reading of this should convince you of how superficial most other counseling and therapy theories are.

Napier, A. Y., & Whitaker, C. A. (1978). *The Family Crucible.* **New York: Harper & Row.**

Napier describes "the intense experience of family therapy" as the cotherapist of Whitaker, a pioneer in the field. The book, which reads like a novel, explores the nuances and dynamics of working with a troubled family. It skillfully interweaves dramatic scenes of one family's therapy with discussions of systems and family dynamics—the "family dance." Napier also shares his own struggles, doubts, discoveries, and joys during the family therapy process.

Perls, F. (1969). *Gestalt Therapy Verbatim.* **Lafayette, CA: Real People Press.**

This is one of the books that made the most sense to me in the early stages of my career as a counselor. Although that was almost twenty years ago, the lessons I learned from Perls through this book still stay with me. Regardless of your theoretical orientation, the vivid image of therapeutic change that this book provides can teach you a lot about the counseling process.

Polster, E. (1987). *Every Person's Life Is Worth a Novel.* **New York: Norton.**

What I like best about this book is the title and the notion of approaching clients as a novelist might—seeing their lives as full of drama and helping them appreciate and confirm the wonder of their existence. Polster is a noted Gestalt therapist who has much to contribute to other theoretical orientations.

Rogers, C. R. (1961). *On Becoming a Person.* **Boston: Houghton Mifflin.**

In this wonderfully insightful book, Rogers reflects on therapy, personal growth, and creativity. You come away from this book knowing both the man and his ideas—with an appreciation for his intellectual journey and dedication to his clients. At one point, Rogers challenges us with the assertion that the good life is not one "for the faint-hearted. . . . It involves the courage to be. It means launching oneself fully into the stream of life" (p. 196).

Shapiro, D. (1965). *Neurotic Styles.* **New York: Basic Books.**

This is a classic and original study. This book is an old favorite of mine and contributed to my interest in the development of personality and the disorders of personality. Shapiro examines the ways of thinking and perceiving, forms of emotional experience, and the behavioral manifestations that characterize the obsessive-compulsive, paranoid, histrionic, and impulsive personality styles. Although the book and its terminology is dated in these days of the *DSM–IV*, I continue to find it helpful in clinical work.

Tzu, L. (1988). *Tao Te Ching* **(S. Mitchell, Trans.). New York: HarperCollins.**

This book of ancient Eastern wisdom is the second most translated book in the world. It has been, and continues to be, a source of inspiration and guidance for my work as a counselor. It emphasizes a gentle method of working with, and relating to, others—and the importance of understanding the paradox of the human condition. If I am stuck with a client, I often turn to the *Tao Te Ching* for a clue. There are many translations, each of them different and most of them difficult to comprehend because of the *Tao Te Ching*'s nonlinear nature. One of the most accessible of the translations is by Mitchell. I recommend spending some time with this book. There is a wealth of knowledge for counselors.

Watzlawick, P., Beavin, J., & Jackson, D. D. (1967). *Pragmatics of Human Communication*. New York: Norton.

This book is the seminal work in communications theory. Virtually no family therapy book written is without the influence of some of the ideas in this book. It must be read sparingly. Great exposition of paradox!

Watzlawick, P., Weakland, J. H., & Fisch, R. (1972). *Change: Principles of Problem Formation and Problem Resolution*. New York: Norton.

A cogent follow-up to some of the ideas in *Pragmatics* (see the preceding entry). You might like it better because it contains "how to do it" informtion.

Weinberg, G. (1991). *The Taboo Scarf and Other Tales of Therapy*. New York: Ivy Books.

Similar to Yalom (*Love's Executioner*), Weinberg is a therapist who details case histories with an emphasis on his personal experience in the therapeutic process. A great "read."

Wood, D. (1992). *Old Turtle*. New York: Pfeifer-Hamilton.

This beautiful children's book presents a magnificent conversation about the nature of God, with different creatures picturing God in their own images. Whether or not you consider yourself a "religious" person, the essence of the story is intriguing in its simple message regarding acceptance and awareness of community and global responsibility. The illustrations are also lovely and may be just what you need when you're feeling bogged down by textbooks and theory.

Yalom, I. (1990). *Love's Executioner and Other Tales of Psychotherapy*. New York: Basic Books.

Irving Yalom writes of his personal experiences working with clients in individual therapy. A fascinating "inside" account of this well-known therapist's work.

American Counseling Association's
Code of Ethics and
Standards of Practice
(Approved by the Governing Council, April 1995)

PREAMBLE

The American Counseling Association is an educational, scientific and professional organization whose members are dedicated to the enhancement of human development throughout the life span. Association members recognize diversity in our society and embrace a cross-cultural approach in support of the worth, dignity, potential, and uniqueness of each individual.

The specification of a code of ethics enables the association to clarify to current and future members, and to those served by members, the nature of the ethical responsibilities held in common by its members. As the code of ethics of the association, this document establishes principles that define the ethical behavior of association members. All members of the American Counseling Association are required to adhere to the Code of Ethics and the Standards of Practice. The Code of Ethics will serve as the basis for processing ethical complaints initiated against members of the association.

CODE OF ETHICS

Section A: The Counseling Relationship

A.1. Client Welfare

a. *Primary Responsibility.* The primary responsibility of counselors is to respect the dignity and to promote the welfare of clients.

b. *Positive Growth and Development.* Counselors encourage client growth and development in ways that foster the client's interest and welfare; counselors avoid fostering dependent counseling relationships.

c. *Counseling Plans.* Counselors and their clients work jointly in devising integrated, individual counseling plans that offer reasonable promise of success and are consistent with abilities and circumstances of the clients. Counselors and clients regularly review counseling plans to ensure their continued viability and effectiveness, respecting clients' freedom of choice. (See A.3.b)

d. *Family Involvement.* Counselors recognize that families are usually important in the clients' lives and strive to enlist family understanding and involvement as a positive resource, when appropriate.

e. *Career and Employment Needs.* Counselors work with their clients in considering employment in jobs and circumstances that are consistent with the client's overall abilities, vocational limitations, physical restrictions, general temperament, interest and aptitude patterns, social skills, education, general qualifications, and other relevant characteristics and needs. Counselors neither place nor participate in placing clients in positions that will result in damaging the interest and the welfare of the clients, employers, or the public.

A.2. Respecting Diversity

a. *Nondiscrimination.* Counselors do not condone or engage in discrimination based on age, color, culture, disability, ethnic group, gender, race, religion, sexual orientation, marital status, or socioeconomic status. (See C.5.a., C.5.b., and D.1.i.)

b. *Respecting Differences.* Counselors will actively attempt to understand the diverse cultural background of the clients with whom they work. This includes, but is not limited to, learning how the counselor's own cultural/ethnic/racial identity impacts her/his values and beliefs about the counseling process. (See E.8. and F.2.i.)

A.3. Client Rights

a. *Disclosure to Clients.* When counseling is initiated, and throughout the counseling process as necessary, counselors inform clients of the purposes, goals, techniques, procedures, limitations, potential risks and benefits of services to be performed, and other pertinent information. Counselors take steps to ensure that clients understand the implications of diagnosis, the intended use of tests and reports, fees, and billing arrangements. Clients have the right to expect confidentiality and to be provided with an explanation of its limitations, including supervision and/or treatment team professionals; to obtain clear information about their case records; to participate in the ongoing counseling plans; and to refuse any recommended services and be advised of the consequences of such refusal. (See E.5.a. and G.2.)

b. *Freedom of Choice.* Counselors offer clients the freedom to choose whether to enter into a counseling relationship and to determine which professional(s) will provide counseling. Restrictions that limit choices of clients are fully explained. (See A.1.c.)

c. *Inability to Give Consent.* When counseling minors or persons unable to give voluntary informed consent, counselors act in these clients' best interest. (See B.3.)

A.4. Clients Served by Others

If a client is receiving services from another mental health professional, counselors, with client consent, inform the professional persons already involved and develop clear agreements to avoid confusion and conflict for the client. (See C.6.c.)

A.5. Personal Needs and Values

a. *Personal Needs.* In the counseling relationship, counselors are aware of the intimacy and responsibilities inherent in the counseling relationship, maintain respect for clients, and avoid actions that seek to meet their personal needs at the expense of the clients.

b. *Personal Value.* Counselors are aware of their own values, attitudes, beliefs, and behaviors and how these apply in a diverse society, and avoid imposing their values on clients. (See C.5.a.)

A.6. Dual Relationships

a. *Avoid When Possible.* Counselors are aware of their influential positions with respect to clients, and they avoid exploiting the trust and dependency of clients. Counselors make every effort to avoid dual relationships with clients that could impair professional judgment or increase the risk of harm to clients. (Examples of such relationships include, but are not limited to, familial, social, financial, business, or close personal relationships with clients.) When a dual relationship cannot be avoided, counselors take appropriate professional precautions such as informed consent, consultation, supervision, and documentation to ensure that judgment is not impaired and no exploitation occurs. (See F.1.b.)

b. *Superior/Subordinate Relationships.* Counselors do not accept as clients superiors or subordinates with whom they have administrative, supervisory, or evaluative relationships.

A.7. Sexual Intimacies with Clients

a. *Current Clients.* Counselors do not have any type of sexual intimacies with clients and do not counsel persons with whom they have had a sexual relationship.

b. *Former Clients.* Counselors do not engage in sexual intimacies with former clients within a minimum of two years after terminating the counseling relationship. Counselors who engage in such relationship after two years following termination have the responsibility to thoroughly examine and document that such relations did not have an exploitative nature, based on factors such as duration of counseling, amount of time since counseling, termination circumstances, client's personal history and mental status, adverse impact on the client, and actions by the counselor suggesting a plan to initiate a sexual relationship with the client after termination.

A.8. Multiple Clients

When counselors agree to provide counseling services to two or more persons who have a relationship (such as husband and wife, or parents and children), counselors clarify at the outset which person or persons are clients and the nature of the relationships they will have with each involved person. If it becomes apparent that counselors may be called upon to perform potentially conflicting roles, they clarify, adjust, or withdraw from roles appropriately. (See B.2. and B.4.d.)

A.9. Group Work

a. *Screening.* Counselors screen prospective group counseling/therapy participants. To the extent possible, counselors select members whose needs and goals are compatible with goals of the group, who will not impede the group process, and whose well-being will not be jeopardized by the group experience.

b. *Protecting Clients.* In a group setting, counselors take reasonable precautions to protect clients from physical or psychological trauma.

A.10. Fees and Bartering (see D.3.a. and D.3.b.)

a. *Advance Understanding.* Counselors clearly explain to clients, prior to entering the counseling relationship, all the financial arrangements related to professional services including the use of collection agencies or legal measures for nonpayment. (A.11.c)

b. *Establishing Fees.* In establishing fees for professional counseling services, counselors consider the financial status of clients and locality. In the event that the established fee structure is inappropriate for a client, assistance is provided in attempting to find comparable services of acceptable cost. (See A.10.d., D.3.a., and D.3.b.)

c. *Bartering Discouraged.* Counselors ordinarily refrain from accepting goods or services from clients in return for counseling services because such arrangements create inherent potential for conflicts, exploitation, and distortion of the professional relationship. Counselors may participate in bartering only if the relationship is not exploitive, if the client requests it, if a clear written contract is established, and if such arrangements are an accepted practice among professionals in the community. (See A.6.a.)

d. *Pro Bono Service.* Counselors contribute to society by devoting a portion of their professional activity to services for which there is little or no financial return (pro bono).

A.11. Termination and Referral

a. *Abandonment Prohibited.* Counselors do not abandon or neglect clients in counseling. Counselors assist in making appropriate arrangements for the continuation of treatment, when necessary, during interruptions such as vacations, and following termination.

b. *Inability to Assist Clients.* If counselors determine an inability to be of professional assistance to clients, they avoid entering or immediately terminate a counseling relationship. Counselors are knowledgeable about referral resources and suggest appropriate alternatives. If clients decline the suggested referral, counselors should discontinue the relationship.

c. *Appropriate Termination.* Counselors terminate a counseling relationship, securing client agreement when possible, when it is reasonably clear that the client is no longer benefiting, when services are no longer required, when counseling no longer serves the client's needs or interests, when clients do not pay fees charged, or when agency or institution limits do not allow provision of further counseling services. (See A.10.b. and C.2.g.)

A.12. Computer Technology

a. *Use of Computers.* When computer applications are used in counseling services, counselors ensure that: (1) the client is intellectually, emotional, and physically capable of using the computer application;

(2) the computer application is appropriate to the needs of the client; (3) the client understands the purpose and operation of the computer application; and (4) a follow-up of client use of a computer application is provided to correct possible misconceptions, discover inappropriate use, and assess subsequent needs.

b. *Explanation of Limitations.* Counselors ensure that clients are provided information as a part of the counseling relationship that adequately explains the limitations of computer technology.

c. *Access to Computer Applications.* Counselors provide for equal access to computer applications in counseling services. (See A.2.a.)

Section B: Confidentiality

B.1. Right to Privacy

a. *Respect for Privacy.* Counselors respect their clients' right to privacy and avoid illegal and unwarranted disclosures of confidential information. (See A.3.a. and B.6.a.)

b. *Client Waiver.* The right to privacy may be waived by the client or their legally recognized representative.

c. *Exceptions.* The general requirement that counselors keep information confidential does not apply when disclosure is required to prevent clear and imminent danger to the client or others or when legal requirements demand that confidential information be revealed. Counselors consult with other professionals when in doubt as to the validity of an exception.

d. *Contagious, Fatal Diseases.* A counselor who receives information confirming that a client has a disease commonly known to be both communicable and fatal is justified in disclosing information to an identifiable third party, who by his or her relationship with the client is at a high risk of contracting the disease. Prior to making a disclosure the counselor should ascertain that the client has not already informed the third party about his or her disease and that the client is not intending to inform the third party in the immediate future. (See B.1.c. and B.1.f.)

e. *Court Ordered Disclosure.* When court ordered to release confidential information without a client's permission, counselors request to the court that the disclosure not be required due to potential harm to the client or counseling relationship. (See B.1.c.)

f. *Minimal Disclosure.* When circumstances require the disclosure of confidential information, only essential information is revealed. To the extent possible, clients are informed before confidential information is disclosed.

g. *Explanation of Limitations.* When counseling is initiated and throughout the counseling process as necessary, counselors inform clients of the limitations of confidentiality and identify foreseeable situations in which confidentiality must be breached. (See G.2.a.)

h. *Subordinates.* Counselors make every effort to ensure that privacy and confidentiality of clients are maintained by subordinates including employees, supervisees, clerical assistants, and volunteers. (See B.1.a.)

i. *Treatment Teams.* If client treatment will involve a continued review by a treatment team, the client will be informed of the team's existence and composition.

B.2. Groups and Families

a. *Group Work.* In group work, counselors clearly define confidentiality and the parameters for the specific group being entered, explain its importance, and discuss the difficulties related to confidentiality involved in group work. The fact that confidentiality cannot be guaranteed is clearly communicated to group members.

b. *Family Counseling.* In family counseling, information about one family member cannot be disclosed to another member without permission. Counselors protect the privacy rights of each family member. (See A.8., B.3., and B.4.d.)

B.3 Minor or Incompetent Clients

When counseling clients who are minors or individuals who are unable to give voluntary, informed consent, parents or guardians may be included in the counseling process as appropriate. Counselors act in the best interests of clients and take measures to safeguard confidentiality. (See A.3.c.)

B.4. Records

a. *Requirements of Records.* Counselors maintain records necessary for rendering professional services to their clients and as required by laws, regulations, or agency or institution procedures.

b. *Confidentiality of Records.* Counselors are responsible for securing the safety and confidentiality of any counseling records they create, maintain, transfer, or destroy whether the records are written, taped, computerized, or stored in any other medium.

c. *Permission to Record or Observe.* Counselors obtain permission from clients prior to electronically recording or observing sessions. (See A.3.a.)

d. *Client Access.* Counselors recognize that counseling records are kept for the benefit of clients, and therefore provide access to records and copies of records when requested by competent clients, unless the records contain information that may be misleading and detrimental to the client. In situations involving multiple clients, access to records is limited to those parts of records that do not include confidential information related to another client. (See A.8., B.1.a, and B.2.b.)

e. *Disclosure or Transfer.* Counselors obtain written permission from clients to disclose or transfer records to legitimate third parties unless exceptions to confidentiality exist as listed in Section B.1. Steps are taken to insure that receivers of counseling records are sensitive to their confidential nature.

B.5. Research and Training

a. *Data Disguise Required.* Use of data derived from counseling relationships for purposes of training, research, or publication is confined to content that is disguised to ensure the anonymity of the individuals involved. (See B.1.g. and G.3.d.)

b. *Agreement for Identification.* Identification of a client in a presentation or publication is permissible only when the client has reviewed the material and has agreed to its presentation or publication. (See G.3.d.)

B.6. Consultation

a. *Respect for Privacy.* Information obtained in a consulting relationship is discussed for professional purposes only with persons clearly concerned with the case. Written and oral reports present data germane to the purposes of the consultation, and every effort is made to protect client identity and avoid undue invasion of privacy.

b. *Cooperating Agencies.* Before sharing information, counselors make efforts to ensure that there are defined policies in other agencies serving the counselor's clients that effectively protect the confidentiality of information.

Section C: Professional Responsibility

C.1. Standards Knowledge

Counselors have a responsibility to read, understand, and follow the Code of Ethics and the Standards of Practice.

C.2. Professional Competence

a. *Boundaries of Competence.* Counselors practice only within the boundaries of their competence, based on their education, training, supervised experience, state and national professional credentials, and appropriate professional experience. Counselors will demonstrate a commitment to gain knowledge, personal awareness, sensitivity, and skills pertinent to working with a diverse client population.

b. *New Specialty Areas of Practice.* Counselors practice in specialty areas new to them only after appropriate education, training, and supervised experience. While developing skills in new specialty areas, counselors take steps to ensure the competence of their work and to protect others from possible harm.

c. *Qualified for Employment.* Counselors accept employment only for positions for which they are qualified by education, training, supervised experience, state and national professional credentials, and appropriate professional experience. Counselors hire for professional counseling positions only individuals who are qualified and competent.

d. *Monitor Effectiveness.* Counselors continually monitor their effectiveness as professionals and take steps to improve when necessary. Counselors in private practice take reasonable steps to seek out peer supervision to evaluate their efficacy as counselors.

e. *Ethical Issues Consultation.* Counselors take reasonable steps to consult with other counselors or related professionals when they have questions regarding their ethical obligations or professional practice. (See H.1.)

f. *Continuing Education.* Counselors recognize the need for continuing education to maintain a reasonable level of awareness of current scientific and professional information in their fields of activity. They take steps to maintain competence in the skills they use, are open to new procedures, and keep current with the diverse and/or special populations with whom they work.

g. *Impairment.* Counselors refrain from offering or accepting professional services when their physical, mental or emotional problems are likely to harm a client or others. They are alert to the signs of impairment, seek assistance for problems, and if necessary, limit, suspend, or terminate their professional responsibilities. (See A.11.c.)

C.3. Advertising and Soliciting Clients

a. *Accurate Advertising.* There are no restrictions on advertising by counselors except those that can be specifically justified to protect the public from deceptive practices. Counselors advertise or represent their services to the public by identifying their credentials in an accurate manner that is not false, misleading, deceptive, or fraudulent. Counselors may only advertise the highest degree earned which is in counseling or a closely related field from a college or university that was accredited when the degree was awarded by one of the regional accrediting bodies recognized by the Council on Postsecondary Accreditation.

b. *Testimonials.* Counselors who use testimonials do not solicit them from clients or other persons who, because of their particular circumstances, may be vulnerable to undue influence.

c. *Statements by Others.* Counselors make reasonable efforts to ensure that statements made by others about them or the profession of counseling are accurate.

d. *Recruiting Through Employment.* Counselors do not use their places of employment or institutional affiliation to recruit or gain clients, supervisees, or consultees for their private practices.

e. *Products and Training Advertisements.* Counselors who develop products related to their profession or conduct workshops or training events ensure that the advertisements concerning these products or events are accurate and disclose adequate information for consumers to make informed choices.

f. *Promoting to Those Served.* Counselors do not use counseling, teaching, training, or supervisory relationships to promote their products or training events in a manner that is deceptive or would exert undue influence on individuals who may be vulnerable. Counselors may adopt textbooks they have authored for instruction purposes.

g. *Professional Association Involvement.* Counselors actively participate in local, state, and national associations that foster the development and improvement of counseling.

C.4 Credentials

a. *Credentials Claimed.* Counselors claim or imply only professional credentials possessed and are responsible for correcting any known misrepresentations of their credentials by others. Professional credentials include graduate degrees in counseling or closely related mental health fields, accreditation of graduate programs, national voluntary certifications, government-issued certifications or licenses, ACA professional membership, or any other credential that might indicate to the public specialized knowledge or expertise in counseling.

b. *ACA Professional Membership.* ACA professional members may announce to the public their membership status. Regular members may not announce their ACA membership in a manner that might imply they are credentialed counselors.

c. *Credential Guidelines.* Counselors follow the guidelines for use of credentials that have been established by the entities that issue the credentials.

d. *Misrepresentation of Credentials.* Counselors do not attribute more to their credentials than the credentials represent, and do not imply that other counselors are not qualified because they do not possess certain credentials.

e. *Doctoral Degrees From Other Fields.* Counselors who hold a master's degree in counseling or a closely related mental health field, but hold a doctoral degree from other than counseling or a closely related field do not use the title, "Dr." in their practices and do not announce to the public in relation to their practice or status as a counselor that they hold a doctorate.

C.5. Public Responsibility

a. *Nondiscrimination.* Counselors do not discriminate against clients, students, or supervisees in a manner that has a negative impact based on their age, color, culture, disability, ethnic group, gender, race, religion, sexual orientation, or socioeconomic status, or for any other reason. (See A.2.a.)

b. *Sexual Harassment.* Counselors do not engage in sexual harassment. Sexual harassment is defined as sexual solicitation, physical advances, or verbal or nonverbal conduct that is sexual in nature, that occurs in connection with professional activities or roles, and that either: (1) is unwelcome, is offensive, or creates a hostile workplace environment, and counselors know or are told this; or (2) is sufficiently severe or intense to be perceived as harassment to a reasonable person in the context. Sexual harassment can consist of a single intense or severe act or multiple persistent or pervasive acts.

c. *Reports to Third Parties.* Counselors are accurate, honest, and unbiased in reporting their professional activities and judgments to appropriate third parties including courts, health insurance companies, those who are the recipients of evaluation reports, and others. (See B.1.g.)

d. *Media Presentations.* When counselors provide advice or comment by means of public lectures, demonstrations, radio or television programs, prerecorded tapes, printed articles, mailed material, or other media, they take reasonable precautions to ensure that (1) the statements are based on appropriate professional counseling literature and practice; (2) the statements are otherwise consistent with the Code of Ethics and the Standards of Practice; and (3) the recipients of the information are not encouraged to infer that a professional counseling relationship has been established. (See C.6.b.)

e. *Unjustified Gains.* Counselors do not use their professional positions to seek or receive unjustified personal gains, sexual favors, unfair advantage, or unearned goods or services. (See C.3.d.)

C.6. Responsibility to Other Professionals

a. *Different Approaches.* Counselors are respectful of approaches to professional counseling that differ from their own. Counselors know and take into account the traditions and practices of other professional groups with which they work.

b. *Personal Public Statements.* When making personal statements in a public context, counselors clarify that they are speaking from their personal perspectives and that they are not speaking on behalf of all counselors or the profession. (See C.5.d.)

c. *Clients Served by Others.* When counselors learn that their clients are in a professional relationship with another mental health professional, they request release from clients to inform the other professionals and strive to establish positive and collaborative professional relationships. (See A.4.)

Section D: Relationships with Other Professionals

D.1. Relationships with Employers and Employees

a. *Role Definition.* Counselors define and describe for their employers and employees the parameters and levels of their professional roles.

b. *Agreements.* Counselors establish working agreements with supervisors, colleagues, and subordinates regarding counseling or clinical relationships, confidentiality, adherence to professional standards, distinction between public and private material, maintenance and dissemination of recorded information, workload, and accountability. Working agreements in each instance are specified and made known to those concerned.

c. *Negative Conditions.* Counselors alert their employers to conditions that may be potentially disruptive or damaging to the counselor's professional responsibilities or that may limit their effectiveness.

d. *Evaluation.* Counselors submit regularly to professional review and evaluation by their supervisor or the appropriate representative of the employer.

e. *In-Service.* Counselors are responsible for in-service development of self and staff.

f. *Goals.* Counselors inform their staff of goals and programs.

g. *Practices.* Counselors provide personnel and agency practices that respect and enhance the rights and welfare of each employee and recipient of agency services. Counselors strive to maintain the highest levels of professional services.

h. *Personnel Selection and Assignment.* Counselors select competent staff and assign responsibilities compatible with their skills and experiences.

i. *Discrimination.* Counselors, as either employers or employees, do not engage in or condone practices that are inhumane, illegal, or unjustifiable (such as considerations based on age, color, culture, disability, ethnic group, gender, race, religion, sexual orientation, or socioeconomic status) in hiring, promotion, or training. (See A.2.a. and C.5.b.)

j. *Professional Conduct.* Counselors have a responsibility both to clients and to the agency or institution within which services are performed to maintain high standards of professional conduct.

k. *Exploitive Relationships.* Counselors do not engage in exploitive relationships with individuals over whom they have supervisory, evaluative, or instructional control or authority.

l. *Employer Policies.* The acceptance of employment in an agency or institution implies that counselors are in agreement with its general policies and principles. Counselors strive to reach agreement with employers as to acceptable standards of conduct that allow for changes in institutional policy conducive to the growth and development of clients.

D. 2. Consultation (see B.6.)

a. *Consultation as an Option.* Counselors may choose to consult with any other professional competent persons about their clients. In choosing consultants, counselors avoid placing the consultant in a conflict of interest situation that would preclude the consultant being a proper party to the counselors' efforts to help the client. Should counselors be engaged in a work setting that compromises this consultation standard, they consult with other professionals whenever possible to consider justifiable alternatives.

b. *Consultant Competency.* Counselors are reasonably certain that they have or the organization represented has the necessary competencies and resources for giving the kind of consulting services needed and that appropriate referral resources are available.

c. *Understanding with Clients.* When providing consultation, counselors attempt to develop with their clients a clear understanding of problem definition, goals for change, and predicted consequences of interventions selected.

d. *Consultant Goals.* The consulting relationship is one in which client adaptability and growth toward self-direction are consistently encouraged and cultivated. (See A.1.b.)

D.3. Fees for Referral

a. *Accepting Fees from Agency Clients.* Counselors refuse a private fee or other remuneration for rendering services to persons who are entitled to such services through the counselor's employing agency or institution. The policies of a particular agency may make explicit provisions for agency clients to receive counseling services from members of its staff in private practice. In such instances, the clients must be informed of other options open to them should they seek private counseling services. (See A.10.a., A.11.b., and C.3.d.)

b. *Referral Fees.* Counselors do not accept a referral fee from other professionals.

D.4. Subcontractor Arrangements

When counselors work as subcontractors for a third party, they have a duty to inform clients of the limitations of confidentiality that the organization may place on counselors in providing counseling services to clients. The limits of such confidentiality ordinarily are discussed as part of the intake session. (See B.1.e. and B.1.f.)

Section E: Evaluation, Assessment, and Interpretation

E.1. General

a. *Appraisal Techniques.* The primary purpose of educational and psychological assessment is to provide measures that are objective and interpretable in either comparative or absolute terms. Counselors recognize the need to interpret the statements in this section as applying to the whole range of appraisal techniques, including test and nontest data.

b. *Client Welfare.* Counselors promote the welfare and best interest of the client in the development, publication, and utilization of educational and psychological assessment techniques. They do not misuse assessment results and interpretations and take reasonable steps to prevent others from misusing the information these techniques provide. They respect the client's right to know the results, the interpretations made, and the bases for their conclusions and recommendations.

E.2. Competence to Use and Interpret Tests

a. *Limits of Competence.* Counselors recognize the limits of their competence and perform only those testing and assessment services for which they have been trained. They are familiar with reliability, validity, related standardization, error of measurement, and proper application of any technique utilized. Counselors using computer-based test interpretations are trained in the construct being measured and the specific instrument being used prior to using this type of computer application. Counselors take reasonable measures to ensure the proper use of psychological assessment techniques by persons under their supervision.

b. *Appropriate Use.* Counselors are responsible for the appropriate application, scoring, interpretation, and use of assessment instruments, whether they score and interpret such tests themselves or use computerized or other services.

c. *Decisions Based on Results.* Counselors responsible for decisions involving individuals or policies that are based on assessment results have a thorough understanding of educational and psychological measurement, including validation criteria, test research, and guidelines for test development and use.

d. *Accurate Information.* Counselors provide accurate information and avoid false claims or misconceptions when making statements about assessment instruments or techniques. Special efforts are made to avoid unwarranted connotations of such terms as IQ and grade equivalent scores. (See C.5.c.)

E.3. Informed Consent

a. *Explanation to Clients.* Prior to assessment, counselors explain the nature and purposes of assessment and the specific use of results in language the client (or other legally authorized person on behalf of the client) can understand, unless an explicit exception to this right has been agreed upon in advance. Regardless of whether scoring and interpretation are completed by counselors, by assistants, or by computer or other outside services, counselors take reasonable steps to ensure that appropriate explanations are given to the client.

b. *Recipients of Results.* The examinee's welfare, explicit understanding, and prior agreement determine the recipients of test results. Counselors include accurate and appropriate interpretations with any release of individual or group test results. (See B.1.a. and C.5.c.)

E.4. Release of Information to Competent Professionals

a. *Misuse of Results.* Counselors do not misuse assessment results, including test results, and interpretations, and take reasonable steps to prevent the misuse of such by others. (See C.5.c.)

b. *Release of Raw Data.* Counselors ordinarily release data (e.g. protocols, counseling or interview notes, or questionnaires) in which the client is identified only with the consent of the client or the client's legal representative. Such data are usually released only to persons recognized by counselors as competent to interpret the data. (See B.1.a.)

E.5. Proper Diagnosis of Mental Disorders

a. *Proper Diagnosis.* Counselors take special care to provide proper diagnosis of mental disorders. Assessment techniques (including person interview) used to determine client care (e.g., locus of treatment, type of treatment, or recommended follow-up) are carefully selected and appropriately used. (See A.3.a. and C.5.c.)

b. *Cultural Sensitivity.* Counselors recognize that culture affects the manner in which clients' problems are defined. Clients' socioeconomic and cultural experience is considered when diagnosing mental disorders.

E.6. Test Selection

a. *Appropriateness of Instruments.* Counselors carefully consider the validity, reliability, psychometric limitations, and appropriateness of instruments when selecting tests for use in a given situation or with a particular client.

b. *Culturally Diverse Populations.* Counselors are cautious when selecting tests for culturally diverse populations to avoid inappropriateness of testing that may be outside of socialized behavioral or cognitive patterns.

E.7. Conditions of Test Administration

a. *Administration Conditions.* Counselors administer tests under the same conditions that were established in their standardization. When tests are not administered under standard conditions or when unusual behavior or irregularities occur during the testing session, those conditions are noted in interpretation, and the results may be designated as invalid or of questionable validity.

b. *Computer Administration.* Counselors are responsible for ensuring that administration programs function properly to provide clients with accurate results when a computer or other electronic methods are used for test administration. (See A.12.b.)

c. *Unsupervised Test-Taking.* Counselors do not permit unsupervised or inadequately supervised use of tests or assessments unless the tests or assessments are designed, intended, and validated for self-administration and/or scoring.

d. *Disclosure of Favorable Conditions.* Prior to test administration, conditions that produce most favorable test results are made known to the examinee.

E.8. Diversity in Testing

Counselors are cautious in using assessment techniques, making evaluations, and interpreting the performance of populations not represented in the norm group on which an instrument was standardized. They recognize the effects of age, color, culture, disability, ethnic group, gender, race, religion, sexual orientation, and socioeconomic status on test administration and interpretation and place test results in proper perspective with other relevant factors. (See A.2.a.)

E.9. Test Scoring and Interpretation

a. *Reporting Reservations.* In reporting assessment results, counselors indicate any reservations that exist regarding validity or reliability because of the circumstances of the assessment or the inappropriateness of the norms for the person tested.

b. *Research Instruments.* Counselors exercise caution when interpreting the results of research instruments possessing insufficient technical data to support respondent results. The specific purposes for the use of such instruments are stated explicitly to the examinee.

c. *Testing Services.* Counselors who provide test scoring and test interpretation services to support the assessment process confirm the validity of such interpretations. They accurately describe the purpose, norms, validity, reliability, and applications of the procedures and any special qualifications applicable to their use. The public offering of an automated test interpretations service is considered a professional-to-professional consultation. The formal responsibility of the consultant is to the consultee, but the ultimate and overriding responsibility is to the client.

E.10. Test Security

Counselors maintain the integrity and security of tests and other assessment techniques consistent with legal and contractual obligations. Counselors do not appropriate, reproduce, or modify published tests or parts thereof without acknowledgment and permission from the publisher.

E.11. Obsolete Tests and Outdated Test Results

Counselors do not use data or test results that are obsolete or outdated for the current purpose. Counselors make every effort to prevent the misuse of obsolete measures and test data by others.

E.12. Test Construction

Counselors use established scientific procedures, relevant standards, and current professional knowledge for test design in the development, publication, and utilization of educational and psychological assessment techniques.

Section F: Teaching, Training, and Supervision

F.1. Counselor Educators and Trainers

a. *Educators as Teachers and Practitioners.* Counselors who are responsible for developing, implementing, and supervising educational programs are skilled as teachers and practitioners. They are knowledgeable regarding the ethical, legal, and regulatory aspects of the profession, are skilled in applying that knowledge, and make students and supervisees aware of their responsibilities. Counselors conduct counselor education and training programs in an ethical manner and serve as role models for professional behavior. Counselor educators should make an effort to infuse material related to human diversity into all courses and/or workshops that are designed to promote the development of professional counselors.

b. *Relationship Boundaries with Students and Supervisees.* Counselors clearly define and maintain ethical, professional, and social relationship boundaries with their students and supervisees. They are aware of the differential in power that exists and the student's or supervisee's possible incomprehension of that power differential. Counselors explain to students and supervisees the potential for the relationship to become exploitive.

c. *Sexual Relationships.* Counselors do not engage in sexual relationships with students or supervisees and do not subject them to sexual harassment. (See A.6. and C.5.b.)

d. *Contributions to Research.* Counselors give credit to students or supervisees for their contributions to research and scholarly projects. Credit is given through coauthorship, acknowledgment, footnote statement, or other appropriate means, in accordance with such contributions. (See G.4.b. and G.4.c.)

e. *Close Relatives.* Counselors do not accept close relatives as students or supervisees.

f. *Supervision Preparation.* Counselors who offer clinical supervision services are adequately prepared in supervision methods and techniques. Counselors who are doctoral students serving as practicum or internship supervisors to master's level students are adequately prepared and supervised by the training program.

g. *Responsibility for Services to Clients.* Counselors who supervise the counseling services of others take reasonable measures to ensure that counseling services provided to clients are professional.

h. *Endorsement.* Counselors do not endorse students or supervisees for certification, licensure, employment, or completion of an academic or training program if they believe students or supervisees are not qualified for the endorsement. Counselors take reasonable steps to assist students or supervisees who are not qualified for endorsement to become qualified.

F.2. Counselor Education and Training Programs

a. *Orientation.* Prior to admission, counselors orient prospective students to the counselor education or training programs' expectations, including but not limited to the following: (1) the type and level of skill acquisition required for successful completion of the training, (2) subject matter to be covered, (3) basis for evaluation, (4) training components that encourage self-growth or self-disclosure as part of the training process, (5) the type of supervision settings and requirements of the sites for required clinical field experiences, (6) student and supervisee evaluation and dismissal policies and procedures, and (7) up-to-date employment prospects for graduates.

b. *Integration of Study and Practice.* Counselors establish counselor education and training programs that integrate academic study and supervised practice.

c. *Evaluation.* Counselors clearly state to students and supervisees, in advance of training, the levels of competency expected, appraisal methods, and timing of evaluations for both didactic and experiential components. Counselors provide students and supervisees with periodic performance appraisal and evaluation feedback throughout the training program.

d. *Teaching Ethics.* Counselors make students and supervisees aware of the ethical responsibilities and standards of the profession and the student's and supervisee's ethical responsibilities to the profession. (See C.1. and F.3.e.)

e. *Peer Relationships.* When students or supervisees are assigned to lead counseling groups or provide clinical supervision for their peers, counselors take steps to ensure that students and supervisees placed in these roles do not have personal or adverse relationships with peers and that they understand they have the same ethical obligations as counselor educators, trainers, and supervisors. Counselors make every effort to ensure that the rights of peers are not compromised when students or supervisees are assigned to lead counseling groups or provide clinical supervision.

f. *Varied Theoretical Positions.* Counselors present varied theoretical positions so that students and supervisees may make comparisons and have opportunities to develop their own positions. Counselors provide information concerning the scientific bases of professional practice. (See C.6.a.)

g. *Field Placement.* Counselors develop clear policies within their training program regarding field placement and other clinical experiences. Counselors provide clearly stated roles and responsibilities for the student or supervisee, the site supervisor, and the program supervisor. They confirm that site supervisors are qualified to provide supervision and are informed of their professional and ethical responsibilities in this role.

h. *Dual Relationships as Supervisors.* Counselors avoid dual relationships such as performing the role of site supervisor and training program supervisor in the student's or supervisee's training program. Counselors do not accept any form of professional services, fees, commissions, reimbursement, or remuneration from a site for student or supervisee placement.

i. *Diversity in Programs.* Counselors are responsive to their institution's and program's recruitment and retention needs for training program administrators, faculty, and students with diverse backgrounds and special needs. (See A.2.a.)

F.3. Students and Supervisees

a. *Limitations.* Counselors, through ongoing evaluation and appraisal, are aware of the academic and personal limitations of students and supervisees that might impede performance. Counselors assist students and supervisees in securing remedial assistance when needed, and dismiss from the training program supervisees who are unable to provide competent service due to academic or personal limitations. Counselors seek professional consultation and document their decision to dismiss or refer students or supervisees for assistance. Counselors assure that students and supervisees have recourse to address decisions made, to require them to seek assistance, or to dismiss them.

b. *Self-Growth Experiences.* Counselors use professional judgment when designing training experiences conducted by the counselors themselves that require student and supervisee self-growth or self-disclosure. Safeguards are provided so that students and supervisees are aware of the ramifications their self-disclosure may have, on counselors whose primary role as teacher, trainer, or supervisor requires acting on ethical obligations to the profession. Evaluative components of experiential training experiences explicitly delineate predetermined academic standards that are separate and not dependent on the student's level of self-disclosure. (See A.6.)

c. *Counseling for Students and Supervisees.* If students or supervisees request counseling, supervisors or counselor educators provide them with acceptable referrals. Supervisors or counselor educators do not serve as counselor to students or supervisees over whom they hold administrative, teaching, or evaluative roles unless this is a brief role associated with a training experience. (See A.6.b.)

d. *Clients of Students and Supervisees.* Counselors make every effort to ensure that the clients at field placements are aware of the services rendered and the qualifications of the students and supervisees rendering those services. Clients receive professional disclosure information and are informed of the limits of confidentiality. Client permission is obtained in order for the students and supervisees to use any information concerning the counseling relationship in the training process. (See B.1.e.)

e. *Standards for Students and Supervisees.* Students and supervisees preparing to become counselors adhere to the Code of Ethics and the Standards of Practice. Students and supervisees have the same obligations to clients as those required of counselors. (See H.1.)

Section G: Research and Publication

G.1. Research Responsibilities

a. *Use of Human Subjects.* Counselors plan, design, conduct, and report research in a manner consistent with pertinent ethical principles, federal and state laws, host institutional regulations, and scientific standards governing research with human subjects. Counselors design and conduct research that reflects cultural sensitivity appropriateness.

b. *Deviation from Standard Practices.* Counselors seek consultation and observe stringent safeguards to protect the rights of research participants when a research problem suggests a deviation from standard acceptable practices. (See B.6.)

c. *Precautions to Avoid Injury.* Counselors who conduct research with human subjects are responsible for the subjects' welfare throughout the experiment and take reasonable precautions to avoid causing injurious psychological, physical, or social effects to their subjects.

d. *Principal Researcher Responsibility.* The ultimate responsibility for ethical research practice lies with the principal researcher. All others involved in the research activities share ethical obligations and full responsibility for their own actions.

e. *Minimal Interference.* Counselors take reasonable precautions to avoid causing disruptions in subjects' lives due to participation in research.

f. *Diversity.* Counselors are sensitive to diversity and research issues with special populations. They seek consultation when appropriate. (See A.2.a. and B.6.)

G.2. Informed Consent

a. *Topics Disclosed.* In obtaining informed consent for research, counselors use language that is understandable to research participants and that: (1) accurately explains the purpose and procedures to be followed; (2) identifies any procedures that are experimental or relatively untried; (3) describes the attendant discomforts and risks; (4) describes the benefits or changes in individuals or organizations that might be reasonably expected; (5) discloses appropriate alternative procedures that would be advantageous for subjects; (6) offers to answer any inquiries concerning the procedures; (7) describes any limitations on confidentiality; and (8) instructs that subjects are free to withdraw their consent and to discontinue participation in the project at any time. (See B.1.f.)

b. *Deception.* Counselors do not conduct research involving deception unless alternative procedures are not feasible and the prospective value of the research justifies the deception. When the methodological requirements of a study necessitate concealment or deception, the investigator is required to explain clearly the reasons for this action as soon as possible.

c. *Voluntary Participation.* Participation in research is typically voluntary and without any penalty for refusal to participate. Involuntary participation is appropriate only when it can be demonstrated that participation will have no harmful effects on subjects and is essential to the investigation.

d. *Confidentiality of Information.* Information obtained about research participants during the course of an investigation is confidential. When the possibility exists that others may obtain access to such information, ethical research practice requires that the possibility, together with the plans for protecting confidentiality, be explained to participants as a part of the procedure for obtaining informed consent. (See B.1.e.)

e. *Person Incapable of Giving Informed Consent.* When a person is incapable of giving informed consent, counselors provide an appropriate explanation, obtain agreement for participation and obtain appropriate consent from a legally authorized person.

f. *Commitments to Participants.* Counselors take reasonable measures to honor all commitments to research participants.

g. *Explanations After Data Collection.* After data are collected, counselors provide participants with full clarification of the nature of the study to remove any misconceptions. Where scientific or human values justify delaying or withholding information, counselors take reasonable measures to avoid causing harm.

h. *Agreements to Cooperate.* Counselors who agree to cooperate with another individual in research or publication incur an obligation to cooperate as promised in terms of punctuality of performance and with regard to the completeness and accuracy of the information required.

i. *Informed Consent for Sponsors.* In the pursuit of research, counselors give sponsors, institutions, and publication channels the same respect and opportunity for giving informed consent that they accord to individual research participants. Counselors are aware of their obligation to future research workers and ensure that host institutions are given feedback information and proper acknowledgment.

G.3. Reporting Results

a. *Information Affecting Outcome.* When reporting research results, counselors explicitly mention all variables and conditions known to the investigator that may have affected the outcome of a study or the interpretation of data.

b. *Accurate Results.* Counselors plan, conduct, and report research accurately and in a manner that minimizes the possibility that results will be misleading. They provide thorough discussions of the limitations of their data and alternative hypotheses. Counselors do not engage in fraudulent research, distort data, misrepresent data, or deliberately bias their results.

c. *Obligation to Report Unfavorable Results.* Counselors communicate to other counselors the results of any research judged to be of professional value. Results that reflect unfavorably on institutions, programs, services, prevailing opinions, or vested interests are not withheld.

d. *Identity of Subjects.* Counselors who supply data, aid in the research of another person, report research results, or make original data available take due care to disguise the identity of respective subjects in the absence of specific authorization from the subjects to do otherwise. (See B.1.g. and B.5.a.)

e. *Replication Studies.* Counselors are obligated to make available sufficient original research data to qualified professionals who may wish to replicate the study.

G.4. Publication

a. *Recognition of Others.* When conducting and reporting research, counselors are familiar with and give recognition to previous work on the topic, observe copyright laws, and give full credit to those to whom credit is due. (See F.1.d. and G.4.c.)

b. *Contributors.* Counselors give credit through joint authorship, acknowledgment, footnote statements, or other appropriate means to those who have contributed significantly to research or concept development in accordance with such contributions. The principal contributor is listed first and minor technical or professional contributions are acknowledged in notes or introductory statements.

c. *Student Research.* For an article that is substantially based on a student's dissertation or thesis, the student is listed as the principal author. (See F.1.d. and G.4.a.)

d. *Duplicate Submission.* Counselors submit manuscripts for consideration to only one journal at a time. Manuscripts that are published in whole or in substantial part in another journal or published work are not submitted for publication without acknowledgment and permission from the previous publication.

e. *Professional Review.* Counselors who review material submitted for publication, research, or other scholarly purposes respect the confidentiality and proprietary rights of those who submitted it.

Section H. Resolving Ethical Issues

H.1. Knowledge of Standards

Counselors are familiar with the Code of Ethics and the Standards of Practice and other applicable ethics codes from other professional organizations of which they are members, or from certification and licensure bodies. Lack of knowledge or misunderstanding of an ethical responsibility is not a defense against a charge of unethical conduct. (See F.3.e.)

H.2. Suspected Violations

a. *Ethical Behavior Expected.* Counselors expect professional associates to adhere to Code of Ethics. When counselors possess reasonable cause that raises doubts as to whether a counselor is acting in an ethical manner, they take appropriate action. (See H.2.d. and H.2.e.)

b. *Consultation.* When uncertain as to whether a particular situation or course of action may be in violation of Code of Ethics, counselors consult with other counselors who are knowledgeable about ethics, with colleagues, or with appropriate authorities.

c. *Organization Conflicts.* If the demands of an organization with which counselors are affiliated post a conflict with Code of Ethics, counselors specify the nature of such conflicts and express to their supervisors or other responsible officials their commitment to Code of Ethics. When possible counselors work toward change within the organization to allow full adherence to Code of Ethics.

d. *Informal Resolution.* When counselors have reasonable cause to believe that another counselor is violating an ethical standard, they attempt to first resolve the issue informally with the other counselor if feasible, providing that such action does not violate confidentiality rights that may be involved.

e. *Reporting Suspected Violations.* When an informal resolution is not appropriate or feasible, counselors, upon reasonable cause, take action such as reporting the suspected ethical violation to state or national ethics committees, unless this action conflicts with confidentiality rights that cannot be resolved.

f. *Unwarranted Complaints.* Counselors do not initiate, participate in, or encourage the filing of ethics complaints that are unwarranted or intended to harm a counselor rather than to protect clients or the public.

H.3. Cooperation with Ethics Committees

Counselors assist in the process of enforcing Code of Ethics. Counselors cooperate with investigations, proceedings, and requirements of the ACA Ethics Committee or ethics committees of other duly constituted associations or boards having jurisdiction over those charged with a violation. Counselors are familiar with the ACA Policies and Procedures and use it as a reference in assisting the enforcement of the Code of Ethics.

STANDARDS OF PRACTICE

All members of the American Counseling Association (ACA) are required to adhere to the Standards of Practice and the Code of Ethics. The Standards of Practice represent minimal behavioral statements of the Code of Ethics. Members should refer to the applicable section of the Code of Ethics for further interpretation and amplification of the applicable Standard of Practice.

Section A: The Counseling Relationship

Standard of Practice One (SP-1)

Nondiscrimination

Counselors respect diversity and must not discriminate against clients because of age, color, culture, disability, ethnic group, gender, race, religion, sexual orientation, marital status, or socioeconomic status. (See A.2.a.)

Standard of Practice Two (SP-2)

Disclosure to Clients

Counselors must adequately inform clients, preferably in writing, regarding the counseling process and counseling relationship at or before the time it begins and throughout the relationship. (See A.3.a.)

Standard of Practice Three (SP-3)

Dual Relationships

Counselors must make every effort to avoid dual relationships with clients that could impair their professional judgment or increase the risk of harm to clients. When a dual relationship cannot be avoided, counselors must take appropriate steps to ensure that judgment is not impaired and that no exploitation occurs. (See A.6.a. and A.6.b.)

Standard of Practice Four (SP-4)

Sexual Intimacies with Clients

Counselors must not engage in any type of sexual intimacies with current clients and must not engage in sexual intimacies with former clients within a minimum of two years after terminating the counseling relationship. Counselors who engage in such relationship after two years following termination have the responsibility to thoroughly examine and document that such relations did not have an exploitive nature. (See A.7.a. and A.7.b.)

Standard of Practice Five (SP-5)

Protecting Clients During Group Work

Counselors must take steps to protect clients from physical or psychological trauma resulting from interactions during group work. (See A.9.b.)

Standard of Practice Six (SP-6)

Advance Understanding of Fees

Counselors must explain to clients, prior to their entering the counseling relationship, financial arrangements related to professional services. (See A.10.a-d. and A.11.c.)

Standard of Practice Seven (SP-7)

Termination

Counselors must assist in making appropriate arrangements for the continuation of treatment of clients, when necessary, following termination of counseling relationships. (See A.11.a.)

Standard of Practice Eight (SP-8)

Inability to Assist Clients

Counselors must avoid entering or immediately terminate a counseling relationship if it is determined that they are unable to be of professional assistance to a client. The counselor may assist in making an appropriate referral for the client. (See A.11.b.)

Section B: Confidentiality

Standard of Practice Nine (SP-9)

Confidentiality Requirement

Counselors must keep information related to counseling services confidential unless disclosure is in the best interest of clients, is required for the welfare of others, or is required by law. When disclosure is required, only information that is essential is revealed and the client is informed of such disclosure. (See B.1.a-f.)

Standard of Practice Ten (SP-10)

Confidentiality Requirements for Subordinates

. Counselors must take measures to ensure that privacy and confidentiality of clients are maintained by subordinates. (See B.1.h.)

Standard of Practice Eleven (SP-11)

Confidentiality in Group Work

Counselors must clearly communicate to group members that confidentiality cannot be guaranteed in group work. (See B.2.a.)

Standard of Practice Twelve (SP-12)

Confidentiality in Family Counseling

Counselors must not disclose information about one family member in counseling to another family member without prior consent. (See B.2.b.)

Standard of Practice Thirteen (SP-13)

Confidentiality of Records

Counselors must maintain appropriate confidentiality in creating, storing, accessing, transferring, and disposing of counseling records. (See B.4.b.)

Standard of Practice Fourteen (SP-14)

Permission to Record or Observe

Counselors must obtain prior consent from clients in order to electronically record or observe sessions. (See B.4.c.)

Standard of Practice Fifteen (SP-15)

Disclosure or Transfer of Records

Counselors must obtain client consent to disclose or transfer records to third parties, unless exceptions listed in SP-9 exist. (See B.4.e.)

Standard of Practice Sixteen (SP-16)

Data Disguise Required
Counselors must disguise the identity of the client when using data for training, research, or publication. (See B.5.a.)

Section C: Professional Responsibility

Standard of Practice Seventeen (SP-17)

Boundaries of Competence
Counselors must practice only within the boundaries of their competence. (See C.2.a.)

Standard of Practice Eighteen (SP-18)

Continuing Education
Counselors must engage in continuing education to maintain their professional competence. (See C.2.f.)

Standard of Practice Nineteen (SP-19)

Impairment of Professionals
Counselors must refrain from offering professional services when their personal problems or conflicts may cause harm to a client or others. (See C.2.g.)

Standard of Practice Twenty (SP-20)

Accurate Advertising
Counselors must accurately represent their credentials and services when advertising. (See C.3.a.)

Standard of Practice Twenty-one (SP-21)

Recruiting Through Employment
Counselors must not use their place of employment or institutional affiliation to recruit clients for their private practices. (See C.3.d.)

Standard of Practice Twenty-two (SP-22)

Credentials Claimed
Counselors must claim or imply only professional credentials possessed and must correct any known misrepresentations of their credentials by others. (See C.4.a.)

Standard of Practice Twenty-three (SP-23)

Sexual Harassment
Counselors must not engage in sexual harassment. (See C.5.b.)

Standard of Practice Twenty-four (SP-24)

Unjustified Gains

Counselors must not use their professional positions to seek or receive unjustified personal gains, sexual favors, unfair advantage, or unearned goods or services. (See C.5.e.)

Standard of Practice Twenty-five (SP-25)

Clients Served by Others

With the consent of the client, counselors must inform other mental health professionals serving the same client that a counseling relationship between the counselor and client exists. (See C.6.c.)

Standard of Practice Twenty-six (SP-26)

Negative Employment Conditions

Counselors must alert their employers to institutional policy or conditions that may be potentially disruptive or damaging to the counselor's professional responsibilities or that may limit their effectiveness or deny client's rights. (See D.1.c.)

Standard of Practice Twenty-seven (SP-27)

Personnel Selection and Assignment

Counselors must select competent staff and must assign responsibilities compatible with staff skills and experiences. (See D.1.h.)

Standard of Practice Twenty-eight (SP-28)

Exploitive Relationships with Subordinates

Counselors must not engage in exploitive relationships with individuals over whom they have supervisory, evaluative, or instructional control or authority. (See D.1.k.)

Section D: Relationship with Other Professionals

Standard of Practice Twenty-nine (SP-29)

Accepting Fees from Agency Clients

Counselors must not accept fees or other remuneration for consultation with persons entitled to such services through the counselor's employing agency or institution. (See D.3.a.)

Standard of Practice Thirty (SP-30)

Referral Fees

Counselors must not accept referral fees. (See D.3.b.)

Section E: Evaluation, Assessment, and Interpretation

Standard of Practice Thirty-one (SP-31)

Limit of Practice

Counselors must perform only testing and assessment services for which they are competent. Counselors must not allow the use of psychological assessment techniques by unqualified persons under their supervision. (See E.2.a.)

Standard of Practice Thirty-two (SP-32)

Appropriate Use of Assessment Instruments

Counselors must use assessment instruments in the manner for which they were intended. (See E.2.b.)

Standard of Practice Thirty-three (SP-33)

Assessment Explanations to Clients

Counselors must provide explanations to clients prior to assessment about the nature and purposes of assessment and the specific uses of results. (See E.3.a.)

Standard of Practice Thirty-four (SP-34)

Recipients of Test Results

Counselors must ensure that accurate and appropriate interpretations accompany any release of testing and assessment information. (See E.3.b.)

Standard of Practice Thirty-five (SP-35)

Obsolete Tests and Outdated Test Results

Counselors must not base their assessment or intervention decisions or recommendations on data or test results that are obsolete or outdated for the current purpose. (See E.11.)

Section F: Teaching, Training, and Supervision

Standard of Practice Thirty-six (SP-36)

Sexual Relationships with Students or Supervisees

Counselors must not engage in sexual relationships with their students and supervisees. (See F.1.c.)

Standard of Practice Thirty-seven (SP-37)

Credit for Contributions to Research

Counselors must give credit to students or supervisees for their contributions to research and scholarly projects. (See F.1.d.)

Standard of Practice Thirty-eight (SP-38)

Supervision Preparation

Counselors who offer clinical supervision services must be trained and prepared in supervision methods and techniques. (See F.1.f.)

Standard of Practice Thirty-nine (SP-39)

Evaluation Information

Counselors must clearly state to students and supervisees, in advance of training, the levels of competency expected, appraisal methods, and timing of evaluations. Counselors must provide students and supervisees with periodic performance appraisal and evaluation feedback throughout the training program. (See F.2.c.)

Standard of Practice Forty (SP-40)

Peer Relationships in Training

Counselors must make every effort to ensure that the rights of peers are not violated when students and supervisees are assigned to lead counseling groups or provide clinical supervision. (See F.2.e.)

Standard of Practice Forty-one (SP-41)

Limitations of Students and Supervisees

Counselors must assist students and supervisees in securing remedial assistance, when needed, and must dismiss from the training program students and supervisees who are unable to provide competent service due to academic or personal limitations (See F.3.a.)

Standard of Practice Forty-two (SP-42)

Self-Growth Experiences

Counselors who conduct experiences for students or supervisees that include self-growth or self-disclosure must inform participants of counselors' ethical obligations to the profession and must not grade participants based on their nonacademic performance. (See F.3.b.)

Standard of Practice Forty-three (SP-43)

Standards for Students and Supervisees

Students and supervisees preparing to become counselors must adhere to the Code of Ethics and the Standards of Practice of counselors. (See F.3.e.)

Section G: Research and Publication

Standard of Practice Forty-four (SP-44)

Precautions to Avoid Injury in Research

Counselors must avoid causing physical, social, or psychological harm or injury to subjects in research. (See G.1.c.)

Standard of Practice Forty-five (SP-45)

Confidentiality of Research Information
    Counselors must keep confidential information obtained about
research participants. (See G.2.d.)

Standard of Practice Forty-six (SP-46)

Information Affecting Research Outcome
    Counselors must report all variables and conditions known to the
investigator that may have affected research data or outcomes. (See
G.3.a.)

Standard of Practice Forty-seven (SP-47)

Accurate Research Results
    Counselors must not distort or misrepresent research data, nor fabri-
cate or intentionally bias research results. (See G.3.b.)

Standard of Practice Forty-eight (SP-48)

Publication Contributions
    Counselors must give appropriate credit to those who have con-
tributed to research. (See G.4.a. and G.4.b.)

Section H: Resolving Ethical Issues

Standard of Practice Forty-nine (SP-49)

Ethical Behavior Expected
    Counselors must take appropriate action when they possess reason-
able cause that raises doubts as to whether counselors or other mental
health professionals are acting in an ethical manner. (See H.2.a.)

Standard of Practice Fifty (SP-50)

Unwarranted Complaints
    Counselors must not initiate, participate in, or encourage the filing
of ethics complaints that are unwarranted or intended to harm a mental
health professional rather than to protect clients or the public. (See
H.2.f.)

Standard of Practice Fifty-one (SP-51)

Cooperation with Ethics Committees
    Counselors must cooperate with investigations, proceedings, and
requirements of the ACA Ethics Committee or ethics committees of
other duly constituted associations or boards having jurisdiction over
those charged with a violation. (See H.3.)

REFERENCES

The following documents are available to counselors as resources to guide them in their practices. These resources are not part of the Code of Ethics and the Standards of Practice.

American Association for Counseling and Development/Association for Measurement and Evaluation in Counseling and Development. (1989). *The responsibilities of users of standardized tests* (Rev. ed.). Washington, DC: Author.

American Counseling Association. (1988). *American Counseling Association code of ethics and standards of practice*. Alexandria, VA: Author.

American Psychological Association. (1985). *Standards for educational and psychological testing* (Rev. ed.). Washington, DC: Author.

American Rehabilitation Counseling Association, Commission on Rehabilitation Counselor Certification, and National Rehabilitation Counseling Association. (1995). *Code of professional ethics for rehabilitation counselors*. Chicago, IL: Author.

American School Counselor Association. (1992). *Ethical standards for school counselors*. Alexandria, VA: Author.

Joint Committee on Testing Practices. (1988). *Code of fair testing practices in education*. Washington, DC: Author.

National Board for Certified Counselors. (1989). *National Board for Certified Counselors code of ethics*. Alexandria, VA: Author.

Prediger, D. J. (Ed.). (1993, March). *Multicultural assessment standards*. Alexandria, VA: Association for Assessment in Counseling.

▲▲▲
▼▼▼

American Psychological Association's *Ethical Principles of Psychologists and Code of Conduct*

INTRODUCTION

The American Psychological Association's (APA's) *Ethical Principles of Psychologists and Code of Conduct* (hereinafter referred to as the Ethics Code) consists of an Introduction, a Preamble, six General Principles (A–F), and specific Ethical Standards. The Introduction discusses the intent, organization, procedural considerations, and scope of application of the Ethics Code. The Preamble and General Principles are aspirational goals to guide psychologists toward the highest ideals of psychology. Although the Preamble and General Principles are not themselves enforceable rules, they should be considered by psychologists in arriving at an ethical course of action and may be considered by ethics bodies in interpreting the Ethical Standards. The Ethical Standards set forth enforceable rules for conduct as psychologists. Most of the Ethical Standards are written broadly, in order to apply to psychologists in varied roles, although the application of an Ethical Standard may vary depending on the context. The Ethical Standards are not exhaustive. The fact that a given conduct is not specifically addressed by the Ethics Code does not mean that it is necessarily either ethical or unethical.

Membership in the APA commits members to adhere to the APA Ethics Code and to the rules and procedures used to implement it. Psychologists and students, whether or not they are APA members, should be aware that the Ethics Code may be applied to them by state psychology boards, courts, or other public bodies.

This Ethics Code applies only to psychologists' work-related activities, that is, activities that are part of the psychologists' scientific and professional functions or that are psychological in nature. It includes the clinical or counseling practice of psychology, research, teaching, supervision of trainees, development of assessment instruments, conducting assessments, educational counseling, organizational consulting, social intervention, administration, and other activities as well. These work-related activities can be distinguished from the purely private conduct of a psychologist, which ordinarily is not within the purview of the Ethics Code.

The Ethics Code is intended to provide standards of professional conduct that can be applied by the APA and by other bodies that choose to adopt them. Whether or not a psychologist has violated the Ethics Code does not by itself determine whether he or she is legally liable in a court action, whether a contract is enforceable, or whether other legal consequences occur. These results are based on legal rather than ethical rules. However, compliance with or violation of the Ethics Code may be admissible as evidence in some legal proceedings, depending on the circumstances.

In the process of making decisions regarding their professional behavior, psychologists must consider this Ethics Code, in addition to applicable laws and psychology board regulations. If the Ethics Code establishes a higher standard of conduct than is required by law, psychologists must meet the higher ethical standard. If the Ethics Code standard appears to conflict with the requirements of law, then psychologists make known their commitment to the Ethics Code and take steps to resolve the conflict in a responsible manner. If neither law nor the Ethics Code resolves an issue, psychologists should consider other professional materials and the dictates of their own conscience, as well as seek consultation with others within the field when this is practical.

The procedures for filing, investigating, and resolving complaints of unethical conduct are described in the current Rules and Procedures of the APA Ethics Committee. The actions that APA may take for violations of the Ethics Code include actions such as reprimand, censure, termination of APA membership, and referral of the matter to other bodies. Complainants who seek remedies such as monetary damages in alleging ethical violations by a psychologist must resort to private negotiation, administrative bodies, or the courts. Actions that violate the Ethics Code may lead to the imposition of sanctions on a psychologist by bodies other than APA, including state psychological associations, other professional groups, psychology boards, other state or federal agencies, and payors for health services. In addition to actions for violation of the Ethics Code, the APA Bylaws provide that APA may take action against a member after his or her conviction of a felony, expulsion or suspension from an affiliated state psychological association, or suspension or loss of licensure.

PREAMBLE

Psychologists work to develop a valid and reliable body of scientific knowledge based on research. They may apply that knowledge to human behavior in a variety of contexts. In doing so, they perform many roles, such as researcher, educator, diagnostician, therapist, supervisor, consultant, administrator, social interventionist, and expert witness. Their goal is to broaden knowledge of behavior and, where appropriate, to apply it pragmatically to improve the condition of both the individual and society. Psychologists respect the central importance of freedom of inquiry and expression in research, teaching, and publication. They also strive to help the public in developing informed judgments and choices concerning human behavior. This Ethics Code provides a common set of values upon which psychologists build their professional and scientific work.

This Code is intended to provide both the generalprinciples and the decision rules to cover most situations encountered by psychologists. It has as its primary goal the welfare and protection of the individuals and groups with whom psychologists work. It is the individual responsibility of each psychologist to aspire to the highest possible standards of conduct. Psychologists respect and protect human and civil rights, and do not knowingly participate in or condone unfair discriminatory practices.

The development of a dynamic set of ethical standards for a psychologist's work-related conduct requires a personal commitment to a lifelong effort to act ethically; to encourage ethical behavior by students, supervisees, employees, and colleagues, as appropriate; and to consult with others, as needed, concerning ethical problems. Each psychologist supplements, but does not violate, the Ethics Code's values and rules on the basis of guidance drawn from personal values, culture, and experience.

GENERAL PRINCIPLES

Principle A: Competence

Psychologists strive to maintain high standards of competence in their work. They recognize the boundaries of their particular competencies and the limitations of their expertise. They provide only those services and use only those techniques for which they are qualified by education, training, or experience. Psychologists are cognizant of the fact that the competencies required in serving, teaching, and/or studying groups of people vary with the distinctive characteristics of those groups. In those areas in which recognized professional standards do not yet exist, psychologists exercise careful judgment and take appropriate precautions to protect the welfare of those with whom they work. They maintain knowledge of relevant scientific and professional information related to the services they render, and they recognize the need for ongoing education. Psychologists make appropriate use of scientific, professional, technical, and administrative resources.

Principle B: Integrity

Psychologists seek to promote integrity in the science, teaching, and practice of psychology. In these activities psychologists are honest, fair, and respectful of others. In describing or reporting their qualifications, services, products, fees, research, or teaching, they do not make statements that are false, misleading, or deceptive. Psychologists strive to be aware of their own belief systems, values, needs, and limitations and the effect of these on their work. To the extent feasible, they attempt to clarify for relevant parties the roles they are performing and to function appropriately in accordance with those roles. Psychologists avoid improper and potentially harmful dual relationships.

Principle C: Professional and Scientific Responsibility

Psychologists uphold professional standards of conduct, clarify their professional roles and obligations, accept appropriate responsibility for their behavior, and adapt their methods to the needs of different populations. Psychologists consult with, refer to, or cooperate with other professionals and institutions to the extent needed to serve the best interests of their patients, clients, or other recipients of their services. Psychologists' moral standards and conduct are personal matters to the same degree as is true for any other person, except as psychologists' conduct may compromise their professional responsibilities or reduce the public's trust in psychology and psychologists. Psychologists are concerned about the ethical compliance of their colleagues' scientific and professional conduct. When appropriate, they consult with colleagues in order to prevent or avoid unethical conduct.

Principle D: Respect for People's Rights and Dignity

Psychologists accord appropriate respect to the fundamental rights, dignity, and worth of all people. They respect the rights of individuals to privacy, confidentiality, self-determination, and autonomy, mindful that legal and other obligations may lead to inconsistency and conflict with the exercise of these rights. Psychologists are aware of cultural, individual, and role differences, including those due to age, gender, race, ethnicity, national origin, religion, sexual orientation, disability, language, and socioeconomic status. Psychologists try to eliminate the effect on their work of biases based on those factors, and they do not knowingly participate in or condone unfair discriminatory practices.

Principle E: Concern for Others' Welfare

Psychologists seek to contribute to the welfare of those with whom they interact professionally. In their professional actions, psychologists weigh the welfare and rights of their patients or clients, students, supervisees, human research participants, and other affected persons, and the welfare of animal subjects of research. When conflicts occur among psychologists' obligations or concerns, they attempt to resolve these conflicts and to perform their roles in a responsible fashion that avoids or minimizes harm. Psychologists are sensitive to real and ascribed differences in power between themselves and others, and they do not exploit or mislead other people during or after professional relationships.

Principle F: Social Responsibility

Psychologists are aware of their professional and scientific responsibilities to the community and the society in which they work and live. They apply and make public their knowledge of psychology in order to contribute to human welfare. Psychologists are concerned about and work to mitigate the causes of human suffering. When undertaking research, they strive to advance human welfare and the science of psychology. Psychologists try to avoid misuse of their work. Psychologists comply with the law and encourage the development of law and social policy that serve the interests of their patients and clients and the public. They are encouraged to contribute a portion of their professional time for little or no personal advantage.

ETHICAL STANDARDS

1. General Standards

These General Standards are potentially applicable to the professional and scientific activities of all psychologists.

1.01. Applicability of the Ethics Code.

The activity of a psychologist subject to the Ethics Code may be reviewed under these Ethical Standards only if the activity is part of his or her work-related functions or the activity is psychological in nature. Personal activities having no connection to or effect on psychological roles are not subject to the Ethics Code.

1.02. Relationship of Ethics and Law.

If psychologists' ethical responsibilities conflict with law, psychologists make known their commitment to the Ethics Code and take steps to resolve the conflict in a responsible manner.

1.03. Professional and Scientific Relationship.

Psychologists provide diagnostic, therapeutic, teaching, research, supervisory, consultative, or other psychological services only in the context of a defined professional or scientific relationship or role. (See also Standards 2.01, Evaluation, Diagnosis, and Interventions in Professional Context, and 7.02, Forensic Assessments.)

1.04. Boundaries of Competence.

(a) Psychologists provide services, teach, and conduct research only within the boundaries of their competence, based on their education, training, supervised experience, or appropriate professional experience.

(b) Psychologists provide services, teach, or conduct research in new areas or involving new techniques only after first undertaking appropriate study, training, supervision, and/or consultation from persons who are competent in those areas or techniques.

(c) In those emerging areas in which generally recognized standards for preparatory training do not yet exist, psychologists nevertheless take reasonable steps to ensure the competence of their work and to protect patients, clients, students, research participants, and others from harm.

1.05. Maintaining Expertise.

Psychologists who engage in assessment, therapy, teaching, research, organizational consulting, or other professional activities maintain a reasonable level of awareness of current scientific and professional information in their fields of activity, and undertake ongoing efforts to maintain competence in the skills they use.

1.06. Basis for Scientific and Professional Judgments.

Psychologists rely on scientifically and professionally derived knowledge when making scientific or professional judgments or when engaging in scholarly or professional endeavors.

1.07. Describing the Nature and Results of Psychological Services.

(a) When psychologists provide assessment, evaluation, treatment, counseling, supervision, teaching, consultation, research, or other psychological services to an individual, a group, or an organization, they provide, using language that is reasonably understandable to the recipient of those services, appropriate information beforehand about the nature of such services and appropriate information later about results and conclusions. (See also Standard 2.09, Explaining Assessment Results.)

(b) If psychologists will be precluded by law or by organizational roles from providing such information to particular individuals or groups, they so inform those individuals or groups at the outset of the service.

1.08. Human Differences.

Where differences of age, gender, race, ethnicity, national origin, religion, sexual orientation, disability, language, or socioeconomic status significantly affect psychologists' work concerning particular individuals or groups, psychologists obtain the training, experience, consultation, or supervision necessary to ensure the competence of their services, or they make appropriate referrals.

1.09. Respecting Others.

In their work-related activities, psychologists respect the rights of others to hold values, attitudes, and opinions that differ from their own.

1.10. Nondiscrimination.

In their work-related activities, psychologists do not engage in unfair discrimination based on age, gender, race, ethnicity, national origin, religion, sexual orientation, disability, socioeconomic status, or any basis proscribed by law.

1.11. Sexual Harassment.

(a) Psychologists do not engage in sexual harassment. Sexual harassment is sexual solicitation, physical advances, or verbal or nonverbal conduct that is sexual in nature, that occurs in connection with the psychologist's activities or roles as a psychologist, and that either: (1) is unwelcome, is offensive, or creates a hostile workplace environment, and the psychologist knows or is told this; or (2) is sufficiently severe or intense to be abusive to a reasonable person in the context. Sexual harassment can consist of a single intense or severe act or of multiple persistent or pervasive acts.

(b) Psychologists accord sexual-harassment complainants and respondents dignity and respect. Psychologists do not participate in denying a person academic admittance or advancement, employment, tenure, or promotion, based solely upon their having made, or their being the subject of, sexual harassment charges. This does not preclude taking action based upon the outcome of such proceedings or consideration of other appropriate information.

1.12. Other Harassment.

Psychologists do not knowingly engage in behavior that is harassing or demeaning to persons with whom they interact in their work based on factors such as those persons' age, gender, race, ethnicity, national origin, religion, sexual orientation, disability, language, or socioeconomic status.

1.13. Personal Problems and Conflicts.

(a) Psychologists recognize that their personal problems and conflicts may interfere with their effectiveness. Accordingly, they refrain from undertaking an activity when they know or should know that their personal problems are likely to lead to harm to a patient, client, colleague, student, research participant, or other person to whom they may owe a professional or scientific obligation.

(b) In addition, psychologists have an obligation to be alert to signs of, and to obtain assistance for, their personal problems at an early stage, in order to prevent significantly impaired performance.

(c) When psychologists become aware of personal problems that may interfere with their performing work-related duties adequately, they take appropriate measures, such as obtaining professional consultation or assistance, and determine whether they should limit, suspend, or terminate their work-related duties.

1.14. Avoiding Harm.

Psychologists take reasonable steps to avoid harming their patients or clients, research participants, students, and others with whom they work, and to minimize harm where it is foreseeable and unavoidable.

1.15. Misuse of Psychologists' Influence.

Because psychologists' scientific and professional judgments and actions may affect the lives of others, they are alert to and guard against personal, financial, social, organizational, or political factors that might lead to misuse of their influence.

1.16. Misuse of Psychologists' Work.

(a) Psychologists do not participate in activities in which it appears likely that their skills or data will be misused by others, unless corrective mechanisms are available. (See also Standard 7.04, Truthfulness and Candor.)

(b) If psychologists learn of misuse or misrepresentation of their work, they take reasonable steps to correct or minimize the misuse or misrepresentation.

1.17. Multiple Relationships.

(a) In many communities and situations, it may not be feasible or reasonable for psychologists to avoid social or other nonprofessional contacts with persons such as patients, clients, students, supervisees, or research participants. Psychologists must always be sensitive to the potential harmful effects of other contacts on their work and on those persons with whom they deal. A psychologist refrains from entering into or promising another personal, scientific, professional, financial, or other relationship with such persons if it appears likely that such a relationship reasonably might impair the psychologist's objectivity or otherwise interfere with the psychologist's effectively performing his or her functions as a psychologist, or might harm or exploit the other party.

(b) Likewise, whenever feasible, a psychologist refrains from taking on professional or scientific obligations when pre-existing relationships would create a risk of such harm.

(c) If a psychologist finds that, due to unforeseen factors, a potentially harmful multiple relationship has arisen, the psychologist attempts to resolve it with due regard for the best interests of the affected person and maximal compliance with the Ethics Code.

1.18. Barter (With Patients or Clients).

Psychologists ordinarily refrain from accepting goods, services, or other nonmonetary remuneration from patients or clients in return for psychological services because such arrangements create inherent potential for conflicts, exploitation, and distortion of the professional relationship. A psychologist may participate in bartering only if (1) it is not clinically contraindicated, and (2) the relationship is not exploitative. (See also Standards 1.17, Multiple Relationships, and 1.25, Fees and Financial Arrangements.)

1.19. Exploitative Relationships.

(a) Psychologists do not exploit persons over whom they have supervisory, evaluative, or other authority such as students, supervisees, employees, research participants, and clients or patients. (See also Standards 4.05–4.07 regarding sexual involvement with clients or patients.)

(b) Psychologists do not engage in sexual relationships with students or supervisees in training over whom the psychologist has evaluative or direct authority, because such relationships are so likely to impair judgment or be exploitative.

1.20. Consultations and Referrals.

(a) Psychologists arrange for appropriate consultations and referrals based principally on the best interests of their patients or clients, with appropriate consent, and subject to other relevant considerations, including applicable law and contractual obligations. (See also Standards 5.01, Discussing the Limits of Confidentiality, and 5.06, Consultations.)

(b) When indicated and professionally appropriate, psychologists cooperate with other professionals in order to serve their patients or clients effectively and appropriately.

(c) Psychologists' referral practices are consistent with law.

1.21. Third-Party Requests for Services.

(a) When a psychologist agrees to provide services to a person or entity at the request of a third party, the psychologist clarifies to the extent feasible, at the outset of the service, the nature of the relationship with each party. This clarification includes the role of the psychologist (such as therapist, organizational consultant, diagnostician, or expert witness), the probable uses of the services provided or the information obtained, and the fact that there may be limits to confidentiality.

(b) If there is a foreseeable risk of the psychologist's being called upon to perform conflicting roles because of the involvement of a third party, the psychologist clarifies the nature and direction of his or her responsibilities, keeps all parties appropriately informed as matters develop, and resolves the situation in accordance with this Ethics Code.

1.22. Delegation to and Supervision of Subordinates.

(a) Psychologists delegate to their employees, supervisees, and research assistants only those responsibilities that such persons can reasonably be expected to perform competently, on the basis of their education, training, or experience, either independently or with the level of supervision being provided.

(b) Psychologists provide proper training and supervision to their employees or supervisees and take reasonable steps to see that such persons perform services responsibly, competently, and ethically.

(c) If institutional policies, procedures, or practices prevent fulfillment of this obligation, psychologists attempt to modify their role or to correct the situation to the extent feasible.

1.23. Documentation of Professional and Scientific Work.

(a) Psychologists appropriately document their professional and scientific work in order to facilitate provision of services later by them or by other professionals, to ensure accountability, and to meet other requirements of institutions or the law.

(b) When psychologists have reason to believe that records of their professional services will be used in legal proceedings involving recipients of or participants in their work, they have a responsibility to create and maintain documentation in the kind of detail and quality that would be consistent with reasonable scrutiny in an adjudicative forum. (See also Standard 7.01, Professionalism, under Forensic Activities.)

1.24. Records and Data.

Psychologists create, maintain, disseminate, store, retain, and dispose of records and data relating to their research, practice, and other work in accordance with law and in a manner that permits compliance with the requirements of this Ethics Code. (See also Standard 5.04, Maintenance of Records.)

1.25. Fees and Financial Arrangements.

(a) As early as is feasible in a professional or scientific relationship, the psychologist and the patient, client, or other appropriate recipient of psychological services reach an agreement specifying the compensation and the billing arrangements.

(b) Psychologists do not exploit recipients of services or payors with respect to fees.

(c) Psychologists' fee practices are consistent with law.

(d) Psychologists do not misrepresent their fees.

(e) If limitations to services can be anticipated because of limitations in financing, this is discussed with the patient, client, or other appropriate recipient of services as early as is feasible. (See also Standard 4.08, Interruption of Services.)

(f) If the patient, client, or other recipient of services does not pay for services as agreed, and if the psychologist wishes to use collection agencies or legal measures to collect the fees, the psychologist first informs the person that such measures will be taken and provides that person an opportunity to make prompt payment. (See also Standard 5.11, Withholding Records for Nonpayment.)

1.26. Accuracy in Reports to Payors and Funding Sources.

In their reports to payors for services or sources of research funding, psychologists accurately state the nature of the research or service provided, the fees or charges, and where applicable, the identity of the provider, the findings, and the diagnosis. (See also Standard 5.05, Disclosures.)

1.27. Referrals and Fees.

When a psychologist pays, receives payment from, or divides fees with another professional other than in an employer-employee relationship, the payment to each is based on the services (clinical, consultative, administrative, or other) provided and is not based on the referral itself.

2. Evaluation, Assessment, or Intervention

2.01. Evaluation, Diagnosis, and Interventions in Professional Context.

(a) Psychologists perform evaluations, diagnostic services, or interventions only within the context of a defined professional relationship. (See also Standard 1.03, Professional and Scientific Relationship.)

(b) Psychologists' assessments, recommendations, reports, and psychological diagnostic or evaluative statements are based on information and techniques (including personal interviews of the individual when appropriate) sufficient to provide appropriate substantiation for their findings. (See also Standard 7.02, Forensic Assessments.)

2.02. Competence and Appropriate Use of Assessments and Interventions.

(a) Psychologists who develop, administer, score, interpret, or use psychological assessment techniques, interviews, tests, or instruments do so in a manner and for purposes that are appropriate in light of the research on or evidence of the usefulness and proper application of the techniques.

(b) Psychologists refrain from misuse of assessment techniques, interventions, results, and interpretations and take reasonable steps to prevent others from misusing the information these techniques provide. This includes refraining from releasing raw test results or raw data to persons, other than to patients or clients as appropriate, who are not qualified to use such information. (See also Standards 1.02, Relationship of Ethics and Law, and 1.04, Boundaries of Competence.)

2.03. Test Construction.

Psychologists who develop and conduct research with tests and other assessment techniques use scientific procedures and current professional knowledge for test design, standardization, validation, reduction or elimination of bias, and recommendations for use.

2.04. Use of Assessment in General and With Special Populations.

(a) Psychologists who perform interventions or administer, score, interpret, or use assessment techniques are familiar with the reliability, validation, and related standardization or outcome studies of, and proper applications and uses of, the techniques they use.

(b) Psychologists recognize limits to the certainty with which diagnoses, judgments, or predictions can be made about individuals.

(c) Psychologists attempt to identify situations in which particular interventions or assessment techniques or norms may not be applicable or may require adjustment in administration or interpretation because of factors such as individuals' gender, age, race, ethnicity, national origin, religion, sexual orientation, disability, language, or socioeconomic status.

2.05. Interpreting Assessment Results.

When interpreting assessment results, including automated interpretations, psychologists take into account the various test factors and characteristics of the person being assessed that might affect psychologists' judgments or reduce the accuracy of their interpretations. They indicate any significant reservations they have about the accuracy or limitations of their interpretations.

2.06. Unqualified Persons.

Psychologists do not promote the use of psychological assessment techniques by unqualified persons. (See also Standard 1.22, Delegation to and Supervision of Subordinates.)

2.07. Obsolete Tests and Outdated Test Results.

(a) Psychologists do not base their assessment or intervention decisions or recommendations on data or test results that are outdated for the current purpose.

(b) Similarly, psychologists do not base such decisions or recommendations on tests and measures that are obsolete and not useful for the current purpose.

2.08. Test Scoring and Interpretation Services.

(a) Psychologists who offer assessment or scoring procedures to other professionals accurately describe the purpose, norms, validity, reliability, and applications of the procedures and any special qualifications applicable to their use.

(b) Psychologists select scoring and interpretation services (including automated services) on the basis of evidence of the validity of the program and procedures as well as on other appropriate considerations.

(c) Psychologists retain appropriate responsibility for the appropriate application, interpretation, and use of assessment instruments, whether they score and interpret such tests themselves or use automated or other services.

2.09. Explaining Assessment Results.

Unless the nature of the relationship is clearly explained to the person being assessed in advance and precludes provision of an explanation of results (such as in some organizational consulting, pre-employment or security screenings, and forensic evaluations), psychologists ensure that an explanation of the results is provided using language that is reasonably understandable to the person assessed or to another legally authorized person on behalf of the client. Regardless of whether the scoring and interpretation are done by the psychologist, by assistants, or by automated or other outside services, psychologists take reasonable steps to ensure that appropriate explanations of results are given.

2.10. Maintaining Test Security.

Psychologists make reasonable efforts to maintain the integrity and security of tests and other assessment techniques consistent with law, contractual obligations, and in a manner that permits compliance with the requirements of this Ethics Code. (See also Standard 1.02, Relationship of Ethics and Law.)

3. Advertising and Other Public Statements

3.01. Definition of Public Statements.

Psychologists comply with this Ethics Code in public statements relating to their professional services, products, or publications or to the field of psychology. Public statements include but are not limited to paid or unpaid advertising, brochures, printed matter, directory listings, personal resumes or curriculum vitae, interviews or comments for use in media, statements in legal proceedings, lectures and public oral presentations, and published materials.

3.02. Statements by Others.

(a) Psychologists who engage others to create or place public statements that promote their professional practice, products, or activities retain professional responsibility for such statements.

(b) In addition, psychologists make reasonable efforts to prevent others whom they do not control (such as employers, publishers, sponsors, organizational clients, and representatives of the print or broadcast media) from making deceptive statements concerning psychologists' practice or professional or scientific activities.

(c) If psychologists learn of deceptive statements about their work made by others, psychologists make reasonable efforts to correct such statements.

(d) Psychologists do not compensate employees of press, radio, television, or other communication media in return for publicity in a news item.

(e) A paid advertisement relating to the psychologist's activities must be identified as such, unless it is already apparent from the context.

3.03. Avoidance of False or Deceptive Statements.

(a) Psychologists do not make public statements that are false, deceptive, misleading, or fraudulent, either because of what they state, convey, or suggest or because of what they omit, concerning their research, practice, or other work activities or those of persons or organizations with which they are affiliated. As examples (and not in limitation) of this standard, psychologists do not make false or deceptive statements concerning (1) their training, experience, or competence; (2) their academic degrees; (3) their credentials; (4) their institutional or association affiliations; (5) their services; (6) the scientific or clinical basis for, or results or degree of success of, their services; (7) their fees; or (8) their publications or research findings. (See also Standards 6.15, Deception in Research, and 6.18, Providing Participants With Information About the Study.)

(b) Psychologists claim as credentials for their psychological work, only degrees that (1) were earned from a regionally accredited educational institution or (2) were the basis for psychology licensure by the state in which they practice.

3.04. Media Presentations.

When psychologists provide advice or comment by means of public lectures, demonstrations, radio or television programs, prerecorded tapes, printed articles, mailed material, or other media, they take reasonable precautions to ensure that (1) the statements are based on appropriate psychological literature and practice, (2) the statements are otherwise consistent with this Ethics Code, and (3) the recipients of the information are not encouraged to infer that a relationship has been established with them personally.

3.05. Testimonials.

Psychologists do not solicit testimonials from current psychotherapy clients or patients or other persons who because of their particular circumstances are vulnerable to undue influence.

3.06. In-Person Solicitation.

Psychologists do not engage, directly or through agents, in uninvited in-person solicitation of business from actual or potential psychotherapy patients or clients or other persons who because of their particular circumstances are vulnerable to undue influence. However, this does not preclude attempting to implement appropriate collateral contacts with significant others for the purpose of benefiting an already engaged therapy patient.

4. Therapy

4.01. Structuring the Relationship.

(a) Psychologists discuss with clients or patients as early as is feasible in the therapeutic relationship appropriate issues, such as the nature and anticipated course of therapy, fees, and confidentiality. (See also Standards 1.25, Fees and Financial Arrangements, and 5.01, Discussing the Limits of Confidentiality.)

(b) When the psychologist's work with clients or patients will be supervised, the above discussion includes that fact, and the name of the supervisor, when the supervisor has legal responsibility for the case.

(c) When the therapist is a student intern, the client or patient is informed of that fact.

(d) Psychologists make reasonable efforts to answer patients' questions and to avoid apparent misunderstandings about therapy. Whenever possible, psychologists provide oral and/or written information, using language that is reasonably understandable to the patient or client.

4.02. Informed Consent to Therapy.

(a) Psychologists obtain appropriate informed consent to therapy or related procedures, using language that is reasonably understandable to participants. The content of informed consent will vary depending on many circumstances; however, informed consent generally implies that the person (1) has the capacity to consent, (2) has been informed of significant information concerning the procedure, (3) has freely and without undue influence expressed consent, and (4) consent has been appropriately documented.

(b) When persons are legally incapable of giving informed consent, psychologists obtain informed permission from a legally authorized person, if such substitute consent is permitted by law.

(c) In addition, psychologists (1) inform those persons who are legally incapable of giving informed consent about the proposed interventions in a manner commensurate with the persons' psychological capacities, (2) seek their assent to those interventions, and (3) consider such persons' preferences and best interests.

4.03. Couple and Family Relationships.

(a) When a psychologist agrees to provide services to several persons who have a relationship (such as husband and wife or parents and children), the psychologist attempts to clarify at the outset (1) which of the individuals are patients or clients and (2) the relationship the psychologist will have with each person. This clarification includes the role of the psychologist and the probable uses of the services provided or the information obtained. (See also Standard 5.01, Discussing the Limits of Confidentiality.)

(b) As soon as it becomes apparent that the psychologist may be called on to perform potentially conflicting roles (such as marital counselor to husband and wife, and then witness for one party in a divorce proceeding), the psychologist attempts to clarify and adjust, or withdraw from, roles appropriately. (See also Standard 7.03, Clarification of Role, under Forensic Activities.)

4.04. Providing Mental Health Services to Those Served by Others.

In deciding whether to offer or provide services to those already receiving mental health services elsewhere, psychologists carefully consider the treatment issues and the potential patient's or client's welfare. The psychologist discusses these issues with the patient or client, or another legally authorized person on behalf of the client, in order to minimize the risk of confusion and conflict, consults with the other service providers when appropriate, and proceeds with caution and sensitivity to the therapeutic issues.

4.05. Sexual Intimacies With Current Patients or Clients.

Psychologists do not engage in sexual intimacies with current patients or clients.

4.06. Therapy With Former Sexual Partners.

Psychologists do not accept as therapy patients or clients persons with whom they have engaged in sexual intimacies.

4.07. Sexual Intimacies With Former Therapy Patients.

(a) Psychologists do not engage in sexual intimacies with a former therapy patient or client for at least two years after cessation or termination of professional services.

(b) Because sexual intimacies with a former therapy patient or client are so frequently harmful to the patient or client, and because such intimacies undermine public confidence in the psychology profession and thereby deter the public's use of needed services, psychologists do not engage in sexual intimacies with former therapy patients and clients even after a two-year interval except in the most unusual circumstances. The psychologist who engages in such activity after the two years following cessation or termination of treatment bears the burden of demonstrating that there has been no exploitation, in light of all relevant factors, including (1) the amount of time that has passed since therapy terminated, (2) the nature and duration of the therapy, (3) the circumstances of termination, (4) the patient's or client's personal history, (5) the patient's or client's current mental status, (6) the likelihood of adverse impact on the patient or client and others, and (7) any statements or actions made by the therapist during the course of therapy suggesting or inviting the possibility of a post-termination sexual or romantic relationship with the patient or client. (See also Standard 1.17, Multiple Relationships.)

4.08. Interruption of Services.

(a) Psychologists make reasonable efforts to plan for facilitating care in the event that psychological services are interrupted by factors such as the psychologist's illness, death, unavailability, or relocation or by the client's relocation or financial limitations. (See also Standard 5.09, Preserving Records and Data.)

(b) When entering into employment or contractual relationships, psychologists provide for orderly and appropriate resolution of responsibility for patient or client care in the event that the employment or contractual relationship ends, with paramount consideration given to the welfare of the patient or client.

4.09. Terminating the Professional Relationship.

(a) Psychologists do not abandon patients or clients. (See also Standard 1.25e, under Fees and Financial Arrangements.)

(b) Psychologists terminate a professional relationship when it becomes reasonably clear that the patient or client no longer needs the service, is not benefiting, or is being harmed by continued service.

(c) Prior to termination for whatever reason, except where precluded by the patient's or client's conduct, the psychologist discusses the patient's or client's views and needs, provides appropriate pretermination counseling, suggests alternative service providers as appropriate, and takes other reasonable steps to facilitate transfer of responsibility to another provider if the patient or client needs one immediately.

5. Privacy and Confidentiality

These Standards are potentially applicable to the professional and scientific activities of all psychologists.

5.01. Discussing the Limits of Confidentiality.

(a) Psychologists discuss with persons and organizations with whom they establish a scientific or professional relationship (including, to the extent feasible, minors and their legal representatives) (1) the relevant limitations on confidentiality, including limitations where applicable in group, marital, and family therapy or in organizational consulting, and (2) the foreseeable uses of the information generated through their services.

(b) Unless it is not feasible or is contraindicated, the discussion of confidentiality occurs at the outset of the relationship and thereafter as new circumstances may warrant.

(c) Permission for electronic recording of interviews is secured from clients and patients.

5.02. Maintaining Confidentiality.

Psychologists have a primary obligation and take reasonable precautions to respect the confidentiality rights of those with whom they work or consult, recognizing that confidentiality may be established by law, institutional rules, or professional or scientific relationships. (See also Standard 6.26, Professional Reviewers.)

5.03. Minimizing Intrusions on Privacy.

(a) In order to minimize intrusions on privacy, psychologists include in written and oral reports, consultations, and the like, only information germane to the purpose for which the communication is made.

(b) Psychologists discuss confidential information obtained in clinical or consulting relationships, or evaluative data concerning patients, individual or organizational clients, students, research participants, supervisees, and employees, only for appropriate scientific or professional purposes and only with persons clearly concerned with such matters.

5.04. Maintenance of Records.

Psychologists maintain appropriate confidentiality in creating, storing, accessing, transferring, and disposing of records under their control, whether these are written, automated, or in any other medium. Psychologists maintain and dispose of records in accordance with law and in a manner that permits compliance with the requirements of this Ethics Code.

5.05. Disclosures.

(a) Psychologists disclose confidential information without the consent of the individual only as mandated by law, or where permitted by law for a valid purpose, such as (1) to provide needed professional services to the patient or the individual or organizational client, (2) to obtain appropriate professional consultations, (3) to protect the patient or client or others from harm, or (4) to obtain payment for services, in which instance disclosure is limited to the minimum that is necessary to achieve the purpose.

(b) Psychologists also may disclose confidential information with the appropriate consent of the patient or the individual or organizational client (or of another legally authorized person on behalf of the patient or client), unless prohibited by law.

5.06. Consultations.

When consulting with colleagues, (1) psychologists do not share confidential information that reasonably could lead to the identification of a patient, client, research participant, or other person or organization with whom they have a confidential relationship unless they have obtained the prior consent of the person or organization or the disclosure cannot be avoided, and (2) they share information only to the extent necessary to achieve the purposes of the consultation. (See also Standard 5.02, Maintaining Confidentiality.)

5.07. Confidential Information in Databases.

(a) If confidential information concerning recipients of psychological services is to be entered into databases or systems of records available to persons whose access has not been consented to by the recipient, then psychologists use coding or other techniques to avoid the inclusion of personal identifiers.

(b) If a research protocol approved by an institutional review board or similar body requires the inclusion of personal identifiers, such identifiers are deleted before the information is made accessible to persons other than those of whom the subject was advised.

(c) If such deletion is not feasible, then before psychologists transfer such data to others or review such data collected by others, they take reasonable steps to determine that appropriate consent of personally identifiable individuals has been obtained.

5.08. Use of Confidential Information for Didactic or Other Purposes.

(a) Psychologists do not disclose in their writings, lectures, or other public media, confidential, personally identifiable information concerning their patients, individual or organizational clients, students, research participants, or other recipients of their services that they obtained during the course of their work, unless the person or organization has consented in writing or unless there is other ethical or legal authorization for doing so.

(b) Ordinarily, in such scientific and professional presentations, psychologists disguise confidential information concerning such persons or organizations so that they are not individually identifiable to others and so that discussions do not cause harm to subjects who might identify themselves.

5.09. Preserving Records and Data.

A psychologist makes plans in advance so that confidentiality of records and data is protected in the event of the psychologist's death, incapacity, or withdrawal from the position or practice.

5.10. Ownership of Records and Data.

Recognizing that ownership of records and data is governed by legal principles, psychologists take reasonable and lawful steps so that records and data remain available to the extent needed to serve the best interests of patients, individual or organizational clients, research participants, or appropriate others.

5.11. Withholding Records for Nonpayment.

Psychologists may not withhold records under their control that are requested and imminently needed for a patient's or client's treatment solely because payment has not been received, except as otherwise provided by law.

6. Teaching, Training Supervision, Research, and Publishing

6.01. Design of Education and Training Programs.

Psychologists who are responsible for education and training programs seek to ensure that the programs are competently designed, provide the proper experiences, and meet the requirements for licensure, certification, or other goals for which claims are made by the program.

6.02. Descriptions of Education and Training Programs.

(a) Psychologists responsible for education and training programs seek to ensure that there is a current and accurate description of the program content, training goals and objectives, and requirements that must be met for satisfactory completion of the program. This information must be made readily available to all interested parties.

(b) Psychologists seek to ensure that statements concerning their course outlines are accurate and not misleading, particularly regarding the subject matter to be covered, bases for evaluating progress, and the nature of course experiences. (See also Standard 3.03, Avoidance of False or Deceptive Statements.)

(c) To the degree to which they exercise control, psychologists responsible for announcements, catalogs, brochures, or advertisements describing workshops, seminars, or other non-degree-granting educational programs ensure that they accurately describe the audience for which the program is intended, the educational objectives, the presenters, and the fees involved.

6.03. Accuracy and Objectivity in Teaching.

(a) When engaged in teaching or training, psychologists present psychological information accurately and with a reasonable degree of objectivity.

(b) When engaged in teaching or training, psychologists recognize the power they hold over students or supervisees and therefore make reasonable efforts to avoid engaging in conduct that is personally demeaning to students or supervisees. (See also Standards 1.09, Respecting Others, and 1.12, Other Harassment.)

6.04. Limitation on Teaching.

Psychologists do not teach the use of techniques or procedures that require specialized training, licensure, or expertise, including but not limited to hypnosis, biofeedback, and projective techniques, to individuals who lack the prerequisite training, legal scope of practice, or expertise.

6.05. Assessing Student and Supervisee Performance.

(a) In academic and supervisory relationships, psychologists establish an appropriate process for providing feedback to students and supervisees.

(b) Psychologists evaluate students and supervisees on the basis of their actual performance on relevant and established program requirements.

6.06. Planning Research.

(a) Psychologists design, conduct, and report research in accordance with recognized standards of scientific competence and ethical research.

(b) Psychologists plan their research so as to minimize the possibility that results will be misleading.

(c) In planning research, psychologists consider its ethical acceptability under the Ethics Code. If an ethical issue is unclear, psychologists seek to resolve the issue through consultation with institutional review boards, animal care and use committees, peer consultations, or other proper mechanisms.

(d) Psychologists take reasonable steps to implement appropriate protections for the rights and welfare of human participants, other persons affected by the research, and the welfare of animal subjects.

6.07. Responsibility.

(a) Psychologists conduct research competently and with due concern for the dignity and welfare of the participants.

(b) Psychologists are responsible for the ethical conduct of research conducted by them or by others under their supervision or control.

(c) Researchers and assistants are permitted to perform only those tasks for which they are appropriately trained and prepared.

(d) As part of the process of development and implementation of research projects, psychologists consult those with expertise concerning any special population under investigation or most likely to be affected.

6.08. Compliance With Law and Standards.

Psychologists plan and conduct research in a manner consistent with federal and state law and regulations, as well as professional standards governing the conduct of research, and particularly those standards governing research with human participants and animal subjects.

6.09. Institutional Approval.

Psychologists obtain from host institutions or organizations appropriate approval prior to conducting research, and they provide accurate information about their research proposals. They conduct the research in accordance with the approved research protocol.

6.10. Research Responsibilities.

Prior to conducting research (except research involving only anonymous surveys, naturalistic observations, or similar research), psychologists enter into an agreement with participants that clarifies the nature of the research and the responsibilities of each party.

6.11. Informed Consent to Research.

(a) Psychologists use language that is reasonably understandable to research participants in obtaining their appropriate informed consent (except as provided in Standard 6.12, Dispensing with Informed Consent). Such informed consent is appropriately documented.

(b) Using language that is reasonably understandable to participants, psychologists inform participants of the nature of the research; they inform participants that they are free to participate or to decline to participate or to withdraw from the research; they explain the foreseeable consequences of declining or withdrawing; they inform participants of significant factors that may be expected to influence their willingness to participate (such as risks, discomfort, adverse effects, or limitations on confidentiality, except as provided in Standard 6.15, Deception in Research); and they explain other aspects about which the prospective participants inquire.

(c) When psychologists conduct research with individuals such as students or subordinates, psychologists take special care to protect the prospective participants from adverse consequences of declining or withdrawing from participation.

(d) When research participation is a course requirement or opportunity for extra credit, the prospective participant is given the choice of equitable alternative activities.

(e) For persons who are legally incapable of giving informed consent, psychologists nevertheless (1) provide an appropriate explanation, (2) obtain the participant's assent, and (3) obtain appropriate permission from a legally authorized person, if such substitute consent is permitted by law.

6.12. Dispensing With Informed Consent.

Before determining that planned research (such as research involving only anonymous questionnaires, naturalistic observations, or certain kinds of archival research) does not require the informed consent of research participants, psychologists consider applicable regulations and institutional review board requirements, and they consult with colleagues as appropriate.

6.13. Informed Consent in Research Filming or Recording.

Psychologists obtain informed consent from research participants prior to filming or recording them in any form, unless the research involves simply naturalistic observations in public places and it is not anticipated that the recording will be used in a manner that could cause personal identification or harm.

6.14. Offering Inducements for Research Participants.

(a) In offering professional services as an inducement to obtain research participants, psychologists make clear the nature of the services, as well as the risks, obligations, and limitations. (See also Standard 1.18, Barter [With Patients or Clients].)

(b) Psychologists do not offer excessive or inappropriate financial or other inducements to obtain research participants, particularly when it might tend to coerce participation.

6.15. Deception in Research.

(a) Psychologists do not conduct a study involving deception unless they have determined that the use of deceptive techniques is justified by the study's prospective scientific, educational, or applied value and that equally effective alternative procedures that do not use deception are not feasible.

(b) Psychologists never deceive research participants about significant aspects that would affect their willingness to participate, such as physical risks, discomfort, or unpleasant emotional experiences.

(c) Any other deception that is an integral feature of the design and conduct of an experiment must be explained to participants as early as is feasible, preferably at the conclusion of their participation, but no later than at the conclusion of the research. (See also Standard 6.18, Providing Participants With Information About the Study.)

6.16. Sharing and Utilizing Data.

Psychologists inform research participants of their anticipated sharing or further use of personally identifiable research data and of the possibility of unanticipated future uses.

6.17. Minimizing Invasiveness.

In conducting research, psychologists interfere with the participants or milieu from which data are collected only in a manner that is warranted by an appropriate research design and that is consistent with psychologists' roles as scientific investigators.

6.18. Providing Participants With Information About the Study.

(a) Psychologists provide a prompt opportunity for participants to obtain appropriate information about the nature, results, and conclusions of the research, and psychologists attempt to correct any misconceptions that participants may have.

(b) If scientific or humane values justify delaying or withholding this information, psychologists take reasonable measures to reduce the risk of harm.

6.19. Honoring Commitments.

Psychologists take reasonable measures to honor all commitments they have made to research participants.

6.20. Care and Use of Animals in Research.

(a) Psychologists who conduct research involving animals treat them humanely.

(b) Psychologists acquire, care for, use, and dispose of animals in compliance with current federal, state, and local laws and regulations, and with professional standards.

(c) Psychologists trained in research methods and experienced in the care of laboratory animals supervise all procedures involving animals and are responsible for ensuring appropriate consideration of their comfort, health, and humane treatment.

(d) Psychologists ensure that all individuals using animals under their supervision have received instruction in research methods and in the care, maintenance, and handling of the species being used, to the extent appropriate to their role.

(e) Responsibilities and activities of individuals assisting in a research project are consistent with their respective competencies.

(f) Psychologists make reasonable efforts to minimize the discomfort, infection, illness, and pain of animal subjects.

(g) A procedure subjecting animals to pain, stress, or privation is used only when an alternative procedure is unavailable and the goal is justified by its prospective scientific, educational, or applied value.

(h) Surgical procedures are performed under appropriate anesthesia; techniques to avoid infection and minimize pain are followed during and after surgery.

(i) When it is appropriate that the animal's life be terminated, it is done rapidly, with an effort to minimize pain, and in accordance with accepted procedures.

6.21. Reporting of Results.

(a) Psychologists do not fabricate data or falsify results in their publications.

(b) If psychologists discover significant errors in their published data, they take reasonable steps to correct such errors in a correction, retraction, erratum, or other appropriate publication means.

6.22. Plagiarism.

Psychologists do not present substantial portions or elements of another's work or data as their own, even if the other work or data source is cited occasionally.

6.23. Publication Credit.

(a) Psychologists take responsibility and credit, including authorship credit, only for work they have actually performed or to which they have contributed.

(b) Principal authorship and other publication credits accurately reflect the relative scientific or professional contributions of the individuals involved, regardless of their relative status. Mere possession of an institutional position, such as Department Chair, does not justify authorship credit. Minor contributions to the research or to the writing for publications are appropriately acknowledged, such as in footnotes or in an introductory statement.

(c) A student is usually listed as principal author on any multiple-authored article that is substantially based on the student's dissertation or thesis.

6.24. Duplicate Publication of Data.

Psychologists do not publish, as original data, data that have been previously published. This does not preclude republishing data when they are accompanied by proper acknowledgment.

6.25. Sharing Data.

After research results are published, psychologists do not withhold the data on which their conclusions are based from other competent professionals who seek to verify the substantive claims through reanalysis and who intend to use such data only for that purpose, provided that the confidentiality of the participants can be protected and unless legal rights concerning proprietary data preclude their release.

6.26. Professional Reviewers.

Psychologists who review material submitted for publication, grant, or other research proposal review respect the confidentiality of and the proprietary rights in such information of those who submitted it.

7. Forensic Activities

7.01. Professionalism.

Psychologists who perform forensic functions, such as assessments, interviews, consultations, reports, or expert testimony, must comply with all other provisions of this Ethics Code to the extent that they apply to such activities. In addition, psychologists base their forensic work on appropriate knowledge of and competence in the areas underlying such work, including specialized knowledge concerning special populations.

(See also Standards 1.06, Basis for Scientific and Professional Judgments; 1.08, Human Differences; 1.15, Misuse of Psychologists' Influence; and 1.23, Documentation of Professional and Scientific Work.)

7.02. Forensic Assessments.

(a) Psychologists' forensic assessments, recommendations, and reports are based on information and techniques (including personal interviews of the individual, when appropriate) sufficient to provide appropriate substantiation for their findings. (See also Standards 1.03, Professional and Scientific Relationship; 1.23, Documentation of Professional and Scientific Work; 2.01, Evaluation, Diagnosis, and Interventions in Professional Context; and 2.05, Interpreting Assessment Results.)

(b) Except as noted in (c), below, psychologists provide written or oral forensic reports or testimony of the psychological characteristics of an individual only after they have conducted an examination of the individual adequate to support their statements or conclusions.

(c) When, despite reasonable efforts, such an examination is not feasible, psychologists clarify the impact of their limited information on the reliability and validity of their reports and testimony, and they appropriately limit the nature and extent of their conclusions or recommendations.

7.03. Clarification of Role.

In most circumstances, psychologists avoid performing multiple and potentially conflicting roles in forensic matters. When psychologists may be called on to serve in more than one role in a legal proceeding-for example, as consultant or expert for one party or for the court and as a fact witness-they clarify role expectations and the extent of confidentiality in advance to the extent feasible, and thereafter as changes occur, in order to avoid compromising their professional judgment and objectivity and in order to avoid misleading others regarding their role.

7.04. Truthfulness and Candor.

(a) In forensic testimony and reports, psychologists testify truthfully, honestly, and candidly and, consistent with applicable legal procedures, describe fairly the bases for their testimony and conclusions. (b) Whenever necessary to avoid misleading, psychologists acknowledge the limits of their data or conclusions.

7.05. Prior Relationships.

A prior professional relationship with a party does not preclude psychologists from testifying as fact witnesses or from testifying to their services to the extent permitted by applicable law. Psychologists appropriately take into account ways in which the prior relationship might affect their professional objectivity or opinions and disclose the potential conflict to the relevant parties.

7.06. Compliance With Law and Rules.

In performing forensic roles, psychologists are reasonably familiar with the rules governing their roles. Psychologists are aware of the occasionally competing demands placed upon them by these principles and the requirements of the court system, and attempt to resolve these conflicts by making known their commitment to this Ethics Code and taking steps to resolve the conflict in a responsible manner. (See also Standard 1.02, Relationship of Ethics and Law.)

8. Resolving Ethical Issues

8.01. Familiarity With Ethics Code.

Psychologists have an obligation to be familiar with this Ethics Code, other applicable ethics codes, and their application to psychologists' work. Lack of awareness or misunderstanding of an ethical standard is not itself a defense to a charge of unethical conduct.

8.02. Confronting Ethical Issues.

When a psychologist is uncertain whether a particular situation or course of action would violate this Ethics Code, the psychologist ordinarily consults with other psychologists knowledgeable about ethical issues, with state or national psychology ethics committees, or with other appropriate authorities in order to choose a proper response.

8.03. Conflicts Between Ethics and Organizational Demands.

If the demands of an organization with which psychologists are affiliated conflict with this Ethics Code, psychologists clarify the nature of the conflict, make known their commitment to the Ethics Code, and to the extent feasible, seek to resolve the conflict in a way that permits the fullest adherence to the Ethics Code.

8.04. Informal Resolution of Ethical Violations.

When psychologists believe that there may have been an ethical violation by another psychologist, they attempt to resolve the issue by bringing it to the attention of that individual if an informal resolution appears appropriate and the intervention does not violate any confidentiality rights that may be involved.

8.05. Reporting Ethical Violations.

If an apparent ethical violation is not appropriate for informal resolution under Standard 8.04 or is not resolved properly in that fashion, psychologists take further action appropriate to the situation, unless such action conflicts with confidentiality rights in ways that cannot be resolved. Such action might include referral to state or national committees on professional ethics or to state licensing boards.

8.06. Cooperating With Ethics Committees.

Psychologists cooperate in ethics investigations, proceedings, and resulting requirements of the APA or any affiliated state psychological association to which they belong. In doing so, they make reasonable efforts to resolve any issues as to confidentiality. Failure to cooperate is itself an ethics violation.

8.07. Improper Complaints.

Psychologists do not file or encourage the filing of ethics complaints that are frivolous and are intended to harm the respondent rather than to protect the public.

History and effective date

This version of the APA Ethics Code was adopted by the American Psychological Association's Council of Representatives during its meeting, August 13 and 16, 1992, and is effective beginning December 1, 1992. Inquiries concerning the substance or interpretation of the APA Ethics Code should be addressed to the Director, Office of Ethics, American Psychological Association, 750 First Street, NE, Washington, DC 20002-4242.

Index

A
Abstracts, 103
ACA Counseling Today, 256
Academic prerequisites, 29
Academic skills, 6, 84–119
    critical reflection, 88–90, 104
    emotion in, 90–95
    heart and mind in, 86–88
    listening, 84
    presenting, 84–85, 110–117
    reading, 84, 95–99
    research, 84, 99–104
    writing, 84, 105–109
Acceptance, 195
Accommodation, 167–168
Admissions process, 28–32
Advertising, 142–143
    for clients, 287–288
    ethics of, 325–327
    job, 255–256
    standards of practice on, 306
Advisors, 37
Alcohol, 130
Altruism, 155–157
Alumni networks, 250, 256
Ambiguity, tolerance for, 111
American Association for Marriage
    and Family Therapy, 22
American Counseling Association
    (ACA), 23, 75
    Code of Ethics, 278–303

getting involved in, 256–257
job listings, 269
liability insurance, 222–223, 241
Standards of Practice, 303–311
Web site, 252
American Mental Health Counselors
    Association, 23
American Psychological Association
    (APA)
    address for, 23
    classified ads, 269
    *Ethical Principles of Psychologists
        and Code of Conduct*, 312–341
    getting involved in, 256–257
    liability insurance, 222–223, 241
    Publication Manual, 6
Analysis skills, 89
Angelou, Maya, 2, 145
Antonovsky, A., 135
APA Monitor, 256
Application
    for assistantships, 74
    for financial aid, 74–75
    to graduate programs, 28–32
Application skills, 89
Applied studies, 48
Apprenticeship, 41–46
Aristotle, 229, 264
Assessment, formal procedures of,
    38. *See also* Evaluation
Assimilation, 166–167

Assistantships, 73–74
Association for Counselor Education
    and Supervision, 256
Association for Support of Graduate
    Students (ASGS), 146
Assumptions
    about interpersonal relationships,
        187, 188–189
    questioning self-, 92
Attachment theory, 70
Attitude, 136, 143, 265
    confronting personal, 233–237
Audience, knowing, 114
Authenticity, 175–178, 199,
        202–205
    being vs. seeming and, 203–205
    exploring, 163
    social masks and, 203
Avoidance, 116
Awareness, 154
    interpersonal, 186–187
    I vs. me, 154–155
    self-, 174, 191–192

B
Baird, B. N., 107, 219, 240
Balance, 60, 65–80, 266–267
    in career, 264
    empathy and, 63
    housing and, 68–72
    pathways to, 67–68
    perspective in, 78–80
    sea star exercise for, 64–65
    wellness and, 76–77
Bartering and fees, 282–283, 320
Basic needs, 5–6
    balancing, 60–61
    comprehensive examinations and,
        45–46
    context for, 67
    determining, 55–56
    inventorying, 62–65
    love and belonging, 57

meeting, 55–83
    personal hierarchy of, 56–59
    physiological, 57
    safety and security, 57
    self-actualization, 57–61
    self-esteem, 57
    unmet, 59
Bateson, M. C., 272–273
Becoming a Therapist: A Workbook
    for Personal Exploration (Kerr),
    50
Becoming Attached: First Relation-
    ships and How They Shape Our
    Capacity to Love (Karen), 275
Being vs. seeming, 203–205
Belenky, M. D., 273
Berenson, B. G., 273
Berman, M., 273
Beyond Counseling and Therapy
    (Clarkhuff, Berenson), 273
Bird cage exercise, 92–93
Blau, D. S., 162–163
Bloom, B. S., 89–90
Bolles, R. N., 251
Bowlby, J., 70
Bowman, Marilyn, 135
Bread and Roses, 55–56
Breathing, 116–117, 131
Buber, Martin, 203–204
Bulletin boards, 37
Burnout, 161

C
Caffeine, 130
Calhoun, L. G., 135
Campbell, Joseph, 7–8
Campus career centers, 250–251,
    256
Capstones, 46
Career Beliefs Inventory, 251
Career Decision Scale, 251
Career genograms, 249–250
Career Magazine, 269

Careers, 243–271
    clock-watchers and workaholics
        in, 264
    counseling in, 251
    degrees and, 251–254
    fitting in vs. standing out,
        260–262
    intentionality in, 254
    job hunting in, 254–259
    lifelong learning and, 260
    passion and, 243–245
    personal characteristics employers
        seek and, 251
    planning, 254–257
    resume design and, 257–258
    transition from student to profes-
        sional in, 246–250
Carkhuff, R. C., 273
Carroll, Lewis, 168–169
Case notes, 105, 107, 109
Center for Credentialing & Educa-
    tion, Inc. (CCE), 51
Challenges, manageable, 91–92
Change
    continuous, 150
    coping with personal, 149–155
    discomfort of, 16
    Groucho paradox and, 165
    significant others and, 210
*Change: Principles of Problem
    Formation and Problem Resolu-
    tion* (Watzlawick, Weakland,
    Fisch), 278
Character, 142–144
Chi Sigma Iota, 41
Chronicle of Higher Education, 256,
    269
Churchill, Winston, 2, 145
Client responsibilities, 224
Client rights, 280–281
Client welfare, 280
Code of Conduct (American Psycho-
    logical Association), 312–341
Codes of ethics, 20–21

American Counseling Association,
    280–303
American Psychological Associa-
    tion, 312–341
    internships and, 223–225
Cognitive scales, 251
Cohen, E. D., 231–232
Cohen, S. P., 231–232
Collaborative learning, 11–12
    research as, 100–101
Colleagues, 218
"Color of Fear, The," 197
Commencement, 50
Committee meetings, 37
Committee selection, 49
Communication, 13–14. *See also*
    Feedback
    during training, 36–38
Community, 183–212. *See also*
    Others
    rituals in, 34
    satisfying needs through, 70–72
"Company Therapist, The," 117
Compensating strategies, 170–173
Competence
    belief in, 111
    internships and, 223
Competence, standards of,
    286–287, 314–315, 317
Competition, 11
*Complete Guide to Graduate School
    Admission, The: Psychology,
    Counseling and Related Profes-
    sions* (Keith-Spiegel, Wieder-
    man), 50
Composing a Life (Bateson),
    272–273
Comprehensive examinations,
    44–46
Computers
    ethics of in counseling, 283–284
    technophobia and, 6
Conditions of worth, 169, 261
Cone, J. D., 50–51

Conferences, 239
Confidence, 116
  for comprehensive examinations, 46
Confidentiality
  ethical dilemmas in, 229–231
  ethics codes on, 284–286, 330–332
  exceptions to, 225, 229–231
  internships and, 224–227
  portfolios and, 39
  of research, 300
  standards of practice on, 305
Conflict, unresolved, 173–174
Conformity, 263
Confucius, 132
Confusion, 92
Congruence, 175–176
Consent. *See* Informed consent
Consultation
  ethics of, 291–292, 321
  privacy and, 331
Coping styles, 170–173
Cornely, Laura, 245
Correspondence, 105, 258
Council for Accreditation of Counseling and Related Educational Programs (CACREP), 44, 52, 252, 254
COUNSGRADS: Counseling Student Listserv, 211–212
Counseling qualities, 194–196
Counseling/therapy
  countertransference in, 173–174
  for trainees, 7, 160–162
Counselor Preparation Comprehensive Examination (CPCE), 44
Counselors, characteristics of good, 111
Countertransference, 173–174
Cover letters, 258
Creativity
  expert thinking vs., 166
  preserving, 260–262

from stress, 134
  taking time for, 65
  uncovering, 262–264
Credentials, 252
  ethics codes on, 288–289
Critical reflection, 87–90, 104
Critical reviews, 48
Critical thinking skills, 100
Critiquing skills, 104
Csikszentmihalyi, Mihaly, 91
Cultural context, 88
  practicums and, 217–218
Cultural influences, 152
Culture shock, 56
Curriculum, 8

D
Damasio, Antonio, 87
Databases
  confidentiality and, 331
  searching, 102–103
Death, causes of, 123
Decision making, 221–222, 248–249
Defensiveness, 144
Defensive strategies, 70–71, 204
Defying the Crowd (Sternberg, Lubart), 262–263
Deikman, A. J., 154
Design skills, 100
Desiring soul, 57
Developing Your School Counseling Program: A Handbook for Systemic Planning (Van Zandt, Hayslip), 240
Developmental stages, 26
Dialectical tension, 91
Discovery of Being, The (May), 179
Disillusionment, 43–44
Dissertations, 48–49, 50–51
Dissertations and Theses from Start to Finish: Psychology and Related Fields (Cone, Foster), 50–51

Distancing behaviors, 196–197
Distress, 125
  meaning and, 136
Diversity
  respecting, 280
  testing and, 295
Divided Self, The (Laing), 153
Doctorate degrees, careers with,
  253–254
Do-gooders, 155–157
Don't Miss Out (Leider, Leider), 81
Dualistic thinking, 26, 39–40
Dual relationships with clients,
  227–229, 281–282, 320
  standards of practice on, 304

E
Edison, Thomas, 265
Educational specialist degrees,
  careers with, 251–253
Effectiveness
  from personal counseling, 160–162
  personality and, 156
Einstein, Albert, 9
Elements of Style, The (Strunk,
  White), 107
E-mail, 37
Embark, 82
Emerson, Ralph Waldo, 132
Emotional arousal, 93–94, 115–116
Emotional intelligence, 86–87
Emotions
  in academic skills, 90–95
  distancing behaviors and,
    196–197
  emotional baggage, 7
  graduation and, 265
  multiplistic thinking and, 42
  in reading, 96
Empathy
  altruism and, 156
  developing, 156–157
  housing and, 69–70

learning, 63
  from stress, 144–145
  through counseling, 160
Employers, relationships with,
  290–291. *See also* Supervision
Equifinality, 67
ERIC, 102–103
Erickson, Milton, 92
Erikson, Erik, 154, 261
Essay questions, 31
*Ethical Principles of Psychologists and
  Code of Conduct* (American
  Psychological Association),
  312–341
Ethics, 20–21, 227–237
  American Counseling Association
    code of, 230–303
  dual roles and, 227–229
  handling dilemmas in, 229–232
  principles of, 227
  resolving issues in, 340–341
Evaluation
  ethics codes on, 292–296, 323–325
  learning to perform, 100
  portfolios in, 39
  of research projects, 49
  standards of practice on, 308
Evaluation skills, 89–90
Every Person's Life Is Worth a Novel
  (Polster), 277
Excellence, 260–262
Exercise, 76–80
  stress management and, 130–131
*Existence: A New Dimension in
  Psychiatry and Psychology* (May,
  Angel, Ellenberger), 276
Existential psychotherapy, 179
Expectations
  of others, 261
  self-, 214–215
  sophomore slump and, 43–44
Experience
  before graduate programs, 28–29
  on resumes, 258

Expertise, dangers of, 165–168
Extracurricular activities, 8

F
Faculty, 32
  advisors, 37
  assistantships, 73–74
  as mentors, 207
  participation anxiety and, 112
  research with, 100–101
  student expectations of, 43–44
Family Crucible, The (Napier,
  Whitaker), 276
Family influences, 248–249
Fear of public speaking, 110–111
Federal Stafford Loans, 74–75
Feedback
  flow and, 91
  giving and receiving, 198–202
  guidelines for helpful, 199–200
  honesty in, 175
  on presentations, 111, 115
Fees
  ethics and, 282–283, 292,
    322–323
  internships and, 224
Field placements, 221–222, 298
Fight or flight response, 127–128
Financial assistance, 72–76, 81
  assistantships, 73–74
  scholarships, 75–76
  student loans, 74–75
  Web sites on, 82
Finkle, J., 81
Fitting in, 214–215
Flexibility, 167
Flow states, 91, 154
Focus, 94, 111
Forensic activities, 340, 338
Foster, S. L., 50–51
Frankl, V. E., 121, 136, 143
  Man's Search for Meaning: An
    Introduction to Logotherapy, 146

Psychotherapy and Existentialism:
  Selected Papers on Logotherapy,
  273
Free Application for Federal Student
  Aid (FAFSA), 74–75
Freud, S., 174

G
Generativity, 261
Genograms, career, 249–250
Genograms in Family Assessment
  (McGoldrick, Gerson), 249
Gerson, Randy, 249
Gestalt Therapy Verbatim (Perls), 277
Getting In: A Step-by-Step Plan for
  Gaining Admission to Graduate
  School in Psychology (American
  Psychological Association), 50
Gilligan, C., 274
Goals
  envisioning, 18–19, 138–139
  journey as destination and, 7–9
  personal growth, 149–155
Golden mean, 264. See also Balance
Gradschools.com, 51
Graduate programs
  beginning, 32–41
  comprehensive examinations,
    44–46
  guides of, 29
  opening rituals in, 33–34
  researching, 81
  selection process for, 28–32
  sophomore slump in, 43–44
Graduate Record Examination
  (GRE), 30
Graduate School (Finkle), 81
"Graduate School Survival Guide,"
  23
Graduation, 50, 265
Greeley, Horace, 7
Grotberg, E. H., 135
Groucho paradox, 41, 164–165

Group work
  confidentiality and, 285
  ethics of, 282
  standards of practice on, 304
"Guide to Selecting Statistics," 118
*Guide to State Laws and Regulations
  on Professional School Counseling, A* (American Counseling
  Association), 252

H
Halonen, J. S., 117
Hard-belly responses, 196–197
Harm, avoiding, 319
Hayslip, J., 240
Health psychology, 76
Helms, J. E., 274
Help
  asking for, 98–99, 103, 112–113
  stress management and profes-
  sional, 131
Henry, W. E., 156
Hero cycle, 205–206
Hierarchy of needs, 57–58
Higher order thinking skills, 88,
  104
High road, taking the, 20–21
Hippocampus, 130
Holmes and Rahe Stress Scale, 146
Honesty, 175, 194, 198–199
Honor societies, 41
Horn, Dan, 81–82
Horney, Karen, 168, 171
Housing, 68–72
Hughes, Langston, 131
Human differences, 318
Humor, 18
  stress management and, 131

I
"I AM" experiences, 178
Identity
  changing, 25
  internship and, 220
  I vs. me, 154–155
  self-concept in, 151–152
*If You Meet the Buddha on the Road,
  Kill Him!* (Kopp), 275–276
"I-It" relating, 204
Imagination, 263. *See also* Creativity
*Imperfect Therapist: Learning From
  Failure in Therapeutic Practice*
  (Kottler, Blau), 162–163
Impostor phenomenon, 41,
  164–165
In a Different Voice (Gilligan), 274
Incompetence, feelings of, 40–41
Independent practice, 253–254
Individuality, 11
Industrial/organizational psychology,
  careers in, 253
Information release, 293–294. *See
  also* Confidentiality
  standards of practice on, 305–306
Informed consent, 293
  explaining to clients, 225–227
  internships and, 223
  minor/incompetent clients and,
  285
  for research, 300–301
  to therapy, 327–328
Ingham, Harry, 201
Initiation stage, 238
Insurance, liability, 222–223, 241
Integrity, 315
Interdependence, 195–196, 262
Interest inventories, 251
Interlibrary loan, 103
*Internship, Practicum, and Field
  Placement Handbook, The*
  (Baird), 240
Internships, 46, 220–240
  agreements, writing, 222
  choosing sites for, 221–222
  confidentiality and, 224–227
  ethical behavior in, 227–237

Internships *(continued)*
  ethics codes and, 223–225
  liability insurance for, 222–223
  making the most of, 239–240
  school, 240
  stages in, 237–238
  support during, 232–235
  time management in, 239
Interpersonal dynamics, 88
  assumptions about, 187, 188–189
  individual history in, 186
  self and, 186–193
  self-awareness of, 174
Interpersonal Process in Psychotherapy
  (Teyber), 179
Interruption of services, 329
Interviews
  graduate program selection,
    31–32
  job, 259
  portfolios in, 39
Irving, John, 265
Isolation, 124
"I-Thou" encounters, 203–204

J
James, William, 154, 274
Job hunting, 254–256
Jobs. *See also* Careers
  during training programs, 72
  work-study, 75
Johari Window, 201
Journals, 15, 26
  in portfolios, 39
  practicums and, 218
  in research projects, 48–49
  stress and, 136–137
  tracking change in, 47
  writing skills through, 108–109
Journey
  as destination, 7–10, 19–20
  training as, 25–54
Jung, C. G., 86, 274–275

K
Kaplan Web site, 51
Karen, R., 275
Katz, J. H., 275
Keith-Spiegel, P., 31, 50
Kerr, D. R., 50
Kiser, P. M., 237, 240
Knowledge skills, 89
Koans, 166
Kopp, S. B., 275–276
Kottler, Jeffery, 155, 162–163
Kozol, J., 276

L
Laing, R. D., 153
Learned resourcefulness, 135
Learning
  as adventure, 19–20
  assimilation and accommodation
    in, 166–168
  attention to, 87
  from clients, 219–220
  creativity undervalued in,
    263–264
  dangers of expertise in, 165–168
  lifelong, 8–9, 260
  outside in to inside out, 47
Learning experiences, 2
Lefrancois, G. R., 260
Legal standards, 20
Leider, A., 81
Leider, R., 81
Lesbian/gay/bisexual clients,
  197–198
Levin, J. D., 151
Lewin, Kurt, 95
Liability insurance, 222–223, 241
Library skills, 102–103
Licensing, 252
Lifelong learning, 8–9, 260
Listening, 84
Literacy. *See* Reading
Literature reviews, 48, 49, 102–103

Love/belonging needs, 57, 80
Love's Executioner and Other Tales of Psychotherapy (Yalom), 278
Lubart, T. I., 262–263
Luft, Joe, 201

M
MacLaine, Shirley, 59
Magic mirror exercise, 18–19
Malcolm, Janet, 16
Man's Search for Meaning: An Introduction to Logotherapy (Frankl), 146
Maslow, Abraham, 56–58, 60
  Toward a Psychology of Being, 276
Master's degrees, careers with, 251–253
May, R., 178, 179, 276
Mbuti people, 13
McConnaughy, E. A., 175–176
McGoldrick, Monica, 249
McLeod, J., 160
Meaning
  interpersonal assumptions in, 188–189
  storytelling as, 136–137
  of stress, 121, 136
Media presentations, 289
Memories, Dreams, Reflections (Jung), 274–275
Mentors, 12, 205–207, 261
Metaphors, 107
Middle Way, 66
Milestones, 25–26, 45
Miller Analogies Test (MAT), 30
Mindfulness
  critical reflection and, 89
  improving, 90
  in reading, 97–99
  stress and, 137
  in writing, 109
Mistakes, 154, 162–163, 264–266
Mitchell, K. M., 156

Modeling behavior, 12–13
Monster.com, 269
Moral reasoning, 228–229
Moving toward/moving against/moving away strategies, 171–173
Multiplistic thinking, 26, 42
Mutuality, 195–196
Myers-Briggs Type Indicator (MBTI), 251

N
Napier, A.Y., 276
National Association of Social Workers, 23
National Board of Certified Counselors, 252
National Counselors Examination, 252
Nature vs. nurture, 135
Navajo legends, 55–56, 66, 67–68
Neimeyer, Gregory, 43
Networking, 239–240
Neurotic Styles (Shapiro), 277
Newsletters, 37
"No," how to say, 132–133
Nondiscrimination standards, 303, 318
Nontraditional students, 87
Nutrition, 76–80
  stress management and, 130

O
Observation skills, 100
Occupational Outlook Handbook, 269–270
Ochwiay Biano, 86
On Becoming a Person (Rogers), 277
Ontological security, 153–154
Openness, 11, 90, 184–186
  handling difficult topics and, 157–160

Opinions, handling difficult topics and, 157–160
Oppenheim, James, 55–56
Oppression, 92–93
Organization skills, 103, 109
    for presentations, 113–114
Orientation, 34
Originality, 49
Others
    being with, 183–212
    demands of, 168–170
    important, in training, 205–210
    learning with/through, 10–13
    resilience from, 75–76
    stress management and, 140
    views of you, 176–178

P
Paperwork, 240
Parrott, L., III, 163
Participation, 12
    anxiety over, 111–113
    forms of, 112–113
    in learning, 8
    in professional organizations, 256–257
    in reading, 97–99
    in relationships, 194
Passion, 243–245
Perfectionism, 40–41, 68
Performance
    emotional arousal and, 93–94
Perls, F., 277
Personal growth
    exploring assets and, 163
    goals for, 149–155
    Groucho paradox and, 164–165
    need for, 155–165
    through mistakes, 162–163
Personality
    counseling from, 42–43
    do-gooder, 155–156
    effectiveness and, 156
    inventories, 251

research skills and, 101
    stress and, 142–144
Personal needs
    coping styles and, 170–173
    ethics of in counseling, 281, 319
Personal problems, 38
Personal statements, 31
Personal time, 15
Perspective, 78–80
Perturbation wave, riding, 91–93
Petersons.Com: The Grad Channel, 51
Physiological needs, 57
Piaget, J., 167
Plagiarism, 337
Planning Job Choices (National Association of Colleges and Employers), 250
Planning skills, 100
Plato, 57, 58
Polster, E., 277
Portfolios, 26, 38–39
    as comprehensive examinations, 45
Practice
    of critical reflection, 90
    in presentations, 111, 114
    in writing, 107–109
Practicums, 214–220
    accommodating to, 217–218
    videotaping during, 218–219
Practitioner tools, 187
Pragmatics of Human Communications (Watzlawick, Bevin, Jackson), 278
Prejudice
    confronting personal, 233–237
    facing, 189
    handling difficult topics and, 157–160
    hard-belly responses and, 196–198
    uncovering personal, 16
Preparation, 111
Preplacement stage, 237–238
Presentations

developing skill in, 84–85, 110–117
ethics of, 289, 326
improving, 113–117
need for skills in, 110
participation anxiety and, 111–113
technology for, 115
Privacy, right to, 284–285
standards of, 330–332
Process groups, 184–186
Professional development, 8–9
conference presentations in, 110
early, 46–48
portfolios of, 39
research in, 100
Professional organizations, 22–23,
254–257
Professional resources, 6–7
Professional responsibility, 286–290
Program development, 48
Progress reviews, 38
Psyching up, 94
Psychnet-UK, 179–180
*Psychotherapy and Existentialism:
Selected Papers on Logotherapy*
(Frankl), 121, 273
PsycINFO, 102–103
Publication, 301–302
ethics of, 338
standards of practice on, 309–310
*Publication Manual of the American
Psychological Association* (Ameri-
can Psychological Association),
6, 49, 106

Q
Quest myths, 11

R
Race Is a Nice Thing to Have, A
(Helms), 274
Racism, 189
Rational soul, 57
Reading, 6

critical, 96
developing skills in, 84, 95–99
to develop writing skills, 108
environment in, 96–97
making time for, 97
participating in, 8, 97
in research, 103
Reciprocity, 195–196
Records, confidentiality of,
285–286, 331–332
Reenchantment of the World
(Berman), 273
Reference books, 6
References, personal, 30, 258
Referral process, 283, 292
ethics of, 321
Reflection
balancing, 65
portfolios in, 39
stress management and, 132
Relationships
collaborative in training, 11–13
counseling, 194–196
ethics of counseling, 280–284
exploitative, 320–321
exploring worldview of, 187–191
growing in, 191–192
as mirrors, 192–193
with other professionals,
290–292, 307
personal history in, 186
self and, 186–193
standards of practice on, 307
with students/supervisees, 296
Relativistic thinking, 26, 46–48
Relaxation, 94, 131
Reporting
accuracy in, 322–323
ethics violations, 303, 341
research results, 301
Required readings, 96
Rescue fantasies, 157
Research
animals in, 337
careers in, 253

Research *(continued)*
  confidentiality of, 286
  deception in, 336
  developing skills in, 84, 99–104
  documentation of, 322
  ethics of, 333–337
  informed consent for, 300–301,
    334–335
  interest in, 104
  literature reviews in, 102–103
  need for skills in, 99–101
  responsibilities in, 299
  standards of practice on, 309–310
Research projects, 46, 48–49
Research reports, 48
Resentment, 44
Resilience, 75–76, 135
ResilienceNet, 146–147
Resolution, need for, 92
Resources, 22–23, 50–52, 81–82,
    117–118, 146–147, 179–180,
    211–212, 240–241, 268–269
  counseling/therapy books,
    272–278
Respect, 195
Rest, 45–46
  exercise and, 130
  stress management and, 129–130
Resumes, 257–258
Rites of passage, 45
Rituals, 26, 33–34
  security from, 79
  traditions and, 34–36
Rogers, C. R., 115, 145, 169, 175,
    261, 277
  on social masks, 203
Roman Spring of Mrs. Stone
    (Williams), 169
Room 42, 180
Rumination, 65. *See also* Reflection

S
Safety/security needs, 57
  housing and, 69–71

ontological security, 153–154
  rituals in, 79
Sage Publications Graduate Survival
    Skills series, 81
Salary negotiations, 259
Santiago de Compostela Camino, 59
Santrock, J. W., 117
*Savage Inequalities: Children in
    America's Schools* (Kozol), 276
Scholarships, 75–76
School counselors, 252
School psychology, careers in,
    252–253
Sea star exercise, 64–65, 140–142
Seeming vs. being, 203–205
Selection process, 28–32
  academic prerequisites for, 29
  for doctoral programs, 253–254
  experience in, 28–29
  exploring options in, 29
  interviews in, 31–32
  making choices in, 32
  personal statements in, 31
  references and, 30–31
  standardized tests for, 29–30
Self-actualization, 57–58, 59–61
Self-concept, 152
Self-Directed Search (SDS), 251
Self-discovery, 15–16
Self-doubt, 164–165, 214–215
Self-esteem, 261
  approval of others and, 169
  Groucho paradox and, 164–165
  need for, 57
  ontological security and, 153–154
  wellness and, 77
Self-exploration, 149–182
  authenticity/clarity and, 175–178
  avoiding "expertise" and,
    165–168
  centeredness and, 168–173
  countertransference and,
    173–174
  need for personal growth and,
    155–165

personal growth goals in, 149–155
Self-image, 154
relational worldview and, 187–191
Self-knowledge
accommodating, 167–168
getting a clear picture in, 175–178
others' views in, 176–178
through counseling, 160–162
Self-system, 154–155
Self-uncertainty, 155
Seminars, 8
Sexism, 189
Sexual harassment, 289, 318–319
standards of practice on, 306
Sexual relationships
with clients, 282, 328–329
standards of practice on, 304
with students/supervisees, 296
Shapiro, D., 277
Significant others, 208–210
financial assistance and, 72
Sixteen Personality Factor Questionnaire (16PF), 251
Social masks, 203
Social Readjustment Rating Scale, 125
Social responsibility, 316
Sophomore slump, 43–44
Spirited soul, 57
Stafford, William, 144
Standardized tests, 29–30
Standards, 286
Standards of Practice (American Counseling Association), 303–311
Steinbeck, John, 19
Steinem, Gloria, 165
Stereotypes, 233–237
Sternberg, R. J., 262–263
Strengths
developing, 261
exploring, 163

focusing on, 16, 139–140
turning stress into, 144–145
Stress, 123–127
accumulation of unresolved, 125–126
character and, 142–144
creativity from, 134
distress and, 125
empathy development and, 156–157
events causing, 125–127
good, 124, 126–127
of helping professions, 124
meaning of, 121, 136
resilience and, 135
responding to, 127–137
turning into strength, 144–145
Stress management, 6–7
assessing stressors in, 138
embracing stress as, 120–148
envisioning goals and, 138–139
gender differences in, 127–128
learning from problems, 18
techniques for, 129–132
using strengths in, 139–140
Strong Interest Inventory (SII), 251
Student Aid Report (SAR), 75
"Student Guide to Financial Aid: Funding Your Education," 82
Student loans, 73, 74–75
"Study Skills Self-Help Information," 118
Subcontractor arrangements, 292
Subject matter knowledge, 114
Success
defining, 132
Groucho paradox and, 41, 164–165
Summary reports, 107
Supervision
ethics of, 296–299, 321, 333
in informed consent, 223–224
internship, 232–234
in internships, 221
licensing/credentialing and, 252

Supervision *(continued)*
　standards of practice on, 308–309
　student expectations of, 43–44
Support
　for comprehensive examinations,
　　45
　in internships, 232–234
　stress management and, 140
Support staff, 208
Survival guides, 4–5
Survivor, 1
Suspense, 94–95
Suzuzi, 166
Synthesis skills, 89

T
*Taboo Scarf and Other Tales of
　Therapy, The* (Weinberg), 278
Tao Te Ching (Tzu), 277–278
Tax records, 75
Teaching
　careers in, 253
　ethics of, 296–299, 332–333
　standards of practice on, 308–309
Technique development, 48
Technology, 6
　ethics of, 283–284
　in presentations, 115
Technophobia, 6
Tedeschi, R. G., 135
Tend and befriend response,
　127–128
Tension, learning through, 91. *See
　also* Stress management
Termination process, 283, 329
　standards of practice on, 304
Testimonials, 326
Tests
　competence to use and interpret,
　　292–293, 323, 324
　conditions of administration of,
　　294
　construction of, 295–296, 323

diversity in, 295
obsolete/outdated, 295, 324
scoring and interpreting, 295,
　324–325
security of, 295, 325
selecting, 294
Textbooks, 96
Teyber, Edward, 179
Thank-you notes, 31, 259
Theory, changes in personal, 47
Thesis, 48–49, 50–51
Thompson, S. C., 136
Thriving
　principles for, 1–24
　resources for, 5–7
　surviving vs., 2
Time management, 6
　demands of others and, 168–170
　exercise and nutrition and, 76–80
　in internships, 239
　personal time and, 15
　during practicums, 217
　for reading, 97
　stress management and, 132
Tolerance for ambiguity, 111
Torrance, E. Paul, 260
Tournier, Paul, 15
Toward a Psychology of Being
　(Maslow), 276
Traditions, 34–36. *See also* Rituals
Training
　ethics of, 296–299, 332–333
　graduate vs. undergraduate, 4–5
Transcripts, 75
Transference, 174
Transformation, personal, 143–144
Transparency, 175–176
　social masks and, 203
Traumatic events, 156–157
Travels with Charley (Steinbeck), 19
Treatment summaries, 105
Truax, C. B., 156
Trust, feedback and, 199–200
Truth, 196–198

Twice-told stories, 107
Tzu, L., 277–278

U
U.S. News on-line, 51

V
Values. See also Ethics
  confronting personal, 233–237
  dealing with different client,
    176–178
  ethics and, 20–21
  exploring for career, 246–248
  handling difficult topics and,
    157–160
  multiplistic thinking and, 42
  needs and, 56
  rituals in, 34
Values Scale (VS), 251
Van Zandt, Z., 240
Varieties of Religious Experience, The
  (James), 274
Videotapes, 47, 218–219
Virtual Classroom, 118
Virtue, 229
Visualization, 116
Vos Savant, Marilyn, 90
Vulnerability, 195

W
Washington, Booker T., 143
Watzlawick, P., 278
Weaving Woman legend, 66, 67–68
Web searching, 102
Weinberg, G., 278
Wellness, 76–77

Well-roundedness, 261–262
Whitaker, C. A., 276
White Awareness: Handbook for Anti-
  Racism Training (Katz), 275
Wiederman, M.W., 31, 50
Williams, Tennessee, 169
Women's Ways of Knowing (Belenky,
  Clinchy, Goldberger, Tarule),
  273
Working stage, 238
Workshops, 239
Work-study jobs, 75
Worldviews, 249–250
Wounded healer theory, 156–157
Writing, 6
  developing skills in, 84, 105–109
  goals of, 21
  internship agreements, 222
  journals, 108–109
  meaning making in, 136–137
  need for skills in, 105–107
  organization in, 109
  personal statements, 31
  practicing, 107–109

Y
Yalom, I., 278
Yerkes-Dodson Law, 93–94
Young, Mark, 26
Young, M. E., 47
Your Guide to College Success
  (Santrock, Halonen), 117

Z
Zeigarnik effect, 94–95, 268
Zen, 166